Courtesy The Experience Music Project, Seattle, Washington

The Hawaiian Steel Guitar
and its
Great
Hawaiian Musicians

Compiled and Edited by Lorene Ruymar
Foreword by Jerry Byrd
Sponsored by the Hawaiian Steel Guitar Association

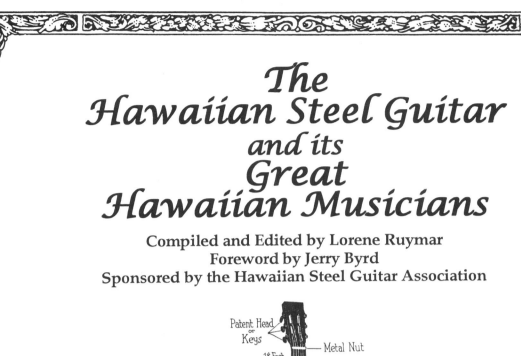

ISBN 1-57424-021-8
SAN 683-8022

Cover design and illustration
Scott McDougall
Seattle, WA

Layout and production - Ron Middlebrook

Table Of Contents

Chapter 1
Origin Of The Steel Guitar

Chapter 2
Travels Of The Steel Guitar Throughout The World

Chapter 3
Mainland Schools, And Cultural Influences

Chapter 4
Hui 'Ohana Kīkā Kila

Chapter 5

Chapter 6

Chapter 7

The Honolulu Serenaders of Indianapolis, Indiana
From Oahu Publishing Company

Dedication

To Merle Kekuku for keeping the tradition of steel guitar alive in the illustrious Kekuku name.

To Dr. Mantle Hood for consenting to kick off this worthy project and giving guidance along the way.

To Billy Hew Len, whose courage and greatness of heart should be made known to every child of Hawai'i.

ACKNOWLEDGMENTS

The following is a list of all those who have contributed articles, illustrations, and vignettes:

Margie Alkire, Henry and Sherron Allen, John Auna, Fred Barnett, Rudolf Barten, Alfred Bentley, Joe Boudreau, Harry Brown, Bob Brozman, Jerry Byrd, Jim Carroll, Walter Carter, Myldred Cooper, Joe Custino, John DeBoe, F. Deininger, Belva and Wes Dunn, Michael Dunn, Warren H. Edgar, Bernie Endaya, Norm English, Dennis Farrar, Rodney Freedman, Kazunori Funao, Cliff Gaunt, Bill Gioia, Betty Glynn, Bob Green, Emperor Hanapi, Rick Hanapi, Herbert Hanawahine, Jim Hanchett, Hudson Hawk, Jimmy Hawton, Alika Herring, Frank Hibberd, Jake Holck, Mantle Hood, Harold Humphry, Jess Hurt, Barney Isaacs, Agnes Kaehalio, Benny Kalama, Kale Kaleiali'i, Sonny Kamahele, Merle Kekuku, Ronnie Kekuku, Paul Kerley, Louis F. Kitchen, Ray Knapp, Ken Kobayashi, Ralph Kolsiana, Jack Korinek, Ernest Kurlanski, George Lake, Kealoha Life, Violet Lilikoi, Fred Lunt, Eric Madis, Thomas Malm, John Marsden, Chuck Matses, Ruby and Miro Maximchuk, Ed Mayer, Bob Mekani, Frank Miller, Louis Mirrer, Tau Moe, Jack Montgomery, Walter Mo'okini, Leona Murphy, George K. Na'inoa, Bob Naukam, Kalaya Nilson, Atsushi Onji, James Kahale Kai Papa, Steve Pascual, Mike Perlowin, George Rout, John Russell, Art Ruymar, Helen Ruymar, Owana Salazar, Greg Sardinha, Clay and Lois Savage, DeWitt Scott, Mike Scott, Margo Shy, Dave Siemens, Danny Sim, Ivan Sinclair, Warren Slavin, Richard R. Smith, Murray Storm, Terry Sullivan, Don Sweatman, Freddie Tavares, Chuck Togstod, Bud Tutmarc, Frank Vice, Dirk Vogel, Sig Vogel, Andrew Volk, Marten Walker, Don Walkerow, Ken Wallace, Bob "Pulevai" Waters, Evan H. Williams, Don Wright, John York, Leonard T. Zinn.

I have tried very hard to keep track of all your submissions and all the help you gave me and I hope the above list is correct. If someone's name has been left out, please accept my sincere apology. I did the best I could.

Special thanks and recognition:

-*to* Owana K. Salazar who served as the Hawaiian language consultant.
-*to* the volunteer workers at the Family History Library of the Church of Latter-Day Saints, both in Salt Lake City, UT and in La'ie HI who never tired of supplying me with marriage, birth, and death records.
-*to* Walter Mo'okini on whose excellent memory I relied for the story of people and places in Hawai'i, past and present.
-*to* the Honolulu Advertiser and the Star Bulletin and all the other editors of publications for their permission to reproduce their articles in this book.

Preface

It was in 1989 when we visited a bank in Honolulu that I struck up a conversation with one of the staff members. I told him about the Hawaiian Steel Guitar Association and our celebration of the centennial of the invention of the Hawaiian guitar. I mentioned Joseph Kekuku and the Kamehameha School for Boys. The young man was amazed at my story. He said, "I was born and educated right here in Honolulu but never have I heard it said that the steel guitar was invented here. I always thought it was a Nashville product which was being forced upon us and I resented that intrusion on our culture." It was then I knew for sure that a book must be written telling the story of this great instrument and the men and women of Hawai'i who played it.

Our members live in 18 different countries, some of them "very mature" people. What we have in common is our love for the steel guitar and the Hawaiian musical culture, and our great admiration for those ambassadors of Hawaiiana who traveled to the four corners of the world carrying the spirit of aloha with them. Our members witnessed it, kept records, treasured the souvenirs. So it is indeed valid for a group such as ours to put together the story as it was enacted on the world's stage.

As we researched the story of the Hawaiian steel guitar, the 'ukuleles story kept crossing our path. It became evident that these two made their entry into Hawaiian music at roughly the same time and there are great similarities in their stories. The 'ukulele story explains some of the discrepancies of the Hawaiian steel guitar story, so we included it.

We have done our best to put together a correct and complete story but, since it was done by human hands we must acknowledge that error and omission must be part of this work as well. For that, we apologize to all who have been slighted or ignored. We would be happy to receive corrections and additional information so that, should a second edition be printed, we can come closer to the truth. Articles which are shown as direct quotations credited to other writers have not always been reported in their entirety. To save space it was necessary to use only that part which referred to our topic and to make small changes in the text to weld together the sections we did use. We were careful, however, not to change the intent or the factual information.

It is not only a collection of rare articles and personal statements but also a kind of testimony that all of us dedicated to the Hawaiian steel guitar have a bond of mutual interest that simply transcends detailed differences of opinion. For that spirit, we are truly grateful. Without it, there would have been no book.

Foreword

By Jerry Byrd

I consider it an honor to be asked to write a foreword to this book. It is a work that should have been written many years ago, and yet, had it been so, it would have preceded its most productive years. The story of "steel" guitar is a romantic one - as is the very sound it emits. Steel guitar has long been in the "underground" of the musical world and remains largely unknown to the masses to this day. In spite of this, it survives and thrives due to those of us who love our instrument and give it our full measure of devotion. The author of this book, Lorene Ruymar, is a classic example of that devotion in this - a "labor of love".

This lady is a <u>dynamo</u> who remains undaunted in spite of the odds. She has done a magnificent job on this book, and with a subject that lends itself to wide debate. Steel guitar can be anything depending on the individual player's desires. It has multiple tunings, multiple strings from 6 to 14, and multiple necks - or "fret boards". It is the most individual instrument in the world, no two players can sound the same. In spite of all this, Mrs. Ruymar has done a herculean job of covering all of these facets of steel guitar so that even a non-player can understand. She is an excellent steel guitarist in her own right and knows "of whence she speaks".

Trying to get information and help of any kind from musicians is next to impossible. Most are simply not interested enough to sit down and do it! Yet, you will see at once that Lorene has had good success in that area and you can read what many of today's players have to say about their music and their careers.

Most important, I think, is that she has substantiated the various claims with documented proof where it is most needed and desired rather than using those worn-out phrases; "it is said" or "it has been rumored" and the like! This is especially true in the area of who 'invented' the instrument and when, etc.

But, really: all that matters is that steel guitar lives on and that it receives the respect that it has earned and deserves. This book will do much to enhance those chances. It is the first of its kind that has gone into the complete story of our instrument. I know of no other that has done so. I, for one, am very proud.

Author's Biography

The author took her formal musical education as a student at the University of British Columbia and for most of her life served as a music educator in the public schools of Vancouver, B.C. She organized and for many years directed a very successful 60-piece school band. She then took further instruction at U.B.C. on 'ukulele and joined the popular movement toward 'ukulele instruction in the classrooms of Canada.

Ruymar's real beginning as a Hawaiian steel guitarist didn't come until 1980 when she met Jerry Byrd who taught her by tape recorded lessons by mail. In 1985 she and her husband Art joined with others to form the Hawaiian Steel Guitar Association which she served as vice president until early in 1986 when she became its president. Shortly after, Ruymar became editor of the club's quarterly newsletter, publishing her first issue in January of 1988 and her last issue in April of 1993. The association had grown too large and it was seen as a progressive move to headquarter it in Hawai'i under the presidency of steel guitar virtuoso Alan Akaka.

Ruymar now serves as HSGA's president emeritus and on the Board of Directors. Her greatest moment as a professional steel guitarist came in May of 1991 when she was invited to perform in the most prestigious show of the Hawaiian steel guitar world - the Steel Guitar Ho'olaule'a in Honolulu.

Lorene Ruymar

What Is A Steel Guitar ?

First, we must define the term "Hawaiian Guitar" which has been used in two ways. Outside of Hawai'i it means a guitar played flat on the lap, with the use of a steel bar to change the pitch. In Hawai'i, it is the early term for the slack key guitar, later named the *kī hō'alu*. Every ship that came to the Islands since Captain James Cook first landed there on January 19, 1778 could have brought the Spanish style guitar with it. No doubt Hawaiians were in contact with the guitar as early as 1818, when King Kamehameha sent 80 of his men to California to fight for the Argentinean navy of Rio de la Plata. (Kanahele p.351) Hawaiians took to the guitar readily and soon adapted the tuning to a straight major chord. This style was referred to as the "Hawaiian guitar", later called the slack key guitar since the strings had been slacked from the original Spanish tuning, and it is now called *kī h ō'alu*. It has six strings and is played in the standard upright position of the Spanish guitar. In Gavan Daws' "Shoal of Time", p. 167 he tells of a Japanese diplomat, visiting Honolulu in 1860, having reported that he heard people playing the "Hawaiian guitar, violin, and castanets". In a 1993 brochure published by Kamehameha Schools' Continuing Education Department, night school courses are offered on "Hawaiian Guitar", which refers to the slack key guitar, not the steel guitar.

The steel guitar came into use some time after the slack key tuned "Hawaiian guitar". The term "steel guitar" refers to a guitar with any number of strings, raised higher off the frets. It is played in the flat or horizontal position with or without supporting legs, and the change of pitch is accomplished by movement of a steel bar held in the left hand.

Thumb and finger picks are used on the right hand. There are many variations of the steel guitar - acoustic, resophonic, electric , with or without pedals and knee levers, with any number of necks ranging from one to four - and many playing styles: country, western, blues, gospel, Hawaiian, jazz, bottleneck, and so on. In this book we refer to the "Hawaiian steel guitar" and we limit our topic to the Hawaiian-ness of the instrument. We include only the acoustic, resophonic, and electric guitars in the original form (no pedals or knee levers). The story of the pedal steel guitar is a long and complex one, best left to the experts in country music to tell. Although the pedal steel guitar can be played in a most authentic Hawaiian manner, it has not been adopted by the Hawaiians to any great extent.

What Is The Hawaiian Style Of Playing?

By Alan Akaka

What do we mean when we say someone is playing "In the Hawaiian style" as compared to standard or country style? There's something very rare, very special that the listener can hear when a Hawaiian plays the steel guitar. It's the essence of Hawaiianness that non-Hawaiians envy and try to copy. Jerry Byrd calls it the Hawaiian mystique. Hawai'i's young virtuoso Alan Akaka tried to define the undefinable for us:

The Hawaiian style of playing is a feeling - an emotion that is nurtured throughout one's life. It's from being a part of the Hawaiian musical culture. In order to play in the Hawaiian style you have to live, eat, and drink Hawai'i. Hawai'i's musical culture nurtures a feeling of nature-given smoothness - a lilting, laid-back expression of aloha. For example, artists can emulate the jazz idiom because of their deep interest and involvement in that culture's music style. However, jazz artists could not be expected to be equally versed in the playing of Hawaiian music unless they are equally involved in Hawai'i's musical culture. If you were to compare a Hawaiian vs. a non-Hawaiian playing, the style of approaching the same composition would be dissimilar. Attacks, phrasing, and glissing would be different.

There are many non-Hawaiian players who have kept in close contact with the Hawaiian music culture throughout their lives and can play in the Hawaiian style as they feel and see it. Therefore, the Hawaiian style of playing the steel guitar is available to those select few who choose to totally embrace it.

A fascinating point of interest, the style of playing a steel guitar matches the style of the artist's singing.

Chapter 1

Origin Of The Steel Guitar

If the reader imagines that the invention of this instrument was a well-documented, highly applauded event, he or she must read on. There are many versions of the story, some erroneous data, and some strongly conflicting theories. But somewhere, amid all the confusion, is the truth. It is up to you, ladies and gentlemen of the jury, to find it.

Music In Hawai'i Before The Steel Guitar

by Miro A. Maximchuk, who received his information from Ben Hokea, Sam K. Na'inoa, A.P. Sharpe, W.J. Murray, B.L. Mecke, George Peate Jr., Eddie Alkire, H.G. Stanley, and the Waikiki Record Co.

"'Ukuleles and guitars should be considered modern-day instruments as far as Hawai'i is concerned. The original instruments prior to these were the musical bow or 'ūkēkē, nose flute or 'ohe hano ihu, and percussion instruments such as the pahu kettle-type drums, conch shell or pū, the hardwood sticks or kāla'au, river-bed stones or 'ili'ili, the large gourd or ipu, the small gourd with rattle and feathers or 'uli'uli, and the bamboo sticks called pū'ili. The only stringed instrument was the primitive bow 'ūkēkē which used three strings made of sinnet or horse hair.

"In 1879 three Portuguese musical instrument makers emigrated to the Islands and introduced a six-string guitar. They later produced the 'ukulele with four gut strings, which immediately gained an undying popularity because of its versatility and convenient size. During the nineteenth century another instrument popular in the Islands was the autoharp.

"The guitar was introduced to Hawai'i in the early 1800's by the whalers. In the 1830's Kamehameha III brought Spanish-Mexicans in to train the Hawaiians as cowboys. They brought with them the guitar, which has always been well loved about the cattle ranches of Hawai'i.

"The innovative Islanders produced a new effect by slacking the guitar strings to a major chord tuning. The strings were plucked, not strummed. The bass carried the basic rhythm and the higher strings carried the melody to simulate the Hawaiian matchless falsetto voice.

"Hawaiian music moved a long way from chants, influenced by the music of immigrants. They played Hawaiian hulas, marches, waltzes, hymns, etc. In addition, Hawaiians adopted the Tuamotu style. Spanish whalers who stopped at the Island of Tuamotu (near Tahiti) taught their style of playing to the natives, who brought it to Hawai'i. From the slack key guitar with its major chord tuning, it was a logical step to the invention of the Hawaiian steel guitar."

Joseph Kekuku
Originator Of The Hawaiian Guitar

by Ken Kapua (Ken Reece), Ken played the steel guitar in the 1920's and 1930's in England. This article was first published in the Banjo Mandolin and Guitar magazine (B.M.G.) in England, August 1933.

"Joseph Kekuku was born at La'ie, near Honolulu, in the year 1874. It was in the year 1885, when Kekuku was 11 years old, that he originated the Hawaiian method of playing the guitar with a steel held in the left hand. Whilst walking along the railroad strumming on a guitar of the regular type, he stopped to pick up a bolt, and somehow or other he slid this bolt on the strings of his guitar, thus producing, in embryo, the well known slur so characteristic of the Hawaiian guitar. From this, Kekuku conceived the idea of the Hawaiian guitar (sometimes, but erroneously, termed the "steel" guitar).

"The bolt was far from being a success, and Kekuku tried the back of a penknife and various other things, until he settled down to using the blade of an ordinary razor with the edge ground down. Mr. Kekuku told me that he tried to practice in secret, but it was not possible, and other natives began playing in the same manner. This created a spirit of friendly competition and made Kekuku more determined than ever to be the first to master this new style of playing.

"It must be borne in mind that he had at that time no knowledge of music, and there were no instruction books available for this method of playing. It took him seven years to master the instrument.

"In the year 1904, Kekuku left the Hawaiian Islands for the U.S.A., and he played in all the theatres of renown, from coast to coast. Whilst in America, Kekuku taught numerous people to play the guitar in the fascinating Hawaiian manner, and he told me that two of his best pupils were Myrtle Stempf and C.S.DeLano, the latter being the first person to write out in musical notation a Hawaiian guitar solo.

"In 1919, Kekuku left the U.S.A. for an eight years' tour of Europe, during which time he played before kings and queens of many different countries, whilst with the "Bird of Paradise" show. He also played at the London Hippodrome in a production called "Leap Year", and was featured in a scene accompanied by (I believe) 40 "Banjulele" banjos, and, so marvelous was his tone production, his guitar was clearly audible to one and all. The number in question was, unless my memory fails me, "Say it With A 'Ukulele".

"Kekuku also played at the Cafe de Paris in a band under the direction of Al Keech, and it was about this time that he assisted Layton and Johnstone in recording some numbers, amongst them being "I'll See You In My Dreams", "Tell Me More", and "When You and I Were Seventeen". I have copies of these records and, although old, they serve to illustrate the wonderfully pure tone he could produce from his guitar. There can be no disputing the fact that Kekuku was a truly fine player and a master of his instrument. For instance, he could play "The Rosary" entirely in artificial harmonics and, I can assure readers from my personal experience, it was a pleasure to see and hear him play this number in this manner. He broadcast from London and other stations on several occasions.

"Mr. Kekuku returned to the U.S.A. about 1927/28 and settled in Chicago, where he opened a music school. For those who are interested, Kekuku used a plain wire 3rd and 4th string in place of the usual covered variety.

"Some time back, I received a letter from Mrs. Kekuku, and it was with the deepest regret that I learned of his death. He died on the 16th of January, 1932, at the age of 58, his death being caused through hemorrhage of the brain, brought on by writing so much music. I am proud to say that Joseph Kekuku was my teacher and my friend, and no one regrets his passing more than I. As Mrs. Kekuku informed me: 'He gave his life for the music he loved.' "

Joseph Kekuku, inventor of the Hawaiian steel guitar?
M. Maximchuk photo

Editor's note: In this article, both Al Keech and C.S.DeLano are mentioned. Later in this chapter each will give his version of the invention. It is interesting to note the similarities and the differences in their stories.

Hawaiian Musical Instruments And Their Origin

by Alvin D. Keech This article was first published in B.M.G., December, 1931.
It was submitted by John Marsden of England.

"Until the arrival of the missionaries, the Hawaiian Islanders had three types of songs: the "Meles," or war songs, the "Hulas", or dance songs and thirdly, the "Dirges", or songs of lamentation. Hawaiian music today is divided into two classes: standard songs such as "Aloha Oe" written by the late Queen Liliu'okalani, and modern Hawaiian songs that can be traced to English and American hymns. The Hawaiian Islanders gave them a peculiar rhythm, and so changed their construction that few persons would recognize them as early missionary hymns.

"It is only of late years that modern Hawaiian musical instruments were invented. The best known of these is the "'Ukulele", the "Taro-patch fiddle", the "Hawaiian Guitar", played with a steel according to the Hawaiian fashion, manipulated with the left hand, and lastly, my own invention, the "Banjulele".

"To work in the great sugar cane fields, many labourers came from the Canary Isles, and it is to them that we owe the introduction of a small Portuguese guitar with six strings. The Hawaiian Islanders found this instrument too large to carry conveniently, so a smaller instrument was designed, with only four strings and the tuning so arranged that anything could be played within the scope of five frets.

"This instrument was played before the last King of the Islands, Kalākaua, whom I cannot remember although I attended his last feast as a small boy. Kalākaua was much amused by the way it was played and the tones produced. Being very diminutive in size and strummed by a very rapid manipulation of the right hand across the strings, it was suggestive of a flea dancing beneath the paw of an aggrieved monkey, so he christened it "'Ukulele", which literally translated is "Uku", a flea, and "lele", to dance—hence a dancing flea.

"The 'Taro-patch fiddle' (or guitar) is a glorified 'Ukulele with five strings, and though not resembling a violin at all, obtained its name from the Hawaiian boys serenading their sweethearts while walking through the taro-patches. The strings of this instrument have now been reduced to four.

"The Hawaiian Steel Guitar was originated by Joseph Kekuku, who was for some time in England under my management and played in the finale of "Leap Year", which included a big "Banjulele" scene, arranged under my personal supervision, with sixty artists playing my "Banjulele" banjos."

Hawaiian Music, Its Origin

by C.S.DeLano
C.S.DeLano published Hawaiian music in Los Angeles, the first to publish a song specifically arranged for steel guitar. This article was first seen in B.M.G. April, 1932. Submitted by John Marsden, England.

"While on a concert tour last April with the DeLano Musical Four, I called on Joseph Kekuku, a native of Hawai'i, who now resides in Chicago. He told me about his visit to Paris, where he spent several years playing and teaching the Hawaiian guitar and 'ukulele, and said that during one engagement there, he made the tone of his guitar carry above the accompaniment of a full theatre orchestra and forty-two 'ukulele banjos.

"Joseph Kekuku is generally acknowledged to be the man who invented the steel method of playing the guitar. He told me that he was walking along a road in Honolulu forty-two years ago, holding an old Spanish guitar, when he saw a rusty bolt on the ground. As he picked it up, the bolt accidentally vibrated one of the strings and produced a new tone that was rather pleasing. After practicing for a time with the metal bolt, Joe experimented with the back of a pocket-knife, then with the back of a steel comb, and still later with a highly-polished steel, very similar to the sort that is used today.

"For more than twenty years the steel-played guitar continued to increase in popularity, although no music had been published for the instrument. Seventeen years ago I wrote music for steel-guitar and 'ukulele in correct notation. My "Hawaiian Love Song" was the first original composition to be published for the Hawaiian guitar. I have also written and published forty-five solos for the Hawaiian guitar in sheet music form."

Kupihea
On Steel Guitar And 'Ukulele

In a newspaper article (Honolulu Advertiser, January 24, 1932),
David M. Kupihea (a fisherman for almost 50 years at the time of the article) made this statement:

"The steel guitar first came into popular use as a sensational feature of Hawaiian music at King Kalā kaua's Jubilee celebration. Sweet Emalie, the most famous of all Hawaiian dancers, was the first to appear in the hula while playing an 'ukulele and with the accompaniment of the steel guitar and 'uke. I played the 'ukulele on that occasion and Gabriel Davion...played the steel. In those days we didn't call the 'ukulele by the name it now has. It was called "pila li'ili'i". It was originally a small imitation of the popular Spanish guitar. Youngsters used to get old cigar boxes or shingles and cut out toy guitars. It was the ideal accompaniment for the hula, and the old gourds and drums were neglected except on special occasions. At first it was purely a Honolulu instrument, not found on the other islands.

"The instrument got its name at a housewarming at the Wilcox homestead at Kalihi. Gabriel Davion had an instrument he had made. It had but three strings. It was such a success that one of the guests, a lady by the name of McKea, asked what they called it. Gabriel stated jokingly that it was a "jumping flea" apparently judging by the way one scratched at it. "What is jumping flea in Hawaiian?" the lady asked, turning to Judge W. L. Wilcox. " 'Ukulele", he replied and the instrument was given the name.

"The real development of the 'ukulele was the work of two Portuguese, Nunes and Santos, who were musical instrument repairmen. Judge Wilcox asked them to make him two 'ukuleles. They continued to build 'ukuleles, developing them into the approximate size and shape of the present instrument."

Kupihea's story of the steel guitar invention is as follows: "James Hoa invented the steel guitar in 1876. In those days we had only the Spanish style guitars and they were scarce. So we used to make our own instruments. I was a musician then even though I was just a youngster. Hoa was the first Hawaiian bandmaster and served under Kamehameha V, Lunalilo, and Kalākaua.

"There was a professional guitarist here at the time. He was William Bradley, a barber. One of the things he did, and which roused the envy of the rest of the guitar players, was to play chimes on his guitar. Hoa practiced it and in experimenting discovered that the back of a comb could be used to block off the chords and to give the chime effect. Then he discovered that the back of a table knife - and finally a pocket knife - was still better. I remember the knife well, it was one of the old style ones called IXL".

In Kupihea's statement about William Bradley playing chimes on his guitar, he does not say the guitar was laid flat on the knees. Also, the word "chimes" in early days (and still in use today among slack key artists) was used to mean "natural harmonics" which were played by applying the left little finger to the fret. Is it possible that Hoa held a slack-key tuned guitar in standard guitar position and produced louder, clearer "chimes" by means of a comb, a table knife, or an IXL pocket knife? I refer you to Dr. George Kanahele's research reported later in this chapter in which he refutes most of the statements made by David M. Kupihea.

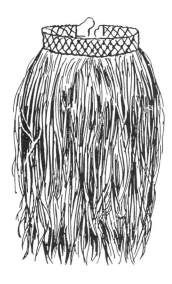  

Harry Duncan On Steel Guitar

On October 17, 1944 the Honolulu Star Bulletin ran a story by Harry Duncan who had been in the islands since 1893, from Scotland. Mr. Duncan spoke of a Joe Schulmeister from Vienna who had sailed to Hawai'i on the same ship in 1893. Schulmeister and his zither became popular with the Hawaiians and on one occasion in 1894, Duncan reports, a Hawaiian watched very carefully, then "One day later the Hawaiian came to Joe and me. He brought a guitar, strung with steel strings. He also had a small piece of metal as a finger piece. He had re-tuned the guitar so that when he pressed down on any fret with the little metal piece and plucked the strings, the strings responded in true harmony."

Reply To Harry Duncan

A response to the Harry Duncan story came from Simeon Nawa'a,
published in the Star Bulletin October 21, 1944.

"No hard feelings, Mr. Editor, but that story is off the beam...I entered the Kamehameha School for Boys in the fall of 1888. The following fall (1889, five years before the time you mentioned), two lads from La'ie, on the windward side of O'ahu, came to our school - Joseph Kekuku, the guitar player and Samuel Na'inoa, the violinist. They were good entertainers, and to our astonishment Joe, besides playing the guitar the ordinary way, would shift to running a hair comb or tumbler on the strings producing a sweet sound, while Sam, the accompanist, followed him with his violin.

"From the information these lads gave, they had experimented on this for some time...We learned also that they were close relatives and Joe took his cue from the violin his mate played.

"Joe wanted to be a mechanic and went to the school machine shop. He was working on something which later appeared to be the first steel bar. He might have seen the 'gouge stone' sharpen in the wood-turning shop, for he patterned this accordingly. Later, he produced the round bar, which is now universally used by all steel guitar players.

"Joe left school a year or so before the year you mentioned and was heard later from the mainland, doing the same stunt, which had elevated the guitar from a thumping strings instrument to that of the leading role of today."

The editor, Riley Allen, concluded with, "As no other account of the origin of the steel guitar is dated prior to 1889, the name of Joseph Kekuku stands as the first steel guitar player and the inventor." The editor added some personal notes about Sam. "Well, there's my friend Simeon Nawa'a's story and he's a truthful man... Sam remained in the school and graduated, to later become the leader of the famous Kawaiaha'o Glee Club."

"The Music of the Hawaiians, the most fascinating in the world, is still in my ears and haunts me sleeping and waking."-- Mark Twain.

The Recorded Voice of Sam K. Na'inoa

When Miro Maximchuk, whom we heard from earlier, was doing his research, he received directly from Sam K. Na'inoa one of four recordings Sam had made. (This is the same Sam K. Na'inoa referred to by Simeon Nawa'a in the previous essay.) In this recording Sam confirms that his cousin Joseph is the inventor of the steel guitar but goes on to take credit for working out a playing style in which the steel guitarist accompanies himself. Sam did not say WHEN that work was done, but we suppose it was during the time 1889-1893, when Sam and Joseph were enrolled at Kamehameha School for Boys, and Joseph was developing the guitar and its playing style. The message on the aforementioned recording is as follows:

> *"Ladies and Gentlemen: This is Sam K. Na'inoa speaking, a real native and direc-*
> *tor of the Sam K. Na'inoa Foundation of Hawaiian Music Studios at 235 West 18th*
> *St. Los Angeles 15 California. Since the origination of the Hawaiian guitar by my*
> *cousin, Joseph Kekuku of La'ie, O'ahu TH (I have the credentials here to prove it)*
> *as far as I know, no one has ever come forward either in words or in writing to ex-*
> *plain the intricate working of this unique instrument. I call it unique because it is*
> *played different from any other instrument in the world..."*

And Sam went on to talk about his work on playing technique. Judging by the materials used and the technology involved, it has been estimated that the recording was made in the late 1930's or early 1940's, at which time Sam must have been in his 60's or 70's.

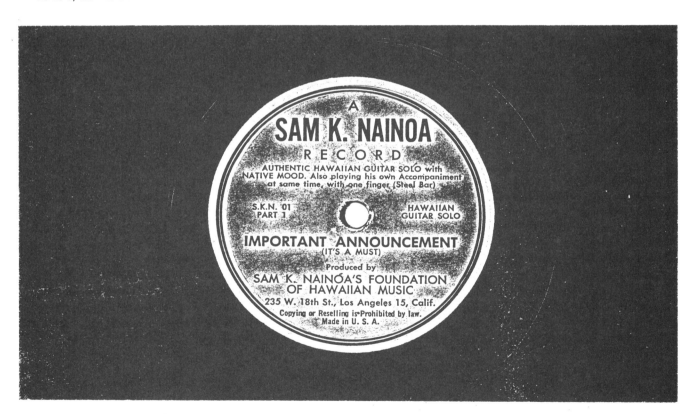

A voice recording made by Sam K. Na'inoa, cousin of Joseph Kekuku, who enrolled at Kamehameha School for Boys the same year as Joseph did, and played violin while Joseph played steel guitar.

Emilie D. Noble
On Steel Guitar And 'Ukulele

In her biography of her late husband Johnny Noble, "Hula Blues" published in 1948, the author states (p.10) that the Portuguese brought the 'ukulele to Hawai'i in 1879. "It was called *cavaquinho* in Portugal and *braghino* in Madeira, the Portuguese island from which this group of people came. It was brought to the islands by Joao Gomes da Silva. As he could not play it, he gave it to his friend Joao Fernandes who won the hearts of the Hawaiians for his playing,...immediately the Hawaiians accepted it as their own, and at once began making them by the hundreds from the wood of the *koa* tree. They called it *'ukulele*- from the word *uke* which means striking on wood, and *lele* meaning jumping or strumming...Later the name became *'ukulele,* probably because of the similarity between *uke* and *uku* which meams flea.

"And then in 1893, Joseph Kekuku of La'ie, on the island of O'ahu, a student at the Kamehameha Boys' School, by accidently dropping a steel pocket-knife on the strings...etc, etc." Emilie D. Noble went on to state that Joseph Kekuku was the inventor of the Hawaiian steel guitar.

Johnny Noble

In his book "Paradise of the Pacific", copyright 1943, two invention stories are told. The first is that in 1895 Joseph Kekuku, at Kamehameha School, accidently dropped a small comb on his guitar during an intermission in a program by the Hawaiian Quintet Club in which he was playing. The second story (the author says it is more likely to be true) was told to Johnny Noble by Kekuku's brother Edwin. It tells of Joseph in his dormitory room opening a package which contained a small knife as a gift. The knife fell on the strings...etc. etc.

Helen Roberts
On Steel Guitar And 'Ukulele

Dr. Roberts, a graduate of the University of Chicago School of Music, was commissioned by the Legislature of Hawai'i in 1923 to make a thorough study of Hawaiian music.

In her "Hawaiian Annual", 1926, pages 77-80, Roberts agrees that the first Portuguese immigrants came from Madeira in 1879, among them three men who were partners in the instrument-making business. They brought with them the guitar and two smaller instruments and commenced to make and sell them in Hawai'i. "The guitar was too large and expensive for the natives to adopt generally, although it was popular, but the two others, the *viola* and the *rajao* were soon in the hands of the peasantry. The *viola* became known as the taro-patch fiddle, from its being found so often in the hands of the natives...in their taro fields; but the *rajao* gained its title of *'ukulele* in a quite different way which has been related to me by persons who knew the circumstances intimately.

"A certain army officer, who early in the 1880's came to make the islands his home...became a master of it and was seldom seen without it. At the court of King Kalākaua, he often amused the gatherings with his expert playing. The Hawaiians loved him and gave him the affectionate nick-name of *'Uku-lele,* literally the jumping flea but figuratively applicable to his nimble movements and small structure, which contrasted markedly with their huge frames and deliberate movements. The instrument became known as *'Uku-leles* instrument and later the name was transferred to it."

In Dr. H. H. Roberts' book "Ancient Hawaiian Music" published in Honolulu, 1926, (p.10) the author told of the steel guitar's invention as follows: "During the years 1893 to 1895, Joseph Kekuku, a young Hawaiian man from La'ie, Ko'olauloa, O'ahu, was attending the Kamehameha School for Boys, in Honolulu. The guitar was a popular instrument among the students who were constantly strumming it. Like school boys all over the world, probably, they were not unfamiliar with the possibilities of the comb as a musical instrument, and one day as he was playing the guitar the idea occurred to young Kekuku to try the effect of a comb placed on the strings. He was delighted with the result and played with his new toy for a time before it occurred to him to try the back of his pocket knife. This second inspiration was even more satisfactory and thereafter the knife was always used when he played the guitar. However, he wanted a more convenient piece of metal, so he appealed to John Padigan*, in the school shop, to fashion for him a piece of steel suited to his needs.

"By this time his singular and beautiful playing had become the talk of the boys, who were all emulating him, and one of them, Tilton, who went to his home on Maui during a vacation, performed on his guitar with the aid of his knife for the benefit of his family. His sister-in-law, now Mrs. Clement Parker of Honolulu, from whom this account was obtained through the kindness of Mrs. Webb, asked him where he learned to play in such a curious manner and he told her that Joseph Kekuku at school had been the first to think of it and had taught the others how to do it. She later met Joseph Kekuku, who verified the statement.

"According to Mrs. Webb, the fashion spread very rapidly after a concert which she attended and at which, if her memory serves her correctly, Kekuku himself played. The audience was delighted and, as she expressed it, 'it took the house,' as it has since taken the musical world. This invention of the Hawaiian schoolboy is the most significant contribution by Hawai'i to music, the introduction of an entirely new technique for the playing of stringed instruments, at least as far as the western world is concerned."

Dr. Roberts' report regarding Kekuku was later verified in a statement dated October 24, 1944 published by the Honolulu Star-Bulletin. "Solomon Kenn was a student at the Kamehameha School For Boys at the time and verified the story, stating that he recalls very vividly the experiments performed by Mr. Kekuku."

*John Padigan is named in the November 1895 issue of the school's publication "Handicraft" as "...J. Padaken is home with us again having recovered from his long illness."

History of Steel Guitar According To Charles E. King

This is taken from the unpublished notes on the History of Hawaiian Music, handwritten by C. E. King for a radio broadcast in the late 1930's. Mr. King was born in Honolulu on January 29, 1874. He graduated from Kamehameha School in 1891, and was leader of the Royal Hawaiian Band from 1932-34, and 1939-40. For his hundreds of compositions, he was known as "The Father of Hawaiian Composers".

Although he was only one quarter Hawaiian, he was extremely well educated in Hawaiian history, music, culture, and language. During a talk he gave in 1937 at the Hawaiian Civic Club, he used very strong language to express his disapproval of those who wrote "Hawaiian music" which was not authentic (Todaro, p.201). He called them "murderers of Hawaiian music." He criticized Webley Edwards, Al Perry, Harry Owens, and the Hawai'i Tourist Bureau for pepping up songs with "new style treatment" on the Hawai'i Calls radio broadcast. As a guardian of traditional Hawaiian music, he may have viewed the steel guitar as a modern intrusion. He moved to New York in 1942 to be nearer to the distribution center of his numerous books and recordings, which were fantastic best sellers.

Mr. King said, "I was a pupil at Kamehameha School from 1887 to 1891 and the principal insisted on the rule that no guitar or 'ukulele was to be allowed in the school. He was in charge of the school until August 1893; Joseph Kekuku entered Kamehameha in 1892." He went on to say that in 1884 when he (KIng) lived in Waihe'e Maui, Gabriel Davion, a native of India "....attracted a great deal of attention because he had a new way of playing the guitar. With the pocket-knife common in those days, the pen knife, he manipulated the strings. Of course there was great interest created and some players used a hair-comb instead of the knife. All the playing was done on one string, and the strings were not elevated by a bar... In a short while, a lead pencil was used which later on was displaced by the use of a steel bar, as in modern days. Joe Kekuku learned the method of playing and left for the Mainland. ...Ka'ai Kaleikoa was the next leading exponent who departed from Honolulu and went East. He, instead of being contented with playing on one string, devised a certain kind of tuning which enabled him to produce chords which enriched the musical effects."

King did not mention the guitar being laid flat on the knees, nor did he support Kupihea's statement that Davion played at the King's jubilee, 1886. He spoke of seeing Davion play in Waihe'e, Maui in 1884, at which time he (King) was 10 years old. We have some indication that Davion's playing did not 'catch on'. See Dr. Helen Roberts' statement about the student named Tilton who, after 1889, took his new skill (learned from Kekuku in school) home to Maui on holidays and "caused a sensation". See also discussion of Armine Von Tempsky's book "Born in Paradise" under title "Mystery Pursued" later in this chapter. The Von Tempsky ranch was on Maui.

King differed from other reports which put the date of Joseph Kekuku's enrollment at Kamehameha School at 1889. If, as he said, he graduated in 1891 and Kekuku enrolled in 1892, the two were not on campus at the same time. According to Kamehameha School records, King entered Oswego Normal School in New York State directly after graduation from Kamehameha. King also did not mention the first known steel guitarists to leave Hawai'i for the mainland in 1899, July Paka and Tom Hennessy. King named Ka'ai Kaleikoa (or possibly Keli'ikoa?) as a leading exponent of the instrument, yet in the four years we gathered information for this book we have found no trace of him under either spelling. Was King thinking of Ernest Kaleihoku Ka'ai who did "depart from Honolulu" to the mainland U.S. in 1906? Although Ka'ai did play the instrument, he was known primarily as a 'ukulele and mandolin virtuoso. Why did King not mention Kekuku's tour of mainland U.S.A. and Canada which began in 1904 or his tour of Europe with the Bird of Paradise show, playing before the crown heads of Europe and causing a sensation with his new instrument?

Simeon Nawa'a said, "Joe wanted to be a mechanic and went to the school machine shop." Perhaps, if King's course of studies did not take him into the area of the machine shop, their paths did not cross. In a letter to HSGA dated October 14, 1992, Kamehameha Schools' Publications Coordinator Lesley Agard said, "In November 1887, the Boys' School opened and within eight months, the Preparatory Department opened with its own dormitory, administration, faculty, classrooms, and sports facilities. The Preparatory was designed to be self-contained. The two student bodies would not intermingle, except for certain occasions."

Loring G. Hudson
The Steel Guitar Story

This was taken from the Kamehameha Schools History by L.G.Hudson, his masters thesis 1935.

"The death of Joseph Kekuku, Jr., '94 in the spring of 1932 brought to mind the discovery of steel guitar playing, so characteristic of Hawaiian music and now in world-wide favor wherever popular music is played. The guitar has always been a popular instrument among the pupils of Kamehameha." Hudson went on to tell that Joseph, while playing the comb as a harmonica at Kamehameha School, dropped it on the strings of his guitar and was "delighted with the new effect". Hudson spoke of the steel bar being built in the school machine shop and other students learning to play. "Mrs. Lahilahi Webb of the Bishop Museum says that she attended a concert given at Mission Memorial Hall at which Kekuku himself played. This was probably one of the first public demonstrations of the steel guitar. Kamehameha boys returning to their home islands carried this technique with them and the steel guitar became endeared to the musical hearts of the people of Hawai'i. In recounting his early experiences, Kekuku said it took him seven years to master the steel guitar."

Herb Ohta San's
Story Of The 'Ukulele

In 'ukulele virtuoso Ohto San's book 'Ukulele O Hawai'i published in 1973 by Kamaka Hawai'i Inc., he points out that the 'ukulele is part of the guitar family, as is the smaller cousin of the guitar, the *Braguinha* or *Machete de Braga* which originated on the Portuguese island of Madeira. Among the Portuguese immigrants who brought the *Braguinha* to Hawai'i in 1879 were men skilled in guitar building who supplied the Hawaiians with copies of the popular little instrument which had taken the fancy of King David Kalākaua. In Hawai'i it was given the name *'ukulele* which means "Jumping flea". One of the men, Joao Fernandes, played it very skillfully, while the others, Augusta Dias, Joe do Espirito Santo, and Manuel Nunes were unable to play it. Nunes took credit for inventing the 'ukulele.

Kanahele's Summary
Of The 'Ukulele Stories

In his "Hawaiian Music and Musicians", (pp 394-398) published by the University of Hawai'i Press, Dr. Kanahele agrees with the origin of the instrument as the *braguinha* but says it arrived in Hawai'i in 1878 and no one including its owner knew how to play it. In 1879 two musicians arrived who could play it: Joao Fernandes and Joao Luiz Correa, and three craftsmen arrived who could build it: Augusto Dias, Jose do Espirito Santo, and Manuel Nunes. The body of the *braguinha* is eight inches long, with four catgut strings tuned to intervals of a fifth. To all the stories presented here he adds one more, that Queen Lili'uokalani did not like the interpretation of 'ukulele as 'jumping flea'. She felt the translation was demeaning to Hawai'i's favorite instrument and preferred a more poetic meaning, from *uku* which also means gift and *lele* which means "to come". Hence, "the gift that came here (from Portugal)".

Dr. Kanahele reported that King Kalākaua took great delight in the instrument, playing, designing, and building his own instruments at the shop of Augusto Dias. He featured it at his jubilee celebration in 1886 which may be the first time it was used by both musicians and dancers together in public. (Note: Here we DO have record of the 'ukulele being played at the king's jubilee in 1886, but we DO NOT have record of the steel guitar being played there.) Kanahele says the construction and repair shop was opened in 1884 by Augusto Dias, and four years later Santo and Nunes went into business making 'ukuleles. Of the three, Santo seems to have been the leading maker of 'ukuleles during this early period. Nunes, for example, was making 'ukuleles only in his spare time, and in 1900 Dias had actually given up entirely. Nunes carried on and by 1910 orders were coming from the mainland at such a pace he had to enlarge the shop. He allowed himself to be described as "the inventor of the 'ukulele". New competitors opened shops, including Samuel K. Kamaka whose shop, opened in 1916, is the only major 'ukulele factory in Hawai'i today.

'Ukulele And Hawaiian Steel Guitar
The New Grove Dictionary Of Musical Instruments (1985)

In the story of the 'ukulele, the words *braguinha* and *braghino* which were used in some of the preceeding articles are not listed by Groves, but *cavaquinho* is. It is listed as "...*cavaco*, a plucked lute mid way between a guitar and a mandolin, used in Portugal. It usually has four strings tuned D.G.B.D or D.G.B.E., although some instruments have six strings tuned like a guitar. A small *cavaco* is called a *cavaquinho* or a *machête*." The name of *machete de braga* may have suffered in its translation to English. See Groves' "*machête de braça* and *machête de rajao*". Both are said to have come from Madeira, Portugal and travelled to other cultures (Hawai'i included) where they were adopted and renamed. The larger of the two, the *machête de rajao*, had five metal strings and became the *taro-patch fiddle* of Hawai'i. The *machête de braça* (about two thirds the size of the *machête de rajao*) had four strings and became known as the 'ukulele in Hawai'i. The only adaptation was the changing of the strings from metal to gut, and the re-tuning to the various 'ukulele tunings. The size remained the same.

Groves reports that the 'ukulele tuning listed in a Hawaiian catalog in 1918 was G.C.E.A. or A.D.F#.B. They state that an older tuning was F.Bb.D.G., in use in 1918. The taro-patch fiddle, according to Groves, began as the five-string *machete de rajao*, but is now strung with four double courses of wire or nylon strings, tuned G.C.E.A.

In the 1886 "Hawaiian Annual", Marques wrote of the musical preferences of the Hawaiians "...of late they have taken to the banjo and that hideous small Portuguese instrument now called the taro-patch fiddle." We note there was no mention of the Hawaiian steel guitar.

What does the Grove's Dictionary of Music say about the Hawaiian steel guitar? "Around 1830 Mexican cattle herders introduced the guitar into Hawai'i. The Hawaiians took up the instrument and incorporated it into their own music with appropriate *slack key* or open tuning in which the strings are all tuned to the notes of a major triad. Joseph Kekuku is said to have been the first person to place the guitar across his knees and to slide a comb (later a penknife) along the strings to produce the glissandos for which Hawaiian music has become known."

Front and back of a Larson Bros. made Taro-patch, c.1917

The story of the 'ukulele demonstrates a point. You will find small discrepancies between the stories, as you do in the steel guitar invention story. On display at the Bernice Pauahi Bishop Museum in Honolulu are two very old, beautifully inlaid 'ukuleles with a card beside them identifying the instrument as being "invented by Manuel Nunes". Very little was changed in the 'inventing' of the 'ukulele. From the *machête de braça* the only change made by the Hawaiians was in the strings - from metal to gut, and the tuning. In the invention of the Hawaiian steel guitar, however, the changes made to the original instrument and to the playing technique were significant.

Groves said the Portuguese tuning of the *cavaco* (*machête*) was D.G.B.D., which is the same as the banjo tuning. It is a major triad on open strings. When the Hawaiians re-tuned their guitars to *kī hō'alu* (also known as *slack key*) tuning, it is very possible that the idea came from the above instruments. The Dobro, an acoustic Hawaiian steel guitar first manufactured in the 1930s, is commonly tuned to G major: G.B.D.G.B.D (6-1, low to high).

Martin made uke, Style O

A.P. Sharpe's
"Spotlight On Hawai'i"

In this publication, dated 1944 and published by Maxlove Publishing Co. Ltd., London England, A. P. Sharpe has no difficulty in crediting Joseph Kekuku as the inventor. On pp 34 -35 he tells of the early Portuguese sailors bringing to Hawai'i a small stringed instrument "probably the European terz guitar" which became the 'ukulele, and full-sized guitars. He says, "There are many stories of how the steel guitar (more usually called the 'Hawaiian guitar' today) came into being - although all agree that Joseph Kekuku was the originator."

Joseph Kekuku's Claim

The following is from a steel guitar instruction book published around 1930. In Joseph's Keluku own words,

"Dear Pupil: I hope you will be pleased with my simple method of playing the Hawaiian Guitar. I originated the Hawaiian Steel Guitar method of playing in the year 1885 at the age of 11 years. At the time, I was living in the village where I was born, a place called La'ie only a short distance from Honolulu. It took me seven years to master the guitar as I had no teachers to show me and no books to refer to for information. In 1904 I came to your beautiful country and played in every theater of renown from coast to coast. In 1919 I went to Europe for a tour of eight years' duration, and during this time I played before kings and queens of many different countries with the 'Bird of Paradise' show.

Since my return to the United States I have traveled extensively, giving instruction to those who wish to learn how to play the enchanting Hawaiian Steel Guitar. Pupils who live in Chicago may now have the privilege of taking lessons from me personally, and I assure you that it is possible to play the guitar wonderfully well after studying my 20 lesson course..."

Musical Ornamentation As History
The Hawaiian Steel Guitar

The following was written by Dr. Mantle Hood[1], Ethnomusicologist and Professor Emeritus of the University of Maryland, Baltimore County. When serving on the staff of the University of Hawai'i, Dr. Hood was one of the founders of the Hawaiian Music Foundation's monthly publication 'Ha'ilono Mele' and served as its first editor, January 1975. Dr. Hood is a former director of the Institute of Ethnomusicology at UCLA. He is renowned for his studies of the musical cultures of Polynesia and Indonesia, among others. At the University of Maryland he offers a seminar in Hawaiian music and recently guided a master's thesis on the life and works of Sol Ho'opi'i, written by his student, Frank Vice.

"Prior to World War II, Hawaiian music claimed enthusiastic audiences throughout the world. In some countries there were local performers of Hawaiian music who had never even visited the Islands. Although that popularity has greatly diminished, it is still surprisingly alive in such places as Japan, Indonesia, Canada, England, Holland, Sweden, and elsewhere in Europe.[2] Without exception, the most famous performers in these countries are masters of the Hawaiian steel guitar.[3] In fact, the sound of the steel guitar is considered the hallmark of Hawaiian music.

"The steel guitar is also highly regarded in Hawai'i itself, and some of the most honored musicians have been virtuosi on the instrument. But for the Hawaiian, the most important aspect of Hawaiian music is the words, the text.[4]

"In the poetic tongue of the Hawaiian language the mele, either oli (unaccompanied chant) or mele hula (accompanied by instruments and often by dance), can be interpreted word-for-word on three different levels of meaning: the literal, the symbolic, and the mystical. Some persons can apply these levels of difference even to syllables of the word.[5] The mele include songs on an endless variety of subjects, and they all may carry these compound meanings.

"After World War II, some of the older generation still spoke Hawaiian, but the young paid it little attention. Many of the songs written in the first third of this century were "hapa haole", a mixture of Hawaiian and English. Most of their meaning could be understood, or the text guessed by an English-speaking audience. Even during this period however, the family mele, treasuries of poetry very personal to some of the great Hawaiian families, continued to be zealously guarded by the elders.[6]

"Early in the 1970's, there was a general renaissance in Hawaiian culture, and young people began studying their language, poetry, music, history, crafts, and so forth. Today, popular songs are written and published in the Hawaiian language. Usually the song writers, especially the younger ones, go to an older Hawaiian for help with the language, sometimes for an entire translation from English to Hawaiian. Singers also consult the elders about proper pronunciation. The current song market, like ancient chant, once again requires a knowledge of the language, if it is to be appreciated in terms of Hawai'i's own assessment of the primacy of the words.

"Let me reiterate two principal points: 1) in parts of the world outside Hawai'i, where Hawaiian music still has an avid following, the sound of the steel guitar is considered the most important aspect of the music; 2) among Hawaiians the words of Hawaiian music are given this honor.

"Are we confronted by two different standards, one for Hawaiians and one for non-Hawaiians? There are still many Hawaiians who cannot speak the language, although they are accustomed to using some Hawaiian words and phrases mixed with English as a type of pidgin.[7] There are also a few non-Hawaiians who speak the language fluently. Does the non-Hawaiian who speaks the language hold some kind of third standard?

"I do not agree with what I sometimes term the 'ethno-mentality', those who might claim that only Hawaiians can truly appreciate Hawaiian music or only Koreans understand Korean music. By inference we should assume that only Germans appreciate Beethoven or Italians understand Verdi. But rather than pursue ethno-ghosts, let us bear in mind that Hawaiian music still enjoys international popularity, however individual listeners may listen to it - or to Beethoven.

"For a moment, let me speak on the Hawaiian side of the issue. No one questions the importance of understanding the language in which a song is written, and Hawaiian poetic language complicates the matter by yielding three possible levels of meaning. Literal competence, therefore, does not guarantee access to poetic symbolism and mystical reference; and these two levels, of course, are usually the ones that carry the intended meaning.

"Now it is a fact that a good many Hawaiians cannot negotiate the more abstract levels of poetic text. They cannot really understand the intended meaning of the words, therefore, until the meaning has been explained to them. It is also a fact, however, that there are less than 100 traditional songs performed over and over, so that someone born in Hawaiian culture grows up learning them by exposure. Even without a language abiity, therefore, the Hawaiian clings to the conviction that the words are the most important part of Hawaiian music. What is he or she hearing, in that case?

"Suppose we return to the Dutchman, the Japanese, the Canadian. What possible understanding could they have of a song text sung in Hawaiian? They, of course, listen to the steel guitar. Is this a possible clue? Might there be other factors beyond language that manage to communicate with native speaker and foreigner alike? Have we implied a polarity between text and steel guitar that is misleading?

"A few years ago, I wrote about the effects of what I termed the 'untalkables' in music, certain aspects of musical practice that defy laboratory measurement.[8] I believe here is another example. Certain untalkables in Hawaiian music seem to transcend language barriers and place of birth.

"In a number of south and Southeast Asian cultures there is a very close affinity between stringed instruments and the human voice. I am thinking especially of India and Java. We shall return to the thought presently.

"The manner in which the text of a Hawaiian song is sung and the manner in which the same song is played on the Hawaiian steel guitar are very similar. It is difficult to say which influences the other, but since the singing voice was present long before the steel guitar, it is probably safe to assume that the instrument is imitating the voice. Quite possibly there has been mutual influence. But this in itself is not surprising, and stylistically what the voice does and what the steel guitar does would seem to be quite talkable indeed. Is there more?

"A recent study by Elizabeth Tatar shows that the Hawaiians follow a sophisticated practice that distinguishes not only five different musical modes in chanting but also ten different, controlled, qualities of the voice.[9] This is evidence of extraordinary sensitivity to the quality of sound itself. Notwithstanding three levels of interpreting a chant or a song, is it not possible that the most important factor is the manner of chanting or singing - or of playing the steel guitar? The six to eight strings of the instrument have quite different sound qualities, depending on gauge and pitch.

"Perhaps in a purely musical idiom of deep emotional expression, quite apart from the text, there is a range of vocal and steel-guitar style that touches an emotional level of meaning independent of, though not necessarily different from, the symbolic and mystical meanings of the text.

"To expose my premise more thoroughly I shall look at some historical roots, a linguistic bridge to the past, a few highlights in the development of the Hawaiian steel guitar and the contemporary scene. Remember, the whole while, we shall really be trying to talk about the untalkables.

"The very remote origins of the Hawaiians began with a dispersion of peoples about 4,000 B.C. from Southeast Asia and Indonesia.[10] Between 4,000 to 2,000 B.C., there were migrations through New Guinea and the Melanesian Islands to Fiji. There, the Polynesians became a cultural unit, although their roots probably derived from diverse origins. During the next 500 years migrations continued to Samoa and Tonga. By 300 A.D., the Marquesas were settled, and by 600 A.D., Hawai'i was settled from the Marquesas. The Cook Islands and New Zealand were settled in 800 to 900 A.D. Between 1,000 and 1,400 A.D. such migrations apparently stopped.

"Around 1,400 A.D., a renewed migration and two-way trade developed between Tahiti and Hawai'i. This traffic and the ali'i or nobility responsible for it are the subject matter of some legends and chants. Other chant styles, some instruments and instrumental and dance styles had their beginnings in Hawai'i itself.

"As a scholar interested in the island of Java for many years,[11] I was surprised, some years ago, to learn that linguists translate "Hawai'i" as "Little Java". the "J" and "H" are common transformations, the "w" is like a soft "v" and "i'i" means "little". I seem to have gone from Big Java to Little Java. Be that as it may, once in a great while, I hear a particular turn of phrase on the Hawaiian steel guitar that stirs some deep but admittedly vague reminiscence of things heard in Java.

"No, I shall not try to show Javanese vocal and instrumental influence on Hawaiian singers and steel guitarists. Neither pesinden nor rebab were in place in Java as early as 4,000 - 2,000 B.C. There is, however, a commonality of ancient origin and the close interrelation of vocal and string styles in both cultures. The voice came before the rebab in Java also.[12] but aurally it is often very difficult to tell the two sounds apart. The rebab leads the singer, who sometimes imitates particular melodic ornaments played on the rebab.

"One or two stylistic coincidences might bear mentioning. The rebab often uses a technique known as mbsut, a glide up to pitch; the reverse, taken from above, is less common. The glide, both rising and falling, is often used by both the Hawaiian voice and the steel guitar. On the rebab, vibrato is used as an ornament. A casual appraisal of steel guitar style suggests that vibrato is the norm, but this may be an over-simplification, because there are many instances in which non-vibrato is used for a particular effect. In other words, it appears that vibrato is the norm and non-vibrato an 'ornament', the opposite of the Javanses style, like a photograph negative - all the details are reversed.

13

"Can a Javanese rebab sound like a singer of the Javanese language? Yes, remarkably so, even when she is singing nonsense syllables. Can a Hawaiian steel guitar sound like a Hawaiian singer? Again, yes, even when the guitarist does not understand the words, at any level.

"There is another question of origin that should be asked; where did the principle of the steel guitar originate? Hawaiians have several competing accounts for attributing its 'invention' to one or another Hawaiian. The man who usually receives the credit is Joseph Kekuku, who is said to have experimented with a comb or the back of his pen knife on the strings of a normal Spanish guitar.[13]

"There is no question that Joseph Kekuku popularized the instrument throughout the United States beginning shortly after 1900, influenced the manufacture of mail-order steel guitars and correspondence courses, and even played for the crown heads of Europe. Joseph Kekuku deserves all the plaudits he receives for launching the incredible development and international popularity of the Hawaiian steel guitar - all the plaudits except one, in my judgment. He did not invent the principle of the steel guitar.

"A newspaper article by Charles E. King gives credit for the application of comb or knife on guitar strings to a young man named Davion.[14] He dates the incident as occurring in 1884; Kekuku was ten years old. Joseph Kekuku claims to have first used the principle in 1885. The opinion by King seems no more and no less reliable than the commonly favored credit given to the Hawaiian boy - until we learn a little farther on in the article that Davion was a stowaway from India. (kidnapped?)

"In 1975, Dr. G C.Deva of the Sangeet Natak Academy contributed a short article on the origins of the Indian guttuvadyam to "Ha'ilono Mele", the newsletter of the Hawaiian Music Foundation.[15] In his article Dr. Deva indicates that the word for the ebony rod or glass slider used in India is *kodu*, the word for instrument is *vadyam* and combined they become: *gottuvadyam*. The earliest mention of the instrument appears to be in Telugu, Sringara Savitri, in the early 17th century (nearly 200 years before the Hawaiian Islands were discovered by Captain Cooke). Deva also speaks of the slide technique being applied to forms of tribal bamboo zithers and shows that a sculptured figure illustrating the technique is in Cave 21, Ellora, dating from the late 6th century A.D. (the depiction is of an *ekatantri*, a type of stick zither with gourd resonator). He suggests that the principle of the slide could be as ancient as 200 B.C.[16]

"Although the preference for a Hawaiian as the inventor of the principle of the steel guitar is understandable, I am convinced that Joseph Kekuku, at the tender age of 10, watched Davion's demonstration of guttuvadyam technique applied casually to guitar and then later exploited the idea in a unique way. Fairly stated, we should say Davion introduced the principle to the Islands and Kekuku developed a Hawaiian version of the guitar that became the steel guitar. In that sense he remains the inventor of the Hawaiian steel guitar, if not to the principle on which it is based.

"For nearly 100 years, the performer on the Hawaiian steel guitar and the singer have developed a similarity of style that immediately identifies Hawaiian music. Some singers use a very wide vibrato, and so may the guitarist, but both employ non-vibrato as an ornament. The glide from below up to the pitch and the reverse practice are standard style elements. Falsetto singing once had great popularity and again is coming back; the Hawaiian steel guitar makes frequent usage of long passages played in harmonics.

"But all these techniques are 'talkables' and can be measured and studied in a laboratory. Earlier I hinted at connections between Hawai'i and India and Java that are very vague, 'untalkable', something beyond an affinity between vocal and stringed instrumental styles. Where or how, then, might these mysterious untalkables function?

"It is not surprising that the untalkables can only be apprehended from listening to pertinent examples of music. The well-known singer Genoa Keawe provides an excellent example of a female voice using a kind of instrumental articulation in her personal style.[17] In the recording 'Lei Aloha, Lei Makamae', a male-female duet. The incomparable steel guitarist Jerry Byrd (the only musician ever elected to the International Hall of Fame for Steel Guitar by unanimous vote) performs both the male and female parts and even manages some accompaniment! There are no singers heard in the entire rendition.[19] The famous Gabby Pahinui - renowned as a performer on the steel guitar, the acoustic guitar, the 'ukulele, and as a singer - is featured taking the vocal line of 'Blue Hawaiian Moonlight' on steel guitar accompanied by a second steel guitar, and continues in the same vein after the voice enters.[20]

"I shall summarize with four attributes of Hawaiian tradition:
(1) a musical marriage between voice and steel guitar in singing and playing songs that have deep emotional content; as talkable examples we mention non-vibrato as an ornament, the ubiquitous glide, the falsetto and harmonics;
(2) a remarkable ability by singer and instrumentalist to imitate the sound of one another; as a talkable, the versatility of the different strings of the guitar;
(3) a personal identification by singer and instrumentalist with the subjects of nature; at this level of personal experience there is not much that is really talkable;

14

(4) all performance is in the oral tradition and the capability of reading music is rare; the talkable: few musicians can read music, and , even when they can, the hundred or less favorites performed are so well known they require no notation.

"The four attributes are enmeshed in a network of complex inter-dependencies between singer and instrumentalist. These nuances comprise a realm of musical ornamentation far subtler than any known in our present conception of musical analysis. They allow a Canadian or a Japanese to hear in the steel guitar what a Hawaiian hears in the vocalized song. They do, indeed, achieve an emotional level of musical meaning independent of, though not necessarily different from, the symbolic and mystical meanings of text. These Hawaiian untalkables transcend time, place and birthright. A backward projection to the ekatantri, the stick zither of India, suggests that since 200 B.C. we have missed the significance of musical ornamentation as history."

---

[1] Reprinted with permission of the author from 1983 Yearbook For Traditonal Music. Vol. 15, 141-148. Dieter Christensen, editor, Seoul: Seoul Computer Press, 1983

[2] Hawaiian Music and Musicians, An Illustrated History, edited by George Kanahele (Honolulu: University of Hawai'i Press, 1979) pp.74-84, 167-172, 178-188, 211-213, 241-252, 347-350, 410-412.

[3] loc. cit.

[4] op. cit., "Chant", pp. 53-58; also see Helen Roberts, Ancient Hawaiian Music (New York; Diver, 1967), passim.

[5] My informant in these matters was Auntie Pilahi Paki, from 1975-1980.

[6] For an extremely rare publication of one of these treasuries see: John R. Kaha'i Topolinski, "Na Mele Ohana (Family Songs)", Ha'ilono Mele, Mantle Hood, ed., Vol. 11, Nos. 1,2,3 (January-March, 1976), 3-6, 2-6, 3, 6.

[7] There are several types of pidgin spoken in Hawai'i; see further Elizabeth B. Carr Da Kine Talk (Honolulu: University Press of Hawai'i, 1972), passim.

[8] Mantle Hood, The Ethnomusicologist (New York: McGraw-Hill, 1971) 297ff.

[9] cf. "Chant" Hawaiian Music and Musicians" pp.53-68.

[10] The following historical highlights are drawn from: Peter Bellwood, Man's Conquest of the Pacific (New York: Oxford University Press, 1979), passim.

[11] Pertinent publications begin in 1954, e.g., The Nuclear Theme as a Determinant of Patet in Javanese Music (Groningen: J. B. Wolters); reprinted: (New York: Da Capo), 1977.

[12] There is probable evidence that the rebab was in usage in Java as early as the 8th century; see further Mantle Hood, "Effect of Medieval Technology on Musical Style in the Orient", Selected Reports, Vol. 1, No. 3, (UCLA: Institute of Ethnomusicology, 1970), passim.

[13] Hawaiian Music and Musicians, pp. 365-368.

[14] Ha'ilono Mele, Vol. 11. No. 10 (Oct. 1976), 5-6.

[15] As the progenitor and editor for the first two years of this little publication I was struggling to launch the beginnings of a modest research journal. The publication began in January, 1975; my editorship ended in December, 1976. Since then, the format has shifted more toward a newsletter than a potential research journal.

[16] Ha'ilono Mele, Vol. 1, No. 5 (May, 1975), 1-2.

[17] Genoa Keawe, on 12" 33 1/3 rpm disc, (no date), GK Records, GK 102; see for example, "Halema'uma'u", Side 1, Band 3.

[18] Hawai'i's Own David Kelii, on 12" 33 1/3 rpm disc, (no date), Maple, Stereo MA-1004; see for example, "Across The Sea", Side 1, Band 3.

[19] Byrd In Hawai'i, on 12" 33 1/3 rpm disc, (no date), Maple, Stereo MA-19002; "Lei Aloha, Lei Makamai", Side 1, Band 6.

[20] The Gabby Pahinui Hawaiian Band, on 12" 33 1/3 rpm disc, 1975, Panini Records, PS-1007; "Blue Hawaiian Moonlight", Side 1, Band 5.

Bibliography

Bellwood, Peter. Man's Conquest of the Pacific, New York; Oxford University Press. 1979.

Carr, Elizabeth P. Da Kine Talk. Honolulu; University Press of Hawai'i. 1972.

Gear, Robert. "Hawaiian Music, Style and Stylists of the Islands," Fretts Magazine (May): 34-35, 1981.

Hood, Mantle. "Effect of Medieval Technology on Musical Style in the Orient," Selected Reports (Vol. 1, No.3): 147-170. 1970.

The Ethnomusicologist. New York: McGraw-Hill. 1971.

The Nuclear Theme as a Determinant of Patet in Javanese Music. Groningen: J.B.Wolters, 1954: reprinted, New York: Da Capo. 1977.

Kanahele, George, Editor. Hawaiian Music and Musicians, An Illustrated History. Honolulu: University of Hawai'i Press. 1979.

Roberts, Helen. Ancient Hawaiian Music. New York: Dover. 1967.

Toplinski, John R. Kaha'i. "Na Mele Ohana (Family Songs)," Ha'ilono Mele, Mantle Hood, ed. (Vol. 11, Nos. 1,2,3): 3-6, 2-6, 3-6. 1976

Origin Of Steel Guitar

by Dr. Donald Mitchell. The following is from "Kika Kila, The Story of the Steel Guitar" which was published by The Hawaiian Music Foundation in August 1973. As a historian and educator on the staff at Kamehameha Schools and at the Bishop Museum, Dr. Donald Kilolani Mitchell was in an excellent position to access the records and interview people with first-hand knowledge.

In Dr. Mitchell's words: "In the village of La'ie, on windward O'ahu in the 1880's, the cousins Joe Kekuku and Sam Na'inoa became close companions through their interest in music. By the time they were eleven years old Joe had become quite skilled with his guitar and Sam was equally proficient on his violin".

He told of young Joseph's experiments in stopping the strings with different objects, then... "In the fall of 1889 life changed dramatically for Joseph and Samuel. They were invited to be boarding students at The Kamehameha Schools in Honolulu...Among their schoolmates was Charles E. King, destined to be one of the greatest composers and publishers of Hawaiian music...

"Joe spent hours in the Kamehameha Schools machine shop designing and making his steel bar with the help of his instructor, John Padigan. At last he produced a slim cylinder of steel about four inches long, convenient to hold in his left hand and able to slide noiselessly along the strings." Mitchell then reported that the strings were changed from gut to wire for more sustain and that Kekuku perfected the playing method, taught fellow students, then travelled the world as a performer.

Mitchell: "Two men, well known in Hawaiian music circles, have suggested that the steel guitar, or the method of playing it, was invented earlier than 1893 and by persons other than Kekuku. There seems to be little evidence to support these claims. David M. Kupihea, keeper of the royal fishponds and an accomplished 'ukulele player, has credited James Hoa with this invention. Hoa used a comb, knife and perfume bottles to play 'chimes' on his guitar. Apparently he did not progress as far as using a steel bar and we do not know that he played melodies.

"Charles E. King named Gabriel Davion, who came to Hawai'i from India, as the discoverer of the style of playing the guitar with his knife about the year 1885. (King graduated from Kamehameha in 1891 and was in college in New York state in 1893 when Kekuku entertained the boys with his steel guitar). King credited Kekuku, however, with inventing the steel bar which gave the Hawaiian guitar the status of a first class musical instrument."

Dr. George S. Kanahele

The following report is taken from "Hawaiian Music and Musicians", published in 1979 by the University Press of Hawai'i.

"There are three conflicting claims attributing the invention of the steel guitar to three different persons: James Hoa, Gabriel Davion, and Joseph Kekuku. Of this trio, Kekuku has been the most commonly mentioned as inventor of the steel guitar - and the evidence is impressive - but it is nevertheless interesting to examine the claims for Hoa and Davion.

"In the case of Hoa, the Honolulu Advertiser reported on January 24, 1932, a statement by David M. Kupihea that James Hoa invented the steel guitar in 1876. Kupihea stated: 'In those days we had only the Spanish style guitars, and they were scarce. So we used to make our own instruments. I was a musician even then though I was just a youngster. Hoa was the first bandmaster and served under Kamehameha V, Lunalilo, and Kalākaua.'

"Kupihea went on to say that 'the steel guitar first came into popular use as a sensational feature of Hawaiian music at King Kalākaua's Jubilee celebration. Sweet Emalie, the most famous of all Hawaiian dancers, was the first to appear in the hula while playing an 'ukulele and with the accompaniment of the steel guitar and uke. I played the 'ukulele on that occasion and Gabriel Davion, whose son is now a well known musician here, played the steel.'

"Kupihea's story is suspect for a number of reasons. First, nowhere else has Hoa's name been mentioned as inventor of the steel guitar. Second, if he was referring to Hoa being the 'first bandmaster' of the Royal Hawaiian Band, it is not true. Hoa was never, in fact, its bandmaster. Third, if Hoa had invented the steel in 1876, why has no one found any mention of it by King Kalākaua, Queen Lili'uokalani, Captain Henry Berger, and others? Berger, who was a keen student of music and a meticulous diary keeper, did not refer to it once. Fourth, no account so far of Kalākaua's Jubilee, which took place in 1886, indicates that the steel guitar was played.

"The important point is that if Hoa indeed invented the steel guitar in 1876, why did no other Hawaiian musicians pick it up? It was not until the 1890's and thereafter that the steel guitar was popularized. This hiatus of 20 years is difficult to explain away - unless it is contended that Hoa merely experimented with a new technique but failed to perfect it, as did Joseph Kekuku later.

"The Davion claim is a little more intriguing. The first and so far the only documented source of the story is a statement by the composer Charles E. King who said during one of his radio station KGU broadcasts in the late 1930's: 'In 1884 I was living at Waihe'e, Maui, and there appeared in the village a group of musicians from Honolulu, one of whom was Gabriel Davion - a young man who was born in India, kidnapped by a sea-captain and finally brought to Honolulu...This Davion attracted a great deal of attention because he had a new way of playing the guitar...'

"Although King was already in his sixties when he recounted his boyhood experience (he was only 10 years old in 1884) with Davion, he was still alert and his memory good. Since we cannot fault him on any other ground, his claim must be taken seriously. The fact that Davion came from India is significant, for he might well have learned the sliding technique using a rod or hard substance from Indian players of the *gottuvadyam*. It would have been a relatively simple matter of using it with a guitar. It is also worth noting that Kupihea mentions Davion as having played the steel guitar with James Hoa at Kalākaua's jubilee. So Davion's talent was known to at least more than one person, if not many. Even if James Hoa did invent (or develop) the steel guitar as early as 1876, or Davion in 1884, still unexplained is the long gap between its first appearance and popularization by other Hawaiian guitarists - a period of 10 to 20 years.

"With Joseph Kekuku, we have no such dilemma. The evidence is more plentiful and convincing that he not only discovered but developed and popularized the new steel guitar technique..."

Dr. Kanahele went on to tell the stories of Joseph's activities in much the same way as others have done earlier in this chapter.

The Kekuku Mystery

by Kealoha Life. This article was submitted by the author for publication in this book.

"With the arrival next year in Hawai'i, of the Centenary of the 'Invention' of the Hawaiian Steel Guitar, reputedly by Joseph Kekuku, I have (after a lifetime of research based on information from musicians who knew him, and who were related to him) printed evidence, conclusively proving that he could not have invented the instrument, from none other than Joseph's own words!

"My first doubts were sparked off by the remark by my lifelong dear friend and musical associate, steel guitarist Pulu Moe, like Joseph, living in La'ie, North O'ahu, and son-in-law of Kekuku, (by virtue of his marriage to Kekuku's daughter Lei Lalana Kekuku) to the effect that many Hawaiians played steel guitar long before his father-in-law did. This is confirmed by authoress Armine von Tempsky, in her fine book about the Parker Ranch, 'Born in Paradise', in the 19th century, saying that her father's 'paniolo' ranch-hands, (Hawaiian cowboys) 'used their jack-knives to play the guitar'. Although Joseph Kekuku popularized the steel guitar on the U.S. mainland, and throughout Europe, (including England), he was apparently not the first, nor the only, player to appear in Europe since Jenny Wilson and Her Hawaiian Troupe appeared in 1894 (although we have no knowledge whether steel guitar was used), and July ('Tulai') Paka was playing steel with Toots Paka's Hawaiians in 1899. We can note that Joseph Kekuku only left Hawai'i in 1904 for the U.S. Mainland and Europe.

"Fifty years ago, this extraordinary 'whodunit' intrigued me, and when I discovered the conflicting and original evidence that follows, I was determined to pursue the enquiry to the end, in completely unbiased fashion..

"When James Hoa reputedly invented the steel guitar in 1876, (witnessed by David M. Kupihea), from possibly copying barber William Bradley, an early steel guitarist, Joseph Kekuku would have been two years old, and when Charles E. King described in a broadcast show how he heard Indian Gabriel Davion playing steel guitar at Waihee, Maui, in 1884, Kekuku only 'invented' the steel guitar the following year, at the age of eleven (!), which was confirmed by Joseph in a leaflet issued by him, while he was instructor at Reid's School of Music in Chicago.

"Charles E. King (with whom I corresponded once), world-famous composer, publisher, bandleader on records and radio, teacher, lecturer, a quarter Hawaiian by descent, was brought up amongst the Royal Family of Hawai'i (his godmother was Her Majesty Queen Emma, and his music teacher was the famous composer Queen Lili'uokalani), and studied at Kamehameha School, when Joseph Kekuku was there. Therefore, his evidence is unimpeachable, when he stated that Joseph could not have practiced with a tumbler (glass) on his Spanish Guitar, after trying a pocket-knife on its strings, as no ukulele or guitar was allowed to be brought into the school. Nor, for this reason, could a metal comb have fallen out of his jacket top pocket onto the strings of his guitar, as some rumors will have it, nor again, could the wrapped gift of a pocket-knife have fallen across guitar strings, as stated by his brother, Edwin Kekuku.

"I saw, and listened to, the 'Bird of Paradise' Hawaiians (with Joseph Kekuku on steel guitar), at the Wembley Exhibition, England, in 1923, at the age of four years, and although I only remember them vaguely (one of Kekuku's musicians remembered me as a little boy, when he worked for me many years later), I shall always be grateful to them for introducing to me, at such an early age, the beautiful singing of the Hawaiians, and the sound of steel guitar, ukulele, and guitar, which caused me to become a professional Hawaiian steel guitarist, solo standard guitarist, solo ukuleleist, and Hawaiian vocalist all my life, which was a 'spin-off' from my career as a government linguist, translator, and philologist.

"However, Kekuku issued so many conflicting dates of his 'invention', in articles and interviews, in addition to the many steel guitar tutors published and available in Europe from the 20's to the 40's, bearing his photo inside the cover, and describing his 'invention' that it is difficult to imagine that he was uncertain of the date. He quoted 1880, 1885, 1889, and finally 1893, the last-named date appearing in the biography of Johnny Noble ("Hula Blues"). Differing descriptions appeared inside the covers of these tutors, such as: "...He heard, and saw, sailors" (described variously as being Dutch, German, Scandinavian, or even Spanish!) playing their guitars with a jack knife, after which he practiced in secret..." It may well be that the first inventor before Kekuku, either Dutch sailors imitating with their pen-knives, the Dutch 'hommel' or German 'hummel', a dulcimer played on pinned legs to a table-top, or even more likely, Scandinavian sailors imitating their national instruments, the Swedish pear-shaped 'hulme' and the Norwegian 8-string 'langleik', which are dulcimers too, played both across the knees with a steel bar. Alternatively, it is just possible that the earliest inventors of the steel guitar could have seen and heard the Japanese 'Bugako Biwa', a lute played with a cherrywood or rosewood bar, and the Japanese 'koto', played with an ivory thumbpick and fingerpicks, imported perhaps by Japanese agricultural workers. As the Spanish gut-string guitar was introduced to Hawai'i from Spain and Mexico in 1830, and the steel-strung guitar imported from the Portuguese Azores Islands in 1865, the Hawaiians had ample time and opportunity to invent the steel guitar before Kekuku, even discounting the fact that Gabriel Davion came from India, and could have easily seen, heard, and played the Indian "Swarabat Sitar", (literally: 'plectrum guitar' in Hindustani), which was played with a quill (like the turkey-quill used in playing the Swedish 'hulme' dulcimer, and the American Appalachian dulcimer); more imprtant, the "Swarabat Sitar" was played with a cylindrical metal tube, it was alternatively played with a smooth, polished stone, and in both methods, used a crystal plectrum or pick, like the "bin" and "bicitrabin" of India.

"An enormous influence on the steel guitar's development was the demonstration of F. Menschen of a zither to King Kalākaua (after which several members of the royal Hawaiian Family became proficient on it; in addition, Her Majesty Queen Liliuokalani and Charles E. King used the zither for composing their famous melodies), and from this zither, stemmed the innovations present in the acoustic Hawaiian steel guitar of the 1920s, namely the A major tuning (the earliest E major tuning being contemptuously dubbed "the ladies tuning"), being popular with the Hawaiian musicians, owing to its attack in their marches; fingerpicks, (metal rather than ivorite), thumbpick, (ivorite), and shallow body (to secure a sharp tone), while from the sailors' dulcimers, perhaps seen by Joseph Kekuku, sprang the hollow-box-neck and slightly pear-shaped shoulders of the Bergstrom Music Co., of Honolulu.

"I used to borrow the cook's zither, to practice, in the boarding-school in the tiny alpine village of Château D'Oex, Switzerland (home of film-actor David Niven, and the next village to Rossiniére, where Her Royal Highness Princess Diana was educated), where I was educated till the age of 16, and soon saw the similarity of the zither to the steel guitar, which I had been playing since the age of 14; many years later, it occurred to me that it was quite logical that the President and Founder of the Rickenbacker (originally "Rickenbacher") Guitar Company was a Swiss!

"My two guitarists in the 'Royal Hawaiian Islanders', touring England during World War II, 'Kimo Koa' (Jim Collins) and 'John Kimoa' (John Hendricks), the former being leader of 'Kimo Koa and his Hawaiians' on records, both played with Joseph Kekuku in the 'Bird of Paradise' Hawaiians at Maxim's Chinese Restaurant, and the old Cosmo Club, in London, and told me two varying stories by

18

Kekuku, of his 'invention', as follows: 1) Kekuku 'accidentally dropped his steel-string guitar across the rail of a little railroad back in Hawai'i, (perhaps a narrow-gauge sugar-cane or pineapple spur?)', which story was confirmed by its appearance in the introduction, word for word, in a tutor dedicated to Kekuku, and 2) the story published by me in the organ of the Hawaiian Music Foundation, 'Ha'ilono Mele', as heard from Kimo Koa, that Kekuku and his musicians were playing on an unspecified beach in Hawai'i, where a private party of tourists sailed by in their yacht, were entranced by the steel guitar sound, and picked up Joseph's group, taking them to New York, where an agent booked them to travel the United States and Europe. The two most startling variations on Kekuku's own story of his invention (eight varying stories by him exist to date!), I discovered recently, and am now convinced that these show that Joseph did not invent the steel guitar. Here they are:

"Alvin D. Keech, Hawaiian inventor of the 'Banjulele Banjo' wrote in an article called 'Say it with a Banjulele' (which I have), that Kekuku playing with him in the show: 'Leap Year' at the London Palladium, was the inventor of the steel guitar, but contradictorily added: 'The steel guitar was invented from the five-string 'Taropatch Fiddle' (not the eight-string taropatch, nor, the later four-string baritone ukulele, also sometimes called the 'taropatch'), used by the plantation serenaders, and which was played with a STEEL 'KILA' MANIPULATED WITH THE LEFT HAND, ACCORDING TO LOCAL CUSTOM.' So, it would seem that for some years before Kekuku's invention, the taropatch serenaders had been playing the five-string taropatch ukulele with a bar, before the size of the instrument had been reduced; Keech's description of the size alteration of the ukulele obviously referred to its reduction to baritone, tenor, and alto longscale, after the reduction in string number to four strings after 1885, since I had a photo of three hula-girls playing, in 1885, a five-string taropatch, larger than the alto longscale and standard ukuleles depicted in the photo, and reproduced by the"National Geographic Magazine" of the mid-forties. (Unconnected with the original Madeiran 'Braguinha', from which koa wood copies were made into the ukulele.)

"Alvin D. Keech states in his article that he was present at H. M. King Kalakaua's feast (at which Gabriel Davion was alleged to have played the Hawaiian steel guitar), and Keech's article proves beyond any reasonable doubt, that others were playing long before Kekuku, as confirmed by his son-in-law Pulu Moe.

"The final chapter in this Agatha Christie style 'whodunit', is added by famous steel guitarist, composer, and publisher C. S. DeLano, who, in his article of April 1932 issue of the English 'Banjo, Mandolin, and Guitar' Magazine, said that when he visited Joseph Kekuku in Paris, Joseph told him that in 1880 (yet another, and differing date!), he was walking along a road in Honolulu, holding an old Spanish guitar, when he saw a rusty bolt on the ground (other stories say he used an old railroad spike); he picked it up, when it 'accidentally vibrated one string, and produced a new tone'. Only then did he experiment with a highly-polished steel bar. Alvin D. Keech and C. S. DeLano both possessed impeccable reliability regarding their statements, and Kekuku, moreover, had worked for Keech, while C. S. DeLano had met him. The following final coincidences (or are they?) have a bearing on this strange and compelling enigma: William and John Kamoku and Sam Kawaihae, of the 'Bird of Paradise Hawaiians' recorded extensively under their own names, such as 'Winner' record label, and accompanied Hawaiian travel-talks and magic-lantern shows with their Hawaiian music, sponsored by lecturer Mrs. Steedman (with whom I corresponded), when all four lived in Wilmslow, Cheshire, England. William Kamoku broadcast at least once over nearby Manchester radio station. Pulu Moe visited William Kamoku (John Kamoku had by then returned to Hawai'i), whom he knew well, in the mid-40's, when he and I were featured steel guitarists with the world-famous Felix Mendelssohn and His Hawaiian Serenaders, on films, TV, and radio, and world-wide distributed Columbia records, concert, and variety stage for ten years.

"Pulu Moe's internationally known steel guitarist brother, (also from La'ie), Tau Moe, visited 'Bird of Paradise' steel guitarist Joseph Pune, at Honolulu's Lunalili Home. Another member of the group, Segis Luawana (also known for his steel guitar recordings under the name of 'Juan Akoni') taught the ukulele to the Duke of Windsor (then the Prince of Wales), and was accompanied on 'Winner' records by Spanish guitarist Lady Chetwynd.

"Apart from Gabriel Papaia (who played plectrum guitar), and July ('Tulai') Paka (who played steel guitar and violin), the others, William Kamoku, Joseph Pune, and Segis Luawana, were all individual recording steel guitarists in their own right. Unlike Kekuku, who used a steel bar, they all used blunted sailors' IXL steel 'jack'-knives (clasp-knives) according to my information from Kimo Koa, and ALL used PIANO-WIRE for strings, these being solidcore, plain, unwrapped strings for securing more sustain with less surface-noise. The most significant fact is that William Kamoku was a 'paniolo'! Strangely enough, the Mormon town of La'ie has the nearby Gunstock Ranch today, and at least one of the Kekuku group was an Hawaiian cowboy!

"In those days, the Hawaiian steel guitar was variously called: 'kikala Hawai'i', 'kikala maoli', 'kikala anuunuu', 'wiola anu'unu'u', and occasionally kikala pahe'e'.

"I hope that this research on the <u>true</u> story of the invention of the Hawaiian Steel Guitar, by one who associated in good friendship, and playing music of the Old Hawai'i, many years ago, with associates of Kekuku, will give as much pleasure and interest to steel guitarists and lovers of Hawaiian music, as the pleasure of compiling it has given me."

Editor's note: The life story of Kealoha Life (as told by Kealoha) was printed in the Hawaiian Steel Guitar Association's July 1989 and October 1989 issues. In that article he stated the following: He was born Alfred Hollis Randell in London, England, in 1919, of Welsh, Australian, and French Huguenot descent. He was educated in Switzerland, during which time he became an expert (self-taught) 'ukuleleist, steel guitarist, and fluent in 10 different languages. (His friend, John Marsden, stated that Life is also fluent in the Hawaiian language.) Aside from performing with his own big band, Life was the featured artist with the very famous Felix Mendelssohn's Hawaiian Serenaders as steel guitarist, Spanish guitarist, 'ukuleleist, Hawaiian vocalist, and Hawaiian dancer. He then spent 20 years as a very popular and successful musician in South Africa, Namibia, and Moçambique. He identified one of the guitar players in "Kekuku's group" as being a South African Griqua (Hottentot) guitarist named Kimo Koa. Life stated that this research report has been published in whole or in part at least 12 times in different magazines and perodicals since 1951.

The Mystery Pursued

When one asks, "Who invented baseball?" the question is not taken to mean, "Who was first to <u>throw</u> an object and who was first to <u>catch</u> a flying object?" No, when we ask, "Who invented baseball?" we mean who designed the diamond and equipment, then called together the sandlot gang and, using the principles of "throw", "catch", "hit", and "run", played the game over and over until the rules "worked". So it is when we ask, "Who invented the Hawaiian steel guitar?" We don't mean, "Who was the first to slide an object over a string to change its pitch?" Many cultures developed musical instruments on which the change of pitch was done by sliding an object over the strings, but those weren't steel guitars. For it to have been done in Hawai'i by someone carelessly moving a metal or glass object over guitar strings and later repeating it for party entertainment is quite conceivable. But that's not inventing an instrument.

To "invent", quoting from a Random House Dictionary, is "...to use known materials to originate or create as a product of one's own ingenuity, experimentation, or contrivance." The U.S. Patent Office defines it this way: "Inventions Patentable: Whoever invents or discovers any new and useful process, machine, manufacture, or composition of matter, or any new and useful improvement thereof, may obtain a patent there for." Just as surely as the game of baseball was *invented* by someone, using principles already known to man, so was the Hawaiian steel guitar *invented* by someone.

When Joseph Kekuku adapted his guitar to the new format, he was probably putting together ideas from different things he'd observed. If both Hoa and Davion played the guitar by sliding an object over the strings, they and their admirers obviously didn't see it as a new instrument. The difference is that Joseph brought into being a new and unique instrument and then worked diligently to perfect the method of playing it, sharing his knowledge with classmates. Some of the new steel guitarists left Hawai'i to show off their amazing instrument before Kekuku did. It's true Joseph didn't follow to the mainland until 1904, but does that take anything away from his invention?

When the Hawaiian Steel Guitar Association decided to celebrate the centennial of Joseph Kekuku's invention, after having the year authenticated by the Bishop Museum, we invited all the other steel guitar clubs to join with us. We were surprised to find our plans politely ignored. It was then that a friend sent us a copy of Kealoha Life's research and explained that it had been widely published and was considered to be the last word on the subject. That explained to us why Kekuku had never been named to the Steel Guitar Hall of Fame.

When steel guitarist Thomas Malm (anthropologist, Department of Social Anthropology, University of Lund, Sweden) visited us we discussed with him the statement in Life's report. "...the first inventor <u>before</u> Kekuku, either Dutch sailors imitating with their pen-knives, the Dutch 'hommel' or German 'hummel', a dulcimer played on pinned legs to a table-top, or even more likely, Scandinavian sailors imitating their national instruments, the Swedish pear-shaped 'hulme' and the Norwegian 8-string 'langleik'..." Thomas hadn't heard of the Swedish hulme but agreed to research it on his return to Sweden.

Thomas sent us reports from 21 different sources, plus two letters. Nowhere did he find record of a 'Hu<u>lm</u>e' and all the following instruments were classified as zithers, not dulcimers. I'll summarize: Hans Grüner Nielsen, in 'Folkelig vals' (Copenhagen) says that in the beginning of the 1800's a 'Hu<u>ml</u>e' introduced to Denmark from Holland was used, but only two known specimens exist, both in museums and "no one can play it or knows how the strings should be tuned...The Humle is a rectangular box with sound holes in it plus a fretboard". (The foregoing was translated to English by Thomas Malm.)   In "The Stringed Instruments of the Middle Ages" by Hortense Panum, published in London (pp.285-8) it is said that the Humle at one time flourished in Sweden but "...in 1917, I met and heard the last Swedish player on this instrument, which has otherwise disappeared. His name was Otto Malmberg". The Humle was pictured as figure-8 shaped, and the "pear shaped instrument of Sweden" was shown as the Hummel (p.286). Grove's dictionary of Musical instruments (London, New York) shows (p.677) the pear-shaped instrument of Sweden as a "...Hommel, a zither used in ...Germany, Denmark, and Sweden in the 18th and 19th centuries." The strings of the zither were not raised and in Scandinavian countries the string pitch was usually changed by the player stopping them against the fret with the fingers of the left hand, not by sliding an object over them.   The strings were sometimes stopped with an object (as in France) but sliding and vibrato were not used.

Thomas put the question on my behalf to Brigit Kjellström of The Music Museum (Music Collections Of The State) in Stockholm. Her reply of March 4, 1992 was, "My answer to Lorene Ruymar's questions, the theory that someone who was playing a Swedish hummel, should have given inspiration to the playing technique of the Hawaiian steel guitar seems to be quite far-fetched."

We were surprised when Paul Kerley of Tucson AZ told us he'd read Armine von Tempski's "Born In Paradise".   Life's exact statement about the book is: "...to the effect that many Hawaiians played steel guitar long before his (Pulu Moe's) father-in-law did. This is confirmed by authoress Armine von Tempsky, in her fine book about the Parker Ranch, 'Born in Paradise', in the 19th century, saying that her father's 'paniolo' ranch-hands (Hawaiian cowboys) 'used their jack-knives to play the guitar.'"
It is indeed a fine book. It was first published in 1940 in New York by Duell, Sloan, and Pearce, Library of Congress Cataloging CT275.V595A33. Armine was born in 1892, she died in 1943. This is hardly a "19th century" story! If our date for the Kekuku invention of the guitar is correct at 1889, the guitar would have been known in the islands for three years before Armine was born.

The ranch which her father managed was NOT the Parker Ranch on the big island of Hawai'i, it was the Haleakalā Ranch on Maui. Yes, Armine did mention her father's paniolos playing the guitar flat on their knees, but it wasn't until page 304 when I estimate she was 25 years old and the year was 1917. I arrive at the estimation from page 200 where she says she is 12 years old and her brother Errol was born, then on page 314 she says Errol is 13 years old. That would make Armine 25 and the steel guitar had been around for 28 years. Her exact words on the subject are, "...Lomi and Kenny took out their guitars and played, using their jack-knives for steels, the long-drawn-out notes sounded like the voices of forgotten people calling to one another across time." In response to Life's claim that "at least one of the Kekuku group" worked as a cowboy on the Gunstock Ranch near La'ie, Merle Kekuku (nephew of Joseph) has stated that there were none that he knows of.

Another interesting point is raised by the Von Tempski book. Accept for a moment the possibility that Davion played the guitar flat on his knees in Waihe'e Maui in 1884. If Davion or anyone else took it seriously, wouldn't the Von Tempski paniolos living on the same island have been doing the same long before 1917? Meanwhile, 10-year-old Joseph Kekuku, living on the far side of another island, O'ahu, is supposed to have copied it??

When my husband and I were visiting at the home of Tau Moe in La'ie, Hawai'i, our conversation turned to the validity of Kekuku's claim. La'ie is Joseph Kekuku's place of birth. Tau grew up there, but left Hawai'i in 1927 to tour the world as so many steel guitarists did. We asked Tau whether he had read Kealoha Life's research on the question. Tau knew and worked with Life in England, so he was a key figure who might be able to unravel the mystery. "Yes," Tau said, "there are some errors in Life's article." First of all, Tau told us that Pulu Moe was NOT his (Tau's) brother, but his half-uncle. He further stated that the wife of Pulu Moe was NOT related to, certainly not the daughter of, Joseph Kekuku. This was in response to Life's words, "My first doubts were sparked off by the remark by ... steel guitarist Pulu Moe, like Joseph, living in La'ie, North O'ahu, and son-in-law of Kekuku, (by virtue of his marriage to Kekuku's daughter Lei Lalana Kekuku) to the ef-fect that many Hawaiians played steel guitar long before his father-in-law did."

February 6, 1992

Ms. Lorene L. Ruymar
Hawaiian Steel Guitar Assoc.
Box 3156
Bellingham, WA 98227

Dear Ms. Ruymar:

Your letters of January 31, 1992 to the State of Hawaii were referred to me. I asked our genealogist, Mr. Kimo Saffery-Tripp to research your request. Mr. Saffery-Tripp searched our marriage record index between 1909 and 1939 and found a record of the following marriage:

Groom: Frank Pulusila, Jr.
Bride: Lalana Kekaa
Date of Marriage: July 15, 1922
Place of Marriage: Laie, Hawaii

Since the marriage occurred less than seventy-five years ago, our vital records law (section 338-18, Hawaii Revised Statutes) prohibits our office from providing more than index information to you.

We are returning the checks that accompanied your letters.

ALVIN T. ONAKA, Ph.D.
State Registrar & Assistant Chief
Office of Health Status Monitoring

Further, should there be a Doubting Thomas among you, we have the word of the State of Hawai'i, Department of Health, and a handwritten note from Pulu's daughter, Mele Moe Daniels.

In a letter to us dated November 11, 1993, Tau said, "To the best of my knowledge, Joseph Kekuku, the La'ie local boy from a little village on the north shore of the Island of O'ahu, Hawai'i (40 miles from Honolulu) was the one who invented the steel guitar."

Hot on the trail of a good mystery, I wrote to Dr. Michael Chun, President of Kamehameha Schools, and asked him for a little help with the next item. It is summarized in Kealoha Life's words, "Charles E. King ...stated that Joseph could not have practiced with a tumbler (glass) on his Spanish Guitar, ...as no ukulele or guitar was allowed to be brought into the school..."

Dr. Chun did not disappoint me, and I'll let you read his letter for yourself.

Along with his letter he enclosed excepts from Dr. George Kanahele's unpublished manuscript The First Hundred Years of the Kamehameha Schools / Bernice Pauahi Bishop Estate which tells of the school's music policy in encouraging students to keep their cultural integrity in using Hawaiian lyrics and singing songs composed by Hawaiians. "...they understood the mana (power) of the mele on the Hawaiian psyche. It was only the convergence of these elements at this highly combustible time that could have forged the musical values and spirit which have given Kamehameha much of its identity and strength - and inventive giants like Joseph Kekuku.'" Discussing the school's choir, he said, "The high quality of its members and their training was borne out by the fact that many members, such as King, Mana'ole, William Keolanui, Matthew Kāne, and Joseph Kekuku, later distinguished themselves in the field of Hawaiian music. Besides the glee club, Richards also organized the school band by 1890, with brass, wind and stringed instruments."

KAMEHAMEHA SCHOOLS / BERNICE PAUAHI BISHOP ESTATE

October 24, 1990

Lorene Ruymar
President and Editor
Hawaiian Steel Guitar Association
Box 3156
Bellingham, WA 98227

Dear Lorene:

Aloha kaua. I read your letter concerning the induction of Joseph Kekuku into the Steel Guitar Hall of Fame with great interest. Since Mr. Kekuku was a Kamehameha student, I feel it is important to accurately record the contributions he made to Hawaiian music and music in general.

I have enclosed some photocopies of articles, photos and documents that may interest you and assist in writing The Story of the Steel Guitar. From what I have learned and experienced, it seems playing the guitar, 'ukulele and other stringed instruments was a popular pastime for KS students throughout its entire 103 year history.

I hope the information helps garner a Hall of Fame spot and postage stamp for Mr. Kekuku, while also clearing up some inaccuracies surrounding the instrument's invention. Best wishes for your worthy efforts.

Me ke aloha pumehana,

Michael J. Chun, Ph.D.
President
The Kamehameha Schools

Enc.

The first band, formed in 1893, played instruments that were either bought with the money contributed by Trustee Cooke or borrowed from a local Portuguese band. Photo courtesy of Kamehameha Schools Bishop Estate

As for getting dates and facts wrong, that happens to the best of us.

In Life's article he tells of his seeing Joseph Kekuku. "I saw, and I listened to, the 'Bird of Paradise Hawaiians' (with Joseph Kekuku on steel guitar), at the Wembley Exhibition, England in 1923, at the age of four years..." However, with a letter dated December 30, 1988 Life sent me his typewritten autobiography titled "An Exciting Life!" which I printed in the July and October, 1989 issues of the HSGA newsletter. In the second paragraph he said, "...I pestered my mother to take me to see Joseph Kekuku's 'Bird of Paradise Hawaiians', at the Ideal Home Exhibition in London, at the age of six."

In articles at the beginning of this chapter, Ken Kapua says the production called 'Leap Year' contained a scene in which 40 Banjuleles performed. Alvin D. Keech, who directed the show, says there were 60 Banjuleles in that scene, and C S. DeLano states that he heard it happened in Paris and the number was a full theatre orchestra plus forty-two Banjuleles. These discrepancies only point out that in trivial matters we humans don't take care to be exactly correct in what we say. Our readers may have noticed the many discrepancies between the invention stories of both the 'ukulele and steel guitar, earlier in this chapter. I don't believe anyone deliberately misinformed you.

See again Life's report of statements made by Al Keech, then re-read Keech's statement near the beginning of this chapter, to see how people mis-report what was said. Among other statements, Life says, "Alvin D. Keech states in his article that he was present at H. M. King Kalākaua's last feast (at which Gabriel Davion was alleged to have played the Hawaiian steel guitar)..." No! It was David Kupihea who made that statement. Keech said only that the 'ukulele was played at the king's feast, he didn't mention the steel guitar. Check also Life's information about the taro-patch fiddle, etc. etc. and compare it with the Groves Dictionary listing.

Life has expressed some dismay at the conflicting tales of the serendipitous invention of the steel guitar. First of all, let's not forget that most of these "variations on a theme" were told by others, not by Kekuku. There's the railway bolt story, the sliding comb, the pocket knife dropping out of a parcel, and so on. As well as careless reporting by others, I believe these were little stories told to entertain those who paid to be entertained. The telling of "little stories" in the entertainment world is not uncommon, they're the little white lies the public delights in hearing. Isn't that why musicians who hadn't a drop of Hawaiian blood in them gave themselves Hawaiian names, and called their band The "Hawaiian" So-and-so's or The "Royal" Whatnots?

Why are there so many dates reported? Because it didn't happen all at one time, but over a span of seven years. The actual invention was just a mundane story of work, trial and error, practice, and more practice. In this matter, we reject the "big bang" theory.

When Tony Todaro published his "The Golden Years of Hawaiian Entertainment 1874-1974" in Hawai'i in 1974, he interviewed over 300 musicians and entertainers. Of those, he named 33 to his "Hawaiian Entertainment Hall of Fame". The first two named were King David Kalākaua and Queen Lydia Lili'uokalani. The seventh named is Joseph Kekuku, of whom Todaro said, (p.195), "One thing is certain - Joseph Kekuku is the undisputed inventor of the Hawaiian steel guitar."

On the one hand we have the speculation of people living far from Hawai'i. On the other, we have the work of trained researchers doing first-hand checking of records and interviewing people in Hawai'i. The first was Dr. Helen Roberts, then Loring Hudson, then Drs. Donald K. Mitchell and Geo S. Kanahele. All came to the same conclusion.

And so, ladies and gentlemen of the jury, I rest my case. The evidence is overwhelming. It is the decision of the Hawaiian Steel Guitar Association that Joseph Kekuku is the inventor of the Hawaiian steel guitar. You are free to decide otherwise.

Joseph Kekuku,
inventor of the Hawaiian steel guitar. Fact? or Fiction?
Jerry Byrd photo

Joseph Kekuku
A Personal Glimpse

It appears that after Joseph left his home in La'ie to travel to far-off lands, the family back home received the occasional letters but he did not return, and much of his life abroad is a mystery. In 1932 Hawaiian music researcher Miro Maximchuk received a letter from a Jim Carroll of Sparta MI who said, "I taught Hawaiian guitar with Joe Kekuku in 1929 - 1930 in the Langdon Brothers Hawaiian Guitar School, 431 S. Wabash Ave., in Chicago, the largest exclusive Hawaiian guitar studio in the U.S. I also took some lessons from him. He was a wonderful player and a most wonderful person. After a short illness, Joseph Kekuku died in Dover, NJ on January 18th, 1932. His ashes were returned to La'ie. Joseph was survived by his father Joseph, his brother Edward, two sisters Miss Ivy Kekuku and Mrs. Violet Meyers, and a daughter Mrs. W. G. Cowart. The original steel used by Mr. Kekuku is now owned by William S. Duncan of Denver. Mr. Duncan, who is now a salesman, was once a vaudeville guitar player. He was presented with the steel guitar by Mr. Kekuku."

We obtained a copy of Joseph Kekuku's will from the Superior Court of New Jersey. It is dated December 12, 1912, by "Joseph Kekuku, of the Borough of Manhattan, City of New York." After the legal preliminaries, it says, "I give and bequeath all my real estate and all my other personal property, of whatsoever name and description which I may posess including life insurance money, due in case of my death to my wife, Adeline E. Kekuku, and I make her my sole and absolute heir. In case of the death of my wife, I leave the above to my next nearest heirs, my dear mother and father, who reside in O'ahu, T.H." His wife, Adeline E. Kekuku was appointed executrix and, although Joseph died in 1932, she was not able to probate the will until December 2, 1937 because of difficulties in locating the three witnesses to Joseph's signature. By the time she was able to probate the will, Adeline had remarried and was "now Adeline E. DeFrance". There is no indication that the Kekukus had children.

Working on the theory that there may have been a previous marriage, we checked the records of the State Department of Health in Honolulu. There is no record of a Kekuku being married in the State of Hawai'i between the years 1885 and 1905.

The Death Certificate, obtained from the State Department of Health - Bureau of Vital Statistics State of New Jersey states that Joseph Kekuku died at 11:20 a.m. on January 16, 1932 and no next-of-kin are listed except his wife, and parents in Hawai'i.

The exact date of Joseph Kekuku's birth remains a mystery. In a leaflet prepared by Kekuku when he was an instructor at the Reids School of Popular Music in Chicago, he stated that he was born in 1874 in the village of La'ie, HI. Kamehameha Schools record his birth year as 1875. A search of the Vital Records Program, State Department of Health in Honolulu, also at the La'ie Family History Center, Church of Latter-Day Saints, in La'ie, also in Utah has not been successful. There are many forms his name could take in their records. It could be listed in the full Hawaiian name *Kekuku 'upenakana 'i-aupuniokamehameha Apuakehau* or in one of the shortened forms *Kekukupena* or *Apuakehau* or in the modern form *Kekuku..* Joseph's father's birth is recorded by the La'ie Family History Center as "Joseph Kekukupena Apuakehau, born June 19 1857 in La'ie, died May 17, 1938, married to Miliama Kaopua." There are seven other members of the Apuakehau family registered with births ranging from 1845 to 1862, but none of them are Joseph Jr. A letter from the Center explains, "Records held by the Health Department in Hawai'i are not considered complete until the 1930's. I have gone through the records we have and find no account of his (Joseph's) birth. This is not unusual for the time period. My own mother, born in 1912, and her 16 brothers and sisters have not one birth record among them."

The only one of the Kekuku family known to have played steel guitar professionally other than Joseph is his nephew Merle Kekuku (son of Joseph's brother Edwin) who lives in Ai'ea, Hawai'i. Merle has stated that he never met his famous uncle, as he was born in 1918 and "Uncle Joe" left Hawai'i in 1904, never to return. He does, however, recall hearing the grownups speaking of Joseph and his persistence in working on his new way of playing the guitar. The family did not realize until many years later that "the kid" had actually made a permanent and important contribution to Hawaiian music, and even then no great fuss was made about it. "We are not ones to blow our own horns," is the way Merle put it.

Dr. Donald Kilolani Mitchell, historian and teacher at Kamehameha Schools, corresponded with Mrs. Kekuku during her husband's fatal illness. She confirmed that Joseph was the inventor of the instrument and said he played his first public performance at the Mission Memorial in La'ie as a boy. After his travels, he settled down in the Chicago area as a highly successful steel guitar teacher. She said, "He was a great teacher and is the possessor of the most beautiful steel guitar in the world."

Steel Guitarist Bob Mekani has a souvenir letter received as fan mail during his radio broadcasting years on Station WMCA, New York. The letter was postmarked Dover N.J. on April 15, 1935 and in the fine English handwriting of Adeline Kekuku, "Dear Hawaiian Boys, I listen to your programe and enjoy very much your Melodies. Please play Joe's solo next Saturday for him who is now in <u>Heaven</u> (as an Easter Offering). 'Ua Like No Like' and 'Mai Poina I'au'. Aloha. Thank you. (signed) Widow of Joseph Kekuku."

We have located a Myldred Cooper of Linden, NJ who knew Mrs. Kekuku during the 1930's, after Joseph had passed away. Adeline had remarried by that time and Myldred gave steel guitar lessons to the new husband. In her letter of June 19th,1992 in which she enclosed a picture of Joseph's grave, Myldred says, "The man that I taught (second husband of Mrs. Kekuku) was named James W. DeFrance. Mrs. DeFrance was an English lady (accent and all). When I knew them (1930's) they lived on Mt. Hope Ave., Dover NJ. Mr. DeFrance was 65 years of age at that time.

I, Mlydred (Hopler) Cooper met Mr. DeFrance in April 1935.

He was the second husband of the wife of Joseph Kekuku, Originator of Hawaiian style of playing guitar.

Mr. DeFrance had taken lessons from Joseph Kekuku until the Hawaiian's death.

I visited their home to teach Mr. DeFrance and became friendly with Mrs. DeFrance.

After the lesson, we would talk and she told me many times how Mr. Kekuku would sit and practice this new style of playing guitar until he perfected it.

I have five pieces of sheet music "Steel Guitar Arrangements" by Myrtle Stumpf published by Southern California Music Co. given to me by Mrs. DeFrance that had belonged to the originator, Kekuku.

Two sheets are initialed J.K.

Witness:
Diana Zeupruflo 8/21/92
Lau M Cox 8/21/92

Myldred Cooper
2816 De Witt Terr
Linden N.J.
07036

Rosellen Grasso 8-21-92

ROSELLEN GRASSO
NOTARY PUBLIC OF NEW JERSEY
My Commission Expires Nov. 12, 1992

Notarized statement by Myldred Cooper attesting to her connection with the widow of Joseph Kekuku.

"I had a chance to buy that National guitar of Mr. Kekuku's, but my mom said 'no' even though I had a little bank account - $300.00 - because I had to save all gift money - birthdays, Christmas, etc.

"The name of the cemetery where Mr. Kekuku is buried is Orchard. You can get there from Blackwell St. to Warren in Dover, NJ.

"I have five pieces of music that belonged to Mr. 'K', arranged in notation in low bass 'A' tuning by Myrtle Stumpf. One sheet has a Christmas stamp on it dated 1928. The songs are all classical selections:

"Traumerei", "Cavalleria Rusticana Intermezzo", "Berceuse", "Sextette from Lucia" (initialed by J. Kekuku), and "Schuberts Serenade" (initialed by J. Kekuku), copyrighted 1915 and 1916. The copies are marked 25¢."

Myldred affirmed in a letter to H.S.G.A., "In answer to: Did Mr. Kekuku invent the steel style of playing guitar? His wife says that he did. He used to play and play at home until he perfected it."

STYLE II
$145⁰⁰

STYLE III
$165⁰⁰

The **Style II** National Silver Guitar is identical in construction to the Style I Guitar but is engraved with a neat floral design completely around the body of the instrument.

Each $145.00

The **Style III** Guitar built in either Spanish or broad neck Hawaiian models is identical to the Style II except that it has an elaborately engraved body with fancy cut pearl position dots.

Each $165.00

Joseph Kekuku's grave marker at Orchard Cemetery, Dover NJ
photo by Myldred Cooper

<u>National Hawaiian guitar, style No. 3</u>
Said by Myldred Cooper to be very similar to the one owned by Joseph Kekuku

Chapter 2

Travels of the Steel Guitar Throughout the World

The Gift Of Aloha From Hawai'i To The World

Within 20 years the *kīkā kila (kīkā = guitar, kila = steel)* had become the new senstation throughout the Hawaiian islands. Then like their forefathers, the fearless navigators of the vast Pacific Ocean, Hawai'i's musicians became its finest ambassadors to every corner of the globe.

The First To The Mainland, The First Recordings

The first documentation we have of a steel guitarist to set foot on the U.S. mainland is in Dr. Kanahele's "Hawaiian Music and Musicians". He tells of not one but two, July Paka and Tom Hennessey, who were taken to the mainland in 1899 by William Kuali'i who was noted for his work in pioneering Hawaiian recordings. Along with Tony Zablan, Tommy Silva, and David Makuakāne, they travelled to San Francisco where they recorded for Edison (see Paka, Hennessey) on the old wax cylinders. Although no samples are known to exist today, this may have been the first recording of Hawaiian music. It is not known which of the two (or whether both) played steel guitar on the recordings.

In our first chapter, Ken Kapua told of Joseph Kekuku's having recorded with Layton and Johnstone while employed by Al Keech in London (1919-1927), the numbers being "Tell Me More", "I'll See You In My Dreams" and "When You and I Were Seventeen". In Hawai'i, the first recordings of steel guitarists were made by the Brunswick Co. in 1928, the artists being M. K. Moke, David Burrows, Kepoikai Lyons, George Ku, etc., but we're getting ahead of our story.

Shortly after their arrival in San Francisco, July Paka married a professional dancer who led them into a whirlwind of success under the name of Toots Paka's Hawaiians. They played in the best places alongside the biggest names in the American entertainment world. They were mobbed by high society, and led the way for many Hawaiian groups to follow. So great was their success, it's been said that they made Hawaiian music a permanent institution rather than a passing fancy. Aside from the costumes and the daring hula dance routines, the greatest attraction was to the beguiling, haunting, teasing music of the steel guitar. Those who heard it never forgot it.

Others To Follow To The Mainland

Paka and Hennessey were followed to the mainland USA by Pale K. Lua, and Frank Ferera followed in 1902, and Joseph himself in 1904., then Ernest Ka'ai in 1906. Other steel players Herman Bishaw, Ben Hokea, Geo E.K. Awa'i and Walter Kolomoku were there by 1915. They all formed groups on the mainland or brought other musicians with them from Hawai'i, to begin making recordings, touring the mainland U.S., and then going abroad. Some of them, like Frank Ferera, Pale K. Lua, Ben Hokea, and Joseph Kekuku never returned to their homeland and so are better known in distant lands than at home.

Toots Paka Troupe, steel guitarist July Paka
M. Maximchuk photo

Frank Ferera
M. Maximchuk photo

Ben Hokea
and his group.
M. Maximchuk photo

Frank Ferera

Pale K. Lua
and David Ka'ili,
both steel guitarists
M. Maximchuk photo

The Second Generation

By 1920 a second generation of Hawaiian steel guitarists had arrived on the mainland: Sol Ho'opi'i, Dick McIntire, Benny "King" Nawahī, Sam Ku West, and many others. The instrument through which Hawaiian music made its most significant impact upon American music was the steel guitar, the first "foreign" musical import to gain a foothold in American pop music.

Sol Ho'opi'i
Ray Smith photo

Benny "King" Nawahī
playing very earliest form of
Hawaiian steel guitar,
converted from Spanish guitar

Sam Ku West playing one of
National's first steel guitars
B. Brozman photo

Keoki E. K. Awa'i, playing earliest form of steel guitar, with his Royal Hawaiian Quartet. Warren H. Edgar photo

Dick McIntire on steel guitar (Rickenbacker), Danny Kua'ana on 'ukulele, Sol Gregory on bass, Danny Santos on guitar. Corliss Johnston photo

The Tau Moe Family

Panama Pacific International, 1915

An event that provided a showcase and fueled the Hawaiian music craze across the country was the Panama-Pacific International Exposition held in San Francisco in 1915. A Hawaiian pavilion was built on the site, and the Hawaiian shows which were staged there several times a day drew the highest attendance of the exposition. The house band was that of steel guitarist George E. K. Awa'i, who later became a music publisher. He was the leader and director of his "Royal Hawaiian Quartet". Many other steel players were featured as guest artists, Joseph Kekuku, Frank Ferera, Pale K. Lua and David Ka'ili to name a few. Hawaiian musical groups featuring steel guitar had played in fairs and expositions across the country since 1901 but none had the impact or attracted as many people as did the Panama-Pacific Exposition. It was followed by an instant boom in Hawaiian music recordings (which out-sold all other pop music recordings), movies with Hawaiian themes, the formation of new Hawaiian musical groups, and the demand for instruction on 'ukulele and steel guitar.

Bird Of Paradise Show, 1912

Earlier than that, in 1912, the first Hawaiian Broadway show "Bird of Paradise" went on stage at Daly's Theater, New York. Its brilliant Hawaiian scenery and dazzling costumes plus the authentic music of the five Hawaiian musicians with Walter Kolomoku on steel guitar made it an instant hit. One reporter referred to the "wierdly sensuous music of the island people". After completing a successful run on Broadway, the show went on the road to tour the U.S. and Canada. It played to packed houses everywhere and nearly always it was the first time the audience heard Hawaiian music and the steel guitar. There were changes of cast and musicians, so other steel guitarists may have taken over at different times.

When the show was reorganized to tour Europe in 1919, its steel guitarist was virtuoso Joseph Kekuku. You must remember that all this time the guitar was not amplified, not even with resonators. It must have been a great challenge to make its voice heard sufficiently from the stage. For eight years the show toured Europe, playing before the crown heads of many countries. It was a total sell-out and European hearts were captured by the sweet teasing sound of the steel guitar. No other instrument in history became the darling of so many countries so quickly. The show was so popular, it was filmed in Hollywood as a movie "The Bird of Paradise" in 1932 and re-filmed in 1951.

Merchant Seamen, Explorers

At this point, we must go back a few years to tell the story of those whose names did not appear in print, but who nonetheless helped to spread the wildfire of steel guitar popularity into the farthest corners of the globe. They are the merchant seamen and unskilled laborers who signed on with the ships stopping in Hawai'i's harbors, taking their guitars and 'ukuleles along to while away long hours at sea. We were told by Alfred Bentley, a steel guitarist of Fiji, "...at the age of fifteen I started to learn the steel guitar. I first heard it when it was played by three Hawaiian crew men from the

Cariso, a ship that stopped every six months at Rotuma to load copra. One evening they took time off and came ashore. They set up their little trio and played until early morning. That was the first time I heard the 'Aloha Chimes' played. The names of the players were: Blake on steel guitar, Wilson on rhythm guitar, and Baker on 'ukulele. I asked Blake about the 'Aloha Chimes' and he gave me a recording of it. I don't remember who made that record, but it was in the early 30's so it could have been Sol Ho'opi'i."

Alf Bentley's brother-in-law, John Fatiaki, conversely became the musician who spread the Hawaiian steel guitar gospel to other people. On the merchant navy vessel S.S.Suva of Fiji, he formed a band among his fellow crewmen and played his 6-string Gibson steel guitar in ports of Japan, India, Australia, Hawai'i, California, and Canada.

A similar story was told by Kale W. Kaleiali'i, born in Hana Maui in 1900. His family had moved to the mainland where his mother died. Conditions at home were so bad that at age 14 he ran away from home and signed on as P.O. Mess on the American Hawaiian Freightliner "S.S. Dakotan" going from the east coast through the Panama Canal to Portland. On what was called the "Dark Gang" was a Hawaiian seaman who played steel guitar, rhythm guitar, and 'ukulele. He kindly befriended his young countryman, taught him to play steel guitar, and helped him to remember the Hawaiian language. In later years Kale toured the American vaudeville circuit, often appearing on the same bill as a young hoofer named Bob Hope. Kyle said that in those days he, with his comic routine on steel guitar, 'ukulele, and novelty instruments such as the theremin etherovox and gut bucket, got more applause than Hope did.

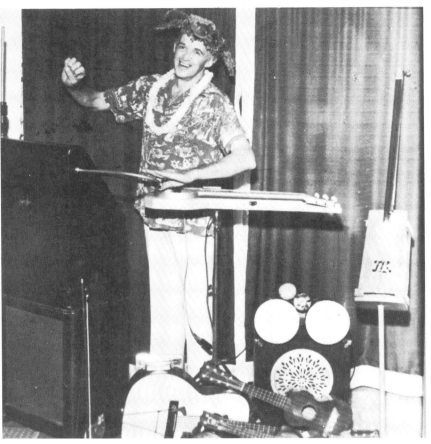

Kale Kaleiali'i, steel guitarist and vaudeville entertainer
K. Kaleiali'i photo

From 1811 on, Hawaiians were brought to the Pacific Northwestern states, and into Canada by the Hudson Bay Co. during the years of exploration and fur trade. Any map of the Pacific Northwest will show you towns that bear Hawaiian names. Most Hawaiians in that era were known simply as "Kanaka Joe" or "Kanaka Sam". Their expertise in canoe handling and swimming made Hawaiians invaluable to the less adept Europeans. The subject has been researched by historian Dr. Jean Barman, University of British Columbia, and reported in her book "West Of The West". The very portable steel guitar could have travelled the river highways of North America without any written record.

Travels To Far Countries.

Ernest Ka'ai is known to have been the first to take his Hawaiian troupe and steel guitar to Australia in 1918, and he did several tours of the Far East and the Orient between 1919 and 1937. Joseph Kekuku was the first to play steel in European countries, and his contemporaries were quick to follow. But, the travels of one steel guitarist from Hawaii were so extensive, his story must be told in detail here, as he must have been the first to play in many countries.

The Tau Moe Family Story

as told by Tau Moe
This story is reprinted from the Hawaiian Steel Guitar Association Newsletter.
Jul. 1990, Oct. 1990, Jan. 1991, Apr. 1991, and Jul. 1991 issues.

This is the story of Tau and Rose Moe who entertained and travelled the world for 61 years of their amazing lives. Let's start at the beginning. Tau was born in Pago Pago, Samoa on August 13th, 1908. His parents were Mormon missionaries. The family, with eleven children, would move from one village to another to start a new church, take leadership, form the choir, and do the lessons. That's how Tau and his brothers became musically literate, being trained by their father. Polynesians have a gift, a natural ear for music, but at that time it was unusual for them to be able to read and write music. The Moe children crept into the church during the week days and each child in turn learned to play it.

Tau was about 11 years of age when the family moved to La'ie, Hawai'i. At that time, in Honolulu, there was a professor Madame Claude Rivier who taught French. She was very interested in Hawaiian and Polynesian music, having lived in Tahiti, American Samoa, Tonga, New Zealand and other Pacific islands. She gave frequent parties and invited the local musicians who were happy to entertain just for the good food. In 1927 she opened her large home at 1136 S. King St. to the public. When a passenger ship arrived, Madame Rivier would go aboard and invite the visitors to her place to be entertained. Tau's uncle Pulu (a dancer in Madame's show) got him a job as a guitar player for $2.00 a day, a lordly sum to Tau and to the people of La'ie. In those days it was a long distance from La'ie to Honolulu. Tau would attend school during the week, then travel over 40 miles to Honolulu to play the weekend shows. He used to take the "sooky" rides but often to save money he'd walk.

The show was a mixture of Tahitian, Samoan, and Hawaiian music. Madame Rivier charged an admission fee and each evening she'd have 100 to 200 people attending her show. This was the beginning of Madame Rivier's Polynesian show group, the first regular tourist show in Honolulu.

When the Royal Hawaiian Hotel opened in 1927, the Johnny Noble band played inside and Tau's group did the opening show in the garden under the palm trees. There were five women and seven men. All had to be musicians, singers, and dancers.

Tau Moe, his first years as a steel guitarist
B. Brozman photo

Tau was fascinated with the sound of the steel guitar, particularly when he heard it playing "Moana Chimes". A nearby music store, "Hawai'i Sail", played recorded music over a loudspeaker for passers-by to enjoy. Tau listened every day, then he would go home and try to imitate the sound. He learned that the steel guitarist on the record. was M. K. Moke, who had a studio just above the record shop. Tau's uncle, who knew Mr. Moke, arranged for him to take one lesson at the outrageous price of $20.00. Moke was a huge man with very big hands, but his touch on the steel guitar was very soft. During that lesson Tau watched Mr. Moke very closely: his movements, his bar positions, his style, and his expression. Moke wrote out the song in numbers for Tau. As arranged, Tau paid the $20.00 to his uncle who, Tau learned later, paid much less to Mr. Moke. BUT!! Here's where cupid played a part. At that lesson Tau met Rose, another steel guitar student of Mr. Moke's. Their courtship began that day.

Rose was born August 11, 1908 in Kohala on the island of Hawai'i. "Ka'ohu" was her father's name. When Rose's mother died, Rose and her two sisters came to live with their brother who was on the Honolulu police force. The three girls were singers and dancers in the Johnny Almeida show when Rose met Tau. Madame Rivier's troupe was ready to leave on December 28th, 1927, travelling by ship, to open a carnival in the Philippines and then go on tour. Tau and Rose were part of the troupe. Little did they know when they left Hawai'i that they wouldn't return to live there for 60 years!

It was at one of Mme Rivier's shows in Honolulu that the owners of the Eddie K. Fernandes Carnival Show had booked the group for one month, and the director of the Manila Carnival invited them to the Philippines for two months to open the carnival at Luneta Park, Manila. Irene West was a great friend of Madame Claude Rivier, so at their farewell performance in Hawai'i at the O'ahu Theater both Irene West and Madame Rivier's groups performed together, as they were booked to travel together. Sam Ku West and Sol Ho'opi'i were the two top steel guitarists in Honolulu at that time. Sam and his brother Dan Ku ('ukulele) and George Kalani (guitarist) made up Irene West's group. George Kalani's wife was the hula dancer.

Tau was not the steel guitarist in the tour group. That was Frank Jona, a Hawaiian. In Tokyo, they met Dan Pokipala who had a big band - 5 saxophones, 4 trombones, etc. Dan convinced Frank Jona to be his steel player, so Tau took over playing steel for Madame Rivier's show. While in India, Madame Rivier met a fast-talking salesman who convinced her to buy a carnival. She turned all her attention to its operation, leaving "the boys" in the band to their own devices. Pulu Moe and the others joined the group of Ernest Ka'ai who was living in Ceylon (Sri Lanka). Unfortunately, the previous owner of the carnival died shortly after, leaving huge unpaid taxes for which the government seized the carnival. M. Rivier had lost her entertainment group as well as her carnival. Tau and Rose stood by her until she found a job with the French consulate in Shanghai, then they carried on touring on their own. Well, by this time it was Tau and Rose and their son Lani.

I'll let Tau tell the story in his own words: "Lani was born in Kyoto, Japan, a beautiful garden city, in 1929. Rose danced and sang in the matinee show, then felt some pain and the theater manager rushed her to Furitsu Hospital which was for Japanese only. Lani was the only foreign kid born in that hospital. They were so kind, bringing gifts of baby clothes and blankets to us. In Japan, the firstborn son is very important. They gave him the name of Yamada. Lani was brought up in the backstage of the theatre, and grew up as a true trouper with show business in his blood.

"Lani would go to school in the morning, then perform in the matinee show, then practice, then do homework. It was a tough life, but when you're young you can do a thousand things. He was five years old when he signed his first contract with a theater in Shanghai. He was a smash hit, singing 'It's Great To Be In Love' and doing a tap dance at the end of the number. Rose made his first costume, a little white satin jacket and black pants, with top hat and tail coat.

"And so we toured throughout all of Asia. Yes, we've been around the world seven times! For example, when we went to Turkey we stayed a year. We'd work three months in Istanbul, three months in Ankara, and so on. We would get into their homes, eat their food, and learn their language. After Asia, we moved into Romania and Czechoslovakia.

"Five years later, we were booked back at the Carnival in Manila, just Rose, three year old Lani, and myself. The agent told us there would be a Hawaiian trio waiting there to perform with us. It was Bob Ka'ai (son of Ernest Ka'ai) and his band. Bob played steel guitar and alto sax, Sid Kanau, the husband of Thelma Ka'ai (Bob Ka'ai's sister), played guitar, and Joe Kānepu'u played steel guitar and rhythm guitar. My next engagement was back at the Taj Mahal Hotel in Bombay, then six months back in Europe. After a few months World War II broke out and the Japanese over-ran the Philippines.

"We always worked as a Hawaiian family, there was never any question of that in our show content. We were fortunate to be of Polynesian origin. We were in Turkey when they started anti-American bombings and riots. Seeing our passport was from Hawai'i, they loved us and didn't bother us. In Germany, at the time of Hitler, people helped us get out. In Munich there was a special house that Hitler used (1938, before the war). He was there at the time, with the S.S. troops stationed outside.

34

We worked in a theater near by. Someone directed us to a restaurant down the street. We misunderstood and walked right into the house where Hitler was staying. The guards stopped us in the lobby and said, 'What do you want?' We said, 'We want to eat,' and they laughed and said, 'Not here!! This area is restricted.' When we were in Frankfurt we drove our car on the wrong side of the frontier. All the guards came out. We smiled and waved, and they did too. That's the Polynesian style.

"We lived in Germany for forty odd years, on and off. We were in Berlin for awhile, then went to Brussels, then over to Belgium where we lived for a long time before we returned to Germany. It was easier for us to travel out of Belgium. We also worked out of Paris for awhile, but Rose didn't like Paris so we shifted to Brussels because it was centrally located. London was near, France, and Germany. It took only 30 minutes from Brussels to get to Germany, 30 minutes to get to Holland, Paris 40 minutes.

"We got stuck during the war, but that's a long story. When the war broke out in Europe, we had an apartment in Berlin. The American Consul called and said we'd better go. We came all the way back through Turkey, Israel, Tel Aviv, Jerusalem, Greece, and Lebanon where we'd been many times before. We bought tickets to take the S.S.Excalibur to take us to Boston, but on the 6th of June before we sailed, Italy declared war. So what did we do? The Mediterranean was closed. The American Consul said our best bet was to go to India. He said, 'I'm getting a bus, to leave for Baghdad tomorrow morning. You can expect four days and nights on the desert. Don't take any luggage.'

"There were about forty Americans on the bus, professors from the university in Beirut. Before we started we bought a lot of French bread, and boiled 3 dozen eggs. By the third day the eggs smelled so badly we had to throw them out. The other passengers had no food, so we shared our bread. There was drinking water on the bus. We arrived in Baghdad in a sand storm. We couldn't breathe. The hotel manager gave us mosquito nets which we got under, and stayed inside until the storm was over. In about 20 days we got a ship to go from the Persian Gulf to India. We had two battleships escorting us. The first night out we had to observe blackout rules, and accidentally rammed an Italian submarine that had come up for air. The Italian sailors had come out on deck naked, and were lying about in the fresh air. When we rammed them, their sub went down and we took them all aboad our ship in their bare skins. They surrendered.

"When we arrived in India (which was British) they wouldn't allow us to stay because our passport said 'Berlin', and Lani spoke only German. Again, the consul helped us. Because I had already bought our tickets for Hawai'i he convinced them we were 'enroute'. So we were allowed to work our way to Calcutta. But, in Calcutta we couldn't leave for home because the Japanese bombed Pearl Harbor. We were stuck in India for the whole war. All Lani could do is talk German and Japanese, but he learned to speak perfect Hindu. We found work in a good 15 piece dance band, based at the Grand Hotel in Calcutta. I played clarinet and steel guitar, Lani played saxophone, Rose was the regular band singer, and I was the band leader and show director.

"We played Glenn Miller arrangements (or my own) but always included Hawaiian music. We would do a session of jazz band music, then some classical music, then a Hawaiian session with me on steel guitar. At 15 years of age, Lani was the jazz singer, a dancer, and the choreographer of the show. Two Russian musicians in the band taught him to play all the band instruments so he could take the part of any absent musician. Later on, I took charge of all the entertainment in the hotel. Show business was very good in India.

"Dorian was born in India in 1946, during the riots between the Muhammadans and the Hindus. The Hindus wanted the British to leave India, but the British thought the Indian government would collapse if they withdrew. The British moved away, to see if the Indians could self-govern. There was an American base near by in case the Japanese invaded Burma. The time came for the baby to be born, but the doctor would not come because of the rioting. On the ground floor of our building there was a Muhammadan furniture store. The Hindus smashed the windows and pulled out all the furniture, burned it and killed the manager. I was filming this with my movie camera from the window up above. The hotel was then surrounded by the army. They took Rose to a hospital, but Lani and I had to do the 6 o'clock evening show. After the show we were taken by two guards in a jeep, tommy guns on the side, to see Rose and the baby. It was about an hour's drive out of the city. We went through floods, and we waded through waist deep water to get to the hospital. The nurse came out with this wrinkled looking 'something' in her hands and said to Lani, 'This is your sister'. He said, 'Oh, my God!' From then on we were the Aloha Four.

"It was because of my steel guitar that we met Mahatma Ghandi of India and of course 'the great' Adolf Hitler. During our stay in Germany in Hitler's time, there was an organization to help orphanages, called 'The Winter Help'. Every night after our show, we would collect donations from the audience. Every year they announced which entertainers collected the most money. For five years the Tau Moe family came out the winners, so Hitler sent for us to come and meet him.

"As for Ghandi, he was a very highly educated man and I enjoyed the 35 minutes we spent talking to him. Before we left I said that it was unusual to see him put on his lava lava from between his legs.

He laughed and said, 'Well, I am better off than you Polynesian people who walk about without shirts.' We laughed and then he said, 'You know, Tau Moe, you are the very first Polynesian I have met.'

"We were the first Hawaiian act ever to come to Egypt. When they heard the steel guitar music they came to our hotel and wanted to see how I played it. They took my fingers in their hands to see the picks. Of course, they all had Sol Ho'opi'i recordings and they were crazy about Hawaiian music and the steel guitar. They kept on taking us to the radio station and our picture was always in the newspapers. They even booked us to appear at the Folks Theater where only Egyptian culture was allowed, just to let the Egyptian people hear the Hawaiian steel guitar music. The same thing happened in Turkey, Bulgaria, and Greece, where I also gave steel guitar lessons.

"Two years later we returned to play at the Variety Theater in Athens. We happened to hear the sound of a steel guitar and four voices singing in beautiful harmony. The song was 'Imi Au Iā 'Oe, the same one I had taught two years before. They sang it so beautifully, except the words were not pronounced clearly. When they found out we were there they nearly mobbed us and we had to get out fast. In Yugoslavia they wanted us to join with them in making a recording, but I didn't want to because it was mostly Western music. Even in the islands of the Mediterranean, Malta, Cyprus, Gibraltar, Lisbon Portugal, and Spain they loved Hawaiian music. We played in Spain about 20 times, also Beirut Lebanon, Baghdad, also Iran where I taught music to 14 boys. The same thing in Italy, we had great success every time we went to Milano, playing at the Puccini Theater with many big Italian opera stars. We made many recordings in Italy. They wanted us to record "O Solo Mio" and "Santa Lucia", to show how it sounds on the steel guitar. We did it and they loved it. In Israel all the slow and pure Hawaiian music was a big hit. It was a 'must' for me to play 'Maui Chimes' and 'Aloha No Wau I Kou Maka'. In Berlin and Vienna we made recordings with the symphony orchestras.

"In Vienna, a doctor always came to our hotel to get us to bring our sweet Hawaiian music to his hospital for drug and alcohol abusers and the insane. We were surprised that 60 percent of the patients were young women. The steel guitar always brought a happy and serene response from the patients while loud music made them worse.

"In May of 1947, we finally got to make a quick stop at home, so Dorian had her first birthday in Hawai'i. Here's how it happened: There was no ship at all to leave Bombay to go to Hawai'i. Finally, a troop transport named the Marine Adders came along, headed for Hawai'i. We bought third class tickets, and had very good luck when we got on the ship. I'd sold all my guitars before leaving India, planning to buy more when we got to the States. What did we find on the ship? A whole crew of Hawaiian boys! They moved us into a first class room! They had 'ukuleles and guitars!!

"We stayed home for a little while, then we went back to Europe where we signed a contract to join Felix Mendelssohn's Hawaiian Serenaders. Felix was an English bandleader, not the classical Mendelssohn. Dorian joined the show when she was three. We stayed in that show a long time, so Dorian was brought up in Europe. She was on national TV, on the BBC, and sang 'Drifting and Dreaming' on the air. They had to wake her up first, as she always slept when we were recording in the studio.

"At five years old, Dorian did tap dancing in the show. Lani studied classical music and dance. He took 13 years of ballet (both modern and classical) in Paris and in Copenhagen. All the while the kids were studying, Rose and I were studying too. Rose became an acrobat and I a tap dancer. Our act consisted of Hawaiian music with steel guitar, then modern music, and ended with acrobatic dancing, which was the shocker, the surprise element. We were billed as The Aloha Four. We did not need a back-up band, we did our own show. We carried our own big band arrangements, so a band from a host country could back us up. Music styles kept changing, so we were best doing our own thing. We found it was the very high class people who loved Hawaiian music most. We worked all stages, from the highest to the lowest. We played the Super Super Club, very difficult to get in there. Very elite, very upper crust, no act could please them. The patrons were lethargic, didn't applaud but they loved our Hawaiian music, our slow sweet music.

"We had to adjust to country, western and other styles, you name it. We recorded, got into discotheque. We worked in southern France, on the Riviera side, where they expected loud music. We did it, but in the middle of the evening we'd stop and I would just play my soft steel guitar. People were so tired of hearing the booming sound all night. We'd do only two or three soft ones on the steel guitar and that was it. People would just bring down the house and call for more. We've seen all stages of life. Every show was special, regardless of where it was. Some of the worst places were dumps but we didn't call them that. We came into places that were so dark you'd fall over things. One time we thought we were in the kitchen and asked the manager where we were to play. He said, 'Right here. I'll move the tables away.' and I said 'Thank you,' because they were paying us good money, regardless of how dumpy the place was.

"Once in England, it was called the Ocean View Country Club and we were prepared for a posh location. It turned out to be a broken down old theater. We were to work in the middle of a huge hall, in a boxing ring. They'd had mud wrestling the night before. Even worse, we were in tuxedos and Rose and Dorian were in sequined dresses, but they had to climb over the ropes into the boxing ring and try to look cool. Shirley Bassey (a big star) had been there not long before us. We thought if she could do it so could we. The first thing we did was 'The Wonderful World of Aloha.' The back-up band was about a mile away from us. We couldn't hear them at all, so we rang the bell to tell them when to stop. The guys in the front row of the audience were reading their newspapers. So we thought, 'If they want it rough, they're going to get it rough.' We turned up our amplifiers to the maximum and banged the drums for dear life. They stopped reading their newspapers and we had their undivided attention throughout the show. At the end, they said, 'Gee, I never knew Polynesians played so loud!' The manager had the audacity to ask us to extend our contract. No way!!

The Aloha Four
Tau on steel, Dorian on rhythm guitar, Rose on rhythm guitar, Lani on 'ukulele and bass. T. Moe photo

"Hilton Hotels took us over to Australia for three years, about twenty years ago. We were on our way back to Belgium via New Zealand, Fiji, Tonga, and Hawai'i when we realised that we were heading back to Europe and had never seen Samoa, the homeland of the Moe family. We stayed at the Rainmaker Hotel in Pago Pago for 15 days, then in Western Samoa for another 15 days. I was surprised to find the villages where my father had established churches were now big towns and services were no longer conducted in grass huts. I proudly played my steel guitar in places where my parents had worked, with our family of 11 children.

"We've even worked in a circus. We did Polynesian music, the only non-circus act in the show. We went with the Josephine Baker show to Venice, with the Bluebird Girls to Paris, and with the Maurice Chevalier show. In Paris we played the Moulin Rouge and the Circus Medrano, and the strip clubs because they paid very well. They hired us because we were 'different', we were colorful. We were guests on many TV shows, also on radio, and we worked the cruise ships from London, the P & O line on the 'S.S. Queen Elizabeth I' and 'S.S. Queen Elizabeth II'. Every facet of stage, we did it. We played for heads of state, for royalty. Lani did a command performance for the King of Yugoslavia when he was young.

"Aristotle Onassis and Marie Callas were our friends. The first time we met Aristotle he offered us a drink, but we Mormons don't drink. He was the director of a casino in Monte Carlo, which is how we got the job in the casino, then in the night club. Onassis would come often to see our show, and learned to offer us pineapple juice. He surprised us by bringing Maria Callas down to see our show. She sat right in the front, wearing a huge hat and she waved at us on the stage. After the show she hugged and kissed us. She told us that she hated tenors, always fought with them. We were good friends with her in the 1970's.

"One day In Yugoslavia I drove to Brussels and bought four tickets to Hawai'i. I told the family, 'We're going home next week'. Lani was making costumes for the opera in Brussels, and designing costumes for the circus. He had a wonderful job. Lani said, 'We're going home! I'm at the top of my career and Dad wants to go home.' Dorian was working in the costume department too, but in other shows as well as our own. It was hard for them to just drop everything and go home. I had a vision we must go home, so we did.

"There are hundreds of steel guitarists who played much better than I, but in many places we were the first to whom the Lord gave the opportunity. People in some remote villages in eastern Europe loved the music and the image of Hawai'i but didn't know where it was, so they reported in the newspapers that we were from Haiti."

Lani on bass, Tau on steel, Rose and Dorian on rhythm guitar, the Aloha Four performed in the HSGA bandstand show, Kapi'olani Park, Honolulu in May, 1991. A.W.Ruymar photo

And so ended the story as told by Tau Moe. In Hawai'i, the story of The Aloha Four is far from over. Tau and Rose, in their early eighties, are still strong and musically active. Lani and Dorian have been able to carry on with their professional careers at the Polynesian Cultural Center in the family's home town of La'ie, and at the university. Tau paid tribute to the genius of Sol Ho'opi'i when he said that in every country they visited the music of Sol had preceeded them. The people knew and loved the steel guitar playing of Sol Ho'opi'i although they had never seen a steel guitar until they met the Tau Moe family.

In Hawai'i the Tau Moe family has made a classic recording, titled "Ho'omana'o I Na Mele O Ka Wa U'i" (Remembering The Songs of Our Youth) on Rounder Records 6028. This recording was produced by steel guitarist Bob Brozman of California who played his National tricone acoustic guitar on the recording. The songs are from the 1920's, played and sung in the musical style of those days and the steel guitar was identical to the one Tau had used in his youth. The album received a very prestigious U.S. national award: it is on the Library of Congress Select List. Only 34 albums per year (all types of music) make it onto this list, yet in Hawai'i the album was nominated for a Hōkū award in the Traditional category and amazingly did not win!

Working with director Terry Zwigoff and the Tau Moe family, Brozman produced a movie based on the lives of these great ambassadors of Hawaiian music. Although it has not yet been released, the film promises to be one of the greatest to come out of Hawai'i. During their many hours of working together on the recording and the film, a strong "musical father and son" relationship has developed between Tau and Bob. Bob Brozman is perhaps the only proponent of the early steel guitar playing style who is still VERY heavily booked throughout Europe, Asia, Africa, mainland U.S.A. and so on. He is carrying on in Tau's footsteps except that jet transportation makes it unnecessary to live in the lands where he performs.

Steel Guitar In Other Lands

Wherever Hawai'i's musical ambassadors travelled, they left behind a legacy of love for their music and a fascination with the steel guitar. Many stories are told in this book of the men and sometimes the women who undertook the long journeys from Hawai'i to distant lands. Now we will investigate some of the stories of people living in those lands who were captivated by the new music.

Steel Guitar Was Loved In China.

Steel Guitarist Bernardo Endaya tells us,

"I was born in Shanghai and so were my sister, my eight brothers, and my parents. Hawaiian music started in Shanghai in the late twenties, but did not catch on until the 30's. At that time there were several amateurs and about 3 or 4 who played the steel guitar professionally. All of our family members were devoted to Hawaiian music.

"During the years between 1937 and 1949 Hawaiian music was very popular in Shanghai. Most radio stations played an hour of it every week. We used to listen to the music of Sol Ho'opi'i, Sol K. Bright, Lani and Dick McIntire, Lena Machado, Harry Owens, etc. There were about three amateur groups, mostly from the Portuguese community, that played in private clubs on a regular basis and sometimes in radio programs. Hawaiian music began to pick up in the ballrooms and night clubs in the early 40's and became very popular.

"The night clubs of Shanghai were packed to capacity every night. The Chinese patrons demanded at least one session of Hawaiian music before the night was over. Our Filipino family dance band always had a steel guitar to play the Hawaiian section. There was only one Chinese vocalist who dared to copy Lena Machado's style of singing and she did a very good job of it. She sang both Chinese and American popular tunes. With the addition of Hawaiian music she was a winner. When the Chinese Communists took over mainland China in 1949, all types of foreign music were gradually forbidden, including the beautiful music of Hawai'i. I left Shanghai in 1952 to play bass in Macao and then Hong Kong. In 1957, I moved to the United States and left the music world for a desk job.

"I can guess how Hawaiian music got to Shanghai. Shanghai was known as the "Pearl of the Orient" and had many foreign communities. There were the French, the English, and the International Concessions with their own schools and their own police and military units. Most buildings were built in the taste of each country occupying the settlement. America had the Fourth Marines stationed in the International Settlement. All types of music were brought into Shanghai by the various foreign communities and adopted by everyone living in the city. Shanghai was, in a sense, a little world all by itself. Whenever it was possible, we used to listen to the Armed Forces Radio Programs and to a program called 'Hawai'i Calls' "

Another steel guitarist who once lived in Shanghai (now Waimea, Hawai'i) Ernest Kurlansky, reported,

"In 1927 a friend of mine came to Shanghai from Honolulu, a cartoonist named Johnny Zane. He operated a Hawaiian Music Studio there, teaching Hawaiian guitar, Spanish guitar, and 'ukulele. During 1935 - 37 there were a lot of Chinese boys from Hawai'i from well-to-do parents who were attending American Missionary Colleges in Shanghai at St.John's University, Ling Nam in Peking. They studied medicine and law, etc. I met most of them through Johnny. They were all evacuated during the Sino-Japanese war together with all other U.S. citizens in August of 1937 on the Dollar Line passenger ship President Hoover, which incidentally was bombed by the Japanese military during its departure from Shanghai.

"Ernest Kawohionalani (Prince Kawohi), Ernest (Bobby) Ka'ai Jr., Billy Lee, Joe Kanapu'u, and Sonny Lewis were all musicians in Shanghai. Ernest Kawohi as he was known then came to Shanghai with Walter Downing, the father of famed beach boy Surfer Downing of Waikiki. Ernest Kawohi played a pancake Rickenbacker with Billy Lee and Joe Kanapu'u at St. George's Night Club. Bobby Ka'ai was the band leader at the Del Monte Night Club. All were evacuated from Shanghai in August of 1937 during the second Sino Japanese War."

Steel Guitar And Hawaiian Music To Japan.

Hawaiian music was first played in public in Japan on March 4, 1881 when Hawai'i's King David Kalākaua visited there and was welcomed by the military band playing Hawai'i's national anthem "Hawai'i Pono'i". Then it wasn't until 1923 when the World's Fair was held in Yokohama that Hawaiian music came in the form of Helen Makela and her troupe of musicians and dancers. We do not know who played steel guitar in that group.

Next came the two Haida brothers, Yukihiko (Haruhiko) and Katsuhiko, both born in Hawai'i and very talented. Their first trip (Yukihiko, the eldest, was 14) to Japan in 1922 resulted in their remaining to build an outstanding musical career. While Yukihiko attended university he formed what might be the first Hawaiian musical group in Japan. Then in 1929 he (with his brother Katsuhiko) formed and directed the Moana Glee Club with up to 50 instrumentalists and singers. It remained the top Hawaiian musical group in Japan until the 1940's. Yukihiko visited Hawai'i in 1933 to study steel guitar under M. K. Moke. He should be known as "The Father of Hawaiian Music" in Japan for his pioneering work.

Many Hawaiian groups toured Japan in the 1920's and 1930's including Ernest Ka'ai Sr., M. K. Moke, David Pokipala, Tau Moe, Andy Iona, and Joe Cravalho. Both Haida brothers kept their Hawaiian musical skills honed by listening closely to these touring steel guitarists and to their recordings. The first Hawaiian recording to find its way to Japan was "Lady of Waikiki" performed by steel guitarist Frank Ferera, 1927. Ernest Ka'ai Sr. brought his son with him, and Ernest Ka'ai Jr. (Bob Ka'ai) remained in Japan to build a musical career in jazz. Steel guitarist David Pokipala also elected to stay for a few years in Japan to teach and perform Hawaiian music.

In 1933 young Buckie Shirakata (born in Honolulu April 16, 1912), with his Aloha Hawaiian Trio, won a trip to Japan. He had learned to play steel guitar from Sol Ho'opi'i. and introduced to Japan the wood-bodied steel guitar, the steel bar, and the A major tuning. He returned to Hawai'i for a short time to finish university, then returned to Japan to stay, bringing with him Japan's first electric steel guitar, a Rickenbacker Electro frypan and amplifier. In 1945 he formed his own group, the Aloha Hawaiians, which was immensely successful. He made over 200 LP recordings and for over 20 years was on the best seller list. In 1965 the Hawai'i House of Representatives honored him for disseminating Hawaiian music in Japan. He is credited with developing a jazzy technique for steel guitar, and new tunings such as A minor, in the style of Tommy Castro. He taught many to play steel guitar, including Ginji Yamaguchi. Ginji and his brother Gunichi Yamaguchi, who was born April 1931 in Tokyo, formed the group Ginji Yamaguchi and His Luana Hawaiians. In 1964 Gunichi (also a steel guitarist) left the group and formed a new group of the same name. He was awarded the Sakura-matsuri prize for a Hawaiian theme song he composed.

A great steel guitar player of the early days was Eiichi Asabuki, born in Japan in 1909. He learned from Yukihiko Haida. Another great, born in 1916 in Tokyo, was Shin Sato who taught Hawaiian steel guitar, 'ukulele, and standard guitar at the Yamaha Music School in Tokyo aside from his career as a performer and recording artist.

During the years of World War II the playing of Hawaiian music was completely forbidden. After the war, in 1945, it made a great come-back. First was Poss (Hideo) Miyazaki (steel guitarist) who formed his group "Coney Islanders" which became one of the foremost Hawaiian groups in Japan. Another was Tatsuo (Tony) Ohtsuka (steel guitarist) with his Blue Hawaiians. Tatsuo (born in Tokyo, 1922) founded the "Kama'aina Club" in 1963 with 500 members. He is best known for the spectacular Polynesian shows he produces. Among many others of the post-war steel guitarists were Gun'ichi Yamaguchi on steel with the group Ginji Yamaguchi and His Luana Hawaiians, and Makoto Shiraishi with his Na Lei O Hawaiians. Touring groups began flooding in from Hawai'i, and the radio show "Hawai'i Calls" was the most popular overseas show received in Japan.

Hawaiian music is perhaps more popular in Japan today than it is in any other country outside of Hawai'i. In Joban, Japan, is the Joban Hawaiian Senta (Center) in which Hawaiian music and dance is presented every day of the year, performed entirely by Japanese. It is the largest amusement complex in the world with a Hawaiian theme.

Hawaiian music and steel guitar lost popularity during the 1970's with the invasion of rock music, but now in the 1990's it is definitely on the up-swing, particularly with the new interest in pedal steel guitars and all the latest in tone enhancing gadgetry.

One of the foremost of modern steel players in Japan is Kiyoshi Kobayashi, born in Hokkaido, Japan on July 7th 1933. His musical training started at the age of four with musical dictation (hearing) training, then piano lessons at five. At fifteen, already a pianist and 'ukuleleist, he began instruction on steel guitar (6 string, Am tuning) from Willy Yamazaki, accompanist for Yukihiko Haida, in the style of Bucky Shirakata. By the age of 20 Kiyoshi had been introduced to the Gibson Electra Harp, learned the Alvino Rey playing style, and created his own 8 string 4 pedal steel guitar with his own changer system.

After working for twelve years for a movie company, Kiyoshi studied modern jazz theory and began to play the 10 string pedal steel, the "Fuzzy Excel" made by Mitsuo Fuji. In 1977 he recorded "E Ku'u Morning Dew", "Kanaka Wai Wai" etc. with an E9th chromatic tuning on Japan Victor SJV 5013 "Romantic Steel Guitar Golden 20", the first time it had been done in Japan. In 1983 he published a method book in three volumes for lap steel and started giving instruction on both styles of steel guitar.

Still the innovator, Kiyoshi has built a 10-string 5 lock lever steel guitar with the Excel company which he uses for live performances, and a 10-string 9 pedal 5 lever Excel double neck for recording. He is equally at ease playing in the sweet traditional manner of the Hawaiians or in his own jazzy style. He has become a "regular" in the very prestigious Steel Guitar Ho'olaule'a, an annual show in Honolulu. The story of Kiyoshi Kobayashi is an insight for the reader into what a musician must be able to do, to be successful and stay at the top in Japan.

Steel Guitar To Australia In The Early 20's.

COLLEANO'S ALL-STAR CIRCUS.

GREATEST ATTRACTION OF ALL TIME.

CORNER TALBRAGAR AND MACQUARIE STREETS.

SHOW WEEK—COMMENCING TO-NIGHT (TUESDAY).

BIGGEST AND BEST CIRCUS PROGRAMME EVER SUBMITTED TO THE PUBLIC OF DUBBO.

COLLECTION OF THE WORLD'S BEST PERFORMERS, Featuring the Great

5 —— ROYAL HAWAIIAN TROUPE ——5

The World's Best Ladder Balancers and Risley Performers.

Supported by 24 —— STAR ARTISTS —— 24,

Including the Famous 6 ——.COLLEANO FAMILY —— 6.

Six Acrobats Extraordinary.

Also Introducing the World's BEST HIGH JUMPING HORSES, including the Famous Pony Jumper—

BLACK JACK (13.1), 6ft. 9½in. (World's Record).

DO NOT MISS THIS GRAND OPPORTUNITY.

Come and Listen—You'll Enjoy it.7.30 — HAWAIIAN BAND — 7.30.

Performance at 8.   Doors Open 7.30.

POPULAR PRICES.

Colleano's circus advertisement, July 5, 1918.   courtesy Evan Williams

Evan Williams tells us that in the early 1920's he got hooked on Hawaiian steel guitar when his parents took him to the annual Agricultural Shows. There would always be a troupe of Hawaiian musicians, glorious voices blending in harmony with the sweet haunting music of steel guitars, and dusky beauties with grass skirts a-swaying. A New South Wales newspaper dated July 5, 1918 advertised Colleano's All-Star Circus featuring a "Royal Hawaiian Troupe". That would coincide nicely with our records of Ernest Kaleihoku Ka'ai's tour of Australia in 1918 with his group of Hawaiian musicians and dancers. There is another account of Queenie and David Ka'ai performing at the Tivoli Theatre (city unknown) in Australia, 1927.

Frank Hibberd of New South Wales, Australia, shares his recollections of steel guitar in Australia as follows: "I started to learn the Hawaiian guitar in 1937. To the best of my knowledge, the solid body electric steel was not known in this country at that date. However, a friend of mine who was a bit of a radio ham found a diagram in Popular Mechanics magazine. It showed a new-fangled "pick-up", made by using two diametrically opposed horseshoe magnets, with a coil of fine copper wire wound around a soft iron core, assembled in such a manner that the whole cumbersome thing could be mounted on the bridge end of a Spanish guitar (strung with steel strings) wired to a telephone jack for the outlet, to a small valve type amplifier. At this stage I was learning the original style Hawaiian guitar; i.e., a Spanish guitar with round sound hole and a nut as it was called here, to lift the strings away from the frets. The method of tuition was strictly by notation, and written in such a manner that the guitarist played his own accompaniment with the melody.

"My friend made a pickup and amplifier for me, and we fit the thing onto to my guitar, trying not to ruin the guitar. Oh yes, we also had to fit a capacitator (2000 ohms, I think) for use as a volume control. My guitar was tuned to plain A major - (1st to 6th) E.C#.A.G.E.C., which I think was the universal tuning in 1937.

"At my next lesson I proudly turned up with my (I thought) magnificent electric outfit. My teacher refused to teach me unless I dismantled all the electrics. He reckoned I had destroyed the authentic sound! I told him to go to hell, and never went back. Unfortunately, without the incentive of going to lessons, I lost interest a bit. Then came World War II, which put a bit of a crimp in proceedings for awhile.

41

"After the war, I was transferred to Melbourne. I can remember in 1946 walking past a music shop and damn me if they didn't have a new kind of Hawaiian guitar in the window! It was the same shape as a Spanish guitar but the body was small, about violin size, made out of solid wood, with a much wider fretboard, all lovely and black and shiny, with a chrome plated cover over the coil, and no visible magnets. It was a case of love at first sight. I couldn't afford it, but I <u>had</u> to have it. I don't remember <u>ever</u> getting so much pleasure from buying <u>anything</u> in my whole life!!!

"I remember the shop assistant saying, 'Can you play it?' Me, 'Of course.' Him, 'Well tune it up and play something.' Oh my God, how embarrassing! I couldn't remember how to do it! I still blush when I think of that occasion. As a result of that the fellow said, 'I suggest you go to Harry Mawson's Hawaiian Academy for a few lessons'.

"What an eye opener that first lesson at the Academy was! Instead of being compelled to learn the fret board by heart, musically, I could play by just reading numbers and following the time value in the treble clef music notes. On top of that, I was able to talk my wife into learning the Spanish guitar at the same place, so while I was learning a particular piece of music, my wife was being taught the correct chords and strums to accompany me.

"On account of my association with Harry Mawson I learned the following. Prior to 1938 Harry Mawson operated a music teaching studio known as the 'Hawthorn Banjo and Guitar Club'. By 1938 the demand for Hawaiian music was so great that he changed it to 'Harry Mawson's Hawaiian Guitar Academy'. He and his pupils used to do a radio broadcast on Melbourne radio every Sunday evening. He even went to the extent of sending selected staff members to Hawai'i to further their knowledge.

"Just before I joined the Academy in 1946 he brought out his first solid body electric steel, made by a young go-ahead firm named Maton Guitar Co. founded by a certan W.A. (Billy) May. I recently managed to speak to Billy (very ancient, with memory lapses now). He claimed to be the first commercial manufacturer of electric steel guitars in Australia. It was in 1937 when Harry Mawson first started to market Billy's guitars under the Silvertone name. Billy May said he made his first electric guitars after talking to an American named Paul Bigsley, who claimed to be the inventor of the Tremolo Lever, which idea, according to Billy, was "snavelled" by Fender and improved upon. (Now bear in mind that Billy is now old and frail, and just possibly could not have his facts right and might be confusing Fender with some other manufacturer. He said to make this clear because he did not want to libel anyone.)

"Billy May said that in the process of developing his electric Hawaiian guitar, he did research in Hawai'i and found that the origin of the traditional Hawaiian guitar came about through climatic conditions in the islands varying from Spain or Portugal, from where the Catholic missionaries brought their instruments. The island climate caused the guitar necks to bow, resulting in the strings being lifted too far from the frets for the native Hawaiians to be able to push down to make contact. To use Billy's words, someone accidentally found that a pleasing sound could be made by sliding a polished steel bar over the strings. (Note: This adds further light to your theory of the Hawaiian music's beginnings!)

"In 1946 I saw what was allegedly the first Spanish guitar fitted with a Tremolo Lever, also the first electric steel with a mechanism, worked by little hand levers, incorporating various gears, rollers, etc. which allowed the player to change his tuning automatically into three different tunings. I did not play the thing. I remember Harry Mawson saying the basic idea was good, but once the strings had been stretched from the original tuning, they were very erratic in returning 'spot on' to the original manual setting, and he gave it the thumbs down! I gather this instrument was the forerunner of today's sophisticated pedal guitar. In 1947 the Academy was also pushing the Dobro Amplified Guitars.

"In my opinion the Hawai'i Calls programs broadcast from Honolulu were the crucial reason for the popularity of Hawaiian music in Australia. As well as Webley Edwards, artists such as Sol Ho'opi'i, Roland Peachey and their ilk were very popular with radio disc jockeys, and let us not forget Bing Crosby and Dorothy Lamour in her famous sarong."

Steel Guitar To Africa.

I could not find any written record of steel guitarists from Hawai'i visiting the continent of Africa, but most surely the instrument did find its way there. In writing his own biography, steel guitarist Kealoha Life (Alfred Hollis Randell) now living in England tells of his early boyhood experience in seeing Joseph Kekuku perform on steel guitar in the "Bird of Paradise Hawaiians" show in London, 1924. Life wrote that years later a guitarist formerly from Kekuku's group, a South African Griqua (Hottentot) named Kimo Koa, joined his (Life's) musical group. So there we have a guitarist from South Africa playing with a Hawaiian troupe in England. It is not difficult to imagine his curiosity about the new way of playing a guitar. It is possible he learned from Joseph Kekuku and later took his knowledge back to South Africa. Life himself spent 20 years playing steel guitar in Africa and America's Jimmie "The Singing Brakeman" Rodgers toured Africa during the 1930's and always had a steel guitarist in his band. We also know of a "Cheerio" Porter who played and taught Hawaiian steel guitar in South Africa. "Cheerio" had played steel since 1920 but we don't know whether he was born in South Africa or moved there later.

Richard Middleton and David Horn, editors of "Popular Music 1: Folk or Popular? Distinctions, Influences, Continuities" report that the Hawaiian steel guitar's conquest of the world did not omit Southern and the bordering areas of East Africa. In Zimbabwe, Malawi, Zambia, and as far as Mozambique "...it led to the revitalisation of an old technique: playing on one string by means of a slide (usually a piece of calabash, a knife, or a small bottle). ...the term 'Hawaiian' was adapted to Bantu as 'hauyani'..." which means the technique of playing a Spanish guitar held flat on the knees with a small bottle or other object as slide. The tuning, high to low, is G.E.C.G.E.C. The editors conclude, "Thus there arose in this area a parallel to the so-called bottleneck guitar style of the southern U.S.A."

California guitarist Mike Perlowin has done a study of Juju music in Nigeria. It's an odd mixture of traditional native music and American rhythm and blues. Perhaps the most popular is King Sunny Adé, rivaled by Commander in Chief Ebenezer Obey. Multiple drummers play counter-rhythms, as many voices harmonize. Above it all is "the wail and cry of the new sound that has taken this oil rich land of contradictions by storm. The sound of the pedal steel guitar. Nearly every band has one." King Sunny Adé is credited with bringing over the first American electric guitars (Spanish guitars) in 1967. Perlowin tells us that the electric steel guitar made its entrance this way: "Demola became interested in Hawaiian music around 20 years ago and in 1974 was able to buy a 6 string lap steel from a sailor. He taught himself to play a few licks in secret, while he played the standard guitar in a neighborhood band. One day in 1977 the band was playing at a gig that was turning out badly and Demola, in an effort to save it, raced home and brought back his steel guitar. Well not only was the gig saved, but within 2 weeks he was brought to the attention of King Sunny Adé who hired him immediately and made him the featured instrumentalist of the band. Their first recordings together were so successful that they went to England and brought back 3 pedal steel guitars (2 Emmons and a Sho-Bud). The pedal steel revolution had begun."

As For Mexico, Central And South America

The Oahu Publishing Co., in one of their articles "Biographies of Outstanding Guitar Artists" stated that Sam Koki (born in 1900), in his early years as a musician, had gone to Panama to play. Finding conditions not to his liking, Sam left without pay. He stowed away in the engine room of a steamer. After being discovered on board, he was allowed to stay on condition that he must entertain the crew.

From 1918 - 1920 David K. Ka'ili, worked as steel guitarist with a band and hula dancers on the "S.S.Sherman", touring Acapulco, Bahamas, Jamaica and many European ports. When he heard that Pale K. Lua (another steel guitarist) was playing and teaching steel guitar in Brazil, he left the cruise ship to join Lua.

The other documented foray of the steel guitar into Latin America involves the great steel guitarist Dick McIntire. After he served time in the American navy, he began his musical career in Tijuana, Mexico in 1923. He played there for five years before moving on to the mainland U.S. A 1928 Mexican recording "Lirios" by S. Cortez is of a trio using the Hawaiian steel guitar playing a romantic Mexican melody with a very non-Hawaiian playing technique. Did Dick McIntire give steel guitar lessons to the locals while in Mexico, or did an admirer in the audience buy a guitar and try to copy Dick?

The First Steel Guitars In Canada

The first known Hawaiian troupe to tour Canada was Irene West's Royal Hawaiians, in the early 1900's. MIro Maximchuk, who made a study of Hawaiian music before 1920, stated that Pale K. Lua and David Ka'ili toured the U.S. and Canada with the Irene West Show before 1913. So we must conclude that the first Hawaiian steel guitarist to be heard in Canada was either Lua or Ka'ili. The second touring group to cross Canada was the "Bird of Paradise" show, and the steel guitarist could possibly have been Joseph Kekuku, since it is known that he toured Europe with that show from 1919 to 1927. They may have toured across the continent to depart from an east coast port. The steel guitarist who preceeded Kekuku in the Bird of Paradise show was Walter Kolomoku who was part of the original cast, beginning in 1912.

However, the steel guitarist who had the most impact on Hawaiian music's acceptance in Canada was Ben Hokea. He was born in Hawai'i in 1898 and was first heard of playing steel guitar in the David Kalama Orchestra on the Matson Line ships between Honolulu and San Francisco. He then toured Canada with Charlie Clark's Royal Hawaiians, arriving in Toronto in 1915 where they stayed for several years. When the group moved on Ben Hokea stayed in Canada, never to return to Hawai'i. He died in 1971 and today his grand daughter Melanie Hokea is a hula dancer in Vancouver.

At first in Toronto, then in 1937 in St.John New Brunswick, and later in Montreal, Ben Hokea taught steel guitar in his music studios during the day and worked as a performer in the evenings. During the summer months he repeatedly toured Canada. His lifetime career included radio and television work, and a considerable number of recordings on Victor, Columbia, and the Starr Co. of Canada labels.

Although Hokea's name stands out as "King of the Hawaiian Guitar" in Canada, it must be noted that the first known instruction on the steel guitar was given by William Miles, a Canadian, who began teaching steel guitar and 'ukulele for the T. Eaton Department Store in Winnipeg in 1903, and later in Toronto. Miles had visited Hawai'i in 1899 as a banjo virtuoso travelling with a circus band. There, he heard his first steel guitar played. In Pasadena CA, 1902, he learned from a Mexican steel guitar teacher who had studied in Hawai'i.

Indonesia, India, And The Far East

Beginning in 1919, Ernest Ka'ai and his Royal Hawaiian Troubadours toured Malaya, Sumatra, Borneo, Java, Burma, and India. The steel guitarist was Herbert Pahupu Byrnes who also toured Australia, India, Malaya, the Dutch East Indies and other countries in Asia. Rather than return to Hawai'i, Herbert and fellow musician Alexander Lonoikamakahiki Lazarus (also known as Alexander Lono Munson) stayed in Java where they married and raised families. They continued to play their Hawaiian music, to teach, and build Hawaiian instruments. They formed their own band and toured Indonesia. Hawaiian music became extremely popular and that area produced many great steel guitarists.

In 1927 - 37 Ka'ai made another extensive tour of the Orient, which would explain why the Hawaiian steel guitar is used so much in Indian film music. Some groups in India, like Garney Nyss and his Aloha Boys, play Hawaiian music on steel guitar, and others such as Brij Bushan Kabra, Sunil Ganguly, Charanjit Singh, Rajat Nandy, and Van Shipley play classical Indian music on the acoustic steel guitar.

Steel guitarist Ed Mayer, who lived for many years in Honolulu, has this to say. "I was born in Indonesia. My parents became great fans of Hawaiian music after one of the wealthy Sugar Barons of Indonesia returned from an observation trip to Waipahu (O'ahu) to evaluate the cane-burning techniques versus fresh-cutting of cane stalks. He brought back with him the Hawaiian group of Ka'ai including a variety of hula dancers. This was the very first Hawaiian group to entertain the extremely wealthy plantation owners. Tau Moe came very soon after the Ka'ai group.

"The Ka'ais were responsible for the forming of several outstanding Dutch Indonesian Hawaiian groups, which all started out with at least one Ka'ai member amongst them. They had such colorful and nostalgic names like - The Hawaiian Big Boys of Batavia, the Hawaiian Syncopators of Surabaja (East Coast of Java), the Hawaiian Silver Strings of Semarang (Central Java), not to be confused with the Hawaiian Silver Kings of Jakarta, the Royal Hawaiian Minstrels, the Southsea Crooners (the original 1935 group - I joined the second generation) of Bandung, etc. etc. It is also an unknown fact that one of the Ka'ai members actually died in a Japanese concentration camp on Sumatra. I heard many stories about Hawaiian groups that were formed in Japanese concentration camps - home made acoustic steel guitars, etc. etc., all manufactured under Ka'ai's supervision."

How Did The Steel Guitar Travel To Tonga?

Dick Sanft is Tongan, a highly skilled steel guitarist performing in the Polynesian show, World of Disney, Florida. Here is his story of how the first steel guitar came to Tonga.
"In the early 1930's a Mormon missionary came to Tonga from Utah. He had with him an item of exceptional silvery beauty, a National tricone steel guitar! He taught young John Tuita to play it, and when the missionary moved on, he left the prized guitar with John. John soon emigrated to New Zealand where he went to school and became an active musician, a contemporary of Bill Wolfgram. Also in the early 1930's a very bright and talented Charlie Sanft left Tonga with a group of missionaries to study music at Brigham Young University, Utah. After two years of study he found the

call of Hollywood too compelling and for the next four years he found himself acting in movies, (doing supporting roles) and sharpening his skills as a musician. It was during that time that he met Dick McIntire and others, and learned to play the Hawaiian steel guitar. He had been away from Tonga six years by the time the authorities learned that he was not fulfilling his role as a student. He was deported.

"On his return to Tonga Charlie took with him his most prized possession, a National tricone steel guitar. There was no electricity in Vava'u, so no recordings are available of the new band Charlie started. He was extremely successful and became one of the island's main tourist attractions. He was my uncle. I listened to him and wanted to do the same. During WWII my father, a German, was interned in a camp as were all Germans in the area. After the war he took his family to New Zealand where I bought my first electric steel guitar. Bill Wolfgram befriended me and helped me put a professional polish on my performance. I played in dance bands, and did a Polynesian show on an Auckland radio station. I worked with Bill Wolfgram and Bill Sevesi as my contemporaries. In 1959 I moved to the U.S.A. where I worked in many west coast cities, then for four years in an Arizona hotel doing the 'Dick Sanft's Hawaiian Revue'. During this time I met and became fast friends with 'Omaha', a Samoan steel guitarist, cousin of Bill Wolfgram.

"I met Dick McIntire's cousin Jimmy Haulani, a great rhythm guitarist who worked with him in Arizona. It was at this time that Dick moved to Phoenix for the dry air. He had tuberculosis. The disease worsened, so he returned to California where he died. I moved on, to find 15 years of employment in the World of Disney, where I work today."

The First Steel Guitar In Europe

The first steel guitar in Europe is possibly the one played by Joseph Kekuku in the Bird of Paradise show which toured Europe for eight years beginning in 1919, unless Hawaiian sailors carried steel guitars there before that. Jenny Wilson and Her Hawaiian Troupe appeared in England in 1894 but there is no evidence that a steel guitar was included. We know that it took root and flourished in Europe. Eventually many Hawaiian-style musical groups emerged. The most visibly successful group based in England was Felix Mendelssohn And His Hawaiian Serenaders. Felix had great respect for the Hawaiian culture and took pains to select only the very best, most authentic musicians. Some of his steel guitarists were Harry Brooker, Roland Peachey, Sam Mitchell, and Kealoha LIfe. Mendelssohn died at the age of 41, in 1952.

The story of steel guitar in Europe and England is told extensively throughout the pages of this book and therefore not repeated here.

The Story Of The Hawaiian Guitar In Sweden

Told to us by steel guitarist Thomas Malm,

"Between 1919 and 1927, the Bird of Paradise troupe toured Europe. One of the members, Segis Luvaun, or 'Juan Akoni' as he also called himself, stayed in Denmark for some time and introduced the steel guitar in that country. Harald Mortensen, a Danish guitarist, was most likely the first Scandinavian to play this instrument. He recorded on "Polyphon" around 1920.

"Luvaun continued to Sweden, where he performed in a revue that was conducted by Ernst Rolf (1891-1932), a very popular cabaret singer. Rolf had already recorded some Hawaiian songs, so he and Luvaun worked together on a recording of "Lilla Lola Lo från Hawai'i" (Little Lola Lo from Hawai'i). This was the first Swedish recording that featured the steel guitar. The Swedish people fell in love with the new exotic sound.

"The first Swedish manual for the Hawaiian steel guitar was published by Sv. Eduard in 1923 by the Nils Axbergs Musikförlag, Stockholm. The title was "Melodi-Album för Hawaiisk Gitarr" (Melody Album for Hawaiian Guitar). In the same year, Charles Elow became the first Swede to make a recording with this instrument.

"In 1937 Yngve Stoor (1912-1985) revolutionized Hawaiian music in Sweden. He imported an electric Gibson lap steel guitar, probably the first electric guitar of any kind in the country. He formed his first orchestra in 1928, and the phenomenal success of this "King of Hawaiian Music" was legendary. He performed, composed, recorded, published, and toured throughout his lifetime. In 'Hawaiian Music and Musicians,' edited by George S. Kanahele, it was said that, 'When Yngve Stoor played the steel guitar every Swede could feel the sunshine beaming through his music. Unfortunately, the popularity of the Hawaiian steel guitar has passed its peak in Sweden, but the interest in the 'ukulele still carries on."

Hawaiian Troupe To Russia.

The very musical Hawaiian family of Hanapi contributed much to the spread of Hawaiian music. In an essay written by one of the brothers, Emperor Hanapi, he tells of his brother Edward who played music professionally for years on the mainland, then the Hanapi family toured the Asia-Pacific area and, in 1917, went to Vladivostok to entertain American troops. A visit in 1992 to Honolulu's Lunalilo Home for Hawaiian Seniors to talk with Emperor Hanapi produced the information that it was brother Mike who played the steel guitar with the family group in Vladivostok, 1917.

"Hawai'i Calls"
The Radio Program

Surely one of the greatest influences in spreading the gospel of Hawaiian music and steel guitar was the very popular radio show Hawai'i Calls, rated the most popular program in radio history. On Saturday July 3, 1935 the first program was beamed to the U.S. west coast. It featured the 11-piece dance orchestra of Harry Owens with Webley Edwards as producer and Master of Ceremonies. The steel guitarist may have been Alvin Isaacs Sr. for a short time, followed by Freddie Tavares. They selected the best musicians and their purpose was to show what real Hawaiian music is like when performed by Hawaiians in Hawai'i. A good percentage of their songs were sung in the English language so that mainlanders could recognize and learn to sing them.

Hawai'i Calls radio show , notice the radio equipment and engineers on the left
Hawaiian Visitors Bureau photo

In 1937 Al Kealoha Perry took over the bandleader's duties from Harry Owens. Benny Kalama, who had joined the group in 1952, took over as musical director when Al Perry retired in 1967. Two generations of Hawai'i's best musicians and singers built their careers around regular appearances on the Hawai'i Calls show. People from China to snow-bound Finland gathering around their shortwave radios got to know these musicians as family friends. It was an honor to appear on the show and occasionally guests from other lands would be featured. The earliest shows were broadcast from the outdoor dance stage at the Royal Hawaiian Hotel, but later the show moved to the Moana Hotel's lanai, under the huge banyan tree just a few feet from the shore. Often the show moved for just one broadcast to other locations, other islands, even aboard the S.S. Matsonia, for special events or for a stimulating change of pace.

Hawai'i Calls cast pose on Waikiki Beach.

Gentlemen in back row: L - R Sam Alama (with guitar), Ed Kenny, Bob Kauahikaua, Bill Akamahou, Sam Kapu, Sonny Nicholas, Danny Kinilau, Andy Bright, Al Kealoha Perry.
Ladies: L - R Annie Ayau, Lani Custino, Punini McWayne.
Front row seated: Director Webley Edwards, Barney Isaacs, Jules Ah See. Hawai'i Visitors Bureau photo

When listening to the show on their shortwave radios, the audience was convinced they heard the pounding of the surf. It was actually the alternating sound waves of their radio sets, but Webley Edwards picked up on the idea and began the practice of holding the microphone out over the waves while the steel guitar sounded its alluring call. This was the irresistible siren song, the "signature sound" of Hawai'i.

At its peak in 1952, Hawai'i Calls was broadcast over station KGMB in Honolulu to 750 stations in the U.S., Canada, Latin America, Europe, Korea, Japan, South Africa, Australia and New Zealand. Several factors brought about its decline. The show had a chronic problem - finances! There were no commercials to bring in revenue so they had to rely on grants from the Hawai'i Tourist Bureau, and later were given funding from the legislature. When you consider the impact the show had on the world in promoting Hawai'i as the place of dreams, the paradise attainable, it was the best bargain the legislature could have bought. But television, country music, and rock had already begun to make inroads into the popularity of Hawaiian music and the number of radio stations carrying the show had begun to diminish when Webley Edwards, creator and backbone of the show, suffered a heart attack in 1972 which made him unable to carry on as M.C. Entertainer Danny Kaleikini tried to carry on in Webley's shoes but funding cuts came at that very crucial time, so on August 16, 1975 the Hawai'i Calls 2083rd and final show was broadcast from the Cinerama Reef Hotel in Waikiki to its very mournful listeners.

Over 300 of Hawai'i's finest singers and musicians were featured on the show, with some of the world's greatest guest artists. The Brights and the Isaacs families contributed several generations of performers to the show. Lani Custino took over in 1949 and remained until the end. Another daughter, Nina Keali'iwahamana performed on the show from 1958 to 1974.

There was an attempt to change to the medium of television before the show folded in 1975, and over 20 shows were recorded on video. The idea never got off the ground as television shows were much more expensive to produce than radio shows and the Hawai'i Tourist Bureau had found other ways to advertise the allure of Hawai'i. In May of 1990 the AIS recording company, under the direction of steel guitarist Alan Akaka, held a grand reunion party of all surviving members of the Hawai'i Calls radio show cast and staff. The offshoot of that was the recording of an audio cassette "Islands Call" done in the style reminiscent of Hawai'i Calls, featuring many of the artists of that show: Iwalani Kahalewai (vocal soloist), Benny Kalama ('ukulele and vocals), Sonny Kamahele (guitar and vocals), Nina Keali'iwahamana (vocals), Merle Kekuku (string bass), Leilani Kuhao (vocals), Punini McWayne (vocals), Walter Mo'okini (vocals and guitar), and three steel guitarists Alan Akaka, Jerry Byrd, and Barney Isaacs. It was the first time for steel guitars to be heard in trio on a recording. "Islands Call" demonstrated that the great stars of Hawai'i Calls are still ready and able to take up where the show left off in 1975, should public funds become available to send Hawai'i's spirit of aloha over the airwaves once more. That was in 1990.

Hawai'i Calls was never broadcast without the sweet sound of the steel guitar backing the vocalists or soaring as a solo instrument. It became recognized throughout the world as the signature sound of Hawai'i. Just as the bagpipes signal "Scotland" to the listener, so does the steel guitar signify "Hawai'i". Not long ago Frank Miller got Barney Isaacs and Benny Kalama together to reminisce. They put together the following list of steel guitarists who appeared regularly on the show:

> *July 3 - October 14, 1935 Alvin K. Isaacs, with Harry Owens*
> *1935-37 Freddie Tavares with the Harry Owens orchestra.*
> *1937 to 1952 David Keli'i*
> *Mid 1950's Jake Keli'ikoa and Jules Ah See*
> *Late 1950's to June 1960 Jules Ah See and Barney Isaacs*
> *June 1960 to 1962 Barney Isaacs and Danny Stewart*
> *1962 to late 1960's Barney Isaacs and Eddie Pang*
> *1970's until "pau" Barney Isaacs and Joe Custino*

In a letter dated May 11, 1989 Freddie Tavares cleared up the mystery about who was the very first steel guitarist on the show. He said, "According to my nearly 80 year old brain memory cells (I'm 76), Hawai'i Calls started on October 14th, 1935 with Harry Owens' Royal Hawaiians, an eleven piece dance orchestra. I was the steel guitarist. The program was played on the outdoor dance floor of the Royal Hawaiian Hotel..."

You will note that Freddie puts the date of the first broadcast as October 14, 1935 while Dr. G. Kanahele in Hawaiian Music and Musicians (p.109) reports that the show opened on July 3, 1935 in the courtyard of the Moana Hotel. Another interesting fact is that Alvin Kaleolani Isaacs (father of Barney Isaacs) joined the Harry Owens band in 1935 and stayed with them until 1940, mostly as a comic singer and dancer. It is very possible that he played steel guitar for Harry Owens from July 3 to October 14 of 1935, when Freddie Tavares took over. If this is true, we would have to report that the Hawai'i Calls radio show was opened with steel guitarist Alvin K. Isaacs and closed with steel guitarist Barney Isaacs, father and son.

As for a reappearance of Hawai'i Calls on the radio waves, read on. The legend of the amazing Phoenix bird is retold with a modern twist in our final chapter.

Hawaiian Music's Conquest Of America

Steel Guitar Did It.

Hawaiian music didn't "take off" in the U.S.A. until the steel guitar came on the scene. The musicians most effected were the blacks in blues and bottleneck playing, and the whites in country music. The steel guitar with its human-voice-like qualities took a role similar to that of the fiddle, accordion, or mouth organ in country music. It mimicked or complemented the vocalist, or it beguiled the listener with beautiful solos. Hillbilly string bands eagerly included the steel guitar as a lead melody instrument along with their mandolins, fiddles, and banjos. The instrument was easily adapted to their existing repertoire, but occasionally a Hawaiian song was added. One example is the "High Low March" by the Shamrock String Band, obviously a mispronunciation of the Hilo March. There were even hillbilly string bands which took a Hawaiian name, such as Nelstone's Hawaiians, or the North Carolina Hawaiians. The acoustic steel guitar led the way, but the later electrified instrument made the greatest break-through of steel guitar into country music.

Expositions, Chautauquas, And Vaudeville

The earliest appearances of Hawaiian music which had the most impact were at the Alaska-Yukon-Pacific Exposition in Seattle, 1909, and the Panama-Pacific International Exposition in San Fancisco, 1915. Then Hawaiian bands joined the Chautauqua touring groups which moved about the country pitching tents in one small town after another during the summer months, from about 1903 to 1930. At the same time, the Hawaiian steel guitar found its way onto the vaudeville stage, which toured the country in a more dignified manner, on a stage under a permanent roof. The Hawaiian groups consisted of five or six musicians with the steel guitarist seated in the center. Their soft unamplified notes required a respectful, worshipful silence from the audience. Wherever the steel guitar went it left behind those who committed themselves to becoming its possessors and its players.

Western Swing

During the depression years (the 1930's) a new musical style developed, a fusion of many musical cultures in the crowded smoky beer parlors of the Texas-Louisiana-Oklahoma region. Migrant workers moving to the oil fields of Louisiana looking for work brought their music with them: jazz, delta blues, Cajun and Creole music. From Texas: polkas, Mexican, western blues, and country. From Oklahoma: Scotch and Irish fiddle tunes. From this delightful mix, Western Swing was born.

Western swing bands from Texas, like Smokey Woods and His Wood Chips used steel guitar for their recordings. Smokey 'The Houston Hipster' Woods featured J.C.Way on steel. They toured the same circuit with contemporaries Adolph Hofner, Bill Mounce, and Cliff Bruner playing blues and western swing. The most famous of the big western swing bands during the 1940's was Bob Wills And His Texas Playboys, with close competition from the west coast with Spade Cooley, billed as the "King of Western Swing." Both bands always featured a top-level steel guitar player.

John York, president of the Western Swing Music Society explains the involvement of the steel guitar,

"With the introduction of amplified Hawaiian steel guitars in the early 1930's it was guaranteed a permanent place in western swing music as a strong solo and background instrument.

The Light Crust Doughboys, 1934.
Leon McAuliffe in front playing the National guitar, Bob Wills playing the fiddle.

"In the 1930's Leon McAuliffe and Bob Dunn were among the first steel guitarists who had the greatest impact, playing with bands such as Bob Wills and the Texas Playboys, and Milton Brown And His Musical Brownies. The Hawaiian influence was very evident. In the 1940's other very well known steel guitarists with definite Hawaiian music roots were: Noel Boggs, Herb Remington, and Earl 'Joaquin' Murphy. They were all in demand by major western swing bands of the day, such as Bob Wills, Tex Williams, and Spade Cooley. Joaquin was the undisputed master, his genius in playing the non pedal steel guitar and his brilliant single string and chord solos are classic.

"It was sad to see the non pedal steel guitar lose prominence in western swing music with the introduction of the pedal steel guitar in the late 1940's. But, today it is very gratifying to see its resurgence, notably with the return of veteran steel player Bobby Koefer and his 1953 Fender triple 8, and Cindy Cashdollor playing her Fender triple 8 with the group "Asleep At The Wheel". Also, the younger musicians are discovering the wonderful and unique sounds of the western swing non pedal steel guitar with the Hawaiian touch.

"When you next listen to a recording of Leon McAuliffe playing Steel Guitar Rag or Pan Handle Rag, listen for the Hawaiian style with a slight difference. Leon's influence came from listening to recordings of Jim and Bob the Genial Hawaiians, and of Sol Ho'opi'i."

Tex Williams' Western Caravan.

Standing L-R Joaquin Murphy, Rex Call, Max Fidler, Cactus Soldi,
Smokey Rogers, Johnny Weiss, Tex Williams, Ossie Godsen, Deuce Spriggens.
Seated Spike Featherstone, Muddy Berry, Bennie Garcie, Pedro DePaul
Inset: Joaquin Murphy. Photo courtesy of John York

Slide And Bottleneck Guitar

More influenced than the country musicians were the blacks who developed the bottleneck guitar style of playing. They imitated the slide sound of the steel guitar by sliding a broken bottle neck, comb or whatever over the strings to give the melancholy blues sound. Their guitar strings were tuned in a major open-stringed tuning, as was used in the Hawaiian slack key tunings. Black skiffle bands imitated the white hillbilly bands by using the "slide" guitar as a lead or solo instrument. For example, we refer to Chasey Collin's Washboard Band and Tampa Red's Hokum Jug Band. Both used what we would recognize as the steel guitar, played either flat on the knee or held in Spanish guitar position with a broken bottleneck or metal cylinder over a finger of the left hand to act as a steel bar. Some people like Hop Wilson, an R & B player from Houston Texas, actually played electric Hawaiian steel. Texas produced a number of blues players who played lap style steel. Black Ace, L.C.Robinson, and Frankie Lee Sims from Dallas used steel players on their records.

Tampa Red

Eric Madis, a blues, jazz, Hawaiian, and bottleneck guitar player (also vocalist) performing in Seattle WA, explained bottleneck guitar playing this way:

"Bottleneck players use a hollow bar over one of their fingers on the fretting hand (usually the left hand). It could be the middle, ring, or little finger. Some players pick with their bare fingers entirely, some flatpick entirely, and some play with a thumbpick and fingers. Muting is done with fingers on the left hand, and/or with the palm of the right hand. Some players use open G tuning (1st - 6th) D.B.G.D.G.D, open D (D.A.G.D.A.D.) the A tuning (E.C#.A.E.A.E.) and E tuning (E.B.G#.E.B.E) and some use concert tuning (E.B.G.D.A.E). Rock players, who do not have to chord (or accompany themselves), often play in concert tuning. If you want to see someone do a good job of early Delta blues bottleneck, just watch Bob Brozman. He's a very fine player of the authentic traditional style.

"The extent to which Hawaiian steel guitar exerted an influence on the appearance and or development of blues bottleneck guitar is clearly unknown. The most that a present-day musical historian could do is present the facts as they are known and leave the conclusion up to the individual.

"Afro-Americans had a tradition of plucked stringed musical instruments prior to arriving in America as slaves. Many African tribes even used zither-like instruments which were often played with hardwood, ivory, or rock sliders. Afro-Americans had a guitar and banjo tradition prior to the appearance of bottleneck slide guitar, much like the Hawaiians had with slack key guitar prior to the appearance of steel guitar. In fact, Afro-Americans also incorporated different tunings in their guitar playing, beside standard concert tuning (E.B.G.D.A.E.). Many tuned their guitars to the D, E, or G tuning. Like the Hawaiians, Afro-Americans developed a rich, syncopated, highly rhythmic approach to fingerpicking that developed into various styles and regional idioms within blues and ragtime guitar. Some of this playing was performed in open tunings and some was not. So, although we think Hawaiian slack key and blues styles both developed in isolation from each other, the parallels between them are quite astounding.

"Although blues slide guitar appeared throughout the southern U.S. shortly after the turn of the century, the area in which it seems to have first appeared (and the area from which the strongest bottleneck/blues tradition emanates) is the northwestern portion of Mississippi known as the Delta. The earliest recorded Delta blues bottleneck players (such as Charley Patton, Tommy Johnson, Son House, Willie Brown and Fred McDowell) acknowledge not only each other, but also a few earlier musicians as major influences in developing the style. Charley Patton's mentor for blues/bottleneck guitar was Henry Sloan, who is reported to have been playing this style by 1897. The famous Memphis Jug Band leader Gus Cannon recalls a well-known blues musician named Alex Lee who lived in Coahoma County, Mississippi and was playing slide guitar prior to 1900. W.C. Handy reportedly heard his first blues in a railroad station in Tutwiler, Mississippi (in the Delta region) in 1903, and he recalls that it was played on a guitar using a pocketknife as a slide 'in a manner popularized by Hawaiian guitarists who used steel bars'. Whether or not these are accurate and credible reports, some of the above-mentioned musicians developed their styles shortly after the turn of the century and claim to have learned completely from others in their immediate vicinity.

"Although July Paka, Frank Ferrera, and Joseph Kekuku arrived on the U.S. mainland from 1899 to 1904, it is highly unlikely that they had any direct contact with black Americans in the Mississippi Delta region. It is also important to remember that these Delta musicians were indentured farm workers (for most purposes, still slaves), very poor, and immobile. However, this does not preclude the possibility that the appearance of bottleneck slide guitar was an attempt by blues musicians to incorporate an aspect of the increasingly popular Hawaiian music into their own music. The Mississippi Delta style of bottleneck blues guitar evolved through outstanding players such as the infamous Robert Johnson, Muddy Waters, and Elmore James. Both Elmore James and Muddy Waters brought their Delta sounds to Chicago after WWII. Both electrified and revolutionized the Delta sound throughout the late 1940's and 1950's, eventually popularizing it on a worldwide basis. In-terestingly, but not surprisingly, James' composition "Hawaiian Boogie" pays tribute to the Hawaiian steel guitar.

"An interesting aspect of bottleneck blues slide guitar is that it took on a somewhat different character in areas of the south outside of the Mississippi Delta. In fact, bottleneck slide guitar was seen throughout the entire south, from Texas to the Carolinas. Some of these early blues musicians acknowledged the influence of the Hawaiian steel guitar and developed their styles during the period around 1910 to 1940, during which Hawaiian music was very popular and influential. It is commonly accepted that many of these players may have listened to, or even observed, Hawaiian musicians performing at various chautauquas, expositions, and in vaudeville theatre from 1904 through the 1930's. Some of the better-known blues slide guitarists whose styles differed from the Delta style were Kokomo Arnold, Tampa Red, Blind Boy Fuller, Robert Wilkins, and Blind Willie Johnson, the latter two of which played their slide guitar 'lap style'. In fact, Kokomo Arnold learned his rudiments in slide guitar from his cousin John Wiggs (who played lap style) and later switched to a bottleneck style.

"In conclusion., there is little doubt that Hawaiian steel guitar has had an influence on many of the blues slide guitarists, even so much as to influence some to play the guitar 'lap style'. In addition, considering the time period in which blues bottleneck guitar developed, it would seem possible (maybe even logical) to attribute its appearance to the popularity of Hawaiian steel guitar. When all the historical facts are considered, this argument may have considerable merit, but is clearly unsubstantiated."

Big Bands.

Most of the top-level big bands connected with posh hotels and radio broadcasting contained a Hawaiian steel guitarist. Harry Owens became leader of the Royal Hawaiian Hotel band in 1934 and soon went on tour to the mainland. Ernest and Freddie Tavares joined the band in 1935 with Ernest mainly on steel guitar. In 1938 they did the sound track to the movie "Coconut Grove" and in 1938 Harry Owens won an Oscar for his song "Sweet Leilani" (composed October 19, 1934, the day his daughter was born) which stayed on the hit parade for 28 weeks. After World War II the band located permanently on the mainland but never in their 20 years did they play one song that was not Hawaiian. They featured sweet, rhythmic, danceable Hawaiian music, reinforcing the popularity of hapa haole music in America. The steel guitar of Ernest Tavares during the band's ten years on CBS TV opened the show with its characteristic glissando.

The Hawaiian Room in the Hotel Lexington, New York, was opened in 1937 and featured none but the best in Hawaiian music. The big bands of Ray Kinney, Lani McIntire, George Kainapau, and many others featured steel guitarists such as Andy Iona, Sam Koki, Hal Aloma, Sam Makia, Tommy Castro, and the list of names seems endless. Aside from playing to packed houses, the band broadcast from the Hawaiian Room over radio, then over television. The monumental success of the Hawaiian Room at the Lexington brought many more "Hawaiian Room"s into being; at the St.Regis Hotel New York, the Roosevelt Hotel in Chicago, the St. Francis in San Francisco, and many more, not to mention the same phenomenon in other countries. Some outstanding non-Hawaiian names that come to mind are: Alvino Rey playing with the Horace Heidt band and later with his own, also Roy Smeck, Nick Lucas, etc. During the 1950's Hawaiian music began to wane in popularity and the era of the big band came slowly to a close. The band that stayed to turn out the lights was Lawrence Welk's band with Buddy Merrill on steel guitar.

Lani McIntire and his Orchestra, with Sam Koki on steel, Al McIntire on bass, other players unknown.
J.C.Korinek photo

Lani McIntire (left, by microphone playing guitar) and his Aloha
Islanders, Sonora records album cover with Hal Aloma on steel

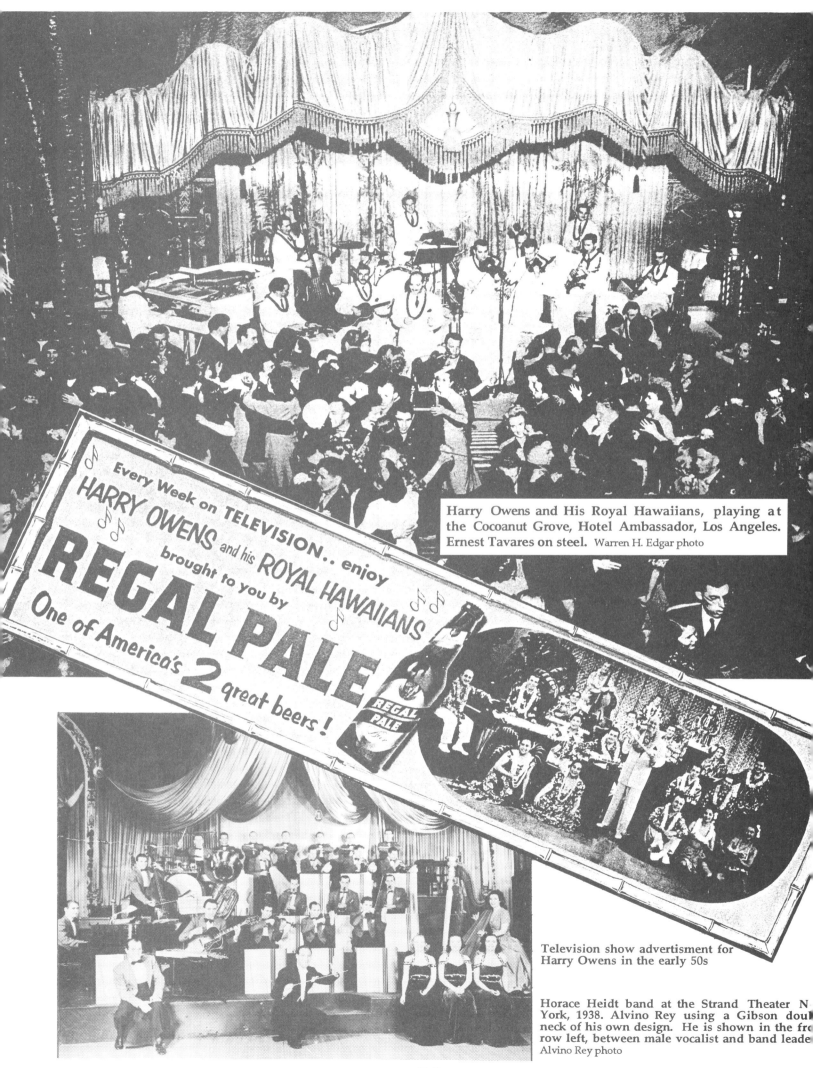

Harry Owens and His Royal Hawaiians, playing at the Cocoanut Grove, Hotel Ambassador, Los Angeles. Ernest Tavares on steel. Warren H. Edgar photo

Television show advertisment for Harry Owens in the early 50s

Horace Heidt band at the Strand Theater N York, 1938. Alvino Rey using a Gibson doul neck of his own design. He is shown in the fro row left, between male vocalist and band leade Alvino Rey photo

54

Alvino Rey's orchestra 1943

Although not considered to be "big band", Bob Wills and His Texas Playboys numbered 22 musicians in 1943, including a large horn section, four fiddles, and a steel guitar.

Country Music

"The Man Who Gave Steel Guitar to Nashville" is the title given to Hawaiian born Rudy Waikuiki (1909 - 1979) who did not play country music. In 1929, while Rudy lived in Flint MI, he taught Hawaiian songs and steel guitar technique to Beecher "Pete" Kirby, who became his most famous student. Kirby, better known as Bashful Brother Oswald to Grand Old Opry fans, made his mark in country music (in 1938) with the acoustic slide Dobro guitar. That is the year "Oz" was hired by Roy Acuff. There's an earlier report of Hoot Gibson's having brought Sol Ho'opi'i to Los Angeles to play with his musical group, in the early 1920's. Hoot, a famous cowoy movie star, became the first to use a Hawaiian musician in a country band, and introduced Sol to Hollywood.

The first electric steel player to become widely known backing a Nashville artist was "Little" Roy Wiggins playing with Eddie Arnold. His sound was somewhat Hawaiian, using what was called the "ting-a-ling" or the "crying sound", the rapid tremolo of first finger and thumb on two adjacent strings embellished by a vibrato of the steel bar. After "Little" Roy, the genius of Jerry Byrd became apparent. Jerry played country music and the standards of the 30's to the 60's, with the Hawaiian touch.

Jerry Byrd, country music star deeply rooted in Hawaiian music.
J. Byrd photo

Even though the business at hand was country music, Jerry always managed to slip in a Hawaiian tune or two wherever possible.

Although other steel guitarists of his time were experimenting with the pedals and knee levers of the new pedal steel guitars, Byrd remained true to the Hawaiian way which demanded much more of the musician in bar technique and in listening skills. A pedal steel player, if his instrument is adjusted correctly, can produce a correct change of harmony by pushing a pedal or kneeing a lever, but one who plays without pedals and levers must slant the bar with his ears and eyes to guide him to perfect harmonic pitch. Byrd developed his own unique style, incredibly smooth and fluid.

Jerry backed most of the great country singers of his day on recordings and in personal appearances, and producing many solo steel guitar recordings. His very earliest, 'Steelin' The Blues' and 'Drowsy Waters' ('Wailana') were sources of inspiration to steel guitarists around the world looking for someone to lead the way. Jerry, the "Master of Touch and Tone" provided that leadership.

Steel Guitar On Radio And Television

In August 1923 radio station WRC became the first in Washington D.C. to broadcast regularly. On November 23rd of the same year Ernest Deale (on steel guitar) and William (Babe) DeWaters as "The Honoluluans" began a regular radio show playing Hawaiian guitar duets. They were the first to play Hawaiian music over a Washington D.C. radio station. On January 4th, 1923 station WBAP in Fort Worth, Texas held what may have been the first hillbilly barn dance radio show. The featured group was Fred Wagner's Hilo Five Hawaiian Orchestra. The American Hawaiian Music Academy of Detroit had as its musical director in the 1920's steel guitarist Jack Raleigh. In 1923 Detroit station WJR participated in the first transatlantic radio broadcast. One number beamed to Europe was Charles E. King's "Na Lei O Hawa'i" with Raleigh playing the steel guitar.

The very earliest radio broadcasts of Hawaiian steel guitar were in Europe (1919 - 1927), when Joseph Kekuku broadcast from London England, and other countries. Johnny Noble's Moana Hotel Orchestra was the first Hawaiian band to perform over Hawaiian radio station KGU. In 1924 it increased its beam so that on April 11th Johnny Noble's band was to be heard in mainland U.S. for the first time. Joseph Lopez was the steel guitarist on that broadcast.

Radio stations hired local musicians in the earlier days, and many did weekly shows of Hawaiian music. George "Keoki" Lake of Edmonton (Canada) tells of their show (1949-1953), which was typical of most Hawaiian radio shows, using the Dick McIntire "Harmony Isle" format: "The Sunset Islanders played soft romantic music while Dick Taylor narrated beautiful poetic descriptions of Island legends, beauty, and the people of Hawai'i. The group consisted of steel guitar ('Keoki'), rhythm guitar, 'ukulele, bass, and vibraharp. The show was broadcast across Canada and in Australia."

The first record we have of Hawaiian music with steel guitar being played on television comes from the Oahu Music Publishing Co. whose graduate students were the musicians on that show. It was on October 23rd, 1939 when the Farnsworth Television and Radio Corporation established its operation in Fort Wayne, IN. The featured musicians were the Honolulu Serenaders who had held a regular radio program spot on Westinghouse Station WOWO for more than two years. Norman English was the steel guitarist.

First Farnsworth TV broadcast, 1939. Carl Van Horn on bass, Walter Peterson MC, Harold Taylor on Spanish guitar, Norman English on steel and Oscar Moser on 'ukulele.
Oahu Publishing Co., permission of Betty Glynn

On The Road With Ralph Kolsiana

by Ralph Kolsiana
As an example of the sort of lifestyle led by many Hawaiians in the pursuit of their musical careers on the mainland, consider the following story.

"I am of Dutch, Brazilian, and Peruvian extraction, born in O'ahu HI 1912, therefore Hawaiian by birth. We moved to Philadelphia when I was 6 years old, but even there I was raised among the Hawaiians of whom there were many in Pennsylvania, Atlantic City, Cleveland, and Chicago. I am one of the original members of the first Polynesian club in Southern California. It was called the "Polynesian Society of Los Angeles". Its members were some of the most popular stars of the day in the Polynesian field, including Joe Keawe of the famous Keawe family, Johnny K. Bright, brother of Sol K. Bright, and Duke Kahanamoku. The first president of the club was the famous bandleader and Hawaiian club owner, a Mr. Gary Spears, well known in Hawaiian circles in the late 40's and 50's, with Geo Piltz as vice president. The famous Telu Mansfield was secretary and head of entertainment. Joe Keawe became president in later years, as did Johnny Bright.

"My father, Walter E. Kolsiana, played clarinet, flute, bassoon, and oboe with the great John Phillips Sousa and I can remember attending many a rehearsal on Sunday afternoon at Rittenhouse Square, where the Declaration of Independence was signed. My father was on the road with the band for a number of years, travelling the world over.

"My brother John and I were both interested in stringed instruments and when my dad returned from his last tour with Sousa, he introduced us to one of his closest friends. He was an old time musician and great steel guitar player who taught at the Royal Hawaiian Studio of Music in Philadelphia. His name was Jimmy Kahanalopua, and his style was similar to that of Sol Ho'opi'i. Jimmy became my teacher, and his guitarist, Henry Kamanuwai, taught my brother guitar. We soon appeared on what was then the first type of talent contestant show out of New York, called the Major Bowes Amateur Show. We took first prize and earned $1,000. Big money in those days! Our first real money! We were all in our early teens then.

"One day (in the early 30's) we received a call for the two of us and Henry Kamanuwai to work six days a week at The Steel Pier in Atlantic City and join Aldridge's Steel Pier Hawaiians which was quite a large group. The owner of the group was Mr. Charles Aldridge who was a German of the old school. His wife was Loke "Rose" Lokelani Kalima of the famus Kalima Brothers family, Loke besides being the director, was the featured dancer, vocalist, and 'ukuleleist. My brother, Johnny Kolsiana, was guitarist and vocalist. Loke's brother Bill Kalima played bass. Clement Akana was guitarist, vocalist, and relief bass player. Pete Kaweikiu played bass and was a classical style vocalist, and Don Ferera (Portuguese Hawaiian, born in Rhode Island) was guitarist and vocalist. I played steel.

"That completed the evening group. There was also a matinee group consisting of a Joe Lopes on steel and vocals, Johnny Watson (an English-Hawaiian boy) on bass and bass vocals, and Ben Ka'ai on guitar with his wife Lucy Kealoha on 'ukulele, with David Na'ole classical voice and guitar. David Na'ole was also a fine steel guitarist. Loke Kalima's brother Bill was among the first of the Hawaiian boys from "The Pier" gang to enlist at the outbreak of WW II and his ship was torpedoed three days out. He was lost at sea.

"At that time the show consisted of the most popular dancers of the day, the Mansfield Sisters (Lulu, Telu, and Luka), and there was also a Samoan dancer, Siva Siva style, Tutasi Salima and a Chief Satini, with knife dancers Chief Kuka Tuitama and Chief Bob Ross. Chiefs Tuitama and Ross had at one time been Jack Dempsey's sparring partners when he was in training, in his prime. Chief Tuitama is still living here in L.A. He is about 89 years old and usually plays the part of an Indian Chief in movies. Chief Satini was the first to play the part of a genie who came out of a bottle as smoke in one of the old Warner Brothers movies. There was also a big water show in the back end of The Pier, featuring a Tahitian girl who jumped off the 85-foot diving board on the back of a beautiful white horse.

"During all this time, Kale Kaleiali'i and I were passing each other on various shows, he on the E.K.Fernandes Show and I with the Steel Pier group and with my own group called the Waikiki Swingsters, the same group I recorded with on the old R.C.A. Victor Recording, Bluebird label. We did 10 sides for them, back in 1936 or 37. The only other professional recordings we've done were all on studio recording tracks for such pictures as the luau scenes in the original motion picture version of "Mutiny On the Bounty" with Charles Laughton and an original Tahitian cast, also the tracks for the marriage luau scene in "Waikiki Wedding" with Bing Crosby and the night club scenes in "The Horizontal Lieutenant" with Debbie Reynolds and Jeff Chandler, a spy picture about World War II in the Philippines.

"While in Florida from 1931-1932 we went on tour with the health food advocate and lecturer, Bernard McFadden and his associate on nutrition, a Professor Paul C. Bragg. We wound up in Miami FL, where we were lured away from his show to work for the New York and Pennsylvania Railroad on what was then known as the "Orange Blossom Special" running between New York and Miami, making all the stops in between.

"It was at this point in the early 30's that we were hired by the infamous gangster Al Capone who caught our act while we were appearing at the posh Hawaiian night club, the Club Lei Lani on the outskirts of Miami Beach proper. After completing our nine month contract there he had us come and play on one of his small islands that were all connected by small arch-type bridges in a group near the Miami area. You may find this as amusing as we did at the time, but he and his cohort were really hung up on Hawaiian music. We were to serenade his guests who stayed over night in the master bedroom of his mansion. This room had alcove-like sections which were closed in by beautiful blue velvet curtains. We would serenade them while they made love after the big party downstairs was over. We did the same at his posh hotel suites in New York city. He called us his 'Boudoir Serenaders'. How is that for unique?

"After playing a few seasons for them, we joined a Hawaiian group based in Reading PA known as Ida K. Miller and Her Hawaiians. We also did broadcasts out of station WEEU and played all of the Police and Firemen's Fairs all over the state and as far as Ohio, Indiana, and Wisconsin. After several years with Ida, we were called to appear at the Mount Royal Hotel in Baltimore under the leadership of a Mr. Lani Kuni then residing in Washington DC. After a long stint there we moved into The Glass Hat in Washington's Biltmore Hotel. Then we worked for awhile at Jack Dempsey's Club at Broadway and 5th in New York City. It was through 'Al' (Capone) that we made the connection with Jack Dempsey, who was also a big fan of Hawaiian music. At the end of that engagement Alan and Pua left and were replaced by Don Ferera on guitar and Pete Kaweikiu who were with me on the Steel Pier engagement. We were booked into the famous Chi Chi Club in Palm Springs CA where we stayed for the next five years from 1945 - 50. We were "The Coral Islanders" at that time.

The Coral Islanders, 1954.
Back row left: Nick Ores, manager, J. Ortega, Spanish guitar. Chief M. Reid, bass. Ralph Kolsiana, double Rickenbacker. Sam Kapuni, Spanish guitar. Johnny K. Bright, vocalist and dancer.
Front row left:: Dancers Melone, Elana, Ku'u Lei, Chief Letuli, Leina'ala Reid, Napua Stevens, and Daisy.
R. Kolsiana photo

"Later in this period 'Al' got us another gig at a famous gangster hangout in Philadelphia down in the center of the third biggest Chinatown in the U.S. While working there we received requests from the likes of Dutchie Schultz, John Dillinger, and Pretty Boy Floyd. They all had one thing in common, Hawaiian music and old standards of the day.

"Finishing there we were introduced by 'Al' to another friend of his known to us only as 'Benny The Bum' whose night club went by the same name. Located up in West Philadelphia at 52nd and Market St. and was frequented by big shots and little shots as well as many city officials. When we worked for Capone in New York and Florida he used to tell us, and I can still hear him saying it, 'Now if you guys ever have any trouble from anybody you just tell Old Al and he'll see that it don't happen again.' This was true especially when we worked down south in Florida.

"During WWII we split up for awhile. My brother John went into the Air Corps and I into the Merchant Marines. During my stint in the Marines we were torpedoed twice. The first time was in the South Pacific in the New Guinea area. We were picked up within a few hours by the crew of a torpedo boat. The second time I was spared was around the Bahamas in the Bermuda Triangle area. I don't think it has any connection but a few minutes before it happened, the other three men and myself observed what appeared to be three fairly large disks with orange, red, and blue lights spinning around the underside. They seemed to play leap frog with each other, then faded out to the horizon. Immediately after, we heard the man in the crowsnest shout, 'Torpedo on the starboard side!!' and once again we ran to the port side and dived overboard. Both times there were just the four of us out of a crew of 144 that survived. Seeing it is a biblical number as well, I gathered that God wanted me to survive.

"We saved ourselves the second time around by forcing our hands and arms through the open sides of orange crates that floated up from the galley. We hung our heads inside and over the ends of the boxes and fell asleep, as we were exhausted from trying to escape the flames which spread quite a distance. After floating for 2 1/2 days in the Atlantic we were picked up by some Cuban fishermen.

"After being discharged I formed a trio with Don Ferera and Peter Kaweikiu and we booked into the Book Cadillac Hotel in Chicago called the Glass Slipper. We did 24 weeks there and then moved into the Mt. Royal Hotel, Baltimore MD, with Lani Kuni, and later went on the road with Jim McKenzie and His Hawaiian Aires. I replaced his former steel player who was a great steel man, Francis Brown of the Hilo Browns. Our guitarist was Mel Peterson and a good violinist named Hayden Hendershot. Mel used to call me 'The Kid With the Solid Touch'. We played all of the air bases and U.S.O. shows and then moved into the Tiki Bar in Portland after the Eddie Bush Trio.

"From there we moved into the Seven Seas Restaurant and Night Club here in Los Angeles following the Andy Iona, Benny Ahuna, and Alan Kila group. After leaving the Seven Seas, I formed a trio to go on the road for one of the most prominent agents at that time, Mr. Jack Warner, one of the famous Warner Motion Picture brothers. I enlisted Allen Kila on guitar/vocals, and Pua Kealoha, a very fine bassist, vocalist, MC, and comedian. We also had a Samoan knife dancer and Siva man named Chief Maka Nua and his wife Leona Maka Nua and her three girls. We went to the Tiki Club in Portland, from there to a theatre in Butte Montana, then to Laramie, Wyoming, to North Dakota, South Dakota, and then to Club Lei Lani, a very posh millionaire's club run by a Mr. Lee in Miami Beach.

"I then joined Max Reid's Tropic Islanders and during that time I created my line of Polynesian artifacts and tikis, masks of the South Pacific, battle clubs, drums, and a line of coconut dishes. During this 5-year period I also went into partnership with the Kelbos brothers of the Kelbos Hawaiian Barbeque Spareribs fame. I did most of the Island decorating of their restaurants both in L.A. and in Miami.

"Through them I was contacted by a Mr. Stephen Crane, the husband of actress Lana Turner, who later was accused of murdering the man who seduced her daughter, a former well-known gangster Johnny Stampanado. Mr. Crane owned the famous Luau Restaurant and Club located on Rodeo Drive, frequented by the rich and famous. My partner Ted Keep and I ran the gift shop and I carved most of the tikis and artifacts as decorations in the club. I designed all the fabrics for Hawaiian shirts, lavalavas, pareos, holokus, muumuus, and sarongs.

"On the more personal side, I am now 80 years old. In my prime I had a four-octave voice. Before the electric instruments, I was playing a German silver flower-engraved 3-resonator National Dobro square neck, 6 strings. My brother John played a Gibson L-5, and Henry Kamanuwai played the old Martin koa wood Dreadnought rhythm guitar. Bill Kalima, our bassist, had an old German swellback bass. In 1934 or 1935 I was presented with one of the first electronic steels that I'd ever heard of, a Rickenbacher "pancake", serial #004! Rickenbacher black bakelite Spanish guitars, also Rick basses and mandolins were used on the job at The Pier. Next, I played a National double 8, and for the past 40 years a 1950 double 8 Fender. My tunings are: A7, E7, Am9, Gm7, Gm9, C13, and E13. The three steel guitarists I most admired were Sol Ho'opi'i, Dick McIntire, and Danny Stewart. I know that if I could get the musicians I have in mind I could produce some great new Hawaiian music. Still searching for the best in life, I remain just another steel guitarist waiting for the ultimate gig. My fondest aloha nu nui iā 'oe nei."

The William "Billy" Hew Len Story

This is a story of an entirely different kind. Told by Jerry Byrd a close friend of Billy, a Hawaiian who made his professional career in Hawai'i. His story glows with the radiance of true courage. It should be read by every kāne, wahine, and keiki in the islands, for this man is truly their national hero. Billy left us on November 23, 1987.

"I heard about this guy long before I met him. His story is inspiring - more so than any other I know of - because he played steel guitar with only one hand! No - it's no trick or an act. He had only one hand. Like many of you, I had heard about other such great musicians as D'jango Reinhardt, who played plectrum guitar with two or three fingers on his left hand; Andy Iona, the great Hawaiian steel guitarist who had no thumb on his right hand; and others of similar circumstance, but not one without a hand! I can hear all of you saying to yourselves the same thing I said when I heard of this; How can anyone play any instrument with only one hand - especially steel guitar? So let me relate to you an amazing story about one Mr. Billy Hew Len. Unlike most stories, this is a true story that will sound like fiction.

"Let me begin by saying that Billy was a master steel guitarist. Brother - he played! He never ceased to amaze me, this real son of Hawai'i. Billy Hew Len was of Hawaiian, Chinese, and Spanish descent; a rather odd mixture, but not uncommon in Hawai'i where many are of six to eight nationalities. There were twelve children in the Hew Len family: nine boys and three girls and they are all musicians or dancers - or both! Also not uncommon in Hawai'i.

"When he was about ten years old, he used to 'swipe' his cousin's guitar while he was at work, keep it all day and when the owner finished work he'd return home only to find his guitar missing. He knew who had it so he'd head for Billy's house in a huff and get his guitar. Same thing the next day. Billy would put a metal nut under the strings, like we used to have to do, to elevate the strings, and he would practise playing steel guitar. This kind of routine continued until he was 15, when he quit school and went to work in a garage. Then one shattering day something happened that would change Billy's whole life. In one terrible moment, a planing machine took all of his left hand - cut it off at the wrist. He was only 17 years old! This could justifiably be termed a tragedy in anyone's life, especially one so young. But I sometimes think that these things happen for a purpose. In Billy's case I'm even more convinced of it.

"So now - he told himself - he was done. What could a guy do with only one hand? One thing was for sure - he could never play steel guitar again. And he did what anyone would do after the shock and the healing process had passed and the dark depths of discouragement took over. He lay around the house or spent the empty hours loafing with the gang down on the corner. What else? One day his mother suggested that they should talk to a man she knew who might be able to help. Billy would not consider it - he just 'flat didn't care about doing anything.' But he later relented and agreed to go, even though 'it was a waste of time.' And so he met the one person who would change his life. His name was Edwin P. Morrell.

"Mr. Morrell was an elder in the Mormon Church and he worked with handicapped people of all sorts and ages. After asking Billy a few questions as to what he wanted to do and what he liked to do ('nothing' were his replies), they stumbled onto the fact that Billy liked to play steel guitar. But when it was explained how a steel guitar had to be played and Morrell suggested they figure out a way to do it, Billy said, 'No way! Not steel guitar.' But he underestimated this man's resourcefulness.

"Later on, after some thought by Mr. Morrell as to how to proceed with the problem, they went to a leather shop - a harness maker in those days. Morrell explained to the man what was involved and gave him a drawing of what he wished him to make - a sort of glove that would fit over the wrist. Then they went to a machine shop - and, again, Morrell had drawings to illustrate what he wanted; this time, a steel bar. It was to be about three inches long, rounded on both ends, and was to have a flange inserted into a slot into which several small holes were drilled. Those were used to attach the bar to the glove with leather laces, and the whole would fit over Billy's wrist.

"When he tried it out later, he was even more positive than ever that it just wouldn't work! 'How could I play and use any vibrato? I'd have to move my whole arm - not only difficult but tiring as well. And the slants - how can I make the necessary forward and reverse slants? Impossible! ' But here is where his strong personality and ingrown desire finally won out. He'd do it - somehow - some way - he would do it!

Billy Hew Len playing his Rickenbacker pancake steel guitar in the early 1950's playing at the Niumalu Hotel, now the Hilton Hawaiian Village Hotel. (Notice the tuning keys: up on one side, down on the other) Trini Hew Len photo

"He joined a band of handicapped musicians and he began the long battle. But at least he was playing music once again. It was decided by Mr. Morrell that Billy needed a new instrument - an electric steel guitar. This was in the late 1930's. They headed for downtown Honolulu and the old Metronome Music Store (still in business). They looked at a relatively inexpensive model - a brand new Rickenbacker 'fry pan'. While they were talking to the salesman they could hear someone upstairs playing a steel guitar. He, too, was trying one of these 'fry pan' looking things, so the salesman called up to him and asked if this lad could come up and listen to him play. This was Bill's first meeting with the great David Keli'i, who later became famous via the Hawaii Calls radio show and on recordings, and who inspired many others to play steel guitar - myself included. So Billy was hearing sounds he'd never heard before! They bought the guitar on the spot! 'But', Billy told me, 'it sure didn't sound that good when I tried to play the darned thing'! It was his main instrument throughout his life.

"When pedal steel guitars came into their own in the 60's Billy started using a Fender 4-pedal, 8-string neck to which he added two additional pedals himself. He used A6th as his basic tuning. Anyhow, he was soon playing at the hotels in Waikiki with his own band, followed by many recording sessions with top Hawaiian groups. He is on more Hawaiian records than any other steel guitarist, including a new album with our brother steelman, Barney Isaacs, entitled 'Steel Guitar Magic' Hawaiian Style. It is a Jack DeMello Presents album No. 31000, and contains 16 of Hawai'i's all-time favorites.

"I asked Billy if he had any regrets over not being able to play with two hands and his quick reply was an emphatic 'No'! I personally feel that as a result of his handicap (or is it?) he evolved, out of necessity, a uniquely original style and sound that he may not have had otherwise. In fact, he may not even have continued in music - as a steel man, especially. He would probably still be in that machine shop!

"Billy enjoyed playing more than anyone I know, always flashing that big smile and giving out an infectious laugh. For about five years, he appeared on alternate nights in the same room as I, the Blue Dolphin Room in the Outrigger Hotel. But he also did luau shows (five or six a week), breakfast musicales, luncheon musicales, cocktail hour gigs, and everything else. Well, like I said, that cat was busy.

"And this story has a happy ending because Billy Hew Len *did* learn to play after what must have been many hundreds of hours of work and mental anguish, despair, impatience, and discouragement. I had these myself and I can well imagine how it was with Billy. He became the most sought-after, most in demand steel guitarist in Hawaii. Hawaii has produced so many great steel guitarists that by sheer numbers their names have become lost in the cruelty of forgetfulness. But Billy Hew Len's name will not be among those lost because he had too much to say musically ever to merit such a fate. It just goes to show how much we mortals can accomplish with a little love and encouragement from somebody who cares. In Bill's case it was his understanding mother and one Mr. E. P. Morrell. "But most of all, it was Billy Hew Len who did it."

Billy left behind his wife Trini and four daughters. One son-in-law, Hiram Olsen, is the great rhythm, lead, and slack-key guitarist who played in the Jerry Byrd Trio at the Halekulani Hotel's House Without a Key, in the days before Jerry retired. The group's name is now the Hiram Olsen Trio and the steel guitarist is Hiram's son, (Billy's grandson) Casey Olsen, bright star of the future.

Trinity Hew Len, Billy's widow, summed up what's been said about her man. These are her words. "His unreal character was expressed through his music that came from 'within his own soul'. He touched many lives through his love and affection for music everywhere and firmly believed in being yourself and he never failed to lend a helping hand to others. Billy Hew Len is the most courageous and talented man I have known...long will his achievements serve to inspire the youth of Hawai'i...

God Bless to All, With Great Respect and Love and Aloha, Mrs. Trinity Hew Len."

The Music Scene In Hawai'i

by Walter Mo'okini. Lest you think that all Hawaiian steel guitar players left the islands and that nothing of note was going on "back home" in Hawai'i, here's a story told by a man with a remarkable memory who knew all the great musicians of his time.

"I played my first steel guitar solo as an eighth grader. The tune was 'Across the Sea' played on a regular Spanish guitar, locally in Hawai'i referred to as a 'gas box', the strings were raised at the bridge with the use of match sticks. My dad taught me my first steel guitar solo. It was not until my sophomore year at the University of Hawai'i that I became seriously interested in the steel guitar. This was due to my association with another student, the late Sam Ka'apuni, who was an outstanding musician, known at the time as a solo guitarist. Sam was a graduate of McKinley High School, and I of Kamehameha Schools. After completing studies at the University of Hawai'i I returned to Kamehameha Schools, as one of its first graduates to teach there.

"Upon receiving our military officers' commission at the University of Hawai'i, Sam eventually served with an Armored Division in Europe during WW II, while I was assigned to the theater of operations in the Pacific as an Infantry Officer, then recalled in 1951 to the Korean conflict with a short tour afterwards in Vietnam.

"While at college, Sam played the steel guitar for the Islanders at the Royal Hawaiian Hotel. Sonny Kamahele's dad was the leader of the group. When Sam joined the Malcolm Beelby Orchestra, which was the featured band in the Monarch Room of the Royal Hawaiian Hotel of which Benny Kalama was a member, I took Sam's place as the steel guitarist for the Islanders. The Malcolm Beelby Orchestra eventually moved to the mainland at Baker's Motel in Texas.

"During this period of time when the Islanders were performing at the Royal Hawaiian Hotel, steel guitar players were evident everywhere. David Keli'i was at Hoffman's Cafe, Tommy Castro at Rathskeller and later with Gigi Royce's Orchestra at the Young Hotel Roof Garden. David Malo played with the Andy Cummings Group at the Hawaiian Town Night Club and Gabby Pahinui later joined Andy. Jake Keli'ikoa was at Maggie's Inn, and later with Don MacDiarmid's Orchestra and eventually with Alfred Apaka, at the Moana Hotel. Pua Alameida (Almeida) started with his dad Johnny, then formed his own band which played at a night club called Club Pago Pago. His stint at the Moana Hotel came some time after this gig. Dan Ka'eka played with Bill Lincoln's group and Eddie Pang later became the steel guitar player.

"Joe Custino was in this circuit of players but performed weekly on a radio broadcast called the Transit Hawaiians. The late Fred Tavares played with the Harry Owens Orchestra at the Royal Hawaiian Hotel while Steppy DeRego was the steel guitar performer for the Ray Andrade Orchestra at La Hula Rhumba. Merle Kekuku played with the original Islanders and later formed a group that played at the Moana Hotel. Billy Hew Len was at the Niumalu Hotel.

"Of course, the program Hawai'i Calls introduced the sounds of Hawai'i throughout the world and the steel guitar stylings of David Keli'i, Jake Keli'ikoa, Tommy Castro, Joe Custino, Pua Alameida, Jules Ah See, to name some of the pioneers, are history now. Jules Ah See, Billy Hew Len, Barney Isaacs, and Mel Abe eventually established themselves with many of the groups. Except for Billy who played almost exclusively for Pua Alameida, Jules, Mel and Barney were the steel guitar virtuosos for Alfred Apaka's Hawaiian Village Serenaders.

"In 1965 I took a group of twenty-five students from Kamehameha Schools to Japan to perform a Polynesian show at a man-made Festival Park in the hills of Kobe called Arima. The group put on two shows a day for about eight to ten thousand people at this summer festival and remained there for ten weeks. The group was invited back the following year for a period of eight weeks. Bill Cazimero (father of the Brothers Cazimero), and his son Roland were members of the group that travelled in 1965 and Bill was the steel guitar player with Roland on the bass.

"In 1967, I took a group of students to Europe sponsored by the U.S. State Department and the Hawai'i Visitors Bureau, and Buddy Hew Len was the steel guitar player. After returning from Europe and while visiting Sol 'Sonny' Kamahele at the Surf Room of the Royal Hawaiian Hotel, I was invited to join Sonny. The group ironically was called 'The Islanders' which was the original musical organization I joined that was led by Sol Kamahele Sr. which was also my advent to Hawaiian music.

"While with Sonny, I doubled on the wood bass and the steel guitar, playing the latter only at the hotel luau sessions. I continued with The Islanders who performed not only at the Royal Hawaiian Hotel but at the Reef, Princess Ka'iulani and Hawaiian Regent Hotels. Later on, The Islanders moved over to the Waikiki Beachcomber Hotel and became the main Hawaiian group with the Tihati Polynesian Review Show. Following this show, The Islanders regrouped at the Halekulani Hotel and are presently esconced there as the cocktail hour band along with the Hiram Olsen Trio. I double on the electric bass and guitar, and do vocals with the trio.

"During The Islanders' tenure at the Surf Room of the Royal Hawaiian Hotel, Joe Custino started as the steel guitar player followed by Mel Abe. As the group moved to the Waikiki Beachcomber Hotel, Mel Abe served as the primary steel guitar person, with Alan Akaka and me sharing some of the workload. At the time the regrouping commenced at the Halekulani Hotel, Eddie Lau started as the steel guitar person followed by Alan Akaka. Alan still continues with the same assignment, however, and Barney Isaacs and Harold Haku 'ole are the alternates.

"I have been on the Hawaiian musical scene for more than 50 years and have seen the changes that have taken place. I have worked with some of the great entertainers and musicians in Hawai'i, such as Renny Brooks, Sam Kapu Sr., Alfred Apaka, Jake Keli'ikoa, Pua Alameida, Joe Custino, Jules Ah See, Benny Kalama, Steppy DeRego, Sonny Kamaka, Barney, Atta and Norman Isaacs, and Gabby Pahinui."

Dan PoePoe on bass, Eddie Kinilau (leader) on 'ukulele, and Walter Mo'okini on steel guitar, with Henry Makua on rhythm guitar playing at a Honolulu wedding reception.
W. Mo'okini photo

64

Steel Guitar Flows Back To Hawai'i

During the 1970's the popularity of Hawaiian music was at its very lowest ebb. The world-wide popularity of rock music is the prime suspect. Steel guitarists have speculated on this phenomenon and blamed many things. Could the over-complication of the instrument by means of too many tunings have been the cause? Could it be that songs with Hawaiian titles and Hawaiian lyrics were too difficult for the haole (non-Hawaiian) audience to pronounce and remember? Another theory for the Hawaiian steel guitar's low profile even in the Hawaiian islands can be drawn from our conversation with vocalist Marlene Sai after a very successful show in the Monarch Room at the Royal Hawaiian Hotel. The show featured traditional songs of Hawai'i, played on trumpet, clarinet, sax, keyboard, electric guitar, and bass. We asked Marlene why it was not played on steel guitar, 'ukulele, semi-acoustic rhythm guitar, and acoustic bass. She agreed that she would have preferred the "more Hawaiian" back-up but pointed out that very few of the steel guitarists of Hawai'i are musically literate. Very few are able to read the score.

The great flood of musical talent that flowed out of Hawai'i has run down to a trickle. There is little employment on the mainland, so the Hawaiian musician stays home to vie for the few gigs being offered there. The days of the grand tours have come to an end. Bookings for special shows abroad can be attended to by air travel, and now a day-time job is a must. On the in-coming tide we see steel guitarists from mainland U.S. and elsewhere moving to Hawai'i in order to keep playing the music style they love best. Ray Knapp, for example, left the mainland in the late 1970's and at first found it very difficult to find employment as a steel guitarist in Hawai'i. He played the cruise ships for awhile, and now has a regular spot playing at a luau in Lahaina, Maui. Ed Mayer moved from Indonesia to Hawai'i but does not have full time employment there as a steel guitarist. John Ely moved from Texas to Maui to pursue his musical career.

The world-famous Jerry Byrd left Nashville in 1972. Born in Lima Ohio, he "went home" to Hawai'i to be immersed in Hawaiian music. He is one of the few who were able to do that successfully. Although he is in semi-retirement now, he can look back over many years of steady contract playing in Hawai'i in the Outrigger Hotel's Blue Dolphin Room, at the Royal Hawaiian Hotel's Surf Room and finally at the Halekulani's House Without A Key. He continues to make recordings and to make short playing tours to Japan and more rarely to the U.S. mainland.

DIAGRAM ARRANGEMENT FOR HAWAIIAN STEEL GUITAR

KILIMA
HAWAIIAN WALTZ
by Keoki Awai

Sherman, Clay & Co.
SAN FRANCISCO

Sole Distributors
OAHU PUBLISHING COMPANY
2108 Payne Ave., Cleveland, Ohio.

Chapter 3

Mainland Schools
And Cultural Influences

Instruction For The Steel Guitar

Along with the huge popularity of Hawaiian music came the demand for instruction on the steel guitar and 'ukulele. The 30's were the years of the Great Depression and little money was available for frivolities such as musical instruments. The acoustic steel guitar had a great timely advantage. It was cheap. You could buy one through a mail-order catalog for $7.00 complete with case and it would come with bar, picks, a metal adapter to raise the strings, and a "How To Play Steel Guitar In Five Easy Lessons" instruction book. For $2.00 more you could buy a tuning pitch-pipe. Another popular accessory was a recording of Sol Ho'opi'i or Dick McIntire and a wind-up gramophone. Many a determined student with a keen ear learned to play with no more help than that.

Many self-taught steel guitar players sought to keep body and soul together during those dreadful days of unemployment by carrying their guitar from door to door, offering to give lessons for $1.00 a week. Too often they were not well enough trained to do any serious instruction and the story is often told of the student who played better than his or her teacher after a few lessons.

A much better contribution was made by the early Hawaiians themselves. Those who had attended Kamehameha School For Boys or any other place of higher education in the islands were often well educated in music and could instruct properly. Many of them composed music and took on impressive positions as music arrangers for radio stations, big bands, and for Hollywood movie studios. They added to their income by opening a small studio where they gave music lessons. Joseph Kekuku taught at Reid's Popular School of Music in Chicago and later at his own studios. Ben Hokea taught in Toronto, Dick McIntire in Los Angeles, Walter Kolomoku in New York, Harlin Bros. in Indianapolis, and so on.

From a February 1928 magazine

Tablature, "The Number System"

In 1916 the first steel guitar instruction book was published by Sherman Clay using J. Kalani Peterson's new invention, the tablature or number system. The Peterson system used six lines which represented the six strings of the guitar. If a student were to pluck the first and second strings, the indication would be two numerals, written on the first and second string lines of the tablature. Exactly what numerals were to be written there depended on what fret the bar was to be placed at. Timing was indicated by a numeral in brackets placed above the note to be played. (2) meant two beats, (3) meant three beats. Or, in the early stages of tablature writing, a tiny quarter note or a half note was placed above the numeral on the tablature staff to tell the player what timing to apply to the numerals. The advantage of the tiny notes was that sixteenth notes or dotted eighth notes could be expressed.

The following are several styles of tablature writing

First line of "Aloha 'Oe" in the Peterson number system. The steel guitarist playing the numbers had to keep an eye on the notation above to get the timing instruction. When a note was the same as the one preceeding it, instead of writing the numerals twice, a series of dashes indicated "play the same again".

Roy Smeck, in 1932, used a system similar to the Peterson numbers, occasionally indicating the picking fingers. "X " indicated thumb pick, ".." indicated second finger, while a single dot indicated first finger.

The Oahu Publishing Company used ties between numbers to indicate eighth notes and put numerals in brackets to indicate half notes (2) and whole notes (4), etc. A dotted eighth note was indicated with a dot over the numeral, and a straight line between numerals meant the player was to slide or gliss the bar between notes. An "R" indicated a rest.

Sol Ho'opi'i wrote his number system (tablature) above the line of notation and indicated timing by placing a properly timed note above each numeral. This was an improvement in that dotted eighths and sixteenths could be indicated.

The number system used at the Langdon Brothers Hawaiian Studios during the years Joseph Kekuku taught there showed the chord symbols for accompaniment written in a straight line across the bottom of the page. Each numeral indicated where the steel bar was to be placed. "O" was the A major chord, "5" was the D chord. If the same chord were to be played for two or more measures, a tiny numeral was placed above, meaning "Play 'O' for 2 measures." If the measure were to be played two beats at fret 2 and two beats at fret 7, it was shown as "(2-7)".

Langdon Brothers Hawaiian Studios
431 S. Wabash, Chicago Web. 0734

The disadvantage of tablature was that many who started on it never bothered to learn music notation and were thus limited to playing only what they could find written in tablature. The obvious advantage was that the student could have instant success, no need to learn the rules of music notation. In later years after it became fashionable to play in many different tunings, a player could switch easily from one unfamiliar tuning to another as long as one could read the tablature written for that tuning. It is also a useful tool for writing a special arrangement. Although the purist can be excused for his or her feelings of disdain for those who are slaves of tablature, one must admit there was good reason for its invention.

The "reason" that I refer to is the method of music notation that was in use in the early years of steel guitar. The first guitars were acoustic, six-stringed, played in the low bass A tuning. The early playing style called for the guitarist to play his own accompaniment. While the tune was carried on the higher strings, a "bass-strum, counter-bass-strum", or an arpeggio pattern was carried on the low strings. In the A major low bass tuning (first string to sixth) E.C#.A.E.A.E. the very lowest note that could be played on the instrument would be E on the sixth string open. On a traditional music treble clef staff, that E would appear on the space below the third ledger line below the staff. The highest OPEN STRING note the instrument could play would be E on the first string. That would be written as E in the top space of a musical staff. Now consider what happened as the bar was moved up the first string to the 24th fret. The written notation to express those notes would climb to ridiculous heights above the staff. E on the twelfth fret first string would be written on the third ledger line above the staff, and E on the 24th fret would be on the space above the sixth ledger line above the staff. When a very high passage came up in a song, some arrangers solved the problem by writing the notes one octave lower than what was intended and putting the direction "8 va" next to the notes, meaning "play this an octave higher than written."

The final bars of "Aloha 'Oe", two lines for steel guitar, A major low bass tuning, bottom line for Spanish guitar accompaniment.

A section of "Hilo March", top line for steel guitar A major low bass tuning, bottom line for Spanish guitar accompaniment.

In this arrangement, the steel guitarist is assisted with indicators "B1, B2, B8 etc." to say at what fret the bar should be placed. Roman numerals indicated which strings the thumb would pluck. This system makes a very "busy" staff line to read.

Below, Hawaiian Guitar book covers from publisher Wm. J. Smith c.1928

It seemed that no system suited the new instrument perfectly, so creative people were inventing new ones. Consider the "Basic Training Method" known as *Lettergram* invented by Kenneth Kitchen who had studios in four towns in northwestern Ohio during the 1940's. He also published his own songs under the name Kenna Halekuki. Look at the second line of his arrangement of "A Shack By A Coral Shore", in A major high bass. Instead of using numerals to show where the bar should be placed, he gave the student the name of the note, what harmony notes should be played with it, and on what string the notes should be played. The student would have to know his fretboard in order to play this method, and would easily make the transition to reading standard music notation. Kenny indicated timing by putting a tiny note above the tablature. Notice how he solved the problem of writing in two octaves. In bar 4, he used lower case "e" to indicate "E" an octave higher. Harmonics were written as diamond-shaped notes. In bar 2, a dotted half note is struck, followed by two strums across the lower strings to keep the flow of the music. An acoustic guitar did not have much sustain, so it was common practice to strum along with the melody in this manner. In bar 5, the line between the two eighth notes indicated a gliss. The numbers 6, 7, 8, 9, 10, 11 indicate the measure or bar number of the song.

Advertisement from "The Motion Picture Magazine" c. late 1920s

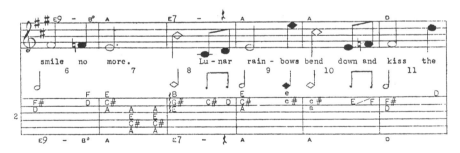

Ken Kitchen's "Lettergram" method of arranging music for his steel guitar students.

submitted by Louie Kitchen, Kenny's son.

The Hawaiian music craze and lack of printed music to support it gave opportunity for many to cash in. No certification was needed, no proof of musical expertise required. The Hawaiian image, usually of a hula girl, on the front of a brochure would bring instant sales. "Play steel guitar in 10 days or your money back" or "Play the Hawaiian steel guitar in five easy lessons" were the promises that brought gold to the pockets.

It would be safe to say that most towns in North America had a steel guitar teacher, and a city of any size in the 1930's and 1940's could boast of several "Hawaiian Conservatories" or "Hawaiian Institutes" of Music. Local radio stations were generous in giving air time, so it was not unusual for senior students and teachers to be heard on regular weekly broadcasts. The following are stories of the largest and most successful schools of music.

69

The Alkire Eharp Method

A highly respected innovator-teacher was Eddie Alkire of West Virginia whose professional career in radio had begun by 1930, playing steel guitar on three different radio stations in the Cleveland area. Eddie published a teaching course with notation written in actual pitch. The new electric guitars with beautiful sustain did not need the bass-strum-strum style of playing to keep the music flowing. All the attention could be focused on the melody, and it made sense to write the music in actual pitch. E on the first string open had formerly been written in the top space of the treble clef staff. In "actual pitch", that same E was written on the lowest line of the staff.

Eddie was a gifted musician. As a freelance writer he contributed hundreds of articles on the Hawaiian steel guitar to trade, school, and special interest magazines. So great was his popularity, he left the Honolulu Conservatory and established his own teaching studio, plus a huge mail order instruction course. By 1939 he had invented a 10-string steel guitar which he called the "EHARP", pronounced "ay-harp". The name was derived from a combination of "EHA" meaning "four" in Hawaiian (since the player used three fingers and the thumb to play it) and "HARP". The playing method involved a very selective choosing of strings (as opposed to the "strum" which is possible on other tunings) which gave it a similarity to the technique involved in playing a harp. The tuning, starting from the first string, was E, C#, B, A, G#, G, F#, F, E, C#. "With the birth of the Eharp," it was said, "the Hawaiian steel guitar had become of age, as much a musical instrument as any other." Eddie organized his musical groups and put them to work recording first for Decca, then for Columbia Recording Studios in New York.

Eddie received many prestigious awards for his development of the Eharp and his instruction course. After a performance in an Artist's Concert at Springfield, Mass in 1941, a critic wrote, "There are few things one never tires of: to listen to Eddie Alkire play is one of them. The influence that the work of this artist has had in shaping a musical future for this new ten-string Eharp is now acknowledged by everyone. Mr. Alkire made a special arrangement of themes from the Tschaikowsky Concerto No. 1 in B flat minor and Symphony No. 6 in B minor. The second selection was the always-fresh "Gavotte" by Czibulka. Not a chord of the original harmonies was changed and the music was greatly enjoyed by the audience."

The Eharp was introduced at the artists' recital, 38th annual convention of the American Guild of Banjoists, Mandolinists, and Guitarists in 1940. Eddie's charismatic personality, his sense of business, and his flair for instruction brought thousands of students to his studios and many more subscribing to his mail-order lessons. He was awarded the Fred Gretch trophy and voted the nation's foremost Hawaiian guitarist. (The four other winners of this prestigious trophy were Tommy Dorsey, Fred Waring, Harry Volpe, and Vincent Gomez.) In 1961 he became the sixth man this century to win the American Guild of Musicians' achievement award for his incomparable contribution to the Hawaiian guitar.

The story of the many instruments Eddie designed and built will be told in a later chapter dealing with the physical development of the steel guitar.

The Oahu Publishing Co.

Undoubtedly the most successful of the guitar schools was the Oahu Publishing Co. of Cleveland Ohio. Perhaps 200,000 students graduated from its guitar courses. Many stayed on with the school to become its teachers and business people, and to establish their own music studios. When Harry G. Stanley started the company in 1926 the Hawaiian music craze had just begun. With his flair for advertising and showmanship, Harry rented space in the classiest areas of town and announced the opening of his studios with flashy advertising. People lined up for blocks to sign up for his courses. When others charged $1.00 a lesson, Harry charged $5.00. When others stayed at the instruction level, Harry branched out into publishing his own magazines and instruction material, and into manufacturing his own guitars for sale. As his brightest students graduated he encouraged them to buy the studios from him so that in time he was supplying up to 1200 studios across the U.S.A., Canada, and other countries without actually running the studios himself. During the worst of the great depression, the Oahu Co. thrived.

The Oahu Publishing Co. can boast of many gifted students who became professionals, such as Wayne Newton and Herbie Remington. By holding annual proficiency competitions for young musicians, the

Oahu Co. maintained high musical standards. They started students on the tablature system but graduated to musical notation, showmanship, and business management training. Although their advertising very successfully used the Hawaiian image - the palm trees, hula girls, leis and orchids - to lure the romantic minded student, the music they used in their courses was varied: standard pop tunes, folk, country, gospel, and Hawaiian.

The story of the Oahu Publishing Co. is best told by one of its principals, Betty Glynn. The following article is reprinted from the Aloha International Steel Guitar Club Newsletter, Dirk P. Vogel, editor. Volume 2 - No. 1. April-May-June. 1989. p.11

The Oahu Publishing Co. -Harry G. Stanley

by Betty Glynn

"Harry G. Stanley and a half-brother, George Bronson, established the original Honolulu Conservatory of Music in Flint, Michigan, in the late 1920's and in Cleveland, Ohio, about 1930. They separated shortly thereafter. George Bronson started his own publishing and instruction business and Mr. Stanley became sole owner of Oahu.

"A popular coast-to-coast NBC and CBS radio program of Hawaiian music was broadcast from Cleveland by the Oahu Serenaders featuring Eddie Alkire, a sensational steel guitarist, Alex Hoapili, a guitarist from Maui, and Mort Searles, 'ukulele virtuoso. They were all instructors at the Honolulu Conservatory of Music. When I enrolled as a student at the Conservatory, Alex Hoapili was my Hawaiian steel guitar instructor and Mort Searles taught me to play the standard guitar.

Honolulu Guitar Club, Lansing Michigan.
Radio station WJIM, February 27, 1936
Norm English photo

"In 1933 Mort Searles formed an all-girl Hawaiian trio. I became a member and we played a one-year series of radio broadcasts. Following this I became an instructor. The Honolulu Conservatory quickly became a nation-wide chain of music studios. The teachers used music courses which were published at the home office in Cleveland. Students were signed up by salesmen from the home office who travelled to various cities upon request.

"It became necessary to separate the rapidly developing publishing business from the studios, so the Oahu Publishing Company was founded by Harry G. Stanley, its president. Its purpose was to publish exclusive teaching methods and to wholesale guitars and musical supplies to the schools. Extensive courses were published featuring the new Oahu Diagram Method (tablature) and new courses in "notes' were written to be taught after the diagram courses. Popular and standard sheet music and folios were produced to supplement the Oahu courses. About this time I transferred from teaching at the Honolulu Conservatory to arranging music at the Oahu Publishing Company and was eventually promoted to Vice President and Manager of the music department.

"Specially-designed electric steel guitars and amplifiers were made by Oahu's own technicians. Other Oahu guitars were produced by three of the finest U.S. guitar factories: Harmony, Valco, and Rickenbacker.

"In 1950 accordion teaching courses were published and accordions were imported from Italy with Oahu trade names: Stanelli and Bernelli. A magazine was published for students and teachers. Originally named 'The Guitarist', it was changed later to 'Music' magazine.

"Meanwhile the Oahu Convention for Teachers and Dealers had been changed in 1942 to the International Guitar League (IGL), a festival of competitions for students of all ages. Thousands of students attended each year with their teachers and played in bands and orchestras (or played solos) to compete for trophies and to improve their skills. As the popularity of these festivals grew, they were opened to all musical instruments and the name was changed to the International Music League (IML)

"By 1968 downtown Cleveland had changed dramatically and it became necessary to leave the building before dark for safety. Music had also changed. Rock and Roll entered the picture introducing a new fad of playing the guitar by ear, rather than by diligent study. So, the company was moved to sunny crime-free Sun City, Arizona.

Beautiful Oahu matched set electric steel and amplifier.
Ron Middlebrook photo

SWANEE RIVER
OAHU ORCHESTRATION FOR HAWAIIAN GUITAR

THE ARTISTS *of today were the* Students of Yesterday

This lesson has been especially prepared for instruction on
PALM HARMONICS

c. 1930

"In July of 1970 Harry G. Stanley died of a massive heart attack, a great loss to the music industry. Mrs. Esther Stanley continued to operate the company, managed by my husband Tom Glynn as president, assisted by Esther and myself, for 16 years until a decision was made by all three to retire and close the Oahu Publishing Company in May, 1985."

c. 1930

Hawaiian Rose

Diagram Arrangement for Hawaiian Steel Guitar

Words by
PAUL B. ARMSTRONG

Music by
F. HENRI KLICKMANN

Arranged for Steel Guitar by
HARRY STANLEY
—
Published by
OAHU PUBLISHING CO.
2108 Payne Ave.
Cleveland, Ohio, U. S. A.
MADE IN U. S. A.

c. 1930

Acoustic guitar given to the beginning student, to become his or her property after successful completion of 52 lessons.

John Russell Photo

International Guitar League

by Norman English

"I first learned to play Hawaiian guitar at the Honolulu Conservatory of Music, 'Clarence Clark Studios' in Lansing, MI. They used the Oahu teaching materials, with the A major low and high bass tuning. At one of their annual competitions, I won first prize for steel guitar playing. Lauritz Melchoir and Al Jolson were guest artists at the Palmer House ballroom and because my student band was also a first place winner, we were presented at the Palmer House on the same program with these great singers. I took the managers and instructors course and started teaching at the Honolulu Conservatory and doing radio broadcasting in 1934-35, station WJIM Lansing. The Oahu Publishing Company held annual conventions for their teachers and dealers, beginning in 1930. The first one I attended was in 1936 and I became deeply involved as the organization grew. As dealers, we purchased from Oahu practically everything that we needed for our studio operation, items such as folding chairs, music stands, lesson music, popular sheet music, strings, picks, bars, guitars, cases, amplifiers.

250 Piece Hawaiian Orchestra, Honolulu Conservatory at Shrine Theatre Show, Ft. Wayne Ind. May 25, 1941. Norm English not only directed the orchestra, but tuned all 250 instruments before each rehearsal and performance. Norm English photo

"In 1941 Oahu decided to break tradition and take their annual convention to the Chicagoland Music Festival. Two railway cars were chartered and 90 Oahu students made the trip. About 2,000 students in all attended the festival and stayed in the Stevens Hotel, later to become the Hilton. The massed band of 2,000 guitar students walking double file from the hotel to Soldiers Field was over one mile long and it did hold up traffic. Special power lines were installed and a crew of electricians worked for days to prepare the stage for the 2,000 electric instruments. Captain Howard Stube was the conductor of probably the largest number of guitarists ever to perform together at one time. The music was arranged by Hank Karch, in four part harmony, and it sounded GREAT! The Chicago Tribune sponsored the festival. Competitions were held and trophies awarded. The organization of the contests, rules, and regulations did not always apply to the nature, scope, and techniques of the Hawaiian guitar, so Mr. Stanley of the Oahu Co. decided to organize the International Guitar League with contests to be held in Cleveland beginning in 1942.

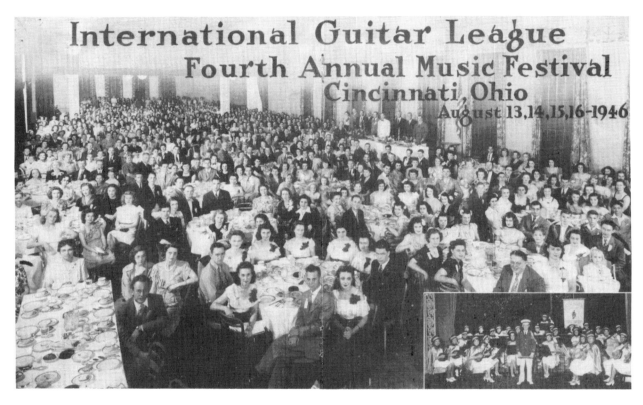

International Guitar League, Fourth Annual Music Festival, Music provided by the "Plectrophonic Band" Cincinnati OH , 1946. Norm English Photo

"The first two days were filled with playing contests followed by a floor show, then a banquet for the awarding of trophies. The third day was set aside for a boat excursion, special luncheon in the banquet hall, afternoon rides in the amusement park, and a picnic supper on the return boat trip to Cleveland, then an evening of dancing. These contest festivals continued during the WWII years, and we very actively participated in fund raising, entertaining the troops and supplying them with instruments.

"During this time I served a term as president of the International Guitar League which later changed its name to the International Music League and included other instruments. In 1949 I served as vice president of the American Guild of Musicians, an organization which dates back to 1901. In the early years of guitar manufacturing there was no agreement on standard fret markings. Originally each manufacturer developed and placed his own patterns of marking the fingerboard. The American Guild of Music was instrumental in convincing the manufacturers to standardize the fingerboard markings in order to eliminate confusion in switching from one fretted instrument to another.

"Clarence Williams, one time president of the International Guitar League, moved to Hawai'i to teach steel guitar. He taught at St.Louis High School where, in 1975, the Hawaiian Music Foundation had established classes for the instruments of Hawaiiana."

Cultural Influences

by Mike Scott. Mike was born in England in 1926. After World War II, in 1949 he formed his first group "The Islanders". After moving to Canada in 1954, he formed The Hawaiianaires, which has become the top Hawaiian band in the Toronto area. Mike was a guest of Sam Makia at the Hawaiian Room in N.Y.C. , and of Hal Aloma at Luau 400, N.Y.C. in the 1950's. He was featured on cross-Canada network TV shows in the late 50's. He played steel for Pua Almeida's group during their 6-month stay in Toronto, also for Ben Hokea as guest artist. Mike's recordings are on the Maple Records label and on several private labels. For assistance in putting together the following facts, Mike wishes to thank Kealoha LIfe, Marty Wentzel, and Eric Madis.

"Hawaiian music means different things to different people. To the Hawaiians it is a number of fairly diverse types of music, both vocal and instrumental involving the use of a wide range of musical instruments. Outside of the Islands, however, Hawaiian music has always been identified by one sound; that of the Hawaiian steel guitar. The prime reason is the long term result of the manner in which the early contingents of Hawaiian musicians presented their music to the outside world. Upon leaving the islands, they usually formed into groups of two. These duets consisted of a steel guitar as the lead instrument and a Spanish guitar playing rhythm. This simple format was used from around 1900 to the late 1920's when a third instrument was added, usually a 'ukulele. The 'ukulele enhanced the sound but did not change the character of what had become accepted as Hawaiian music.

"The second reason is the very distinct and unique sound of the steel guitar itself, the 'once heard never forgotten' aspect of it. Although the generally accepted basic pattern of Hawaiian music was established close to a century ago, it has not changed much in its identity except in Hawai'i itself. The steel guitar, however, has undergone considerable change over the same period, the greatest being its electrification in the early 1930's. For the first time it could be heard above the crescendos of the big orchestra.

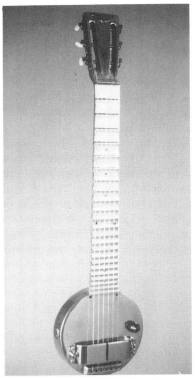

Rickenbacker Electro frypan early 1930's
Tom Gray photo

"As a result of this innovation, the steel guitar attracted the attention of exponents of other types of music, the most notable being country and western. It found fertile ground also in western swing, big band, and jazz. Two derivatives of the steel guitar have been taken in: first, by the blues music circles, in the case of the 'bottleneck' or 'slide' guitar and, second, blue grass musicians who use the Dobro, a modification of the acoustic steel guitar.

"As the electric steel guitar was used for various types of music other than Hawaiian, demands were made for changes in its basic 6-string design. More strings were added, up to 14 on a single neck. Multi-necks (two, three, and even four banks of strings), foot pedal and knee lever tuning and chord changers, solenoids, foot operated volume controls, tone enhancers, the list goes on and on. Although these modifications were influenced by non-Hawaiian music, some of them 'flowed back' to be embraced by Hawaiian music.

"The steel guitar's presence, in all its modifications, in so many kinds of music has had a definite and permanent influence on the musical culture of North America and elsewhere in the world. Its greatest impact was in the popularization of Hawaiian music in the first half of this century, and in country music in the second half.

"Let us focus on the Hawaiian aspect of the steel guitar, for after all it was in Hawai'i and through the genius of a Hawaiian that the instrument came about. How did the cultures of other lands influence it, and how did it make cultural changes in return? In Hawai'i, there's an expression that is used when the conversation gets around to a steel player who left the islands to play and reside in California. They are sometimes called 'west coast style players'. What is the difference? In Hawai'i the musical message was imparted by the vocalist and the traditional role of the 'steel' was as back-up. On the mainland artists like Sol Ho'opi'i, Dick McIntire, and Andy Iona played a lot more lead steel guitar in their performances than did their counterparts back home. Hence, the term 'west coast style'.

"The true follower of Hawaiian music immediately recognizes the very distinct style of the Dutch-Indonesian steel players, which is understandably quite different from those in Hawai'i or California. They are of a different culture, speak a different language. They did not enjoy close contact with Hawaiian musicians, but learned from recordings or short wave radio. Differences in playing styles between German, French, and English players are more subtle than in the case of the Dutch-Indonesians, yet each is distinctly different from the other. German audiences expect the steel guitar, even in Hawaiian music, to sound crisp and zither-like and some feel that the group must include drums and accordion. In Sweden, Yngve Stoor always had an accordion in his orchestra when it served as a dance band, but the steel guitar was considered absolutely essential. In the late 1920's recordings of acoustic Hawaiian steel guitars played by Gino Bordin (a Frenchman) and Len Fillis (of South Africa) there is a noticeable cultural difference. Gino Bordin's music has an exuberant Latin flair while the music of Len Fillis is far more plodding and stolid. Cultural differences influenced their playing styles.

"Again how could we fail to quickly identify the Japanese steel player with his very distinct and unique style. Some have used a tuning which resembles a diatonic scale and the steel guitar is made to sound like their *koto*, playing Japanese traditional songs such as 'Sakura'. One only has to listen for a few moments to the playing of Sunil Ganguly from India to realize how far the steel guitar has strayed from its roots. Yet again there is the very careful and structured playing of Yngve Stoor from Sweden. Ironically, two of Stoor's songs have been translated into Hawaiian and Fijian after he visited the Pacific islands eighteen times and appeared on television and radio all over the Pacific. As reported by Swedish steel guitarist Thomas Malm, the Hawaiian steel guitar was so popular, one radio producer stated that there was more Hawaiian than traditional Swedish music being broadcast in Sweden during the 1970's.

"As in North America in the case of country music, the steel guitar has become part of the folk music of other lands. In Indonesia the steel was until recently an integral part of Krontjong music, in South Africa it is heard in Boeremusik, and in other parts of that vast continent the pedal steel has been introduced into juju music, as fans of King Sonny Adé will tell you.

"In recent times, steel guitars have become very popular in the movie industry of India, often dominating the score in a film's background music. The music played on the steel is not Hawaiian, it's Indian. But then there's Garney Nyss And His Aloha Boys who do play Hawaiian style, and there's Brij Bushan Kabra who plays classical Indian music on the acoustic steel guitar. Quite a culture shock, musically speaking! Ed Mayer of Honolulu, who grew up in Indonesia, has this to add: 'The Indo steel guitarists developed their own style which was mainly influenced by the late greats, Sol Ho'opi'i and Andy Iona - then further developed by George DeFretes of Jakarta and then later again copied by Rudi Wairata.

"The greater percentage of the world's steel guitarists are not Hawaiian, which means they are influenced both by their own culture and by that of Hawai'i. Most imaginative players will take on the style of a third culture as well, often from the U.S., European, and Latin American music scenes. To name a few, Len Fillis, Kealoha Life, Roland Peachey, Yngve Stoor, Gino Bordin, George DeFretes, Rudi Wairata, Harry Brooker, Sammy Mitchell, Jerry Byrd, Marcel Bianchi, and Wout Steenhuis. Also, let's not forget musicians like Sol Ho'opi'i, Elsie Jaggers, and Bud Tutmarc who have departed into the realm of religious music.

Harlin Bros. Hawaiian Orchestra
Indianapolis Indiana, mid 1930s
John Quarterman photo

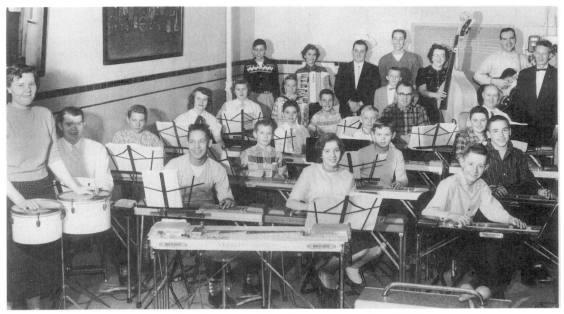

Harlin Bros. still going strong in 1955
Jay Harlin, inventor of the Multi-Kord pedal steel guitar,
stands at far right with bow tie. Jay's 15 pedal guitar stands in front.
John Quarterman photo, John is 3rd row back 2nd from left

Hawaiian Music, Steel Guitar, And Hollywood

"From the early 1900's to the 1930's phonograph recordings had great impact in spreading the gospel of steel guitar and Hawaiian music. Up to the time of the Wall Street crash of 1929 the sale of Hawaiian recordings had boomed, in fact during one period they outsold recordings of any other single type of music. During the depression years, record sales dropped to only a fraction of what they had been and many people didn't have the phonograph on which to play them. As if on cue, a less expensive medium of entertainment made its appearance in the form of the talkie movie. People in unheard-of numbers sought the escape that the movies had to offer. What better fantasy than a musical romance on an island in paradise? Where else but Hawai'i or the South Pacific?

"One of the first South Seas movies was "The Pagan", released in 1929 featuring actor singer Ramon Navarro who both introduced and sang 'The Pagan Love Song'. This was probably the first 'hit' Hawaiian-type song to be introduced via a sound movie. It soon became popular around the world and was eagerly seized upon by Hawaiian steel guitar players who found it ideal material for the instrument and made it an all-time standard.

"1932 saw the release of "Bird of Paradise" with Dolores Del Rio and Joel McCrea. In this movie there is a considerable amount of acoustic steel guitar played by the one and only Sol Ho'opi'i. In addition to other Hawaiian melodies, 'Mauna Kea' and 'Imi Au Iā 'Oe' can be heard in the background weaving the story together. As time passed, Hollywood improved on its Hawaiian/Polynesian theme with stars like Dorothy Lamour and Bing Crosby. The new songs that each succeeding movie introduced and the sound of the music, soft strings with the glissandos of a steel guitar riding over them, created a Hawaiian music addiction. Huge box office receipts told Hollywood moguls they were onto something very good.

"In the 1937 movie "Waikiki Wedding" starring Bing Crosby and Shirley Ross, four new Hawaiian songs were introduced, the two most important being 'Sweet Leilani' and 'Blue Hawai'i'. As Crosby sang these songs, he was backed up superbly with steel guitar and idyllic scenery. The Decca record company released Bing Crosby's recordings of all four of the new Hawaiian songs, 'Sweet Leilani' and 'Blue Hawai'i' being backed by Lani McIntire's Hawaiians with orchestrations by Sam Koki and steel guitar by Bob Nichols. These two recordings sold around the world in unheard-of numbers. 'Sweet Leilani' rose to number one on U.S. popular radio charts and stayed in that position for twenty eight weeks, and world wide sales of the record rocketed to millions. Harry Owens, composer of 'Sweet Leilani', was awarded an Oscar for the best movie song of the year. Thousands rushed to buy steel guitars and begin instruction. Both 'Blue Hawai'i' and 'Sweet Leilani' have been recorded in excess of one hundred times.

"The Hurricane", a movie released in 1937 starring Dorothy Lamour was also a tremendous hit. It introduced 'Moon of Manakoora', another evergreen for the steel guitar player. This movie was something of a phenomenon in that, although superbly performed by Sam Koki, it contained only sixteen bars of steel guitar in its entire length but for some inexplicable reason it had a tremendous impact on those who were susceptible. This writer has personal knowledge of two members of an audience of "The Hurricane" who, after seeing the movie, went immediately to music stores to purchase steel guitars.

"Most of the great Hawaiian steel guitar artists of the 1930's and 40's worked in Hollywood. To name a few would be appropriate at this time.

Sol Bright had speaking roles in "South Sea Rose" 1929, "Charley Chan's Greatest Case" 1933, "Flirtation Walk" 1934, and "White Woman".

Hal Aloma played with Tommy Dorsey in MGM's "Ship Ahoy".

Sam Koki performed in "The Hurricane" 1937, "Waikiki Wedding" 1937, "Paradise Isle" 1939, "Bamboo Blonde" 1939, and "Beyond The Blue Horizon" 1942.

Sol Ho'opi'i was featured in the 1932 release of "Bird of Paradise", "Flirtation Walk" 1934, "Hawaiian Buckaroo" 1938, "Navy Blues" 1941, "Waikiki Wedding" with Bing Crosby, and "Song Of the Islands" with Betty Grable and Victor Mature.

Andy Iona played steel guitar in "Hawaiian Buckaroo", plus "Honolulu" 1938 and "Moonlight in Hawai'i" 1941. He played 'Hola E Pae' from "Honolulu" in a later movie "I Dood It!" starring Eleanor Powell.

Freddy Tavares, steel player for Harry Owens' Royal Hawaiians and his Royal Hawaiian Hotel Orchestra played in "Coconut Grove" 1938, " Hawaiian Nights" 1939 with the song 'Hawai'i Sang Me To Sleep', "It's a Date" 1940, among other steel players in "Song Of The Islands" 1942, and "Lake Placid Serenade" 1944. The songs in "It's A Date" were 'Rhythm Of The Islands' and 'It Happened In Kaloha'.

Danny Stewart's steel guitar artistry can be heard in the movies "Aloma Of The South Seas" 1941 and "From Here To Eternity" 1953.

Barney Isaacs played steel extensively (the song was 'Waipio') in the film "Donovan's Reef" 1963.

Ralph Kolsiana states that he worked on the sound track of "Mutiny On The Bounty", "Waikiki Wedding", and "The Horizontal Lieutenant".

Joe Custino played steel in "Gidget Goes Hawaiian".

Mike "Malihini" Scott and his Hawaiianaires were chosen to play the part of a Hawaiian band playing background music in a restaurant scene in the movie "Life With Mikey" starring Michael J. Fox. Filming of their section took place in the Hilton Hotel, Toronto, on November 6, 1992.

"Credit also goes to the great stars who did much to promote the cause of steel guitar and Hawaiian music through their performances. Among the many are Bing Crosby, Dorothy Lamour, Francis Langford, Jane Frazee, Arthur Godfrey, Hilo Hattie, and Harry Owens.

"In all, including productions made for television, short subject films and videos, probably close to 200 movies have been produced dealing in some degree with Hawai'i and the south seas. Most but not all of them featured Hawaiian music or steel guitar. It's rather interesting to note that Harry Owens and his camera man travelled widely over the South Pacific in 1956, shooting in full colour enough footage to produce thirteen half-hour television shows. We believe they were basically of the travelogue type with beautiful background music provided by Harry Owens' Royal Hawaiians featuring Eddie Bush on steel guitar. Tragically, none of them were ever shown on television or released in any other form. It is believed, however, that they are still in existence.

"Hawaiian musicians with their steel guitars made their impact on many cultures from the turn of the century until the 1960's. Now it is high time for a new impact, one that will once again give this beautifully melodious instrument the universal popularity it enjoyed in the past and surely deserves in the future."

from the Paramount Picture
WAIKIKI WEDDING

BING
SHIRLEY ROSS

Featuring Bing Crosby, Bob Burns, Martha Raye, Shirley Ross, and including the following songs: SWEET IS THE WORD FOR YOU, IN A LITTLE HULA HEAVEN, BLUE HAWAII, OKOLEHAO (O-Koa-Lee-How)

Chapter 4

Hui ʻOhana Kīkā Kila

Steel Guitarists

We will attempt to list just those steel players who came from Hawaiʻi, and those who went to Hawaiʻi to pursue a career in Hawaiian music. We are well aware that this list is incomplete and therefore make apologies to those who have been omitted. We could draw only from those names that appeared in print on album covers, periodicals, or books, or if someone had first-hand knowledge to share with us. There were also a great many excellent steel guitarists in other lands who were not Hawaiian or born in Hawaiʻi. We found it necessary to draw the line there or the list would go on forever. I have no doubt a few will slip through my net. When in doubt, we went the "inclusive" rather than the "exclusive" route. If you wish to learn more about the steel guitarists, two excellent reference books are: Tony Todaro's "The Golden Years of Hawaiian Entertainment" 1974, and Dr. George S. Kanahele's "Hawaiian Music and Musicians", 1979.

Information about steel guitarists in Hawaiʻi today was gleaned by sending questionnaires to recognized musicians in the islands. The amount of information recorded for any one steel guitarist has no bearing on his or her importance or expertise. In some cases, we have a name only. It's listed in the hope that our readers will fill in the gap. Some steel players listed are very young. Give them time. The information gathering process will continue even after this book is printed. We welcome our readers to send us corrections and new data.

ABE, MASAO "MEL"- born 1912 Waimea, Kauaʻi. Self-taught. Performed on USO European tour, at Honolulu Harry's Club Waikiki in Chicago for many years, then in Hawaiʻi with Benny Kalama's "Hawaiian Village Serenaders", replaced Jules Ah See in the Alfred Apaka show after Jules passed away. Then with Sonny Kamahele at Royal Hawaiian Hotel. Took over as steel guitarist with "The Islanders" in the Surf Room of the Royal Hawaiian Hotel after Joe Custino left, moved with the group to the Waikiki Beachcomber Hotel. Recorded with Sonny. Recently worked regularly with the Tihati show at the Beachcomber Hotel. Played in the Steel Guitar Hoʻolauleʻa in 1984.

Mel Abe at his double Fender Stringmaster, shown with Walter Moʻokini far left, then George Lake, and Alan Akaka on far right.
George Lake photo

AH SEE, JULES CRYLES - born 1924 Lahaina Maui. Played with many groups at the best hotels in Hawai'i , was a regular steel guitarist on Hawai'i Calls radio shows in the mid 1950's. Played steel guitar for Alfred Apaka's "Hawaiian Village Serenaders". Was considered one of the greatest steel guitarists developed in Hawai'i. He was a child prodigy, sneaking out of bed at two years old to listen to the grownups playing. Began musical career in early teens with Johnny Almeida, father of Pua Almeida. He did bird and animal imitations on his steel guitar and effectively imitated such legendary players as David Keli'i, Tommy Castro, Andy Iona, Dick McIntire, and Sol Ho'opi'i. Many of the local steel guitarists look upon Jules as a model to emulate. At times he used the pedal steel. He was a trend setter. Deceased 1960.

The Moana Serenaders, 1952 with Jules on steel guitar backed by Andrew Bright on guitar, Benny Kalama on bass, and John Leal.
Richard Choy collection courtesy of Island Guitars

AH SING, PETER HENRY - Contemporary. Played on the S.S.Constitution, a cruise ship which tours the Hawaiian islands. Played with the Royal Hawaiian Band, with Ainsley Halemanu and Kekua Fernandes, and with the Leina'ala Simerson group at the 1991 Steel Guitar Ho'olaule'a. It is his style to play strum chords in preference to passing chords. A popular steel guitarist, a fine singer, and great all-around musician who plays many instruments.

Peter Ah Sing with Leina'ala Simerson group,
Steel Guitar Ho'olaule'a 1991
Clay Savage photo

AHUNA, ALBERT - Contemporary. Born in Laupahoehoe on the Big Island, now of Hilo. Inspired by Hawai'i Calls, began learning steel guitar at age of 12. Played with Waterfront Gang of Stevedores, at the Hilo Yacht Club, Volcano House, Jungle Jim's in Hilo and in Maui.

Albert Ahuna at second annual Hawaiian Steel Guitar Ho'olaule'a, Honoka'a 1992 John Murphy photo

AHUNA, BEN - Born on the Big Island in early 1900's, played at Seven Seas restaurant, Los Angeles for many years. He was known as a bass player more than as a steel player.

AHUNA, KIHEI - Born in Hilo, HI. Taught by his father Albert Ahuna to play steel guitar, he is also an excellent slack key guitarist.

Kihei Ahuna, steel guitar ho'olaulea, Honoka'a 1992
John Murphy photo

AKAKA, ALAN- Born in 1956, son of Senator and Congressman Daniel Akaka. Alan started as a clarinet player in the Kamehameha Schools band then got his degree as a Music Educator, University of Hawai'i. In 1973 he became the first student of Jerry Byrd, then did tourist promotions for Aloha Airlines, and later with Eddie Kekaula at the Princess Ka'iulani Hotel. In 1979-1985 he was featured at the Royal Hawaiian Hotel with the Jerry Byrd Trio, the Leina'ala Simerson Serenaders, and with Tihati's Royal Hawaiian Troupe, also with Sonny Kamahele at the Halekulani Hotel in 1984. In 1986 he organized his own group "The Islanders" including at different times Sonny Kamahele, Benny Kalama, Barney Isaacs, Walter Mo'okini, Kaipo Asing, Merle Kekuku, and Byron Yasui. Alan played in the Jerry Byrd Steel Guitar Ho'olaule'a every year since it began in 1982. Recipient of Hawai'i Music Foundation's music scholarshiip. He plays regularly at the Halekulani Hotel with "The Islanders", taught steel guitar at Kamehameha Schools (summer school) and St. Louis High School, was assistant bandmaster at Kahuku High School, then at University of Hawai'i, and received wide acclaim for his great steel work on Benny Kalama's album. Produced his own album "How D'Ya Do", then "Islands Call" with himself, Barney Isaacs and Jerry Byrd as steel guitarists. In 1991 took over producing Steel Guitar Ho'olaule'a after Jerry Byrd retired. He continues to shine as another beacon in the future of steel guitar in Hawaiian music, taking leadership in promoting concerts and gala events featuring the steel guitar. In 1992 he returned to Kamehameha Schools as bandmaster, and in 1993 he assumed leadership as president of the Hawaiian Steel Guitar Association, which publishes a newsletter to members in 18 different countries.

Alan Akaka, producer of Steel Guitar Ho'olaule'a, 1991
Clay Savage photo

AKAMAHO, BILL - Played at the Royal Hawaiian Hotel.

AKANA, JOE -

AKINA, VINCENT - born in Honolulu, now working as steel guitarist in San Francisco.

AKUNA, DR. ISAAC - Contemporary. Born in Honolulu, a practicing dentist who studied steel guitar under Jerry Byrd. Played in the 1992 steel guitar ho'olaule'a.

AKO, SAMUEL K. - An accomplished piano player for a Billy Gonsalves group called the Paradise Serenaders with whom he also served as the steel guitar performer. Has recorded on steel with the group.

ALAPA, ELWOOD - Born 1912 in Honolulu, passed away in 1986. Played with the Nautical Hawaiians in the early 1930's, and in Turtle Bay and La'ie. Played with the Firemen's band in the 1940's and 50's

ALLECANTE, IDA - She travelled the world with Alice and Tom Pahu (parents of Violet Pahu Lilikoi) during the 1920s, taking Hawaiian music with them everywhere. Their choreographer was Mildred Leo Clemmens who was first cousin of Mark Twain. Ida played the lap steel.

ALLEN, HENRY KALEIALOHA - Born in Hilo, 1933, moved to Honolulu in 1941, lived in Manoa. Graduated from McKinley High in '52, where he studied music. Worked in most of the hotels in Honolulu, then went to Los Angeles in 1956 to work with the best Hawaiian musicians at the Seven Seas in Hollywood. Henry is now living in Lahaina, Maui, where he formed his own company, Polynesian Promotions. Henry is a writer, arranger, and composer of Hawaiian music. He produces and directs his own Polynesian spectacular shows and was chosen to perform in the "Artists in the Schools" program. He travels extensively with his group and is quite popular in Japan.

Henry K. Allen with Fender double Stringmaster
H. Allen photo

ALMEIDA, PUA (ALAMEIDA) - born 1922 Honolulu. An outstanding steel guitarist, accompanist and solo guitarist, and singer. His steel guitar style was unique. He started playing in his father's band (Johnny Almeida) then went on his own. As leader of a big band, "The Sunset Serenaders", he performed in Hawaii at the Queen's Surf, Don the Beach-Comber's, Lau Yee Chai's, and at the renowned roof garden of the Alexander Young Hotel. In 1947 Pua and his band left for Hollywood where they performed at the famous Seven Seas Club and at the Pago Pago Club in Colton CA. He recorded and toured extensively, particularly to Japan. Beginning 1958, for 16 years they played regularly at the Moana Surfrider Hotel and the Surfrider Hotel in Honolulu. Pua played steel guitar frequently as a guest on the Hawaii Calls show, and with Sam Koki, Danny Stewart, Andy Iona, Sam Ka'apuni, Harry Baty, Sonny Kamahele, and Ernie and Freddie Tavares. Deceased

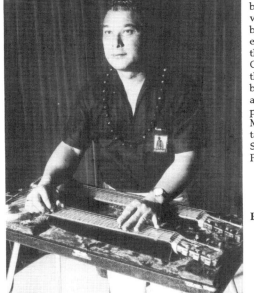

Pua Almeida with his two Rickenbacker frypans

ALOMA, HAL (ALAMA) - born 1908 Honolulu. Played with Lani McIntire, then to New York City with Tommy Dorsey. On TV with Arthur Godfrey, Ed Sullivan, Perry Como. Toured Canada, England, USA. Band leader at Polynesian Village for the Disney World FL grand opening. With Tommy Dorsey in MGM film "Ship Ahoy". Changed his name to Aloma after the movies "Bird of Paradise" and "Aloma of the South Seas" came out in the 1930's. Played with Lani McIntire's band.

Harold Aloma with Bakelite Spanish guitar, 1935

AMARAL, ROBERT LOPAKA - Born Aug 20, 1927, Honolua Maui. One of the last surviving steel guitarists on the Island of Lana'i. A self-taught steel guitarist, he followed the stylings of Alfred Kimakea, Jr. Kaopuiki, and Benny Rogers. He also admired Gabby Pahinui and Billy Hew Len. Began playing professionally in 1947 for Elaine and Sam Kaopuiki's halau group and many luaus and functions on Lana'i. He is a retired captain of a barge tender, and harbor master on the Island of Lana'i.

AMONG, ALEXANDER (ALEC) - Contemporary. The steel guitar is his secondary instrument. For a time, the Among brothers had a quartet in which Alec played steel. He is a highly skilled musician and arranger and plays all instruments in the Hawaiian style.

Alec Among, Bandstand show Kapiolani Park, May 1990
A.W.Ruymar photo

ANDRESEN, EDWIN B. - Born in Hawai'i . Member of Musicians Assoc. of Hawai'i Local 677, A.F.M., living in the Kailua area, now retired.

ASERCION, CARL "KALANI" - Born 1909 in Hawai'i, of Philippine descent. He began as a violinist, but changed to steel guitar in his early youth. Popular steel guitarist and educator in Chicago area. His most successful student was Beau Sterling, steel guitarist and entertainer in the Chicago area. Kalani played a 7-string frypan, his group was known as "Kalani And The Paradise Islanders". Produced an album with his group name for the title, on Replica label. Backed Eddie Howard on the Paradise Isle album, Mercury Records. In addition to Club Waikiki, he played at the Chase in St. Louis, the Blackstone in Chicago, the Fremont in San Francisco, and at Chicago's famed Edgewater Beach Hotel where he aired a weekly half-hour show on WGN radio. He died in 1990.

Carl Asercion with his Paradise Islanders B. Sterling photo

AU, THOMAS - Steel guitarist of La'ie, HI, born in 1913. Started playing steel in 1946, copying Sol Ho'opi'i records. Played steel to raise funds for his church, later going on tour with church members. Played at the Reef Hotel poolside 1970-71 and at the Polynesian Cultural Center 1977-1984.

Tommy Au, jamming at the home of Tau Moe, La'ie
A.W.Ruymar photo

AUNA, ALEY KAHA'AWI - Born June 27, 1927 In Honoka'a. Learned to play steel from Hawai'i Calls show and recordings of David Keli'i admired Joe Custino and Jules Ah See. Began at age 14 on an Epiphone Electar 6. Among many other instruments, played piano and vibes. Played at the Naniloa, Volcano, and Maunakea Hotels. Played the Hawai'i Calls show as guest with family orchestra The Auna's Hawaiians, at age 16. A captain in the Vietnam conflict, and served as a reserve Chief Custodian of National Guard Installations on the Island of Hawai'i until he passed away in 1976. Brother of John Auna.

AUNA, JOHN KEAHIALOA - Born in Waipio Valley. Contemporary musician of the Big Island, a hero of World War II. Began playing steel in public at age 14, playing with his family as guests on the Hawai'i Calls radio show in 1943. During the late 1970's, early 1980's John's trio and brother Glen Auna's show combined to perform four days a week in the Windjammer Lounge, Kona Hilton. He has performed in Germany and France during his military years, then in Maui, Kaua'i, Illinois, Washington, Alaska, and Japan. As Hawai'i 's special representative for HSGA, John organized many promotional events to stimulate interest in steel guitar in both the Kailua Kona area, and in Hilo.

John K. Auna on stage at ho'olaule'a in Honoka'a, 1992
L.Ruymar photo

AWAI, KEOKI E.K. - born 1891 Hawai'i, knew Joseph Kekuku. One of the earliest steel guitarists, had to fashion his own adapter, bar, and picks. Recorded extensively. Played acoustic steel with his Royal Hawaiian Quartet at the Pan-Pacific International Exposition, San Francisco 1915. Published the first steel guitar book for Sherman, Clay in 1916 and wrote steel guitar arrangements using the Peterson numbering system. In 1917 his Volume 1 "Superior Collection of Steel Guitar Solos" was printed, containing thirty Hawaiian selections, followed quickly by Volume 2. He is the composer of the Kilima Waltz. Deceased at age of 95, December 1981.

AWEAU, LEMUEL - Born Jan. 31, 1939 in Honolulu. Graduated from U. of Hawai'i with bachelors degree in Music Education (Secondary). Served as music teacher, Farrington High 1974-90, now going into administration. Lives in Kaneohe, worked at the Hawaiian Village. His first love is the steel guitar, but he is an all-round musician and novelty player as well. Played bass with Elaine Ako Spencer Trio at the Willows until it closed late in 1993, plays steel guitar with the Clyde Lono group at the Hilton Hawaiian Village and the Moana Surfrider Hotel. He also plays steel and arranges for the Dan Kaleikini Show at the Kahala Hilton Hotel.

Lemuel Aweau
L. Aweau picture

AYLETT, GEORGE - Born in Hawai'i, spent lifetime on mainland. Not much is known except that he was in Vancouver, Canada during the 1930's, performed and taught steel guitar. A well educated and highly skilled musician.

BAILEY, "SPEEDY" - Young contemporary steel guitarist of Honolulu, has been playing professionally for four years, uses tunings: B11, C6, and G.

Speedy Bailey played steel for the Punahou Alumni Association
S. Bailey photo

BAKER, FREDDIE- born in Hawai'i, living in Albuquerque, New Mexico. Worked throughout the west coast area, played with many Hawaiian groups, some of the greatest. Has toured the U.S. extensively. Appeared on the Steel Guitar Ho'olaule'a show in 1985. While in Hawai'i, played with "The Islanders" with Sol Kamahele, Pua Almeida, Bill Lincoln, and many others.

BARNETT, FRED - Born in Brooklyn NY in 1950. An excellent contemporary steel guitar player who plays electric steel as well as the National tricone. Made his musical debut with the musical comedy group "Kokonuts". Inspired by a recording he heard of Jerry Byrd. Moved to Hawai'i (Kaua'i) in 1981, where he met Ernie Palmeira who got him started playing Hawaiian style. Later moved to O'ahu where he took lessons from Jerry Byrd. He and his wife Janjoy started their own band and entertain with fun songs under the name "Wiki Waki Woo". They made two recordings 'On Okie Dokie Bay' and 'Along Hawaiian Shores'.

Fred Barnett at HSGA convention Honolulu, 1987
Clay Savage photo

BISHAW, HERMAN - slightly younger than Joe Kekuku. Left Hawai'i by 1915 for tours of the mainland, Europe, and the Orient.

BRIDGES, GEORGE K. - Member of Musicians Assoc. of Hawai'i Local 677, A.F.M., lives in Kamuela.

BRIGHT, IAUKEA ANDREW - Born Honolulu June 30, 1952. Contemporary musician, does radio work at station KCCN, Honolulu. Appeared on the Steel Guitar Ho'olaule'a show in 1988, was steel guitarist in the group that visited Russia on a musical cultural exchange in 1989. Recorded with Joe Recca, Pekelo, Del Beazley, Sean Na'auau, and Frank Kawa'i Hewitt. Performs with group "Lihau" at Moana Surfrider Hotel. Nephew of Sol Bright.

BRIGHT, SOLOMON KEKIPI - born 1909 Honolulu, left us April 27, 1992. Sol's musical debut was made in his sister Hannah's dance band as a drummer and dancer, in 1926. In 1928 he moved to the mainland to play with Sol Ho'opi'i, and to learn to play steel guitar. He formed his own group, "Sol K. Bright and His Hollywaiians". They played the San Francisco World's Fair 1938-40, and he produced shows in the best entertainment centres on the west coast. Between 1943 and 1945 he served in the Merchant Marines, entertaining in every port. He toured Canada, the U.S., and Japan, and did promotional work on radio and TV. He recorded extensively for Victor Records, sometimes with Sol Ho'opi'i and Dick McIntire. From 1946 to 1950 Sol was the entertainment director at the Fairmont Hotel on Nob Hill in San Francisco, some of his shows being broadcast by radio to Hawai'i. He had speaking parts in four Hollywood films, "South Sea Rose (1929)", "Flirtation Walk (1934)", "White Woman", and "Charlie Chan's Greatest Case (1933)". Although he had no formal music training, he was a very successful songwriter, his most famous songs being 'Hawaiian Cowboy' and 'The Hawaiian Scotsman', which he sang and performed on the bagpipes. His last twenty years were spent at home in Hawai'i where he often teamed up to perform with the great David Keli'i. He was named by Tony Todaro to the Hawaiian Entertainment Hall of Fame.

**Sol Bright performing his composition "The Hawaiian Cowboy",
Bandstand H.S.G.A. steel guitar show, Honolulu 1989.**
A. Ruymar photo

BROWN, BUDDY - of Hilo Hawaiians. Deceased.

BROWN, CHARLIE "TINY" - Born about 1901 - deceased about 1950. Brought in new playing techniques and new tunings. Was first to play A minor tuning on acoustic guitar. He didn't really teach anyone to play, but the young ones who hung about and learned from him were: Jules Ah See, Tommy Castro, Jake Keli'ikoa, David Keli'i, Gabby Pahinui, and Jake Kaleikini. He was so good that when he walked into a party all would go quiet and the steel player would turn over his instrument to Tiny immediately. He stayed in Hawai'i and played "Taxi" dance bands at Danceland, also did buskering. Played at Hoffman's Cafe on Hotel Street between Nu'uanu and Bethel St. Played up on balcony with two others in the Wonder Bar. People came just to see whether the balcony would hold for one more night. "Tiny" was 5'8" tall, but over 400 pounds. "Tiny" wrote a Melody in Eb which was played for many years without lyrics until Andy Cummings put words to it and called it "Tiny Brown". "Tiny" had the unique ability of playing a standard tuned guitar both right and left handed with equal ease.

BROWN, FRANCES KALANI. - a very fine steel guitarist and singer. He was one of the "Browns of Hilo", born around 1920. He began his career playing for tourists in Waikiki with the "Stonewall Boys". Played with Jimmy McKenzie's "Hawaiian Rhumba Orchestra" in Portland OR in early 1940's, at the Tiki Hut. He was drafted for service in WWII. In 1965 he was reported in Fretts Magazine as still doing club work in Cleveland.

Jimmy McKenzie's "Hawaiian Rhumba Orchestra" L-R, Herchel (Hayden) Hendershot on fiddle. Charles K. Kamaka, bass and vocals. Frances K. Brown, steel guitar and vocals. Mel Peterson guitar, vocals and M.C. Jimmy McKenzie 'ukulele, vocals and leader. Appearing at the "Tiki Hut", Portland OR. 1943 R. Kolsiana photo

BROWN, NEPHI - A graduate of the Kamehameha Schools, Nephi made his steel guitar debut at Alan Akaka's Steel Guitar Ho'olaule'a in 1993. He is a student of Jerry Byrd's, lives on the Big Island of Hawai'i and performs regularly on the South Kohala Coast.

BURROWS, DAVID- An accomplished musician and one of the few steel guitarists who could sight read musical scores. Now deceased.

BUSH, EDDIE - Worked with Dick McIntire and was every bit the steel guitarist that Dick was in many ways. Took over the Harmony Hawaiians after Dick died. Was steel guitarist for the Harry Owens TV shows in Los Angeles, 1951-54. Took over from Freddy Tavares who played steel with the Harry Owens Band during the 1930's and 40's. Truly one of the most under-rated steel players and falsetto singers ever, in Hawaiian music.

BYRD, JERRY - Born 1920 Lima, OH, Jerry joined the Renfro Valley Barn Dance during his high school years. At that time it was one of the biggest country music shows in the U.S. When the show moved to Kentucky Jerry had to stay home and finish school. In 1939 he re-joined the group, then moved to Detroit 1942 to work on radio station WJR. He worked with Ernest Tubb, then with Red Foley on the Prince Albert NBC part of the "Grand Ole Opry", moving to Cincinnati to play on the "Midwestern Hayride" for three years during which time he did his first recording as a soloist on the Mercury label, in 1949. He did an early morning radio show there, on WLW starting at 5:00 am, then moved back to Nashville in 1952. During his career in Nashville, he played with Chet Atkins, Marty Robbins, Hank Snow, Roy Clark, Ernest Tubb, Red Foley, Hank Williams, Patti Page, Burl Ives, Jimmy Wakely, Guy Mitchell, and many others. He has recorded 25 solo albums and over 60 with local artists. He is a songwriter, rhythm guitarist, vocalist and bass player, producer, musical director, teacher, author, arranger, historian, and manufacturer's consultant. First steel guitarist inducted into Steel Guitar Hall of Fame, 1978. The Jerry Byrd Fan Club was organized by Millie Annis in 1948 and ran until 1972.

His first musical influences had been from listening to recordings of Dick McIntire, Sol Ho'opi'i, Andy Iona, etc. so Hawaiian music remained his first love. He refused to convert to pedal steel. He was the first Hawaiian style steel guitarist to record as featured soloist with full 58-piece symphony orchestra. It was Boudleaux Bryant's "Polynesian Suite" with the Mexico City Symphony Orchestra. In 1972 he moved to Hawai'i to dedicate his life to teaching young Hawaiians to play steel guitar. Toured extensively, most frequently to Japan. Performed in Outrigger Hotel's Blue Dolphin Room, Royal Hawaiian Hotel's Surf Room, Halekulani Hotel's House Without a Key, then retired to continue teaching and recording. Made first and only Hawaiian style steel guitar instruction video cassette. Wrote many instruction books, including the most comprehensive Steel Guitar Method ever produced for the non-pedal instrument, in English and Japanese. Instigated and produced Steel Guitar Ho'olaule'a 1982 - 1989. On his 70th birthday, he received two prestigious awards: a Special Commendation from Governor Waihe'e of Hawai'i and a framed memento of a "Special Tribute To Jerry Byrd" read into the Congressional Record, from the Floor of the House, in Washington D.C., by Hawai'i Senator Daniel Akaka, on April 12, 1989.

Known as the "Master of Touch and Tone", Jerry ranks with Sol Ho'opi'i and Dick McIntire for having inspired the most steel guitarists and earned the love of his listening audience all over the world.

Jerry Byrd playing double ShoBud at his last Steel Guitar Ho'olaule'a, 1989
A.W.Ruymar photo

BYRNES, HERBERT PAHUPU - Could be first steel guitarist to Indonesia, as he played with Ernest Ka'ai's Royal Hawaiian Troubadours on their tour of Australia, India, Malaya, the Dutch East Indies, and other countries in Asia, beginning in 1919. Herbert did not return to Hawai'i, but settled in Java where he continued to perform on steel guitar, teach Hawaiian music, and to build and sell Hawaiian instruments. He and fellow Hawaiian musician, Alexander Lonoikamakahiki Lazarus (known as Munson) formed their own Hawaiian band in Java and toured Indonesia extensively. They were interned in a Japanese prisoner of war camp in the 1940's where Herbert died.

CAMACHO, JAMES - Born in Honolulu in the 1920's, played steel in his sister's group, Julia Nui and Her Kama'ainas. Played the A tuning exclusively, was a very popular performer with the hula groups in Honolulu, but known more for his bass playing. Played for many years with Jimmy MacKenzie who was called the Mayor of Waikiki and owned one of the original tour companies in Hawai'i .

CARVALHO, JOSEPH - Deceased. Basically a sax man for the popular bands in Hawai'i, Ray Andrade, Harry Owens, Ernie Tavares' Special Orchestra, and others. However, when he joined the Malcolm Beelby Band at the Royal Hawaiian Hotel, he played the steel guitar. Some other members of that band were Benny Kalama and Sam Ka'apuni.

CARVALHO, PAT - Contemporary, studied with Jerry Byrd. Pat moved from Kailua to Florida, plays more Spanish guitar than steel. Last heard of playing at World of Disney, Orlando FL.

CASTRO, TOMMY (THOMAS KOANI) - born 1912 Anahola, Kaua'i. Played steel in Ray Kinney's Orchestra in the Lexington Hotel, New York. Then, in Honolulu, steel guitarist for Alvin Isaacs' Royal Hawaiian Serenaders Quartet in 1940's. Some of the best Hawaiian music ever recorded was done by this group consisting of Alvin Isaacs, George Kainapau, Tommy Castro, and Benny Kalama. When Tommy left the group, a very young Alvin Kaleolani (Barney) Isaacs took his place in his papa's quartet. Tommy played at Rathskeller* in 1937-38, then later with Gigi Royce's Orchestra at the Young Hotel Roof Garden. Song arranger for Lena Machado. Could write the notes of a song as he heard it. Played in the A minor tuning, was one of the early innovators of the modern tunings in Hawai'i. He used minor 6ths, major 6ths, major 7th tunings interchangeably on a single 6-string neck. Most tuning changes were done during the playing of a song. His fill-ins were simple but very effective and unique. He played the melody line on a single string frequently. He was an admirer and friend of Duke Ellington and played many of his melodies when he used his various tunings. Was able to do some of the big band arrangements that Ray Kinney and Alfred Apaka eventually recorded.

*The Rathskeller was a famous dive on Alakea Street in Honolulu, owned by the Healani Yacht Club, operated by Herman Clark, a close relative of Duke Kahanamoku and father of the two Clark brothers who were professional football players.

Tommy Castro
R. Choy collection, courtesy of Island Guitars

CASTRO, VINTON KAMAI - Young contemporary, "up and coming" steel guitarist in Hana area, Maui. Student of Jerry Byrd.

Vinton Kamai Castro

CAZIMERO, BILL - Played steel in Honolulu, often backing Eddie Kekaula as he performed on the streets at the Waikiki Shopping Plaza. He's the father of the famous Brothers Cazimero, total musicians and entertainers in the contemporary Honolulu scene. In 1965 Bill played steel in a Polynesian show at Festival Park in Arima, Japan. The group was sponsored by a Japanese Royu Development Co., under the direction of Walter Mo'okini.

CHENEY, STEVE - Born in Salt Lake City, Utah. Contemporary musician. Comes from a musical family and plays with authority and with a real Hawaiian style. Has worked with many groups and on numerous shows with some of Hawai'i's top performers. Played in the Steel Guitar Ho'olaule'a in 1984.

CHING, CLARENCE "DUKE KALEOLANI" - born on Kaua'i. Duke is related to Jules Ah See, and plays in his style. He was steel guitarist for Don Ho in the 60's playing at the Barefoot Bar and at Honey's. Duke now lives in Hollywood and is kept busy doing casuals with his group "The Islanders"

Duke Kaleolani Ching playing his Fender quad, HSGA Joliet convention 1991 backed by Bob Waters L and Walter Mo'okini R. L. Ruymar photo

CHUNG-HOON, HAROLD - Member of Musicians Assoc. of Hawai'i Local 677, A.F.M., lives in Waianae.

CHURCHER, REX - Member of Musicians Assoc. of Hawai'i Local 677, A.F.M., listed as steel guitarist.

CLASON, CALVIN - Member of Musicians Assoc. of Hawai'i Local 677, A.F.M. listed as steel guitarist.

CONN, ELIZABETH L. - Member of Musicians Assoc. of Hawai'i Local 677, A.F.M., lives in Ai'ea. Listed as steel guitarist.

CORREA, DAVID "KAWIKA" - Born in Kahului HI, 1918. Listed as steel guitarist with the Musicians Assoc. of Hawai'i, Local 677 A.F.M. Made his home in Waipahu, deceased Jan. 6, 1994.

CRAVALHO, JOE - toured Japan in the 1920's and 1930's. Played tenor sax as well as steel.

CUSTINO, JOE - Born in 1915, Agana Guam, moved to Hawai'i in 1922. Was steel player in high school band during sophomore year, taking the place of Aiwohi who went to mainland with Harry Owens. Outstanding steel player during the pre-World War II and post-war period in Hawai'i. Was steel guitarist for The Islanders at the Surf Room of the Royal Hawaiian Hotel. Toured Japan for six months in 1963, with Sol Bright bandleader. Played with Sonny Kamahele, Benny Kalama, Merle Kekeke, Walter Mo'okini and many others. Played on the Hawai'i Calls radio show during the 1970's until its closing date in 1975. He retired to Kaua'i, and passed on in 1992. One of his fondest memories was playing four-part harmony on steel guitars with Jules Ah See, each playing two strings.

Joe Custino with his prized Rickenbacher original, Kaua'i 1992
A. Ruymar photo

DANIELS, CHICK - Born in the 1930's, died about 1988. An active steel player in Honolulu, wrote "Lei Aloha".

DeLANO, C.S. - Contemporary of Joseph Kekuku. DeLano's 'Hawaiian Love Song' was the first original composition to be published for the steel guitar. He wrote and published 45 more songs for the guitar, also a good Hawaiian Guitar Method. Toured U.S. mainland with a quartet "The DeLano Musical Four".

DE REGO, JOSEPH "STEPPY" - Born in Honolulu, now living in Kailua, O'ahu. Excellent steel guitarist, accompanist, and bass player. While Freddie Tavares played with the Harry Owens Orchestra at the Royal Hawaiian Hotel, Steppy was the steel guitarist for the Ray Andrade Orchestra at La Hula Rhumba. Played with Tommy Castro, Alvin Isaacs Sr., Benny Kalama, Pua Almeida, David Keli'i, Fred Tavares, Alfred Apaka, Walter Mo'okini. Now retired.

DE TORRE, JACK - Played steel with Duke Lukuwela and Johnny Pineapple.

DIAMOND, CHARLIE - We learned about him from a picture in the March 1980 issue of Ha'ilono Mele showing Charlie Diamond as steel guitarist in a group with David Keao'ahu, William "Brownie" Ruther, and Henry Kua. The picture was taken in the early 1930's. Shortly after the picture was taken, Charlie died.

DILLINGHAM, PETER - Contemporary. Born in Hawai'i about mid-1920's. A well-known and respected steel guitarist in Hawai'i. Plays pedal steel.

Peter Dillingham playing Sierra pedal steel, HSGA bandstand show 1989, with Andy Cummings on 'ukulele, Bill Pa'alani in background tuning up.
L.Ruymar photo

EMERSON, KEN - Contemporary, played with Moe Keale. A disciple of the legendary Sol Ho'opi'i, his playing is exciting and imaginative. Ken has recorded several discs with his brother Phil as "The Emerson Brothers", as well as with other local recording artists. Played in the Steel Guitar Ho'olaule'a 1984. Ken specializes in playing the pre-electric style (1915-1940) steel guitars, and tours the island schools telling *na keiki* the history of their Hawaiian instruments. He likes to collect and restore the old guitars, and on each guitar play the songs that were current during its heyday. Ken taught himself to play by listening to radio broadcasts. He studied with Aunty Alice Namakelua, Raymond Kāne, and Gabby Pahinui.

Ken Emerson, circa 1988.
A. Ruymar photo

EWALIKO, WILLIAM - Early 1900's, Honolulu. Falsetto singer, accomplished steel guitarist, the first to record using slack key guitar and violin in his group.

FERERA, FRANK (FERREIRA) - Portuguese, born 1885 Honolulu, another contemporary of Joseph Kekuku's, left for the mainland in 1902. He is credited with inventing the triple picking style, using a third finger pick plus thumb pick. He and his wife Helen Louisa recorded extensively (using Martin acoustic guitars) and were in great demand in clubs, hotels, theatres, and on tour. In addition to Hawaiian, they recorded popular music, Italian, Mexican selections, marches and social dance music. When Louisa died, Frank took Anthony Franchini as his new recording partner. They recorded Hawaiian guitar duets as "Franchini and Ferera" and were ranked among the top musicians of the day. Frank Ferera's steel guitar was the first to be heard on a recording in Japan. The song was 'Lady of Waikiki' by Irving Berlin, issued in 1927. This is said to be the recording which inspired Japan's Kazunori Murakami to take up playing the steel guitar. Of all Hawaiian recordings made between 1915 and 1930, it is said Frank Ferera appeared on at least a quarter of them, using his own name or "The Hilo Hawaiian Orchestra".

Frank Ferera

FO, MIKILANI - A brilliant female steel guitar player in Hawai'i. Born May 31, 1924, she was the daughter of August Fo and Sarah Pokipala, and grand daughter of Dan Pokipala. She was taught steel by her father but soon surpassed him. She played a 6-string Epiphone Electar Zephyr square neck and was great in everything she did, 'ukulele, guitar, bass, piano, steel guitar, and excellent vocals. She won Arthur Godfrey's 'ukulele playing contest and went to New York City to be featured in his show, then landed a contract at the Blue Angel. She played in shows with Kale Kaleiali'i and Ralph Kolsiana at the "Waikiki" on Catalina Island many times. She dropped dead on the stage in Reno Nevada in 1959, at the age of 35.

A 1949 or 1950 newspaper clipping reported that Mikilani did not actually appear on Arthur Godfrey's TV show on the mainland, although she had come from Hawai'i under contract to do so. Against Godfrey's wishes, she had gone out singing and playing her 'ukulele in club after club, including the prestigious "21 Club", just the night before she was to appear on his show. As a result, he cancelled her contract. A personal friend, Bob "Pulevai" Waters, said, "Miki was the most singly talented person I have ever known, but she was so full of carefree happiness that she couldn't refuse a party!"

Mikilani Fo, steel guitarist
and all-round
instrumentalist and
entertainer
Bob Waters photo

FREEDMAN, RODNEY - Born in Honolulu, 1927. Plays steel guitar with the Paradise Serenaders trio with B. Gonsalves. Plays the Germaine's Luau show, the Hawaiian Civic Club, and other luau shows, conventions, etc. in the Pearl Harbor area. Rodney's idols are Pua Almeida, Billy Hew Len, and Alex Among.

Rodney Freedman, HSGA convention in Honolulu, 1991
Clay Savage photo

FUKUBA, CHARLIE - Born in Honolulu, 1955, contemporary musician of Waimanalo. Was featured on many of the Tony Conjugacion albums, performed with the Kipapa Rush Band, recorded two albums one of which won the Hōkū award in 1986. Plays with "Ho'olaua'o" at the Moana Surfrider Hotel. Plays a Rickenbacher frypan.

FURUSHIMA, SCOTT - Born 1963, plays trombone and euphonium in Royal Hawaiian Band. Started Kahala Surf Serenaders in 1991 with Barney Isaacs on steel, Aaron Mahi (bandmaster of RHB) on bass, also Benny Kalama, and Kaipo Asing. Strongly dedicated to keeping the old "Hawai'i Calls" style of music alive, especially the music of Alvin Kaleiolani Isaacs. Scott is now learning to play steel, Barney Isaacs his teacher gave him the name "Ho'oheno".

GASPAR, JULIAN - Recorded with Kāne Leo's Kalima Brothers. There were five Kalima brothers, with Julian on steel guitar.

GIOIA, BILL (GOYA) - Contemporary. Spent most of his years (1940-1960) playing steel and vibraharp with Hawaiian bands on the mainland, then 1960-1992 in Hawai'i. His working with Sam Koki was his happiest musical experience.

Bill Gioia
B. Gioia photo

GOUVEIA, ALBERT - Member of Musicians Assoc. of Hawai'i Local 677, A.F.M.

HAIDA, YUKIHIKO (HARRY) - born 1909 Honolulu. Studied steel with M.K. Moke. Moved to Japan where he pioneered in Hawaiian music as teacher, bandleader, composer and promoter. Had strong influence on musical trends, known as "Father of Hawaiian Music" in Japan. He was Japan's first steel guitarist.

HAKU'OLE, HAROLD - Contemporary steel guitarist with jazzy style. Played with just about every professional musician in Hawai'i as steel guitarist or on rhythm guitar, bass, whatever. Played in the 1986 Steel Guitar Ho'olaule'a, plays at the House Without A Key, Halekulani Hotel, Waikiki, and on the weekly radio show "Sounds of Aloha".

Harold Haku'ole, bandstand show Honolulu 1990,
Alex Among and Merle Kekuku in background
A.W.Ruymar photo

HANAPI, MIKE KELI'IAHONUI - born 1898 Honolulu. The Hanapis were a very musical family. Mike's father (who graduated from Kamehameha Schools in the same class as Charles E. King) was a singer, his wife a singer and composer. All the brothers were musicians. Frank played professionally on the mainland, Edward toured Asia, went with Mike into Vladivostok with a troupe in 1917, Emperor was also a professional. The greatest of them was Mike who, at age 14, left Hawai'i to join brother Frank performing at Chicago World's Fair in 1912, then on to New York City. There he joined Bill Kalama's Quartet as steel guitarist, doing tenor and falsetto vocals. Made one of the first falsetto recordings while with the Kalama Quartet. Recorded and performed falsetto extensively, causing fascinated Americans to call it yodelling. Eighteen years later moved to Hartford CT where he opened a music studio and performed on weeky radio with his band. In 1938 he and his wife returned to Hawai'i, taught music at Bergstrom's on Fort Street along with Ernest Ka'ai, Jr. and Red Hawk. Joined Royal Hawaiian Band, sang in Glee Club with Lena Machado, Jack Kealaluhi and the Pokipala brothers. Passed away in 1959. His message to young musicians was that they must learn to read music if they are to succeed.

HANAWAHINE, HERBERT KEWIKI JR. - Born in O'ahu, April 4, 1937. Contemporary steel guitarist, plays in style of Benny Rogers, was steel player for the great Genoa Keawe, Hawai'i's First Lady of Song. Played at Paradise Cove Luau, and at the Honolulu Cafe, among many other places. Recorded with Hawai'i's top artists including Linda Dela Cruz, Kealoha Kalama, David "Feet" Rogers. Played in the Steel Guitar Ho'olaule'a almost every year.

Herbert Hanawahine, H.S.G.A.
convention Joliet IL, 1993
Clay Savage photo

HAO, VALENTINE K. - A regular member of the Royal Hawaiian Band during his tenure with the organization. He was an outstanding steel guitar player and used a variety of tunings while performing. He played with all the prominent local groups and doubled on other instruments. A very capable vocalist, he is presently working on the mainland.

HEIM, DANNY KALANI - Toured mainland with Hawaiian Beach Boys during World War II, in 1944. They played the theatres in a stage show called "Hawai'i Calls", in New York and along the east coast.

Danny at the Steuben Inn, Milwaukee, 1944
Mandolin Bros. Ltd. cover photo of 1992 catalog

HEMINGSON, DENNY - moved to Hawai'i about 1987 from Minnesota, took instruction from Jerry Byrd. Plays steel guitar at the Hale Koa playing and singing Hawaiian style, and at Pink's Garage playing country music. Uses synthesizer with multi-instrument voices.

HENNESSEY, TOM - travelled to U.S. mainland with July Paka, 1899, made first ever Hawaiian recordings on Edison wax cylinders in San Francisco. None known to exist today. Tom was also a solo mandolinist and slack key guitarist. They are the first steel guitarists we know of to travel to the US mainland. Had music published by Roach-Frankland of Cincinnati, OH.

HERRING, ALIKA KAMALANI'OKEAUKAHA - Born July 17, 1913 in Waialua, O'ahu. Began playing steel guitar professionally at age 15. An outstanding player in the Sol Ho'opi'i style. Played mostly for radio stations in early 1930's on the mainland. Worked with Eddie Paoli (brother of Bob Paoli) on radio station in Shawnee OK 1934-35. Played in dance bands in the mid western states, and with Hawaiian groups in the San Francisco - Oakland and Chicago areas. Used a National Tri-cone resonater guitar with special microphone and amplifier. Toured the U.S. with father-in-law and two brothers-in-law, "The Kailua Hawaiians" doing vaudeville and theater work. Last position before retiring was with the Los Angeles County Parks and Recreation Dept. playing Hawaiian shows in various parks in the county. By profession, an astronomer who did the research on Mauna Kea before the astronomical observation complex was built there.

L - R, Jerry Byrd, Wally Henke,
Alika K. Herring, Fred Lemay.
Front row: Frank Hashimoto,
George Goforth.
Middletown, OH 1951
A. Herring photo

HERRING, KAWIKA "TEX" - brother of Alika, born Honolulu HI in 1909, died 1940 in Oklahoma City. Mother: Liliana Kahanu, father Jesse D. Herring. Played steel guitar and slack key, was leader of Herring's Hawaiians, a popular radio group in the US midwest in the late 1920's and early 1930's.

HEW LEN, BILLY - born 1921 Honolulu. With John K. Almeida at U.S.O. shows, entertained troops during WWII. Played with all the best bands in Hawai'i, band leader at Moana Hotel for 14 years, at Niumalu Hotel, steel guitarist with Brooks at Niumalu Night Club, present site of Hilton Hawaiian Village Hotel, 1950. Made numerous recordings with top entertainers including the late Pua Almeida. His spirit and musical excellence overcame his physical disability - loss of left hand in his youth. Had a leather glove-like fitting which held the steel bar in playing position. Played pedal steel guitar for a short time, as possible solution to his disability. Probably Hawai'i's most exciting steel guitarist. Totally unpredictable with his "off the cuff" jazz style of playing while retaining the Hawaiian feel and identity. Played in almost all the Steel Guitar Ho'olaule'as. Billy has been called "the most creative risk taker to ever play." Deceased 1987. (See his life story in another chapter.)

Billy Hew Len playing Rick frypan, leader of the group. Kalākaua Aylett on Spanish guitar. Eddie Pang on 'ukulele, David Kupele on bass. Early 1950's, Niumalu Hotel, now the Hilton Hawaiian Village.
Trini Hew Len photo

HEW LEN, ALBERT "BUDDY" - brother of Billy Hew Len, a contemporary steel guitarist and all-round professional musician. He and brother Billy learned to play from "Tiny" Brown. In 1941 left Farrington High School to serve in the Pacific, places like Enewitok and Bikini. Formed his music groups and entertained on those islands. Back in Hawai'i, played with Johnny Almeida, then with Johnny's son, Pua Almeida And His Moana Serenaders at the Moana Hotel for many years. In 1967 he toured Europe as steel guitarist with a group sponsored by the U.S.State Department, under the direction of Walter Mo'okini. Until it closed in 1993, played bass daily at the Willows Restaurant with the Elaine Ako Spencer Trio. He has performed with Sonny Nicholas, Sonny Kamahele, Sonny Kamaka, Gabby Pahinui, Bill Lincoln, Renny Brooks, Sam Kapu Sr., HaroldHakuole, Harold; Haku'ole, and many more.

Buddy Hew Len, guest artist at HSGA steel guitar convention, Joliet IL 1992
B. Hew Len photo

HIRONAKA, CHARLES - Member of Musicians Assoc. of Hawai'i Local 677, A.F.M., listed as steel guitarist.

HO, RICHARD D. S. JR - Member of Musicians Assoc. of Hawai'i Local 677, A.F.M., listed as steel guitarist.

HOAPILI, ALEX - born in 1898, left Hawai'i at age 20 to tour the mainland in Hawaiian musical groups. Joined the Oahu Publishing Co. in Cleveland, first as an instructor then as arranger and composer of music for students of the Oahu steel guitar instruction course.

HOKEA, BEN - born 1898 Honolulu, a beach boy and a wrestler, taught by Pale K. Lua to play steel guitar. Played in David Kalama's orchestra on Matson Line cruise ships between Honolulu and San Francisco. Stayed in San Francisco to join the troupe of

nine, Charlie Clark's Royal Hawaiians. The group toured the U.S., finally settling in Toronto. Hokea decided to live there, taught steel guitar at the Y.M.C.A., Margaret Eaton's School, De LaSalle College and in major centres near Toronto. He opened his own Ben Hokea's School of Hawaiian Guitar with branches in Hamilton, St.Catherine, London, and Toronto. Gave concerts at Massey Hall with 200 of his students. He later moved to Montreal where he wrote music for the George Peate School of Music. In 1937, left for St.John, N.B. where he opened a music studio. He entertained Canadian troops until end of WWII. Spent his final days in Montreal, where he recorded on Victor and Columbia records and travelled extensively across Canada doing vaudeville shows.

Ben Hokea

HOLCK, JACOB PAHULA - A good steel guitar player, excellent 'ukuleleist and singer. Was the last steel guitarist to play with Sterling Mossman group when they closed at the Barefoot Bar. Jake produced several recordings with other musicians. He was a keen supporter of Hawaiian Steel Guitar Association activities promoting the steel guitar in Honolulu. Passed away late in 1991.

Jake Holck, Bandstand steel guitar show Honolulu 1989.
A.W.Ruymar photo

HOLOKA'I, DAVID KELI'I - Born in Hawaii, early 1900's. Performed the mainland circuit with wife Lulu, a singer and dancer whose father was the famous Hawaiian singer Alfred Unauna Alohikea. David Ka'ili, steel guitarist who teamed up with Pale K. Lua, was David Holoka'i's half uncle.

HO'OMANAWANUI, MICHAEL - Member of Musicians Assoc. of Hawai'i Local 677, A.F.M., resident of Waimanalo.

HO'OPI'I, DAVID KA'AI'AI - Passed away in Honolulu, 1990. Brother of Sol, but known as Ka'ai'ai, not Ho'opi'i. Tau Moe tells us that when he returned to Hawai'i for one year in 1947 both Sol and David were performing as steel guitarists at a big Chinese restaurant near A'ala Park on the river side.

bass, "Longy" David Kanikuahine Ka'ai'ai, steel, Sol Ho'opi'i Ka'ai'ai, guitar, Charley Kaplil 'i, guitar ,Joe Kaleikilo, steel guitar, David Ho'opi'i Ka'ai'ai. Photo dated March 12, 1948 R. Choy collection, courtesy of Island Guitars

HO'OPI'I, SOL (SOLOMON HO'OPI'I KA'AI'AI) - born 1902 Honolulu, the first of 21 children, a musical genius at age of 3. His idols were Joseph Kekuku, Pale K. Lua, and David Ka'ili. Played first professional engagements in San Francisco, 1919. He traveled there with two friends as stowaways on a ship. Passengers enjoyed his music so much they paid the fares. Dubbed "King of Steel Guitar" and "Fritz Kreisler of the Steel Guitar". Recorded with Lani McIntire in group " Novelty Trio". Taken to Hollywood by

Hoot Gibson in early 1920's to play in country music band. Played first an acoustic Martin (with a very flamboyant style), then a black bakelite Rickenbacker electric. He might have been the first to play an electric steel guitar before an audience, as he played the Fry Pan prototype at a private party given for the purpose of raising funds to begin production of the instrument. Was in great demand in Hollywood as musician, actor, and technical director. Known as the "Hollywood Hawaiian", when Mary Pickford had to play a scene requiring her to cry, she would insist on Sol's steel guitar playing to give her the proper emotion. Sol also played on radio and in night clubs, Los Angeles area. In later life, beginning 1938, he dedicated himself to gospel music and evangelism and produced some of the best music of his career. Sol's extensive recordings were popular around the world and inspired many to play the steel guitar. He was the trend setter that no one could equal. His complex style was the most sophisticated in Hawaiian music. He had strong influence on country music, was copied by steel guitarists the world over. He suffered blindness near the end of his life, but continued to play, teach the gospel, and compose religious songs. He died at age 51, was named to the Steel Guitar Hall of Fame in 1979.

Sol Ho'opi'i, a trend-setter and innovator, perhaps best known steel guitarist throughout the world. B. Dunn photo

INGANO, BOBBY - Contemporary. Plays beautifully, in the style of David "Feet" Rogers. Guest artist in steel guitar ho'olaule'a show, 1994.

Bobby Ingano, Bandstand steel guitar show Kapiolani Park, 1991 L.Ruymar photo

IONA, ANDY (ANDY AIONA LONG) - born 1902 Waimea, Kaua'i. To the mainland in 1921. Composer of many successful songs, played with Johnny Noble's band, moved to California worked in movie studios. He could do an entire orchestra arrangement without working on an instrument, then turn it over to the band and they would play it with no hitch. Formed own group, "The Islanders" with Sam Koki, broadcast radio shows coast to coast with big name stars, worked in New York. Played for the Sonja Heinie Ice Skating Show. Helped create the Hawaiian Room, Hotel Lexington N.Y., played the opening night with his band and stayed on for many months. Played excellent steel with thumb of right hand missing, due to an accident in the machine shop at school. Joined staff of Oahu guitar studios, published instruction books. Also an excellent jazz musician and saxophonist. Arranger, composer, and musician for Hollywood film studios. Some of his best known compositions are: South Sea Island Magic, Sand, How D'Ya Do, Ku'u Ipo. Named by Tony Todaro to the Hawaiian Entertainment Hall of Fame. He died November, 1966.

Andy Iona, on
Oahu Publishing
Staff demonstrat-
ing Oahu guitar
Oahu Publishing Co.
photo permission by Betty
Glynn

ISAACS, ALVIN KALEIOLANI - born 1904 Honolulu. Successful composer, band leader, singer, recording artist. Alvin taught himself to play steel guitar, following the stylings of Pale K. Lua and Joseph Kekuku. Began musical career at very young age. Organized his first big-time orchestra, the K.M.M. Syncopators, in 1929. Played in the Ray Kinney and His Serenaders band in the early 1930's. Formed the original Royal Hawaiians orchestra, later joined Harry Owens Band. May have been first steel guitarist on Hawai'i Calls radio show. Supplied the music for NBC nation-wide "The Voice of Hawai'i", took his band The Islanders on U.S.O. tours. As a quartet, he and Tommy Castro, Benny Kalama, and George Kainapau performed at Royal Hawaiian Hotel, made many recordings and sell-out mainland tours. Guest star on Bing Crosby's radio shows, did several Hollywood movies with Harry Owens.

Isaacs, leader of "The Islanders",
steel guitarist in Ray Kinney's band, father of Barney Isaacs.
B. Isaacs photo

ISAACS, BARNEY (ALVIN KALEOLANI JR.) - born 1924 Honolulu. Son of Alvin Isaacs. Barney was the regular steel guitarist on Hawai'i Calls radio show from 1960 until it closed in 1975, and when it reopened in 1992. Played steel in movie "Donoivan's Reef". Played with Sterling Mossman, and on Danny Kaleikini's show at Kahala Hilton. Known as "Dean of Steel Guitar", member of the executive board of Musicians' Assoc. of Hawai'i, recognized as one of Hawai'i's top guitarists. The only steel guitarist included in the group representing Hawai'i at the Smithsonian Institute's Folklife Festival, Washington DC,1989. Played on the Steel Guitar Ho'olaule'a show every year since it began in 1982. Was steel guitarist for the Kahala Surf Serenaders at the Kahala Hilton, O'ahu. In July 1994 Barney was officially declared to be one of Hawai'i's living treasures. Passed away February 12, 1996.

Barney Isaacs playing Frank Miller's triple Fender Stringmaster, Joliet
HSGA convention 1991, Art Ruymar playing rhythm back-up. L. Ruymar photo

JAKAHI, JACK T. - Member of Musicians Assoc. of Hawai'i Local 677, A.F.M.

JIM AND BOB, THE GENIAL HAWAIIANS - see Paoli, Bob

JONA, FRANK - played in Madame Claude Rivier's Hawaiian revue which left Hawai'i in 1928 to tour the Orient. In Tokyo they met Dan Pokipala who was also on tour with his big band. He convinced Frank to leave Madame Rivier and finish the tour with him. Tau Moe took Frank's spot in the Rivier show.

KA'A'A, SAM - An excellent steel guitar, rhythm guitar, 'ukulele player, and singer. Performed with Gigi Royce's Band at the Young Hotel Roof Garden as a guitar player and singer. Also a member of a very popular trio in Honolulu, The Boy Friends. Moved to mainland U.S., performed in Chicago and Miami area. Deceased.

KA'A, BILL - Played steel for George Kainapau in Kona. Deceased.

KA'AI, BOB (ERNEST JR.) - a fine musician and steel guitarist, toured with his father, but elected to stay behind in Japan for a few years to organize a jazz orchestra and a Hawaiian music trio. He was the band leader at the Del Monte Night Club, Shanghai, and played ten different instruments as well as the Hawaiian guitar. Made recordings in the U.S., wrote steel guitar method books, associated with Aloha Publishing Co., Dallas TX. Returned to Hawai'i to teach at Bergstrom's on Fort St. during the 1940's and 1950's.

KA'AI, ERNEST KALEIHOKU SR. - born Jan. 1, 1881 Honolulu. In 1904 formed first modern dance band in Honolulu, ran a major talent agency in Hawai'i, had as many as 12 dance bands playing under his direction in hotels and cruise ships. First performance on the mainland was in 1906 at the Yukon Exposition in Seattle, which was followed by a tour in 1911. First to tour Australia and New Zealand in 1918 with a show. Later, 1919 - 1923, toured Malaya, Sumatra, Borneo, Java, Burma, India, Africa, and Great Britain. In 1927-37 toured the Orient extensively. Took his children on tour with him. A mandolin and 'ukulele virtuoso as well as steel guitarist. Wrote two excellent music method books for the Hawaiian guitar, "Songs of Old Hawai'i" in E7th tuning, and "Ka'ai's Enchanted Melodies for Hawaiian Guitar", using notation and Peterson tablature system. He wrote many selections of sheet music published by Roach-Frankland of Cincinnati, Ohio. He passed away in 1964 at Miami Springs, Florida. Named by Tony Todaro to the Hawaiian Entertainment Hall of Fame.

KA'AI'AI - see Ho'opi'i

KA'ALEKAHI, HENRY K. SR. - Contemporary. A very capable steel guitar player, has been in the Hawaiian music scene for over 50 years. He has travelled extensively on promotional tours with the local airlines and the Hawai'i Visitors Bureau. Presently he performs with local groups and with the Greeters Groups at the Honolulu International Airport.

Henry K. Ka'alekahi with
double 8 Fender
J. Auna photo

KA'APANA, LEDWARD - Born in 1948 in Pahala Kau on the Big Island into a very musical family. Learned to play slack key guitar (ki hō'alu) from his uncle Fred Punahoa and was influenced by great musicians of previous generation like Atta Isaacs, Gabby Pahinui, and Raymond Kāne. Formed family group of musicians the Hui 'Ohana with twin brother Nedward, cousin Dennis Pavao, and mother Tina Ka'apana. Became a virtuoso, a trend-setter in music, later formed his own group 'I Kona'. Bought a very old wooden acoustic steel guitar from a San Francisco pawnshop. Taught himself to play steel. He plays brilliantly, with high spirits in the manner of Gabby Pahinui. He has many recordings, first with the Hui 'Ohana, then with I Kona, and is much in demand for overseas touring. Ledward is one of our best hopes for reaching Hawai'i's younger generation.

Ledward Ka'apana playing Hilo acoustic
steel guitar at Malia's Cantina, Honolulu 1990
A.W.Ruymar photo

KA'APUNI, SAM - An outstanding musician and arranger. Learned to play steel guitar in amazingly short time and performed with the original 'Islanders' led by Sonny Kamahele's father, at the Royal Hawaiian Hotel. He later joined the Malcolm Beelby orchestra playing in the Monarch Room at the Royal Hawaiian and traveled with the band to play at the Bakers Hotel in Texas. After World War II he returned to Los Angeles and performed with Andy Iona, Danny Stewart, Sam Koki, David Keli'i, Harry Baty, Ernie and Freddie Tavares, and Pua Almeida. He is also a composer, had the ability to listen to a melody on the radio, write down the melody line then add a four part harmony immediately, without using any instrument. Now deceased.

KA'AUA, ARCHIE - The primary steel guitar player for the Hilo Hawaiians. Uses the C6 tuning.

KA' EKA, DAN - He was the selected steel guitar player for Bill Lincoln's group. When Eddie Pang joined the group, Dan assumed the guitar chores and became a permanent member of the singing trio. When Eddie Pang left the group, Walter Wailehua joined up as the steel guitar player. Dan also worked with Napua Sevens and Lena Machado.

KAHALEWAI, KAMUELA - Member of Musicians Assoc. of Hawai'i Local 677, A.F.M.

KAHANALOPUA, JIMMY - born in Honolulu around 1900 or earlier. Steel guitarist, but played other instruments with John Phillips Sousa band. Director of the Royal Hawaiian Studio of Music in downtown Philadelphia, where he taught Ralph Kolsiana. His style was similar to Sol Ho'opi'i's.

KAHANALOPUA, JACK - brother of Jimmy. Excellent rhythm guitarist and steel guitarist. Played in Sousa band, taught guitar lessons. The two brothers worked together throughout their musical career.

KAHIAMOE, ANELA - Contemporary. Taught by Jerry Byrd, now playing on a cruise ship in Hawaiian waters.

KAHUE, KIMO - deceased brother of Philomena Kaneakua. Played a twin neck Fender steel guitar and entertained at V.F.W. bases until his death at age 63, 1987.

KAIALUA, ALBERT - Born in Honolulu, stayed there for his musical career. Was a polished steel guitarist.

KA'ILI, DAVID LUELA - Born June 17, 1890 in Kahana, O'ahu, HI Contemporary of Joseph Kekuku. One of the very earliest steel guitarists to tour the U.S., England, India, Australia (1927) Jakarta Indonesia, and the Far East, with wife "Queenie" (who was a great singer, often called "Hawai'i's Sophie Tucker"), Pearl Akana, and their band. Toured with Irene West's Royal Hawaiian Troupe. Teamed up with Pale K. Lua to make recordings for Columbia records, playing as a duo with Ka'ili on Spanish guitar. Popularized "Hilo March" in the 1920's by recording it. Wrote songs which were published by Roach-Frankland of Cincinnati OH. Performed in a side show at a carnival in Manila with Tau and Rose Moe in February and March 1934, before the Moes left for Europe. Also performing in Manila at that time was Billy K. Lee, father of composer singer Kui (Kuiokalani) Lee. Because of the impending Japanese invasion, American citizens were evacuated from the Philippines and Singapore. In a phone call, January 1994, Billy Lee stated that he left on an American ship in June 1937 and shortly before that time, David Ka'ili had been killed in a Japanese POW camp. David had bought a restaurant and night club, and had tried to stay in the Philippines because of it. Ka'ili's niece, Lydia Ludin, agrees that her uncle died in the Philippines but believes it was later than 1937. Tau Moe reported that when he visited Hawai'i in 1947 they met Queenie who told them that her husband David had been killed in the Philippines.

David Ka'ili on left,
Pale K. Lua seated with steel guitar.
Mike Scott photo

KA'ILI, DAVID KAHANAMOKU - Born in Lana'i December 23, 1897, his father David Joseph Ka'ili, his mother Benoita, a cousin of Olympic champion swimmer Duke Kahanamoku. David grew up in the Punchbowl area of Honolulu, attended Kamehameha School. Came to mainland at age 12 with Harry Sinclair of Sinclair Oil. Left Sinclair to join Pale K. Lua in Dayton OH where for five years they performed and recorded together for Decca, Columbia, and Victor. Pale Lua played steel on most recordings, with Ka'ili

on rhythm guitar, but a few numbers did feature the Ka'ili steel guitar, a Dobro: Hilo March, Kohala March, and Drowsy Waters. Played at the World Fair in San Francisco in 1914 for the "Hawai'i Calls" show. Lua moved on, Ka'ili formed his own band and from 1918-1920 they did Polynesian shows on the S.S.Sherman and other ships, stopping in Acapulco, the Bahamas, Montego Bay Jamaica, Brazil, France, England, Norway, Spain, and others. Picked up the calypso style which remained a part of his music from then on. Hearing that Lua was playing and teaching in Brazil (first steel guitarist in Brazil), Ka'ili left the ships and re-joined him. Returned to Hawai'i when 20 years old, played with Harry Owens at the Royal Hawaiian during the time Harry wrote "Sweet Leilani" for his daughter. Moved to New York area, played at dude ranches, then to S. Dakota, then settled in Des Moines IA where Dave married Helen, and worked at the Pepsi Cola plant. Kept up his musical career, doing radio shows and giving instruction. Knew McIntire brothers, was friend of Sol Ho'opi'i. Played for many dignitaries like Presidents Roosevelt, Taft, Wilson, and Harding, also for Dorothy Lamour, Bing Crosby, Bob Hope, etc. The above is taken from a letter written by David Ka'ili himself, with assistance by Wes Jordan in late 1992.

David K. Ka'ili playing Weissenborn acoustic steel guitar, with Glenn Kruchlow on Spanish guitar and Herman Teaterman on 'ukulele, Des Moines IA, early 1930's.
D. Ka'ili photo

Oldest living steel guitar player, David K. Ka'ili at age 96 with David Jr. and grand daughter
D.Ka'ili photo

KAIMOKU, HENRY PELEKANE - Born 1925 in Hawai'i.

KAINAPAU, GEORGE - Born May 22, 1905 in Hilo, passed on in January 1993. Primarily known as one of the greatest of falsetto singers, he was also a 'ukuleleist and steel guitarist. This statement was confirmed by his wife Ruth Simpson Kainapau in a written tribute to him, published in the Kapalakiko Calendar of Hawaiian Events. He was taught by Sol Ho'opi'i, but he rarely played the steel guitar in public. His career began on the Matson Liner, "Maui" in 1926, then a tour of the Islands with Sol Ho'opi'i. His first appearance on the mainland was in 1928 with Sol at Grauman's Chinese Theater in Hollywood. During his lifetime he sang with all the top Hawaiian bands in the best hotels, both on the mainland and in Hawai'i. He sang on the Hawai'i Calls show from 1940 to 1947, toured with Andy Iona in the Hollywood Ice Revue 1951-52, and sang with Bing Crosby on radio station KNX. He sang Harry Owens' "Sweet Leilani" with Bing Crosby in the movie "Waikiki Wedding" in 1937, and sang with Sol Ho'opi'i in "Flirtation Walk". He also sang "Mauna Kea" in the movie "Bird of Paradise", 1932.

KALAMA, BENNY (BENJAMIN KAPENA) - Born 1916, North Kohala, HI. Not known primarily as a steel guitar player, Benny did play it in 1938 with the Malcom Beelby Orchestra, as a pinch-hitter until Sam Ka'apuni, then Walter Mo'okini took over on steel. He is most often seen playing in Waikiki on 'ukulele or bass. His first job after graduation from McKinley High was with Leonard "Red" Hawk and the Waikikians, who replaced Harry Owens at the Royal Hawaiian Hotel when Owens left for the mainland. When Don McDiarmid's orchestra moved to the Royal, Benny joined him, then stayed on at the Royal to play with Wally Lavque's band. During this time Benny played with the musical greats: Alfred Apaka, George Kainapau, Alvin Isaacs Sr., and steel guitarist Tommy Castro.

Heading for the mainland, he appeared in several movies and made numerous recordings, touring with the Royal Hawaiian Serenaders. Prior to Pearl Harbor, Benny (as director and arranger) broadcast a very popular weekly program on radio KGU, called the "Voice of Hawai'i" which was heard on the mainland.

Benny re-joined Don McDiarmid at the Kewalo Inn and La Hula Rhumba, at the same time coaching and arranging music for Alfred Apaka. From 1952 - 1955 Benny worked with Andy Bright's dance band at the Moana Hotel. In 1955 he worked with Alfred Apaka in Las Vegas, then for 15 years at the Henry Kaiser's Hawaiian Village where his excellent arrangements had much to do with Alfred's rise to stardom. During this time he also served as music director and arranger for the world-famous "Hawai'i Calls" radio broadcast, from 1952 until it closed.

Now in his late 70's, he plays at the Halekulani's House Without a Key usually with Walter Mo'okini in Alan Akaka's "Islanders", often with Barney Isaacs and Sonny Kamahele, Merle Kekuku or Harold Haku'ole, and always in the stage band for the annual Steel Guitar Ho'olaule'a. He was named by Tony Todaro to the Hawaiian Entertainment Hall of Fame.

KALEIALI 'I, KALE - Born 1900 Hanna Maui. Toured mainland U.S. first with Bird of Paradise show (but not as steel player), then as a duo with his wife. Returned to Hawai'i with E.K. Fernandez show, nearly wiped out by big wave of 1946. Back on mainland, organized and performed in all-girl combo "Diamond Head Melodions", then "The Trade Winds Revue" teamed up with another steel player, Ralph Kolsiana, doing the vaudeville circuit. Often on the same bill as Bob Hope, a black-face "hoofer" at the time. As a musical clown, Kale specialized in novelty instruments: harmonica, tin whistle, jews harp, musical saw, taropatch, theremin etherovox, toy balloon, tire pump, gut bucket, ukalaika, steel guitar, etc. Left this world in 1989.

KALEIHUA, BILL -

KALEIKINI, JACOB P. SR. - Born in Honolulu 1915. Was married to Samoan knife dancer Siliwa, a very popular dancer in Hawai'i, Reno, and Las Vegas. Jake started steel guitar career in 1930's at Lalani Hawaiian Village, located on Kalakaua Ave., between Paoakalani and Kapahulu streets. Before the show, he climbed the palm tree to throw down coconuts, pounded the poi, took the pig out of the imu, helped serve the luau food, and played steel guitar in the band. During the show he shook a piece of tin roof to make thunder and blew burning kerosene out of his mouth behind the hula dancer during the volcano eruption scene, and played steel guitar. To San Bernardino CA in 1946 to perform in new night club "Club Pago Pago" with all-girl orchestra, where he met Tau Moe Family. Then, played on S. S. Lurline as bass player for four years. Back in Hawai'i, he played at the Waikiki Beach Comber Restaurant, and in later years volunteers as musician at Elks Club to raise funds for charity. Excellent falsetto singer.

Jake Kaleikini playing bass at HSGA convention in Honolulu, 1991
Clay Savage photo

KAM, LAWRENCE H. - 1928 - 1992. A self-taught steel guitarist, played with the Ebbtides and taught many others to play. He was a graduate of U. of Hawai'i, U. of S. California, and Cornell Law School. While at U.S.C. he formed a musical group and played steel guitar at campus parties. At Cornell he formed "The Case Notes" and played for graduations and faculty functions. He became state budget director, assistant dean of the U. of Hawai'i Law School, a Honolulu deputy city attorney, and deputy prosecutor. He and Governor William Quinn were a musical duo. When the Governor was asked to sing, Larry would back him on 'ukulele or steel guitar.

KAM, SOLOMON - Born in Honolulu in 1927, Solomon Kam is self-taught. He started by playing in churches. His musical career, interrupted by WWII, was resumed in 1972 with an invitation to play with John K. Almeida (Pua's father) and his Old Timers. He has also played with groups: Na Kupuna, Aina Koa, Leo Nahenahe, Makua Ali'i, and the Honolulu Hawaiian Civic Club. Since 1986, after retiring as an electrical engineering designer, Sol has been serving as a kupuna, teaching Hawaiian studies and playing steel guitar at Queen Lili'uokalani Elementary School.

Christmas party at Hickam Air Force Base, Officer's Club, Honolulu December 1975. L to R, Johnson Aila, John Kamealoha Almeida, Solomon M.L.Kam on Fender double, Daniel Spencer, Shirley Leu, Angie Lau, and Frank Lau S. Kam photo

KAMA, DAVID - Now deceased. A steel player from the big island.

KAMA, HAROLD - steel guitarist of Hilo. Plays very much like "Feet" Rogers.

KAMAHELE, SONNY - born 1921 Honolulu. Singer, recording artist, band leader. Started with his father's band in Honolulu, then to Hollywood with Harry Owens TV shows and with Hilo Hattie. Returned to Hawai'i to join Benny Kalama's Hawaiian Village Serenaders, Alfred Apaka show, then Royal Hawaiian Surf room, later Halekulani's House Without a Key with his own band. Plays steel guitar on occasions and is well schooled on this instrument. An outstanding accompanist, vocalist, and solo guitarist. Called "An amazing talent who never ages".

Sonny Kamahele playing steel at Bandstand show 1989, backed by son King, and Merle Kekuku on bass.
L.Ruymar photo

KAMAKA, SONNY - Born in Honolulu, was one of the original members of the Richard Kauhi quartet, and a very accomplished steel guitarist. He is well schooled on steel guitar, an outstanding accompanist and solo guitarist. Presently playing the steel at the International Hotel, Kihei, Maui.

KAMAKAHI, DENNIS D. - Vocalist, guitar player, and composer with Eddie Kamae's Sons Of Hawai'i , not known as a steel player, but is listed as such with the Musicians Assoc. of Hawai'i Local 677, A.F.M.

KAMANO, JOHN - Member of Musicians Assoc. of Hawai'i Local 677, A.F.M.

KANEAKUA, ALEXANDER - lives in Papakolea district of Honolulu, is still playing the steel guitar. He is a former steel guitarist for Genoa Keawe and is the brother of the late Joseph Kaneakua.

KANEAKUA, JOSEPH - Born in 1916, the late husband of entertainer Philomena Kaneakua. Played steel guitar professionally until his death in 1971, performed primarily at military bases on O'ahu.

KAPUA, KEN - a contemporary of Joseph Kekuku, knew him personally and learned to play steel guitar from him. See his article in Chapter 1 "Origin".

KAUA, ARTHUR - Played steel guitar with the Hilo Hawaiians.

KAUA, TAPU - not only a gifted hula dancer and excellent lead guitarist, Tapu played the sweetest steel guitar this side of heaven. At age 16 she danced in a Hawaiian show on the Boardwalk, Atlantic City and since then was a popular entertainer up and down the Atlantic coast. She worked with Hawaiian entertainers Sam Makia, Johnny Pineapple, and Francis Raccismo and was a long time fixture at the popular Hawaiian Cottage in Merchantville, NJ. She passed away in 1991.

KAULIA, PUNI - One of the finest harmonics players on steel guitar, about 1910-1965. Played with Julian Hawaiians on radio station KGU, a popular group in 1930-1940's. Played with all groups in Honolulu of the time.

KAWOHI'ONALANI, ERNEST (PRINCE KAWOHI) - Known as Ernest Kawohi. Went to Shanghai with Walter Downing, where he played a pancake Rickenbacker with Billy Lee and Joe Kanapu'u at St. George's Night Club. On returning to Hawai'i in 1937, Ernest played on the Roof Top of the Alexander Young Hotel with Joe Gigi Royce's orchestra. He later joined Harry Owens' band and went to the mainland with him. Ernest Kurlansky reports, "I last saw him in 1954 when he recorded a disc at 'Hawaiian Luau' and presented a copy to Ed Michaelman who worked at Radio Station KGMB in Honolulu. I believe he lives in Los Angeles now."

KEALOHA, ALBERT L. - Member of Musicians Assoc. of Hawai'i Local 677, A.F.M., lives in Ai'ea.

Al Kealoha on steel guitar with "Na Kupuna" plaers. L-R, Jimmy Papa, Jimmy Kanae, Ike Manewa, unidentified, and Al Kealoha J. Papa photo

KEALOHA, YLAN K. - Early days steel guitarist, wrote steel guitar arrangements for publishing companies, said to be the inventor of the A7th tuning.

Ylan K. Kealoha extended the nut and saddle to make a 7 string out of his acoustic steel guitar, note extra tuning key Warren H. Edgar photo

KEANA'ĀINA, SAM - Born to a very musical family in Hilo but raised on the slopes of Hualalai Mountain. At 18, he started teaching himself to play the steel guitar, with Jerry Byrd as his idol. He started playing at luaus in Kona, went on tours to Japan, California, and around Hawai'i. Also played in Kona at the Mauna Kea Beach Hotel, King Kamehameha Hotel, Kona Hilton, Kona Lagoon, and Kona Surf. Plays C6 tuning with low A.

Sam Keana'āina playing steel in ho'olaulea, Honoka'a 1992
John Murphy photo

KEAO'AHU, DAVID (LANI) - From a picture printed in the March 1980 issue of Ha'ilono Mele, submitted by the wife of David Keao'ahu Lani. It was a publicity picture from 1930 showing Charlie Diamond as steel guitarist, David Keao'ahu, William "Brownie" Ruther, and Henry Kua all on rhythm guitars. She said they played together on radio stations KGU and KGMB. Then David, Henry Kua, and Dan Pele played on the radio as the Kunu Wai Trio. The letter, written in 1980 from a Seattle address, says "David and Henry still play for parties and for friends, along with John Kaleo and Frank Kapuni Ani. Dan Pele lives in Kaua'i. David is a great steel guitar player, also 'ukulele and guitar, and he is studying the autoharp."

KEAWE, FRANCES - played in many circus and vaudeville travelling shows on the mainland U.S.

KEENE, JOHN S. - Member of Musicians Assoc. of Hawai'i Local 677, A.F.M., lives in Kaneohe.

KEKUKU, JOSEPH (*KEKUKU'UPENAKANA'IAUPUNIOKAMEHAMEHA APUAKEHAU)- born 1874 La'ie, O'ahu. Invented the steel guitar circa 1889. His story is told throughout this book.

> * The Kekuku name in its original form means "The staff of the net that surrounds the Kingdom of Kamehameha" or more simply "Keeper of King Kamehameha's fishing net."

KEKUKU, MERLE (KEKUKU'UPENAKANA'IAUPUNIOKAMEHAMEHA APUAKEHAU) - Born in La'ie March 26, 1918, lived in Ai'ea, left us January 7, 1994. Nephew of the inventor Joseph Kekuku and the only active steel guitarist of the Kekuku family. He and Walter Mo'okini learned to play steel guitar in the late 1930's by visiting bars, listening and watching their elders play the instrument. During college years he studied the fundamentals of music, and chose the D9th tuning. Merle is a very good steel player and has backed many of the best musicians as rhythm guitarist, 'ukuleleist or bass player. He played with the original

"Islanders" and later formed a group that played at the Moana Hotel. In 1956 and 1957 Merle hosted a radio show "Polynesian Serenade" on station KIKI featuring music of the earlier years. Played in the Jerry Byrd Steel Guitar Ho'olaule'a 1989, 1991, 1992 and 1993, plays at Pearl Harbor Hawaiian Civic Club. He has become a steel guitarist in demand for radio and TV interviews and special shows having to do with the story of steel guitar in Hawai'i. Travelled with Jerry Byrd trio to St. Louis to perform in Steel Guitar Hall of Fame ceremony and receive commemorative plaque at the induction of his uncle Joseph Kekuku to the Hall of Fame, September 4, 1993.

Merle Kekuku playing 6-string Teisco, HSGA steel guitar convention Joliet IL 1993, backed by J. T. Gallagher and Julie Haunani Waters A.W.Ruymar photo

KELI'I, DAVID (KELI'IHELEUA) - born Lahaina, Maui. Long-term steel guitarist with Hawai'i Calls, from 1930's to 1952. His steel guitar was blended with the sound of the ocean waves, which established it as the signature sound of Hawai'i to listeners around the world. Played at the Stardust Hotel with Nalani Kele 1960-1972, at Hoffman's Cafe, and at the Eagle Cafe. Guest spots and luaus, much in demand as freelance steel guitarist. Many years with Al Kealoha Perry's Singing Surfriders. Recorded on many Hawai'i Calls albums and with other artists for 40 years, but made only one solo album. Voted by Guitar Player Magazine "Outstanding Steel Guitarist on Las Vegas Strip". David was inducted into the Steel Guitar Hall of Fame in 1990. He was "Hawai'i's ali'i of the Hawaiian steel guitar", the epitome of perfection. His recordings and Hawai'i Calls albums will be a living testimony to his genius. Played in the Steel Guitar Ho'olaule'a in 1983. Named by Tony Todaro to the Hawaiian Entertainment Hall of Fame.

David Keli'i playing Trotmore frypan, made by Ira Trotter of Nashville TN
Bob "Pulevai" Waters photo

KELI'I, SUE (KELI'IHELEUA) - wife of David Keli'i, a steel guitar player in her own right. Played with Rodney Arias, Waikiki, in the 1970's, also with the Al Harrington show. She is presently playing steel with Wayne Panoke's Halau Hula O Kaho'onei of Las Vegas.

Sue Keli'iheleua at Scotty's Steel Guitar International convention, St.Louis 1990 on the occasion of David Keli'i's induction into the Hall of Fame. Sue is next to the presenter, DeWitt Scott Jr., who holds the plaque. Next to Sue is her daughter. Far left: Speedy West, Jimmy Day, then Jerry Byrd. Clay Savage photo

96

KELI'IKOA, JACOB - was considered one of Hawai'i's best. He played a single 6-string neck with a C6th tuning (with a Bb in the lower strings) that had the local steel guitar enthusiasts going crazy. He liked to emulate a brass section, to sound like a brass band. He was very quick in his playing movements, and loved to play jazz. He was famous for his rendition of "Anytime, Anyday". Started with Don MacDiarmid's band and also with small combos at local night spots Barbecue Inn and Maggie's Inn, then played with Alfred Apaka and the Moana Serenaders during World War II years, with the Kalima Brothers, and with Hawai'i Calls radio show during the early 1950's with David Keli'i. He started a trend in styling that is still used by players today. Jules Ah See and Alan Akaka idolized him, taking on some of his playing style. He passed away at the age of 44 in the early 1960's.

KERR, ANNIE - Formed the Annie Kerr trio 1928 - 1934 with Healani Doane, Irma Kaeck, Milla Yap, Thelma Anahu, Irmgard Farden Aluli and her sister Diana Farden Fernandes, a most popular female singing group of the time. Was possibly Hawai'i's first wahine steel guitarist to form her own group and play professionally..

Annie Kerr, from recording made by surviving members of the group in honor of Annie.

KIA, ABRAHAM - Member of Musicians Assoc. of Hawai'i Local 677, A.F.M., a resident of Honolulu.

KIM, PAUL - Contemporary. Student of Jerry Byrd. Made his debut at the 1988 Steel Guitar Ho'olaule'a. Presently playing with Clyde Lono. Lives in Kailua. He shows great promise.

Paul Kim, HSGA scholarship student, on the occasion of his graduation, 1988
P.Kim photo

KINILAU, ERIC - Born Honolulu Jan. 9, 1962. Very promising student of Jerry Byrd. Lives in Kane'ohe. Awarded first place award at 11th annual King David Kalākaua Invitational Hula Festival, group musicians category, in memory of Kekua Fernandes.

Eric Kinilau with Fender double 8
E. Kinilau photo

KNAPP, HOWARD RAY - born 1928, Springfield OH. A newcomer to Hawai'i whose first love is Hawaiian music. Ray was first inspired by Jerry Byrd and played various spots in Honolulu. Played for many years in the Mai Tai Hawaiian Club in Indianapolis IN, also on TV with a country music show there. Staff musician on WFBM-TV and radio in 1956. In Hawai'i, played on cruise ships S.S. Constitution and S.S. Independence, circling the islands for five years. Presently at the Old Lahaina Luau in Lahaina, Maui. Played in the 1983 Steel Guitar Ho'olaule'a. Dubbed "Kanape" by the Hawaiians.

Ray Knapp, playing with house band, American Hawai'i Cruiser S.S. Independence, 1986
R.Knapp photo

KOANUI, MICHAEL KALAMAKU - Contemporary. Played for the Tihati productions in Honolulu, then played steel for a Polynesian show at the Hyatt Regency, Waikoloa, on the big island. Previously played with Dennis Pavao who was one of the Hui 'Ohana. Steel guitarist for 'Pandanus' recordings. Presently serves as lead guitarist for the Tihati Polynesian Show at the Princess Ka'iulani Hotel. Has done some guest spots in shows on mainland west coast.

KOKI, SAM - born 1900 Honolulu, died 1968. Composer, arranger, steel guitarist. Joined Bud Miller Band while still in school, moved to mainland where he was very successful with big bands in the best hotels, New York, Los Angeles, San Francisco. Played in Panama for awhile. Formed "The Islanders" with Andy Iona and two other Hawaiians, played over CBS radio. Recorded with Lani McIntire's band. Joined staff of Oahu School of Music. Joined radio KHJ staff band, retired to Hawai'i. Did musical arrangements for 'Sweet Leilani' for Bing Crosby's Oscar winner. Many credits in films for composing and arranging.

Sam Koki, 1940's New York,
L.T.Zinn photo

KOLOMOKU, WALTER - slightly younger than J. Kekuku. Played in first Hawaiian Broadway stage play "Bird of Paradise" which later toured U.S., Europe and Canada. It opened in New York 1912, featuring five Hawaiian musicians including Walter's steel guitar which was reported in the press as making "wierdly sensuous" music. The play reorganized and moved to Europe where Joseph Kekuku joined it, in 1919. It was the first Hawaiian show to be seen in Europe, very well received. It was later filmed in 1932 and 1951 under the same name. Kolomoku opened a music studio in New York and taught steel guitar lessons, recorded for RCA Victor.

KOLSIANA, RALPH - born Aug. 25, 1912, O'ahu. Learned steel from Jimmy Kahanalopua in Philadelphia, worked at Steel Pier in Atlantic City with Aldridge's Steel Pier Hawaiians, then with his own group the Waikiki Swingsters. Recorded for RCA Victor. Did steel on the sound track of movies "Mutiny On The Bounty", "Waikiki Wedding", and "The Horizontal Lieutenant". After playing casuals and contract bookings all over the U.S.A., Ralph settled in California, playing with Kale Kaleiali'i's "Tradewinds Revue". (See his life story in another chapter.)

KU, DANNY - steel player on Matson Lines, composed 'Tutu E', the Grandmother's hula.

KU, KALAMA - See Koanui, Michael Kalamaku

KULUA, SAM - See Sam Ku West

KUPAHU, HENRY I. JR. - Member of Musicians Assoc. of Hawai'i Local 677, A.F.M., steel guitar player in Honolulu.

KUPELE, DAVID M. - Member of Musicians Assoc. of Hawai'i Local 677, A.F.M.

KUPO, LEONARD - Contemporary. Steel guitar player on the island of Maui who performs at hula shows and in local hotels. Originally he was a bass player, but became a steel player for Emma Sharpe's Hula Troupe in Lahaina. In addition, he played with a trio at the Sheraton Hotel at Lahaina and with such players as Sonny Kamaka, Danny Kapoi, and Henry Allen.

LAFAELE, JUNIOR - Born Honolulu 1973, a beginning student with Jerry Byrd.

LAFFERTY, BRIAN - Contemporary. A student of Jerry Byrd.

LATU, HANALEI -

LAU, EDWARD T. J. - Born in Honolulu, played steel in the islands throughout his life. He was often seen backing Eddie Kekaula, playing on the street level of the Waikiki Shopping Plaza. When The Islanders regrouped and began playing at the Halekulani Hotel's House Without a Key, Eddie Lau was the steel guitarist, followed by Alan Akaka. He is a recognized steel player and a recording specialist, used the pedal steel guitar.

LAUAHI, MOKE - Born about 1900, deceased 1989. Performed on early cargo-passenger combination ship travelling around the islands. Ship called "Hualalai".

LEE, ELMER - Well known in Waikiki during the 30's and 40's. He was the steel player and leader of his group called The Elmer Lee Hawaiians. He used the A tuning entirely. His was one of the popular groups that played regularly for the well-to-do or exclusive clientele in Honolulu.

LILIKO'I, EDWARD KAWAIPUILANI - Early in his career, Edward played with Alice and Tom Pahu. After that he extended his steel guitar talents, playing with such greats as Andy Cummings, Pauline Kekahuna, Vickie I'i Rodrigues, Sam Alama, Genoa Keawe, Joe Ike'ole and Gabby Pahinui. He and his wife Violet Pahu Liliko'i have raised their children to be fine musicians, playing practically every instrument known to Hawaiian music.

LILIKO'I, EDWARD KEONAONA - Son of Edward and Violet Liliko'i, he learned to play the steel by watching his father. He would just go into his room and play! Currently resides in Maui and plays steel guitar at the Maui Sheraton Luau Show. Edward is a Disc Jockey for KPOA Radio in Lahaina, Maui and operates his own booming Karaoke business.

LIM, ELMER - Reported in Ha'ilono Mele, April 1978 as being one of the most talented young steel guitar players in Hawai'i, having just become a member (at the age of 17) of the Makaha Sons of Ni'ihau. Lim's steel stylings were compared to those of David "Feet" Rogers of the Sons of Hawai'i. The group had just cut their third recording, with Lim playing solo on "Sand".

LIM, KOHALA - Of Lim family (well known as musical family) of Waimea.

LONG, ANDY IONA - see IONA, ANDY.

LOPES, COCONUT JOE (JOSEPH LOPEZ) - Johnny Noble's Moana Hotel Orchestra was first Hawaiian band to perform over Hawaiian radio station KGU. The station increased its beam so that on April 11, 1924 the band was heard in mainland U.S. for the first time. Joseph Lopez was the steel guitarist on that broadcast. In 1936 Charles King began his program of Hawaiian music broadcast on KGU with Coconut Joe featured on steel. Ralph Kolsiana told us of a Joe Lopes who played steel guitar in the early 1920's for Aldridge's Steel Pier Hawaiians, at the Steel Pier in Atlantic City.

LOVEY, LOUISE (LUI CONN) - Stage name "Lovey Lou", married name Conn. Excellent female steel guitar player in Hawai'i, pre and post-World War II period. Played at Waikiki Tavern, a block from the Moana Hotel. She lived in the Pearl Harbor area, was an active professional musician in the 1950's.

LUA, PALE (PAUL) KEALAKUHILIMA - Born February 6, 1895 in La'ie O'ahu. Was a noted violinist with the Royal Hawaiian Band Glee Club before he learned to play steel guitar. Went to Cleveland OH in 1910 where he was immediately caught up in a very successful career as steel guitarist on recordings and on stage. He recorded for "His Master's Voice" and Columbia, working as a duo with David Ka'ili, on Spanish guitar. Lua is thought to be the first to record with Spanish guitar accompaniment. He and Ka'ili worked together in the famous troupe "Irene West's Royal Hawaiians". They toured the U.S. and Canada before 1913 with Irene West And Her Royal Hawaiians, also Europe and parts of Indonesia. In Canada, Lua was called "King of the Hawaiian Guitar" by his student, steel guitarist Ben Hokea. He spent some time teaching steel guitar in Brazil, where he was joined by his old friend David Ka'ili. Lua's last years were spent in New York where he passed away in the early 1920's. His family now lives two doors away from the Tau Moe home in La'ie, Oahu.

Pale Lua with acoustic steel guitar, backed by David Ka'ili
M. Maximchuk photo

LUA, LEONARD - Born in Honolulu, played in Hawaiian Hut, and Tahitian Hut in San Francisco.

LUNT, FRED - Born in Kula, Maui 1946.. Took up slack key guitar at age 15 and began steel guitar in 1974. His teachers were "Pops" (George) Rogers, David "Feet" Rogers, and Jerry Byrd. Plays steel for "Kalua" who is a singer and slack key artist who learned from and patterns his music on Gabby Pahinui.

Fred Lunt playing National 6-string with "Kalua", Bandstand show 1990.
L.Ruymar photo

LUVAUN, SEGIS (JUAN AKONI, SEGES LUVAUN, SEGIS LUAWAN) - Toured Europe with the "Bird of Paradise" troupe along with Joseph Kekuku, 1919-1927. Stayed in Denmark for some time, introducing steel guitar to that country. Moved on to Sweden around 1920, where he performed in a revue that was conducted by Ernst Rolf. Teamed up with Rolf in 1920 to make the first Swedish recording featuring the steel guitar, 'Lilla Lola Lo från Hawai'i' on the Ekophon label. Later recorded on Beka, two melodies 'Kilima Waltz' and 'Hawaiian Butterfly' that made the Swedes fall in love with the new exotic sound of the steel guitar. (We are not sure that he was born in Hawai'i.)

LYONS, AUWAE N. K. "FRECKLES" SR - Member of Musicians Assoc. of Hawai'i Local 677, A.F.M.

LYONS, "SPLASH" KEPOIKAI - Born 1905 Wailuku, Maui. Composer of many songs, recording artist. In 1949-50 played at Don the Beachcomber's Night Club (now the International Market Place) Kalākaua Ave., Honolulu. Played with numerous groups before his long engagement at the Edgewater Hotel in Waikiki. Also played Elks Club. Had an excellent steel guitar style of his own. He was Waikiki's renowned beach boy.

McINTIRE, DICK - "Born around 1900 in Hawai'i of a Hawaiian mother and Irish father. He joined the U.S. navy in 1919 and served on the Scout Cruiser, U.S.S. Birmingham along with brother Lani, and soon had a Hawaiian orchestra formed which was the envy of the Pacific fleet. After leaving the navy, he began his musical career playing in Tijuana, Mexico for five years 1923 - 28, then the three brothers, Lani, Dick, and Alfred formed a large band in California. Dick began his radio career in the mid-30's on station KFSD in San Diego with a program called "Harmony Isle". Formed a trio in Los Angeles with brother Lani and Dan Ku'uana, which became very famous. Opened several teaching studios, using Dickerson guitars. Movie stars came for lessons, in-

cluding George Brent. In Hollywood, Dick played in most of the Hawaiian films being made at the time. He was one of the best-liked band leaders in hotels and night clubs throughout the country. He recorded over 300 records backing Bing Crosby, Frances Langford, Ray Kinney, and Lena Machado, mostly on the Decca label. It is only after listening to his many recordings that one can appreciate the beautiful tone, perfect intonation, and above all the 'heart' and feeling that this consumate artist put into his playing. Listen to his backing on Crosby's Song Of The Islands or the instrumental breaks on Flowered Isles, Kukuna O Ka Lā or Royal Hawaiian Hotel. He made only a few completely instrumental recordings, but some of those are gems; e.g., Hilo March, Luana, and Forever And Ever. He mainly stayed in Los Angeles where he played in many places including Ken's Hula Hut and the Seven Seas in Hollywood. He played for awhile in New York's Ambassador Hotel, the Biltmore Hotel, and in Reno at The Tropics, a most exclusive night club.

"On a guest appearance in Detroit he was presented with a new black and white Rickenbacker by the sponsor of the concert, but no matter which guitar he played it was difficult to detect any significant change in the tone he produced. On the long scale frypan he played, the horseshoe magnets were much thicker than on regular production models, so it

Dick McIntire with the "Harmony Hawaiians" demonstrating a Dickerson guitar, Jun. 31,1939 B. Dunn photo

might have been custom built for him. There is speculation that he might have filled the hollow necks of some of his guitars with plaster of Paris to get greater sustain. His tunings were E7, C#m7 and F#9. To this day, he still inspires many steel guitarists to emulate his beautifully expressive, distinctively legato style. In the late 1940's he moved to Arizona where he hoped to recover from a chest condition. In May 1951 he passed away. He was inducted into the Steel Guitar Hall of Fame in 1982. Many Hollywood and Hawaiian greats attended his funeral at the Chapel of Inglewood Cemetery and his theme song 'Aloha Tears' was played.

"A favorite anecdote concerns a party at which Dick, Sam Koki and others were playing their guitars. Dick broke a thumb pick and was unable to persuade the others to lend him theirs. He went into the bathroom and returned with a toothbrush. With a huge grin he broke off part of the toothbrush handle and, heating it over the stove, fashioned himself a perfectly practical pick and took up playing where he left off. His music is as fresh today as it was in the 1930's and we have no doubt at all that a hundred years from now someone else will echo these same sentiments." (This tribute was paid to Dick by an ardent admirer, Jack Montgomery of Toronto. Imitation is the sincerest form of flattery, and Jack shows his sincerity by playing strictly in the Dick McIntire style, to the delight and awe of his fellow steel guitarists.)

Dick McIntire on the
cover of sheet music, 1938

McINTIRE, LANI - Born December 1904 in Honolulu, died 1951. Brother of Dick McIntire. He joined the navy with brother Dick and served on the same ship. Lani was known as a singer and band leader, but actually did play steel guitar very well. It is said that he played steel for the sound track of one movie, but the name of the movie is unknown. He appeared as vocalist and band leader in "Waikiki Wedding", "Honolulu", "Hurricane", "South of Pago Pago" and sang with his own orchestra at numerous night clubs, hotels and radio shows. He composed many popular songs, one of which was The One Rose. The Lani McIntire Hawaiians were the resident band at the Lexington Hotel's Hawaiian Room in New York from 1947 to 1951. He recorded with Bing Crosby, Ray Kinney, Bob Nichols, Eddie Bush, Hal Aloma, Sam Makia, Sam Koki and many others.

**Lani McIntire with
10-string Alkire steel guitar.
Standing: Charles E. King,
Eddie Alkire, and Sam Makia**
John Marsden photo

MAHUKA, VALENTINE K. SR. - Member of Musicians Assoc. of Hawai'i Local 677, A.F.M., lives in Honolulu.

MAKIA, SAM (MAKEA) - Vocalist and steel guitarist with Lani McIntire's band at the Hotel Lexington NYC, then steel player with Johnny Pineapple's band, then played bass with Ray Kinney at the same hotel.

MAKEKAU, SOLOMON UKI - One of the early players, not much is known about him.

MAKEKOA, NANI - Female steel guitarist, had a quartet in Honolulu with two other ladies, plus Al Camacho on bass. This was possibly in the 1940's.

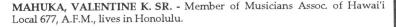

Nani Makekoa on steel guitar,
Al Camacho on bass.
M. Kekuku photo

MAKINI, BUSTER - Contemporary. Steel player in Kailua Kona area of the big island of Hawai'i .

Buster Makini playing steel at John Auna's house party, 1989. Buster was busy building a canoe, consented to come over for "just a few numbers".
A.W.Ruymar photo

MAKUA, SAMUEL KAMOHOALI'I - Born Dec. 10, 1916, Na'alehu Ka'u. Played steel in high school group, then in 1937 in bars on Hotel St., Honolulu, especially when the fleet of navy ships came into Pearl Harbor for military exercises. Played with Walter Wailehua, Tiny Brown, Puni Kaulia, Gabby Pahinui, David Nalu, etc. During the 40's and 50's played with Sam and His Islanders, Ed Machado and His String Masters, Bill Cazimero at China Town Grill and Black Cat Cafe. Sam was the first to play country music in Hawai'i, with his four pedal "Custom Wright" steel guitar. Played Country with military personnel musicians at Hoffman Cafe, Club Hubba Hubba, Swing Club, Black Cat Cafe, Gibsons Bar, etc. from 1952-62. At the age of 75, he is still active, playing casually with the Ko'olau Hui Entertainers.

Sam Makua with his double 8 Fender, April 1992
S. Makua photo

MALO, DAVID - see DAVID NALU

MAYER, DR. EDWARD M. - Born in Indonesia, Ed was raised with Hawaiian music surrounding him. His parents became avid Hawaiian music fans after the Ernest Ka'ai Hawaiian troupe performed there in the late 1920's. Members of the Ka'ai group stayed in Indonesia to teach steel guitar. Tau Moe and his touring group followed shortly thereafter. Ed played steel guitar in Holland with Rudi Wairata's Mena Muria Minstrels, doing radio and TV broadcasts and making recordings, between 1951 and 1955. He moved to the U.S.A in 1957 and played with the Cal Tjader Quartet in San Francisco, then with "Poki and His Polynesians", led by Ben Pokipala from Honolulu, until 1972. After moving to Hawai'i, Ed carried on with his steel guitar work, forming his own group "The Hawaiian Minstrels". They made a recording for Maple Records (Maple MA-0106). He operates his "Indo" recording studio and has mastered and mixed several projects for major labels. Because he has a full-time profession he is under no pressure to play his steel guitar in unfavorable conditions, and so calls himself "a happy steel guitarist". Ed has the largest collection of steel guitars in the Hawaiian islands. He moved to Baltimore MD in 1992.

Ed "Ekualo" Mayer playing Rickenbacker frypan, Bandstand show 1990. George Lake on rhythm guitar,.
L. Ruymar photo

MAYOGA, JOHN JR - 1929-1990. John learned to play steel from Gabby Pahinui. At 18, he played professionally at the Fisherman's Wharf in Honolulu with George Archer and his "Timme Hana's". He was a contemporary of David Keli'i and Arthur Isaacs. During the 1960's he moved to the Big Island and continued to perform, then returned to O'ahu at the Hilton Hawaiian Village for 14 years with the Ginger and John-John trio. His performance in West Hawai'i was well known in all major hotels. He played the guitar, 'ukulele, and bass and was an accomplished singer as well. In earlier years, his Rickenbacher guitar was sold to Benny Rogers for $15.00. Benny gave it to "Feet" Rogers who played it in Eddie Kamae's "Sons of Hawai'i".

John Mayoga, played in the Gabby Pahinui style.
J. Auna photo

MEKANI, BOB (ROBERT) - Born on Moloka'i Dec. 27, 1918, his name legally 'Mechanik' but took his Hawaiian mother's maiden name, Mekani. Learned steel guitar at age of ten by copying records on windup phonograph. Moved to New York, studied and performed on steel guitar. Became an engineer with Grumman Aircraft until he served in the navy during WWII. Before the war, he joined the Hawaiian Federation of America for whom he did radio broadcasts on stations WMCA, WNYC, WJZ and NBC with

his own groups, The Hawaiian Revelers and Mekani's Imperial Hawaiians, and with Bill Hering's South Sea Islanders. Also played USO Canteen shows. Among others who worked for the Federation were Charles E. King (whose performance was a short dissertation on early Hawai'i) and steel guitarists Adeline Mikula, Robert Yap and Ronnie Elliott. Bob Mekani often "subbed" for musicians in the Lexington Hotel, NY. With a later group "The Beach Combers" he performed on WNEW, WMCA, and the NBC network for the Norman Pierce (poet of the air) program. Since retiring, is busier than ever playing Hawaiian style only, with partner Rex Rieke. Bob has among his souvenirs a letter written by Adeline Kekuku, widow of Joseph Kekuku requesting a song to be dedicated to her deceased husband.

Bob Mekani (steel guitarist) playing bass, with Rex Rieke (left) on steel guitar, with dancers.
R. Mekani photo

MOE, PULU - Born in Samoa, grew up in Hawai'i. Half-uncle of Tau Moe. Toured the Far East, then Europe, settling in England. Played with Kealoha Life in their own groups and with Felix Mendelssohn's prestigious band doing recordings, radio and stage shows. Retired to Hawai'i in 1953 where he died in 1962.

MOE, TAU - Born 1909 Pago Pago, Samoa. Grew up in La'ie, O'ahu. Toured world for 60 years, beginning 1928. Took steel guitar for the first time into MANY countries, made many recordings. A living treasure of Hawai'i . Life story told in another chapter of this book. In a letter dated January 19, 1991, Tau cleared up some misconceptions about the family relationship. "My Grandfather and Grandmother have two children. One of them was my father, Chief Savea Moe. My Grandmother passed away and my Grandfather married again. They have six sons. She was Pulu Moe's mother, so Pulu Moe is my uncle, that is Pulu Moe's elder half-brother is my father. Pulu Moe's first wife Lalana Keka'a is not the daughter of Joseph Kekuku. Louisa Reyes, Pulu Moe's second wife, is now married to a German business man. Louisa has two sons now living here in Hawai'i with their families." Pulu's third wife bore him one son, Paul.

Tau Moe played his National acoustic steel guitar in the traditional way, bandstand 1991
L. Ruymar photo

MOKE, M. K. - One of the first steel guitarists, born in North Kohala on the Big Island. Among his many steel guitar students in Honolulu were Harry Haida, and Rose and Tau Moe. Recorded on Brunswick label, toured Japan with Hawaiian show, played in Johnny Noble's band. He is known for his rendition of the original Moana Chimes.

MONROE, J. J. - Member of Musicians Assoc. of Hawai'i Local 677, A.F.M. Listed as steel guitarist.

MONTE, JOHN G. - Member of Musicians Assoc. of Hawai'i Local 677, A.F.M. Listed as steel guitarist.

MONTGOMERY, JESS - Contemporary. Plays steel guitar in Anahola, Kaua'i area. Began playing in 1982, performed with Ilima Rivera at the Sheraton Poipu Beach, Howard Toki at the Sheraton Coconut Beach, and Rick Hanapi at the Coco Palms. Favorite players are Sol Ho'opi'i and David Keli'i.

Jess Montgomery, HSGA convention in Honolulu, 1989
A.W.Ruymar photo

MO 'OKINI, WALTER - Born in Lahaina, Maui, 1917. Taught by his father, he began on an acoustic koa wood guitar with a pocket knife for a bar, and match sticks to raise the strings. He learned also by copying Sol Ho'opi'i recordings. Replaced Sam Ka'apuni as the steel guitarist for the original "Islanders" at the Royal Hawaiian Hotel. Played with Sonny Kamahele, Benny Kalama, Alfred Apaka, Joe Custino, Jake Keli'ikoa, Buddy Hew Len, Sonny Kamaka, Merle Kekuku, Harold Haku'ole, Jules Ah See, Pua Almeida, and Steppy DeRego. Played with Mel Abe at the Royal Hawaiian Hotel's Surf Room, returned to the "Islanders" playing at the Royal Hawaiian, The Reef, the Princess Ka' iulani, and Hawaiian Regent Hotels, also at the Waikiki Beachcomber Hotel for the Tihati Polynesian Show. Plays all other back-up instruments and sings. Presently with Alan Akaka's "Islanders" at the Halekulani's House Without a Key, as bass player. Ernest and Freddie Tavares were Walter's brothers-in-law.

**Walter Mo'okini, backed by Bob "Pulevai" Waters,
Joliet HSGA convention 1991** A.W.Ruymar photo

NA'EOLE, DAVID (NA'OLE) - Ralph Kolsiana told of a David Na'ole, classical voice and guitar, who played with Aldridge's Steel Pier Hawaiians at the Steel Pier in Atlantic City in the early 1920's at the same time as Ralph did. Ralph said, "David was also a fine steel guitarist."

**David Na'eole on steel guitar,
other musicians and the occasion not known.
This picture is part of the "On Char"
Collection, Bishop Museum,
recognized by Ralph Kolsiana**
November 1989 issue O.H.A.

NA'INOA, GEORGE K. - Born in O'ahu, 1932, played bass, 'ukulele, rhythm guitar, and 6-string steel, C6th tuning. Played with Sonny Chillingworth years ago. Now living in California. He is the nephew of Sam Na'inoa who entered Kamehameha School for Boys at the same time Joseph Kekuku did.

NA'INOA, SAM K. - Born La'ie Hawai'i. Cousin of Joseph Kekuku, enrolled at Kamehameha School in the same year, played violin while Joe played the steel guitar. Became a steel guitarist as well, taught steel in his music studio in Los Angeles and states that he shared in developing the playing technique. Said in a vocal recording that he had documentation to prove Joseph Kekuku was the inventor of the Hawaiian steel guitar.

NALU, DAVID (NALO) - Born around 1915, now deceased. Began professional career during high school years. The original steel guitarist with Andy Cummings' Hawaiian Serenaders around 1948 at the Hawaiian Town Night Club, before Gabby Pahinui. Did recordings with Napua Stevens, along with Steppy DeRego on guitar, Walter Mo'okini on 'ukulele, and Jacob Carter on bass. He was also a writer of early Hawaiiana.

**David Nalu, steel player with Andy
Cummings' Hawaiian Serenaders**

NAMAKELUA, ALICE K. - Born in Honoka'a Aug 12, 1892, deceased in late 1980's. She is known primarily as a vocalist, slack key guitarist, and composer of nearly 200 songs, but did play steel guitar as well. She was strong in her knowledge and teaching of the Hawaiian language and spent much of her life working with children as playground director in the Honolulu Parks Dept.

NAWAHĪ, "KING" BENNIE (BENJAMIN KEAKAHIAWA NAWAHĪ) - Born 1899 Honolulu. As a youth, played for nickels and dimes in the park, contemporary of Sol Ho'opi'i who was doing the same thing. Played with his older brother Joe's group on the liner S.S. Matsonia, then on Orpheum vaudeville circuit, U.S. mainland. He was a great showman (he'd play 'Turkey In The Straw' on the steel guitar, with his feet). Played hot jazz style on steel, also known as 'ukulele and mandolin virtuoso. Is known best for his recordings with The Red Devils, The Georgia Jumpers, and with his own group King Nawahi's Hawaiians. One of his first west coast groups, King Nawahi and The International Cowboys, included a young Roy Rogers, not yet famous. Played the part of Little Jakie in the New York stage production "The Big Parade", later made into a movie "What Price Glory" (but not with Benny). Suc-cessful music career on west coast, although suddenly stricken blind in 1935. He became a national hero when, in 1946, he swam the 26-mile channel between Santa Catalina Island and San Pedro in 22 hours, following a ringing bell.

NELSON, CARLYLE - Adopted the steel guitar and performed with groups at the origi-nal Halekulani Hotel. He was an accomplished violinist and performed with the Honolulu Symphony and occasionally with the Harry Owens Orchestra. He was the husband of Clara Inter, better known as "Hilo Hattie".

NICHOLAS, SONNY (JOSEPH PAPAPA HALEMANO NICHOLAS, JR) - born 1920 Hana, Maui. Sonny was a popular musician, singer, and bandleader in the islands. At times he had his own band. He was a regular on the Hawaii Calls broadcasts (but not as a steel guitarist). Promotions and entertainment director for Aloha Airlines and Seattle World's Fair, 1962. With Benny Kalama's Tapa Room Show, Hawaiian Village Hotel. Played with Ed Cane and Don Paishon at the Royal Lahaina Hotel in the early 1980's. While seriously ill, Sonny made the great effort to fly from Maui to O'ahu to play his "Last Aloha" on stage at the HSGA steel guitar convention.

Sonny Nicholas at 1989 HSGA convention, Honolulu, played his final public performance, and was gone soon after. Jerry Byrd played rhythm back-up. L.Ruymar photo

NICHOLS, BOB - An active steel player in Los Angeles for many years, performed with all the area's musicians including George Archer's Pagans and Augie Goupil's Tahitians. In 1951 played at the Tahitian Hut with Sam Ka'apuni, and Harry Baty. Played with Lani McIntire's band during 30's and 40's. One of the very best steel players ever, with a style similar to David Keli'i's. After many years with Lani McIntire's band, he ended his career playing music on the cruise ships in the Pacific, where he started his career. Deceased.

NOSAKA, CHARLES K. - Contemporary steel guitarist, Hilo HI. Joined Aloha Hawaiian Trio along with Buckie Shirakata, went with him to Japan on a prize trip awarded the group by a Honolulu radio station. Arrived in Japan in 1933, stayed until 1934 touring and performing. Played steel for an all-male dance group in Hilo, the "Sweet Things", and in the 1992 Merrie Monarch hula festival, Hilo.

Charlie Nosaka at John Auna's steel guitar show, Kailua Kona 1990. A.W.Ruymar photo

OLSEN, CASEY - Born Hawai'i 1967, son of Hiram Olsen, grandson of Billy Hew Len. Casey took steel guitar lessons from Jerry Byrd and showed outstanding ability from the start. He went from student to professional in eight years. At age 17 played steel guitar on one of Hawai'i's Grammy award winning TV shows "Hawai'i's Super Kids". Began his musical career upon graduation from Roosevelt High School. Played every Steel Guitar Ho'olaule'a since his debut in 1983. In 1989 stepped into Jerry Byrd's very big shoes as Jerry retired from playing with his trio at the Halekulani Hotel's House Without a Key. The group re-formed as the Hiram Olsen trio and Casey shines brilliantly as one of Hawai'i's stars. In February 1994 Ca-sey replaced Barney Isaacs on the Sounds of Aloha radio show, previ-ously known as Hawai'i Calls.

Casey Olsen, steel guitarist at the Halekulani Hotel's House Without A Key, shown here with his father Hiram Olsen, Spanish guitarist and leader of the Hiram Olsen Trio, with Kalani Fernandes on the right, bass and vocals. May 1990 L.Ruymar photo

OPUNUI, CHARLIE - Worked with many different bands in Honolulu, also known as a violinist. When not playing steel, played rhythm back-up in local bands. Excellent all-round Hawaiian musician. Also played with Freddy Tavares, Bob Nichols, and others with the Royal Polynesians in California.

OPUNUI, PETER - Born 1898 in Honolulu, not known to be related to Charlie Opunui. Better known as violinist with Johnny Noble's band, and as clarinetist with Royal Hawaiian Band and Glee Club. Played steel guitar privately and on casual gigs.

OZAWA, AKIRA -

PA'ALANI, BILL - Born in Hawai'i, played casuals around Honolulu, regularly at the Elks' Club, and in Bishop Museum concerts. Deceased 1989.

Bill Pa'alani playing double Fender at HSGA Bandstand show, Kapiolani Park, 1989. George Lake on bass.
A.W.Ruymar photo

PAHINUI, GABBY (CHARLES PHILIP KAHAHAWAI PAHINUI, JR) - Born 1921 Kaka'ako HI. Died in 1980. Gabby was called "King of the Slack Key, Master of the Steel Guitar, and Lord of the Folk Singers". Worked professionally with different orchestras in Waikiki, played steel guitar for Andy Cummings for 18 years, then with the Sons of Hawai'i for several years. Made excellent recordings. In 1954 he played steel for Sterling Mossman at the former Queen's Surf. Gabby was a trend setter, a super-star with raw talent. Better known as a slack-key guitarist, his first love was steel guitar although he never recorded a solo album with it. Can be heard playing steel on some Maile Serenaders recordings. Gabby's nickname is said to have come from the gabardine pants he always wore, and from his hair style.

**Gabby Pahinui,
a most beloved and admired Hawaiian musician.**

PAHINUI, CYRIL L. - Contemporary. Son of the great Gabby. Cyril is more of a slack key guitarist but does play steel guitar.

PAKA, JULY "TULAI" - He and Tom Hennessey were possibly the first steel guitarists to leave Hawai'i for the mainland, in 1899. Recorded on Edison cylinders with four other Hawaiian musicians (in San Francisco), which could be the first recording of Hawaiian music. July was the son of the well-known singer Juliana Walanika, a favorite of Queen Lili'uokalani. He married a professional dancer, "Toots" who led them into a whirlwind of success under the name of Toots Paka's Hawaiians. They played in the best places alongside the biggest names in the American entertainment world, were mobbed by high society, and led the way for many Hawaiian groups to follow. So great was their success, it's been said that they made Hawaiian music a permanent institution rather than a passing fancy.

PALAMA, EDDIE - Local Hawaiian boy who lives in Kaneohe, learned steel guitar from his family and other musicians, a relative newcomer to steel guitar but one who will be around a long time. He has a simple basic Hawaiian style of playing and his technique in playing harmony is tops. Played in the 1983 Steel Guitar Ho 'olaule'a, has made some recent recordings. He plays in the old fashioned style, played with the Danny Kaleikini show.

Eddie Palama playing at the Tapa Terrace, Hilton Hawaiian Village, Honolulu, January 1993
R. Sanft photo

PALEKA, HERMAN - Contemporary steel guitarist of Kapa'a, Kaua'i. Teaches in the local elementary school as well as playing casual gigs.

Herman Paleka, Anahola Kaua'i, May 1992
A. Ruymar photo

PALMEIRA, ERNEST - Born in Kaua'i in 1930, Ernie is a paniolo, a Hawaiian cowboy. He learned to play mandolin and steel guitar at age 17. Got his first job playing at the Club Blue Lei on a National 6-string steel, using a tuning he got from Billy Hew Len. Toured with airline promotions to Caracas Venezuela. Played in Kaua'i at Lovell's Tavern, then Lincoln's Tavern with falsetto singer Kai Davis. Ernie's trio plays at the Hilton Kaua'i Hotel, also at the Fern Grotto, and at the Coco Palms Hotel, Wailua in the Larry Rivera Show.

Ernie Palmeira at the Larry Rivera Show, Coco Palms Hotel Wailua Kaua'i, May 1992
A. Ruymar photo

104

PANG, EDWARD K. - Played on Hawai'i Calls radio show early to mid 1960's. Played on Leina'ala Heine group in the Orchid Room, a night club. Was steel player with Bill Lincoln after Dan Kaeka left, has moved to California.

PAOLI, BOB and HOLSTEIN, JIM (of "Jim and Bob, The Genial Hawaiians"). Most active as musicians during 1930's to 50's, best known for appearances over Chicago radio and station XER in Del Rio, Texas. They were sponsored by Doc Brinkley who promoted the sale of monkey glands. Bob was the steel guitarist, Jim backed him on the harp guitar. No musician playing an acoustic steel guitar in standard high bass A tuning ever carried the instrument to such perfection. His taste and understated technique are unrivalled, with an almost theatrical sense of control and timing, and blazing jazzy steel breaks. He seems to have used a triple resonator square neck National on his recordings. He and Sol Ho'opi'i were the inspiration to mainlanders who copied their styles, particularly in the early days of country music.

PARELIUS, ARTHUR - Born in Boston MA September 26, 1926. Played for over 15 years at Germaine's Luau and for longer with the Royal Hawaiian Band. Toured with the band, playing solo steel, to Toronto, New England, New York City, Chicago, Milwaukee, Hiroshima Japan, and throughout the Islands. Played with many island groups in his younger years. Art is believed to be the first and perhaps the only Hawaiian steel guitarist to perform in Carnegie Hall, on July 16th 1988. His solo was Maui Chimes, "Maui No Ka Oi".

Art Parelius, steel guitarist with Royal Hawaiian Band. June, 1992 A.Parelius photo

Mac Pavon, 1959, with Paul Goupil's Tahitians. M. Pavon photo

Mac Pavon plays a triple 8 Fender with adaptations. **1989** M. Pavon photo

PAVON, MAC - born in Waimea, Kaua'i Sept. 10, 1908. His first appearance in Honolulu as a musician was playing tenor banjo with "Banjo Harry" in 1927. Hearing a recording of Sol Ho'opi'i converted him to steel guitar. Moved to California 1939, played steel for Lena Machado at the State Fair in Sacramento with Lou Machado, then in Sacramento with Eddie Duke's Hawaiians at Donovan's, one of the best clubs. Shared the stage with Jack Benny, Hilo Hattie, George Brent, met Charlie Chaplin, Errol Flynn, Paulette Goddard. Played at Lake Tahoe, with Sol Bright and Hilo Hattie's shows, with Honey Kalima in Reno, Paul Goupil's Tahitians at the Fairmont in San Francisco and in Vegas, then played the cruise ships Lurline, Mariposa & Monterey, Royal Viking Lines, Holland America Lines, Crown Odyssey, and S.S.Rotterdam cruising to islands of Polynesia with Kimo Baird's Spirit of Polynesia. Mac has a most complicated and unique tuning of his own invention and plays skilfully but also humorously in the Spike Jones style. At the age of 86 he is still going strong. Played in Alan Akaka's Steel Guitar Ho'olaule'a 1992 and 1993

PERRY, AL - Played steel in Hawai'i and in California in the late 1930's. Played at the Polynesian Society gatherings at Whistling Hawai'i in Hollywood. Not to be confused with Al Kealoha Perry who was leader of the Singing Surfriders and musical director of Hawai'i Calls in Hawai'i and did not play steel.

PETERSON, J. KALANI - Toured the U.S. in the 1930's. Developed a well-known steel guitar course and a number system or "tablature", used by George K. Awai in his method books, Sherman Clay Publishers, 1916. Title: "Peterson System of Playing the Guitar with Steel in the Hawaiian Manner Designed for Self-Study", edited by N. B. Bailey.

PIENA, RALPH - Member of Musicians Assoc. of Hawai'i Local 677, A.F.M.

POKIPALA, DAN - Composer of 'Nani Wai'ale'ale', father of David and Charlie, grandfather of Mikilani Fo. Played in the first band at the Moana Hotel in 1911.

PUNUA, EDWARD - Born 1970, student of Barney Isaacs. Shows great promise, has the Hawaiian touch in his playing. Is also an excellent rhythm guitar and 'ukulele player, and vocalist. Plays steel with his family's Polynesian show on Kaua'i when he can, but works as an accountant in O'ahu, where he plays casuals.

Edward Punua with his teacher, Barney Isaacs, photographed at the Bandstand show, Honolulu 1991. L. Ruymar photo

105

RALEIGH, JOHN M. - Member of Musicians Assoc. of Hawai'i Local 677, A.F.M.

REIS, LAWRENCE B. - Member of Musicians Assoc. of Hawai'i Local 677, A.F.M. plays steel in Wai'anae area.

ROGERS, BENNY - Brother of George Rogers. One of the great Rogers family of steel players. Played steel for Genoa Keawe for many years in the 1940's and 50's, played on almost all of her recordings until his death. His wife also played rhythm guitar and sang with Genoa. Benny had a style typical of the Rogers family, very Hawaiian with excellent harmonics. Deceased.

ROGERS, DAVID "FEET" - born 1935, son of George Rogers, died 1983. "Feet" was steel player in Eddie Kamae's Sons of Hawai'i, known for his use of the D tuning and excellence in harmonics. Much-recorded, highly successful group, organized in 1960. Eddie said the steel enhanced the natural beauty of their music, made it distinctive at a time when steel was no longer popular. The group did not perform when "Feet", a merchant seaman, was not in town, so great was their respect for his contribution to their sound. His music was a simple pure Hawaiian style always delicately played and beautifully expressed. His best work can be heard in all of the Sons of Hawai'i albums. Deceased.

ROGERS, GEORGE - A true master steel guitarist. Played for Mormon church activities, was very secretive about the tunings he used, even with his immediate family! He could be called one of the greatest of all steel players. He was very religious and refused to play in many places. He played many Mormon functions at La'ie and elsewhere. Deceased.

SALAZAR, OWANA - Contemporary, born in Honolulu, Hawai'i. After graduating from Kamehameha Schools, she spent two years at the University of Hawai'i at Manoa, majoring in music. Owana is an excellent performing artist, including singing, hula, 'ukulele, both standard and slack key stylings with the guitar, and shows great promise of becoming one of the best wahine steel guitar players Hawai'i has ever known. As an HSGA steel guitar scholarship recipient, she graduated after three years of study with Jerry Byrd. Owana began her career as a performer at the age of fifteen as a member of the Concert Glee Clubs at Kamehameha Schools. Throughout her career, she has performed with: Ed Kenney, Herb Ohta San, Charles K. L. Davis, Billy Gonsalves, Genoa Keawe, George Naope, Hoakalei Kamau'u, Mahi Beamer, and Jerry Byrd. Aside from doing radio and television shows, she has toured to Japan, New Zealand, and to 14 US states. She has been nominated several times for Na Hōkū Hanohano awards. Owana has produced several of her own recordings, has been a guest star on the new Hawai'i Calls radio broadcast, and is a "regular" in the Annual Steel Guitar Ho'olaule'as. She is a direct descendent of Keoua Nui, father of King Kamehameha The Great, and bears the rightful title of Princess Owana Ka'ohelelani Mahealani-rose Salazar.

Owana Salazar,
shown performing at
HSGA Honolulu convention, 1991
Clay Savage photo

SANCHEZ, ROBERT A. - Born in Honolulu, spent time on the mainland and in the military. Played slack key guitar from about 17 years old. Took steel guitar lessons from Kimo Pekelo at St.Louis High School, also with Jerry Byrd. Played parties and casuals with Nā Hōkū Pā, including Andy and Paul Rodrigues.

Robert Sanchez plays
Rickenbacker bakelite 6-string
at HSGA bandstand show,
May 1991
A.Ruymar photo

SANG, LANI (AH MOOK SANG) - prominent in late 1940's and early 1950's on the west coast U.S.A., and in Waikiki. He composed 'Mapuana', which was sung by Ray Kinney on a recording with brother Roy Sang's Hawaiians.

SARDINHA, GREGORY "ROCKY" - Born 1953, Honolulu. Another prominent and talented student of Jerry Byrd. Greg has become a successful and popular steel guitarist in Hawai'i. He is a frequent performer on the annual Steel Guitar Ho'olaule'a and has been associated with numerous Hawaiian shows and Hawai'i's top artists such as Cyril Pahinui, Karen Keawehawai'i, and Danny Kaleikini. The versatility of his playing can be found in his recordings with various Hawaiian artists and bands where he has blended the steel guitar with Hawaiian, contemporary, and rock music.

Greg Sardinha playing 8-string frypan at
Bandstand show, 1989. A.W.Ruymar photo

SHEA, ERNIE - Born in Honolulu, started playing professionally with Lovey Lou and her group in 1951. Did some work in Camden NJ with The Invitations, then formed the trio The Torchmen for a Royal Hawaiian Hotel engagement, then at the Princess Ka'iulani Piano Bar, Honolulu, for a year. Back to San Diego, produced and directed Polynesian shows for a year, played with combos at Del Webb's Ocean House, Highway House, Mission Bay's Ilandia Hotel, Stardust Lounge, and appeared in TV specials in San Diego. Returned to Hawai'i 1965, formed the Ernie Shea Trio at the Merry Monarch, also at Kanaka Pete's, Lahaina Maui and at Ka'anapali Hotel, Maui. Back to Honolulu where he played at La Salon Rouge, Little Club, Reef Hotel, Ala Moana Hotel, Embassy Lounge, Ambassador Hotel and in many other places. Known more as a pianist than as a steel guitarist.
While on the mainland he won a guest spot with a trio on the Ed Sullivan Show after winning first prize in the "All-Army Talent Contest" at Schofield Barracks, O'ahu. He also won first prize in Europe with his own group while in the military service.

SHIRAKATA, BUCKIE - Born 1912 Honolulu. With his Aloha Hawaiian Trio, won a trip to Japan in 1933. He had learned to play steel guitar from Sol Ho'opi'i and introduced to Japan the wood-bodied steel guitar, the steel bar, and the A major tuning. He returned to Hawai'i for a short time to finish school at the university, then back to Japan to stay. Buckie brought with him Japan's first electric steel guitar and amplifier. He made over 200 recordings and for over 20 years was on the best seller list. In 1965 the House of Representatives honored him for disseminating Hawaiian music in Japan. He taught many Japanese to play steel guitar.

SHIRAKATA, TSUTOMU - Member of Musicians Assoc. of Hawai'i Local 677, A.F.M.

STEWART, DANNY KALAUAWA - Born and raised in the Makiki neighborhood in Honolulu, he was truly a giant in Hawaiian music. His beautiful singing voice and many excellent compositions speak for themselves. In 1925 he left Hawai'i with Johnny Noble's stage show "Pele and Lohiau". He spent many years playing in the Los Angeles area, working for five years at Universal Studios, recording with Joe Guerrero and Sol K. Bright, and with many others as vocalist, composer, steel guitarist, or on any other instrument. He was part of the same music circle as the likes of Andy Iona, Sam Koki, Ernie and Freddie Tavares. For seven years he worked with the staff band at radio station KHJ. He recorded with Alfred Apaka and George Kainapau, also with Bing Crosby (Harbor Lights, Beyond the Reef, Mele Kalikimaka, etc) He played the background music for films, including "From Here To Eternity" and played in all the big hotels on the east and west coast. When Jules Ah See passed away in June 1960, Danny was invited to come home to Hawai'i to take his place in the Hawai'i Calls radio show, alternating with Barney Isaacs. Danny passed away in 1962.

SWERDLOW, MIKE - Kamuela, HI. Mike plays country style as well as Hawaiian style steel guitar. He learned steel guitar from John Auna, is now playing in the Polynesian Show at the Kona Hilton.

Mike Swerdlow plays double 8 Fender steel at Honoka'a Ho'olaule'a, 1992
J. Murphy photo

TAI, JIMMY HAULANI - Chinese Hawaiian, born in Hawai'i. He played in southern California in the 1930's and 40's.

TAPIA, WILLIAM - Member of Musicians Assoc. of Hawai'i Local 677, A.F.M.

TAVARES, ERNEST - Born in Hawai'i, he was one of the first to develop the pedal device that led to the pedal steel guitar. He died in Feb. 1986. His brother Freddie wrote of him, "He and I joined Harry Owens' Royal Hawaiian Orchestra in 1936, I on steel guitar and he on alto and baritone saxes, clarinet and flute. Ernest and I both settled permanently in Los Angeles in the early 1940's. Ernest was a phenomenal musician and has played professionally the following: steel guitar, guitar, 'ukulele, string bass, electric bass, clarinet (any size), sax (any size), flute, piano, and organ. He also sang beautifully and was a fine arranger and song writer."

TAVARES, FREDDIE - born 1913, Maui HI. In 1937, played broadcasts of Hawai'i Calls radio show with Harry Owen's Royal Hawaiians, then came to Los Angeles with the band, which recorded extensively and backed some of the greats like Bing Crosby and Dorothy Lamour. He played all the 'ukulele in Elvis Presley's film "Blue Hawai'i", and did the opening steel guitar riff in the Looney Tunes cartoons. In 1953, began work with Leo Fender designing and building guitars, pedal steel guitars, and electric bass guitars. He played pedal steel in full chord style, with the soft Hawaiian sound. Freddie on steel and brother Ernest on bass played on Bud Dant's very first Hawaiian album "Isle of Enchantment" at Decca Records, in 1957. Played in the Steel Guitar Ho'olaule'a in 1985 and 1986. Planned to return to Maui, but died in 1990. Was inducted into Steel Guitar Hall of Fame in 1995.

Freddie Tavares, steel guitarist, in Harry Owens' vocal quartet.
L to R, Harry Owens, Ernest Kawohi, Freddie Kaulana Tavares, Gil Mershon
F. Tavares photo

TEMPLETON, CHRIS - Contemporary steel guitarist of Anahola, Kaua'i. Has done some touring to Japan and the mainland. Studied with Jerry Byrd in Hawai'i and with pedal steel guitar teachers in Nashville TN.

(L.) John Ely, steel guitarist, (R.) Chris Templeton, steel guitarist., 1992
J. Ely photo

TOKUMOTO, DWIGHT - Born and educated in Hawai'i, now living in San Francisco. Plays excellent steel guitar for Kapalakiko Hawaiian band, also slack key guitarist and vocalist.

Dwight Tokumoto plays frypan with Kapalakiko Hawaiian Band. Seen at Steel Guitar Northwest meet, Napa CA 1990.A.W.Ruymar photo

TOM, GRIFFORD KAMAKA - Born Honolulu October 27, 1952. Plays steel guitar at the Ala Moana Hotel with Jeff Apaka's group, plus casuals in Honolulu, has done some teaching of steel guitar at Kamehameha Schools. A tireless worker for the "cause" of steel guitar in Hawai'i. Has bachelor's degree in Hawaiian studies and elementary education, U. of Hawai'i.

Grifford Kamaka Tom, playing 8-string frypanL.Ruymar photo

TTORP, YUUGEN EDOURD - Listed as steel guitar player, Musicians Assoc. of Hawai'i Local 677, A.F.M.

VALDRIZ, JERRY - Contemporary. Student of Jerry Byrd. Now playing casuals and practicing law in Wailuku, Maui.

VILLAVER, ALBERT - Now in his early sixties, Albert has been playing for many years primarily at private luaus and church functions on O'ahu.

VINCENT, MANUEL - Member of Musicians Assoc. of Hawai'i Local 677, A.F.M. Manuel is now retired in Pearl City. He's one of the pioneers of the steel guitar in Hawai'i.

VISSER, ULULANI - Kailua, Kona. Hula dancer, vocalist, plays bass, 'ukulele, and Spanish guitar. HSGA scholarship student of Jerry Byrd, made her steel guitar playing debut at the Hulihe'e Palace luau organized by John Auna for HSGA, May 1991.

Ululani Visser, apprentice steel guitarist
U. Visser photo

WAILEHUA, WALTER - His style was beautifully Hawaiian, but he was also an excellent jazz guitarist, which influenced his steel guitar solo playing. He started off as steel player for The Islanders Junior Group of which Sol Kamahele, Sr. was the leader. He later replaced Eddie Pang in the Bill Lincoln group, did almost all the steel work for singer Bill Lincoln, sharing the spot with David Keli'i. Deceased.

**Bill Lincoln, leader, 'ukulele.
Dan Kaeka Spanish guitar.
Walter Wailehua on Multi-Kord steel guitar.
Johnson Aila, bass.**
Bob "Pulevai" Waters photo

WALLACE, SAM - Steel guitar player for the Honolulu Police Glee Club and The Islanders at the Royal Hawaiian Hotel. Most of The Islanders were retired police officers and Sol Kamahele, Sr. was the leader of both groups. Sam was an outstanding instructor of life saving with the Red Cross water safety program. Sam was also an excellent rhythm man and singer and a graduate of Kamehameha School for Boys, a classmate of Randy Oness. Deceased.

WELLS, CLAIR - Elder steel guitarist who plays with the Napua Strings (kama'aina entertainers) regularly at the Beachcomber on Kalākaua Ave. Clair plays a 6-string Fender steel guitar and enjoys playing the old songs of Hawai'i nei.

WEST, SAM KU (SAM KULUA) - Toured US mainland with Irene West (promoter) in the 1920's and 30's, recorded extensively. Took name "Ku West" at Irene's suggestion, as an informal adoption. Went to Manila with Irene West Show and Madame Rivier's show which included Tau and Rose Moe, in 1928.

YAP, ROBERT - Native Hawaiian of Chinese extraction. He had an exceptionally fine touch on the steel guitar, could produce the sweetest sounds. A teacher of the Spanish guitar and steel guitar, an arranger of music. Worked for the New York Academy of Music which supplied demonstration records played by Yap, some of which were his arrangements. Deceased.

ZANE, JOHNNY - Born Honolulu circa 1927. A cartoonist and steel guitarist. Moved to Shanghai 1935, operated a Hawaiian music studio teaching all Hawaiian instruments to Chinese Hawaiian students studying there. Evacuated 1937 before Japanese invasion.

- Chapter 5 -

Physical Development Of The Steel Guitar

The following is a rough sketch of the activities of several manufacturers in their efforts to produce the perfect Hawaiian steel guitar. The ultimate, I suppose, would be one which would play by itself, sparing the musician the exquisite torture of reverse bar slants and the agony of working hard to become proficient. These stories are not complete in detail nor are the pictures a complete collection of all the models put out by any manufacturer. Our purpose is to provide an overview and to show the beautiful instruments owned by our proud contributors. Some books have been written which give the total story of a given manufacturer. They are listed in our bibliography section.

The Very Earliest Hawaiian Guitars

The VERY first were converted Spanish guitars. The adaptations were: a "nut" installed to raise the strings higher off the fretboard, the use of a steel bar and finger and thumb picks, and changing the strings from gut to steel. When manufacturers realized that the new instrument was here to stay they began building a special Hawaiian model with a permanent string-raising nut, and reinforcing the necks by making them square and stockier. Since it was not to be played in the manner of a Spanish guitar, the neck could be made wider and even hollow for more resonance. Raised fret markings were no longer necessary, and many were inlayed into the fretboard or painted on. Two of the first we know of were named Hilo and Bergstrom, built of koa wood or of mahogany, built in the Hawaiian islands. Another was the Weissenborn guitar, built by Hermann Weissenborn in Los Angeles of koa wood. Some early examples have bird's-eye maple backs and sides. Spruce tops were optional but rare, in four styles of trim, no. 4 being the must beautifully decorated with rope binding. Kona Hawaiian guitars were made for Los Angeles music teacher and publisher Charles S. De Lano (perhaps made by Weissenborn). Knutsen Hawaiian guitars were made by Chris Knutsen in Los Angeles. MaiKai Hawaii guitars, the maker and origin of these guitars is unclear at this time. Lyon & Healy offered a number of steel string guitars with high nuts. Re-

gal guitars of Chicago built a special Hawaiian model with body no longer guitar-shaped but extended toward the nut for extra volume and tone.

While most Hawaiian music enthusiasts rushed to buy the specially-built Hawaiian style guitars, those with less cash in their pockets simply adapted the standard or Spanish style guitars by slipping matches or pencils under the strings to raise them off the fretboard.

HOW TO CHANGE REGULAR GUITAR INTO HAWAIIAN GUITAR

Any regular Guitar (also called: Spanish or Standard) may be changed for Hawaiian or Steel style of playing by applying the following instructions:

1. Loosen the strings and slip the Extension Nut over the original Guitar Nut. Adjust strings in the grooves to lie firmly. The strings now are raised above the fingerboard and will not touch the frets when the steel bar is being used.

From a 1936 Nick Manoloff Hawaiian Guitar Method

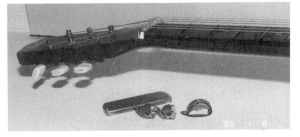

The very first steel guitars had metal adapters (or matches or pencils) slipped over the nut to raise the strings higher, and were played with a flat bar, metal finger picks, and tortoise shell thumb pick. A.W. Ruymar photo

Soon guitars were built in the *Hawaiian* style, with the strings permanently raised and the fret markings carved in or painted on. For extra strength, the square necks were a continuation of the body rather than attached to it.
A.W. Ruymar photo

Hilo Hawaiian guitar built in the 1920's Larry Petree photo

Side view Hilo Hawaiian guitar with squared sturdy neck, permanently raised strings. Larry Petree photo

Ledward Ka'apana plays his Hilo acoustic guitar with a pick-up. It's marked #3622, style 625, made of mahogany. A.W.Ruymar photo

1930's Weissenborn #6042 owned by Michael Dunn. Back and sides are koa wood, the top might be spruce. The strings pass over a bone bar on the curved bridge. A. W. Ruymar photo

Above: W. A. Greenfield poses with his first Hawaiian guitar, and with a second nicknamed the "hambone" (lower left) which has the neck cut away on one side. It is supposed that his steel bar kept bumping into the enlarged neck as he played on the first model. Harry Brown photo

Left: Hawaiian guitar built in 1926 by W.A. Greenfield of Edmonton Alberta Canada no longer resembles a guitar but has the neck greatly enlarged for more sound. Harry Brown photo

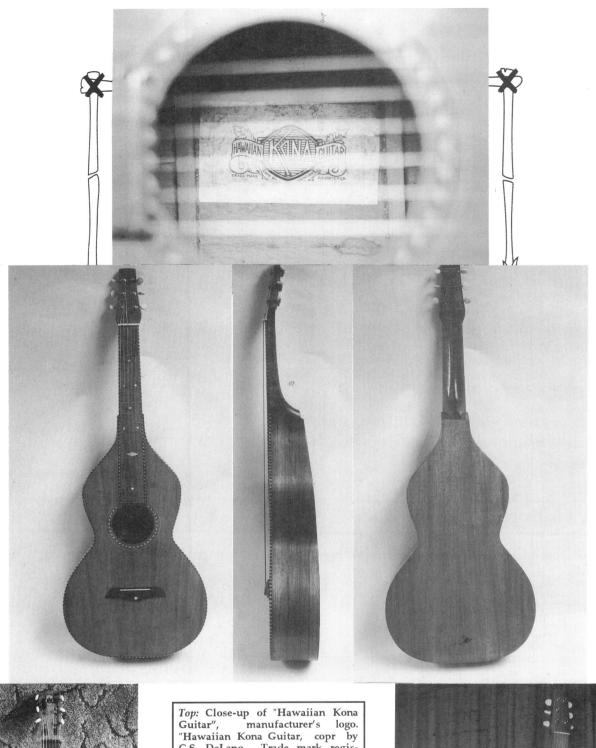

Top: Close-up of "Hawaiian Kona Guitar", manufacturer's logo. "Hawaiian Kona Guitar, copr by C.S. DeLano. Trade mark registered."
Left: "Kona" guitar, It is of Hawaiian koa wood, 950 mm long, 340 mm wide, and 110 mm deep
Center: "Kona" guitar, side view
Right: "Kona" guitar, back view
Atsushi Onji, Kyoto, Japan, photo's

Kale Kaleiali'i poses with his Weissenborn guitar made of koa wood and round back mandolin
L. Ruymar photo

Maikai Hawaii
Ron Middlebrook photo

C. F. Martin Guitar Co.

This company built Hawaiian steel guitars from 1920 to 1941 and they didn't try amplification of any sort. The only style concessions they made were as follows: the frets were ground down so as not to protrude and catch on the steel bar, the bridge maintained a straight saddle even though Spanish guitars went to the slanted saddle, the bridge was slightly forward of the Spanish position, and the nut and saddle were left high. Some of their Hawaiian guitars were made of mahogany or rosewood. They felt that koa was not superior to mahogany in tone, but used it only in Spanish guitars and 'ukuleles because of its beauty and because Hawaiians preferred it. Any style number containing a K was made of koa, and if it contained an H it was a Hawaiian steel guitar. The only Hawaiian models listed in "C.F.Martin & Co. A History" by Mike Longworth are: 0-18K, 0-28K, 2-17H, 0-17H, 0018H, 00-21H, and 0040H.

Right: Martin 0-28K Koawood Hawaiian guitar, 1928
Left: Martin 0-18K Koawood Hawaiian guitar, 1930

Washburn, (Lyon & Healy)

Catolog sheet circa 1920
Washburn guitars showing their Hawaiian models. The top guitar is a 9 string model. Only one model, the Bell-shaped Hawaiian guitar model 5260 was made of Koa (not shown), the other Hawaiian guitars were made of rosewood and flamed mahogany.

Pseudo-Hawaiian Guitars

The Hawaiian Tremeloa

The steel guitar attracted inventors bent on "improving" the instrument. One variation of the Hawaiian guitar was the Hawaiian Tremeloa. The advertisement claimed: "The Hawaiian Tremeloa might well be called the Original Hawaiian Instrument - a Single Melody String upon which anyone can play without months and years of special training. The soft sweet vibrant tones of Hawaiian music are produced as if by magic. The Bass Chords complete the Harmony and permit a wide scope of musical effects.

Directions for playing: The instrument is placed directly in front of player so that bass chords are convenient to player's left hand and the single melody string can be played with right hand throughout its length without difficulty.

"Playing melody string: When the instrument is packed the roller rests in two felt holders. Lift the roller out of these holders and place it on the melody string. By so doing, a spring on the opposite end

The Hawaiian Tremeloa Jim Hanchett photo

of the roller bar forces the bar at right angles to the string. To play, take the celluloid pick between your right thumb and forefinger and move it until it is on the black line of the desired note and then pluck the string. The sliding of the roller as you move the celluloid pick produces the Hawaiian slide effect. Moving the pick a short distance back and forth rapidly after plucking the note produces the Hawaiian tremolo. Playing the bass chords: There are four groups of bass strings. Drawing the thumb over any one group produces a chord. A thumb ring may be used." The owner said of it, "It is played on the lap with the larger portion away from you. It was manufactured in the mid-twenties... The sustain is fantastic and it's awesome with amplification."

Hawaiiphone

This interesting 33 inch long, 16-stringed instrument was also advertised as a "could be" Hawaiian steel guitar. The sign near the tailpiece boasts "This is an Original Marx Instrument" while the manufacturer's logo inside the body states "HAWAIIPHONE. Sold by Our Advertisers Only. Price $35.00. Marxochime Colony, New Troy Michigan. Patent allowed." As the owner, Jess Hurt of Toledo OH, does not have the instructions, I will describe the markings to you and perhaps you will figure it out.

I would imagine the instrument is placed flat on the player's knees with the numbered fretboard farthest away. Although the numbers go to 15, there are actually 24 frets as some numbers are repeated inside a circle, to denote a sharp/flat fret. The strings are tuned A, D, F#, A. This is perhaps (?) the set of four strings that would be played with a steel bar.

The remaining 12 strings are also grouped in sets of four perhaps to be plucked with the thumb as bass accompaniment notes, in the manner of a zither. The two sound holes are separated by what appears to be a bridge. The marking at the bridge indicates the four string sets as 3, 1, 2, and 4. Set 3, is tuned to the D major chord. Set 1 is tuned to the A major chord. Set 2 is the E7th chord, and Set 4 is the B7th chord. These four chords would be the ones most often used in Hawaiian songs, Key of A.

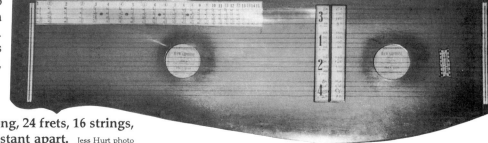

Hawaiiphone, 33 inches long, 24 frets, 16 strings, equi-distant apart. Jess Hurt photo

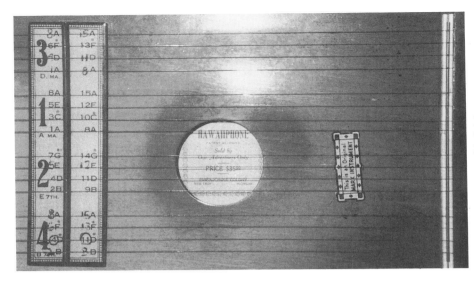

Hawaiiphone fretboard.
The 16 strings are grouped by fours.
Jess Hurt photo

Performers on the acoustic Hawaiian guitar felt the need for more amplification. If you keep track of the dates as the story unfolds, you will see that many people were working on the problem of amplification in different ways, all at the same time.

Resonator Amplification Of Guitars
National And Dobro

The National Guitar Company

Going back to the later 1920's, George Beauchamp (pronounced Beecham), an excellent steel guitarist, tinkered with different ways of attaching a phonograph horn to his steel guitar and actually used one in his shows for a time. Living not far away from George's home in Los Angeles was the violin repairman and inventor, John Dopyera. (Both spellings *Dopyera* and *Dopera* are used by the family). There were actually five Dopyera brothers who worked in John's shop, but he and brother Rudy were the main inventors. The Dopyeras had already tackled the problem of amplifying the steel guitar when Beauchamp took his idea to them and worked with them to develop it farther.

The plan was to find a material that would vibrate so as to reproduce and amplify sound. They had the most success with aluminum, spun as thinly as possible. They built aluminum cones with fine aluminum diaphragms and attached them to the inside of a metal bodied (bell brass) steel guitar and found they worked much as the mica disc did in a phonograph. If one was successful, why not try more? Three cones produced the best results, so a shiny new all-metal non-electric but beautifully amplified steel guitar was born! It was patented in 1926 with improvements in 1928 and 1929. The National "tri-cone" or "triplate" was a huge success. Sol Ho'opi'i and his trio were the first to demonstrate it in public. Besides Hawaiian guitars with varying degrees of ornamentation, Spanish tri-cone guitars, mandolins, and 'ukuleles were also built. In 1928 a new company was formed with George Beauchamp and the Dopyera brothers as principals. It was the National String Instrument Corp.

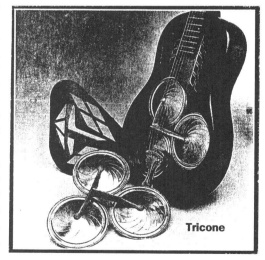

Tricone

Not far from the National factory was Adolph Rickenbacher's Manufacturing Company. He was a highly skilled production engineer and machinist, working in both metal and plastics. Production of National instruments was going at such a great speed, it wasn't long before Adolph was building the metal bodies for the National guitars.

To offer a wider variety of lower priced instruments, George Beauchamp invented the single-resonator guitars which he patented in 1928 as the Triolians. (Some say it was actually Dopyera's work.) The first were built of wood. Single resonators (much larger in diameter than the tri-cones) were installed in 'ukuleles, mandolins, and Spanish guitars, and National's sales skyrocketed.

The Dobro Guitar Company

Sad to say, disagreements brought about the resignation of John Dopyera from the company. By 1929 he and his brothers started their own company known as Dobro (using the first letters of Dopyera and Brothers). Their products were so similar to the National instruments that lawsuits for patent infringement followed. Dobros were made of either metal or wood bodies, with a single resonator. They were very popular in vaudeville where nearly every show contained a Hawaiian act, often not very authentic.

Dobro And National Merge

In 1933-1934, the Dobro and National guitar companies settled their lawsuits and merged, under the name of National - Dobro Corp. with offices in Los Angeles, Chicago, and New York. Although both companies operated at the same address, they kept their products, their markets, and their books separately. George Beauchamp left the company to join forces with Adolph Rickenbacher.

Somewhere during those years it became fashionable to tune the Dobro (1st to 6th string) D.B.G.D.B.G., rather than the accepted A major tuning E.C#.A.E.C#.A. This change is thought to have come from banjo players, since the first three strings of the banjo are tuned D.B.G. Tuning the strings one full tone lower meant less tension, less possibility of bowing of the neck.

National Guitars Compared To Dobro Guitars

"The Soul Of Dobro", note spider bridge

What was the basic difference between a Dobro and a National resonator guitar? It was mostly in the placement of the bridge. On the National, the bridge was on a wooden button (biscuit) fixed to the apex of the resonator cone. The single point of stress at times caused the cone to collapse. The Dobro had an eight-armed cast aluminum spider, which resembled a gas stove burner and supported the bridge, taking the tension off the resonator. The resonator cone was mounted so that the cone opened toward the top of the instrument. The earlier (1927-1941) Nationals with Hawaiian necks (square, for extra strength) were made with triple resonators. The triple resonator Nationals had three small cones placed in a triangular pattern, two of which were placed under the bass strings, the third under the high strings. The bridge was a T-shaped piece of cast aluminum, each point resting on a cone. Under the cones were thick felt pieces. The treble resonator vibrated separately from the two bass resonators, producing an echo effect. The cones also rose and fell slightly, producing a vibrato. A silver plated Hawaiian triple resonator guitar produced a sound unsurpassed by any other instrument.

National Tricone Styles. National's silver guitars were beautifully engraved and designs were designated as follows: Style 1 was plain, not engraved. Style 2 had a rose pattern, Style 3 bore the lily of the valley pattern, and Style 4 was the most ornate with the chrysanthemum pattern. These were National's top-of-the-line products. Two later-year (1936 and on) tricone models were known as Style 97 and Style 35. On both of these the scenes were sand blasted, not etched, and then airbrushed with colored enamel. Style 97's design was a female surfrider with palm tree, Diamond Head, and the moon or sun in the background, the guitar's neck is wood, not metal. Style 35's design is of a seated minstrel plucking a long-necked 4-string instrument, the guitar's square neck made of metal.

National Single Cone Styles. Lower priced steel guitars were produced with one large resonator located in the center of the body. It was stamped from aluminum and supported a wooden bridge and saddle. The strings passed through the bridge to the tailpiece, almost level from nut to bridge. This was the Style O, an economy-priced model which sold well during the years of the Great Depression. Style O designs were sand blasted rather than engraved Hawaiian scenes which came in variations of the palm tree, sea, mountain, clouds, moon, and stars motif. The bodies were of brass, with two f-holes on the front. The large single resonator cover plate had nine sets of small circular holes, each set in grid formation with 6 or 7 rows across and 6 or 7 rows down, or patterns of rectangular slots.

The Triolian was meant to be a low-priced tricone, but went into production with a single resonator, and a wood or steel body with f-holes. It was decorated with stencilled Hawaiian or floral scenes and polychrome lacquer usually with red and blue highlights.

The Duolian was the lowest-priced model, very similar to the Triolian except for the absence of flowers and Hawaiian scenery. It had a single resonator in a metal body, with two f-holes. It was decorated with an unusual crystalline paint designed to make the metal appear to be wood. As the guitar aged, the color changed from gold to green to brown, then black.

National's single cone Hawaiian guitars were built with 12 frets up to the body from 1930 - 1934, increased to 14 frets up to the body from 1935 - 1941. Both had 20 frets in all. During the years between 1927 and 1941 National produced almost 8000 instruments, the best of which were made of German silver and called "National Silver Guitars". The Hawaiian musicians were their best customers. The National logo is a shield with "National" in script on an angle across it, with minor changes on certain models.

Dobro Steel Guitar Designs. For decoration and design, most Dobros had a resonator coverplate with a series of rectangular holes arranged in four semi-circular patterns. Some Dobros also had decoration etched on the back, of Hawaiian scenes, the Dobro logo, or just geometric patterns. The Dobro logo has the word "DOBRO" on a curled banner with an ancient Greek lyre beneath it.

Dobro Guitars Under Other Names. Regal guitars, built in Chicago, used Dobro resonators with the permission of the Dobro Company. Dobro family members built many guitars under other brand names, such as: Norwood Chimes, Angelus, Broman, Montgomery Ward, and Penetro. After WW11: Hound Dog, DB Original, and Replica 66. Regal is thought to have built Alhambra, Bruno, More Harmony, and Orpheum. Magn-o-tone was built by both Regal and Dobro. Production was halted by a shortage of materials during World War II, but in the 1960's Dobro production started again by Rudy, Emil, and John Dopyera under the name "Original", by the new company name of O. M. I. Co. of Long Beach, CA. (Original Musical Instrument Co.) The new serial numbers started at 001, using three digits. In 1967 Semi Mosely bought the rights to build Dobro guitars under the brand name Mosrite. In early 1994 the O.M.I. Co. was bought by the Gibson Guitar Corporation which promises to carry on production of the same line of guitars.

National models. In the 1940's and 1950's National had continued to make small resonator guitars with solid bodies, sometimes with an electric pickup. They also made some guitars shaped like ironing boards with resonators on top and bottom. The last resonator guitar built in the 1960's had a red fiberglass body with single resonator.

When the new electric instruments came on the market everyone rushed to buy one, and the acoustic instruments went out of fashion. Years later some players who liked the tone of the older acoustic instruments began liberating them from the hock shops where the vaudeville players had left them., and they are now enjoying a new popularity. "Bashful" Brother Oswald of Roy Acuff's Smokey Mountain Boys and TV's Grand Ole Opry never did abandon his Dobro. Among players who took up the National and Dobro steels were such great blues performers as Bukka White, Blind Boy Fuller, Memphis Minnie, Tampa Red, Leroy Carr, and Bob Brozman. Perhaps the most influential stylist was Josh (Buck) Graves of the Flatt And Scruggs Band with his unique blend of blues effects and banjo techniques. Rock stars have become fascinated by the shiny resonator instruments. Today, these vintage round-necked and square necked guitars command extremely high prices.

National Style No. 1

National Triolian

Dobro Model 76

Dobro Model 106

Production Of Resophonic Guitars In The 1990's

Dobros By O.M.I. Co.

Still operating at 18108 Redondo Circle, Huntington Beach CA, the O.M.I. Co. has picked up on the renewed demand for both wood and metal bodied resonator guitars, tricones and single cones. The all-metal bodies are available in round (Spanish) necks with radiused fingerboards, or square (Hawaiian) necks with flat fingerboards. They can be ordered with "Biscuit bridge-cones" or with Dobro spider resonators. Coverplates come in a variety of designs, and metal bodies are engraved, etched, or plain. Hand engraved designs are the rose pattern, the lily of the valley, and the Dobro special. In 1970 steel guitars in 8-string (model 63) and 10-string (model 10) styles were offered, later discontinued. Model 36S, a bell brass (plated) steel guitar with rose pattern engraving sold for $558 in 1971, and for $1849 in 1994.

National Reso-Phonic Guitars Inc.

The same National resonator instruments of the 1930's could be back in production again were it not for the fact that all 24 of the original dies have been destroyed. Two young enthusiasts, McGregor Gaines and Don Young, have begun the work of re-inventing the components. At first they worked as employees of O.M.I. but because of differences of opinion have formed their own company, National Reso-Phonic Guitars Inc., as of 1988 and "National" is their registered trademark. Their shop is in San Luis Obispo, CA. Their first creations are the single resonator Style O, Triolian, and Duolians, with the ultimate goal being the re-creation of the National Tricone.

To learn the whole story of the National and Dobro acoustic guitars, the reader is urged to refer to "The History and Artistry of National Resonator Instruments" by Bob Brozman, and "The History of Dobro Guitars" by John Quarterman and Tom Gray, both books published by Centerstream Publishing.

The "Continental", "Beltona", and Other Makers

The Saga Musical Instrument Company in San Francisco is the distrubutor of the "Continental" guitar, a fine tricone resonator limited production model, also offered by Bell Brass Guitars in Spokane WA. The guitars are built by Acoustic Musical Instruments in West Germany. An exact copy of the early National tricone, Style 1, it is a Spanish (round neck) guitar. At present the company has no plans to produce Hawaiian (square neck) models.

The "Beltona Triplate" is being produced in a small factory in the city of Leeds, England. It looks exactly like the early National tricone, and is of best quality. No Hawaiian models are being built at present.

Some of the finest resophonic guitars are being built today by these makers: Beard Guitars, Michael Terris, I. L. Guerney, and Tim Scheerhorn (who also makes a custom Weissenborn Hawaiian guitar).

National tricone steel guitar, Style 4 chrysanthemum pattern, played by Bob Brozman. A.W. Ruymar photo

Close-up of National Acoustic Style #3, lily of the valley Bob Brozman photo

National Tricone Style #2 rose engraved patten. Serial 1350 Al Brisco photo

National tricone steel guitar played by Tau Moe. The engraved pattern is difficult to discern. A.W. Ruymar photo

National Tricone Style #4 chrysanthemum engraved pattern. Serial 1927, built in 1929. Owned by Michael Dunn. A. W. Ruymar photo

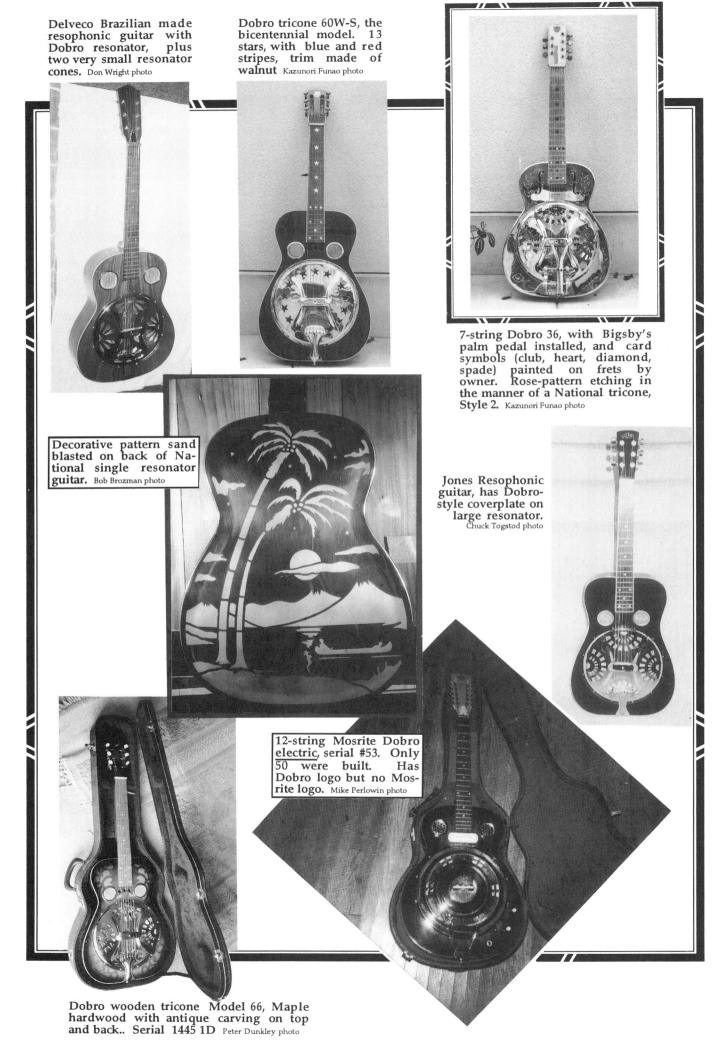

Delveco Brazilian made resophonic guitar with Dobro resonator, plus two very small resonator cones. Don Wright photo

Dobro tricone 60W-S, the bicentennial model. 13 stars, with blue and red stripes, trim made of walnut Kazunori Funao photo

7-string Dobro 36, with Bigsby's palm pedal installed, and card symbols (club, heart, diamond, spade) painted on frets by owner. Rose-pattern etching in the manner of a National tricone, Style 2. Kazunori Funao photo

Decorative pattern sand blasted on back of National single resonator guitar. Bob Brozman photo

Jones Resophonic guitar, has Dobro-style coverplate on large resonator. Chuck Togstod photo

12-string Mosrite Dobro electric, serial #53. Only 50 were built. Has Dobro logo but no Mosrite logo. Mike Perlowin photo

Dobro wooden tricone Model 66, Maple hardwood with antique carving on top and back.. Serial 1445 1D Peter Dunkley photo

Steel Guitars Go Electric

With tongue in cheek, furniture maker W. G. Greenfield of Edmonton Alberta built what he dubbed the first "Electrical Special" steel guitar in 1926. It was not only electrified but it boasted of a double neck, two sets of six strings. Its deep acoustic construction actually did give it a great resonant voice but the player had only to switch on the built-in electric light bulb to enthrall the audience. Imagine the effect in a darkened theatre when the light bulb shone out of the sound-hole to light up the face of the player! The sound, of course, remained unchanged. This remarkable instrument is now in the possession of Michael Dunn of Vancouver, B.C., formerly owned by Bob Brozman of Ben Lomond CA.

W. G. Greenfield's
"Electrical Special" built
just for fun in 1926.
A. W. Ruymar photo

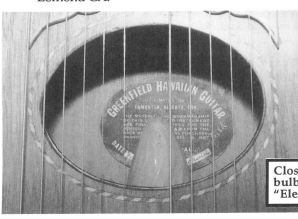

Close-up of orange colored light bulb inside sound hole of the "Electrical Special"

Gibson Guitar Co.

by Eric Madis, guitarist, vocalist and songwriter, of Seattle WA:

"The question of who first applied the AC-DC to the guitar will probably be argued as long as the question of who first accidentally dropped a comb/knife/whatever, on the strings of his guitar as it sat on his lap. However, credit goes to the classical mandolin virtuoso Lloyd Loar, who was Gibson Guitar Co's primary research and development engineer from 1919 - 1924. In that short time he designed the majority of Gibson's early successes: mandolins, banjos (the great Mastertone series), mandolas, and the L-5 guitar. He developed the elevated finger rest (on all arch-top guitars), the elevated fretboard, the f-hole design, the intonation-adjustable bridge, tone-rings and floating heads for banjos, etc. He actually had electric guitar designs, electric pickups, and prototypes in the mid- 1920's which were ahead of their time.

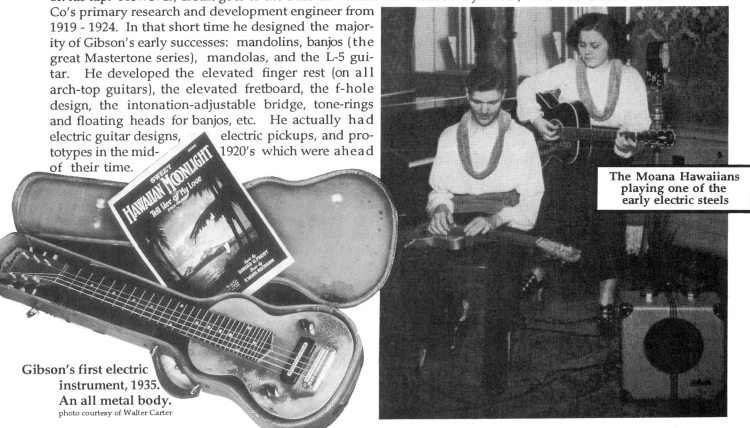

The Moana Hawaiians
playing one of the
early electric steels

Gibson's first electric
instrument, 1935.
An all metal body.
photo courtesy of Walter Carter

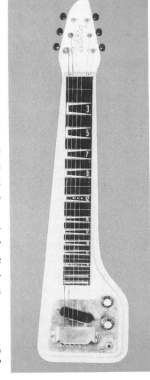

"Walter Fuller, who joined Gibson in 1933, found some of Loar's pickups lying around at the factory. They were comprised of a diaphragm stretched over one fixed anode and contained in a bakelite cover. The diaphragm's vibrations induced a fluctuation in current which could then be amplified. The pickup had two problems (requirement of a very short amplifier cord and sensitivity to moisture), both of which could have been easily corrected had Gibson seen a market for electrification at that time. Loar's electric prototypes never found their way into production. Several players in the late 1920's tried to amplify their guitars, by fixing a record player pickup to the underside of the soundboard, with poor results. It was 1931 before any real interest in the electric guitar resurfaced, with the introduction of the Rickenbacher Frying Pan. Needless to say, that instrument changed forever the look and sound of Hawaiian music.

"Later, in 1933, Loar formed the Vivi-Tone Company in Kalamazoo MI and developed some of the earliest hollow, solid body, and semi-hollow electric guitars ever produced. He was indeed a visionary, producing ideas for electric instruments that are now being utilized, such as electric violins consisting of only a neck, head stock and tuners, a stick body, and pick-up. Loar's problem was business. He didn't have the business acumen nor the business personnel to make his designs successful commercially. "

1961 Gibson lap steel, natural Korina wood, serial 34946
Steve Evans photo

The Rickenbacker Company

In 1931, with the pressures of lawsuits, decreasing sales, and the depression upon them, George Beauchamp (who was still the general manager at National) and his new ally Adolph Rickenbacher turned their attention to developing an electrically amplified steel guitar. To do this, they formed a new and separate company, Ro-Pat-In, in October of 1931. The idea of electrification wasn't new, many others were working on the same idea. Beauchamp must have seen an electric guitar built around 1928 by Hank Kuhrmeyer of the Stromberg-Voisinet Co. The instrument was advertised in the same 1929 catalog that announced National's new Triolian. Kuhrmeyer's electric guitar was not very successful as it was built on the principle of amplifying body vibrations rather than string vibrations. By 1931 Beauchamp, Paul Barth, and Adolph Rickenbacher had developed and marketed the first truly successful electric guitar. It was the Model A-22 nicknamed the "Frying Pan", "The Panhandle", the "Pie-pan" and the "Pancake" because of the shape of its aluminum body. Its pickup design became the industry standard.

Adolph Rickenbacher in 1972 with first frying pan

Acceptance by the public was slow at first, due in part to the depression. The first person to play one in public was Jack Miller who played it at Grauman's Chinese Theater in 1932, in Orville Knapp's orchestra. They immediately went on a tour across the country, which gave the frypan good exposure and public approval. Another who gave it a very early boost was Alvino Rey who played an Electra steel guitar in the Horace Heidt band, and the first Hawaiian we're aware of who played it was Andy Iona. The first recording with an electric steel that we know of today was done in New York on Feb. 22nd, 1933 by a group called the "Noelani Hawaiian Orchestra". It was on Victor Records, the titles "Dreams of Aloha", "Hawaiian Ripple", "Alekoki", and "Hawaiian Love". The steel guitarist was not identified. The steel guitar had often been seen in dance bands previously, but when electrification gave it more volume and sustain its romantic voice was in demand in the modern dance band.

The difference between the frypan and other inventions was in the two magnets which faced each other with the vibrating strings passing through them. The first were of cast aluminum, heavier, considered to have the best tone. Later frypans were built of sheet aluminum (for lightness) and soldered together. The aim was to produce a rigid body which would not vibrate as wood does, so that all vibration was in the strings and passed on to the pick-up. To keep the hollow neck rigid but light, it was stuffed tightly with newspapers. Bakelite is a dense synthetic material, so in 1935 it was used to build the next model. Earlier models were signed with the true German spelling, "Rickenbacher", later simplified to "Rickenbacker". In 1934 they built a 7-string steel guitar, then 8, then 10 strings.

When the 7-string models were first built, it was for the purpose of adding the flatted 7th interval on the lowest string so that seventh chords could be played. By 1950 they were making double and triple necks. Both the aluminum and bakelite models expanded and contracted due to temperature changes, which means they went out of tune. To solve the problem, the company put metal inserts into the necks to make them more rigid. The fryan's prototype was built of maple, 31 and 3/4 inches long, 7 inches wide, 1 and 5/8 inches thick. It is on display at the company's Santa Ana, CA office.

While the work on the new electric guitar was going on, George was still the general manager at National. When he and Rickenbacher formed their new company, Ro-Pat-In Corp., Makers of Electra String Instruments, the board at National voted to oust him. It wasn't long before the Dopyera brothers were back on the board at National (1933) and both companies - National Dobro and Rickenbacher - continued to work together, sometimes co-operatively, sometimes not. For both companies, steel guitars were the biggest sellers of all their instruments.

In 1934 the Ro-Pat-In company's name was changed to the Electro String Instrument Corp, making Rickenbacker Electro instruments. Then the company was sold to F.C.Hallin 1953 who moved it to the present address, corner of Stevens and S. Main in Santa Ana, California. In 1965 Mr. Hall changed the company name to Rickenbacker, Inc. and in 1984 it was changed to its present name, Rickenbacker International Corp. It is now under the leadership of John Hall, F.C. Hall's son.

c. 1960 catalog

c. 1937 catalog

Jerry Byrd and Speedy West
having fun a 1958 NAMN show.
Forest White from Fender looking on.

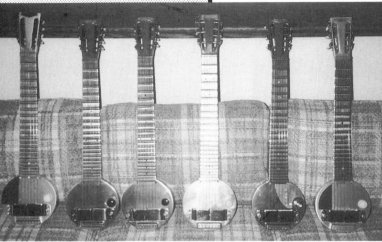

Rickenbacher frypan,
6-string, 1937
Ed Mayer collection

7- string
Rickenbacker
Leo Rajotte collection

**A rare assembly of
7-string frypans.
The one fourth from the
right once belonged to
Dick McIntire.**
Dirk Vogel collection

Rickenbacker Electro N.S.,
6-string student model with
custom pick-up, 1952..
Stamped from high-grade
metal, finished in two-tone
grey baked enamel finish.
Ed Mayer collection

Four long-scale frypans, the
two in the middle were once
owned by Dick McIntire.
Dirk Vogel collection

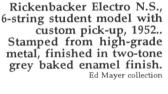

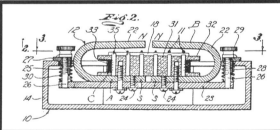

From patent filed
June 2, 1934 by
George Beauchamp
detailing the pickup

6-string
Rickenbacker J6
Rudolf Barten

Academy
Rickenbacker
6-string 1948
Ed Mayer collection

Rickenbacker
all chrome 6-string,
1940, serial 131321
Ed Mayer collection

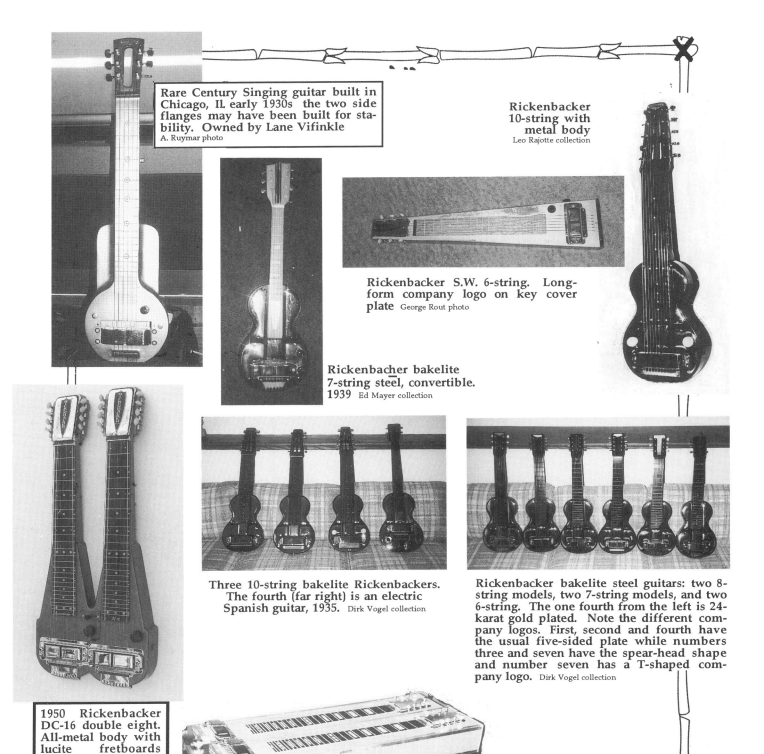

Rare Century Singing guitar built in Chicago, IL early 1930s the two side flanges may have been built for stability. Owned by Lane Vifinkle
A. Ruymar photo

Rickenbacker 10-string with metal body
Leo Rajotte collection

Rickenbacker S.W. 6-string. Long-form company logo on key cover plate
George Rout photo

Rickenbacher bakelite 7-string steel, convertible. 1939
Ed Mayer collection

Three 10-string bakelite Rickenbackers. The fourth (far right) is an electric Spanish guitar, 1935.
Dirk Vogel collection

Rickenbacker bakelite steel guitars: two 8-string models, two 7-string models, and two 6-string. The one fourth from the left is 24-karat gold plated. Note the different company logos. First, second and fourth have the usual five-sided plate while numbers three and seven have the spear-head shape and number seven has a T-shaped company logo.
Dirk Vogel collection

1950 Rickenbacker DC-16 double eight. All-metal body with lucite fretboards and chrome head covers.
Bobby Black photo

Rickenbacker Console 208 (double 8) with polished metal cappings on ends and edges of body. The triple necks were model 508 (three sets of 8 strings) and model 518 (with 8, 10, and 8 strings). Note the bar pattern fret markers.
Leo Rajotte collection

The question of who first invented the electrified steel guitar has often been debated. Many give credit to a Texan named Bob Dunn who, in 1935, strung his Martin guitar with magnetized strings, raised them off the neck, attached a Volutone pick-up to the sound hole, and plugged the whole apparatus into an amplifier. He first played it in the Milton Brown And His Musical Brownies orchestra. However, it appears that Rickenbacker actually had the jump on him by several years.

First Dobro Electric

In the early stages of the electrification of Dobro instruments, it is recorded that Art Stimpson, a Dobro player and inventor from Spokane WA had visited the factory in Los Angeles in 1931 with an idea for attaching a magnetic telephone pickup to a six-string guitar. He had actually built an electric guitar and performed with it on radio. In August of 1932 the Dopyeras put the first acoustic bodied electric Dobro on the market. They did not build many, as the pickup was so weak two large amplifiers were needed. In late 1933 or early 1934 a more successful cast aluminum Hawaiian Dobro was put on the market with a stronger pickup. By 1933 they were advertising all-electric Dobro guitars and amplifiers for $135.00, "No blare! No distortion!" They were built of wood with one huge cone and two very small cones.

National Electric Guitars

National did not get into the business of building electric steel guitars as quickly as their competitors did. In 1933 they became interested when two gentlemen, Messrs. Kirkoff and Hoter visited their shop and showed them an electric pick-up. By 1934, before National merged with Dobro, they had their first electric model on the market. After the merger, National built solid body electric steels of bakelite and plastic-covered wood with all the variations of strings and multi-necks that were built by their contemporaries. Two of National's electric models were the New Yorker of black and white celluloid over wood, and the Chicagoan built in 1939 of blond wood.

During this time, the company changed hands several times and produced guitars under various names: National, Supro, Valco, Kay, and Seeburg. Dealerships were handled by Gretsch. In 1968 the company folded. John Dopyera died in January, 1988 at the age of 94. Other family members continue to build the family guitar under the name of Original in comparatively small numbers. The Dopyera brothers came out with one last model built in the authentic 1929 style, called the Hound Dog, and one with a metal body that sounds more like a Dobro than a National.

Dobro electric, mid-30's. One-piece aluminum alloy casting, has natural high polish finish contrasted with black paneling, metal frets with pearl position inlays. "Dobro" with lyre cast in aluminum body. Same guitar is on display in Roy Acuff museum marked "very rare".
Ken Autenrieth photo

National New Yorker long scale. Positive tone control, three positions. Exceptionally good harmonics, lively tone and response. Ken Autenrieth photo

National 6-string, 1949
Ed Mayer collection

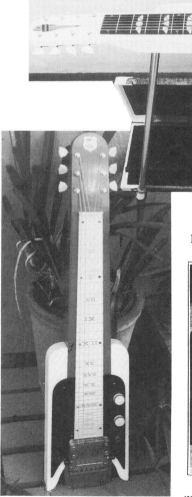

National 8-string, Serial 39932, has three adjustable legs.
Ken Gibson photo

TEAM OF "PRINCESS & WILLIE" KAIAMA
Native Hawaiian Artists of Stage and Screen
From the 1940 National catalog

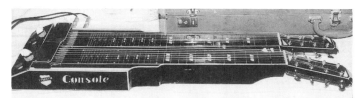

Double 8 National Console
A. Ruymar photo

Three National
6-strings,
outer ones
Triplex Chord
Changer 1949,
center New
Yorker model
1946 Ed Mayer collection

National Grand
Console double
eight, 1946.
Three tone
choices, individu-
ally adjustable
pole pieces to
assure correct
balance between
strings. This
model comes also
as a triple neck.
Ed Mayer collection

Supro 6-string
(National
Dobro) solid
cast body, split
bar pick-up,
rosewood
fretboard
with pearl
button
markers.
Volume
control only.
Ivan Sinclair photo

Supro 6-string
(National),
1955
Ed Mayer collection

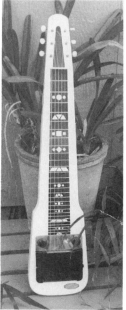

Supro 6-string
(National)
1965
Ed Mayer collection

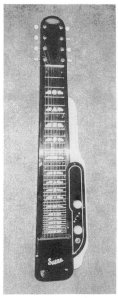

Supro 8-string,
has three legs
George Rout photo

From the 1940 National catalog

TRIPLETS
HERMAN, JOE & WILLIAM PLUT
Talented 12-year-old brothers • Chicago

The True Facts On The Invention Of The Electric Guitar And Electric Bass

By Paul H. "Bud" Tutmarc

"I have been urged by many persons over the years to write the TRUE FACTS regarding the creation of the very first electric guitar, which was a Hawaiian guitar because the inventor was an accomplished artist on that instrument. I am speaking of my father, Paul H. Tutmarc.

"My dad (born May 29, 1896) had a love for the Hawaiian steel guitar from the time he was 15 years old, and played a Knutsen. We moved to Seattle in 1928 where he was the tenor soloist in several of the downtown theaters. He worked on the Fanchon & Marco circuits and was an instructor of the Hawaiian guitar.

"In late 1930 or early 1931, Art Stimpson from Spokane WA, came to Seattle especially to meet my father. Art was an electrical enthusiast. He had been tinkering with a telephone, wondering how the vocal vibrations against the enclosed diaphragm were picked up by the magnet and coil behind the diaphragm and carried by the wires to another telephone. My father became interested, noting that tapping on the telephone was also picked up by the magnetic field created behind the diaphragm. He was encouraged to see if he could build his own magnetic pickup.

"He started with a rather large horseshoe shaped magnet and wound some coils with the smallest wire he could obtain, which was either No. 38 or No. 40. I remember seeing this first magnetic pickup of his. It was all wrapped up in friction tape and about the size of a grapefruit.

"A brilliant young radio repairman, Bob Wisner, helped my dad rewire a radio to get some amplification of his magnetic pickup. My dad then started working with an old round-hole flat-topped guitar and discovered the pickup would pick up the sound from a plucked string and carry it through to the adapted radio. So, this large pickup was eventually installed INSIDE the guitar with a polepiece sticking up through a slot he cut in the top of the guitar near the bridge, and the electric guitar was on its way. Dad made a solid body for his electric guitar idea and his first one was octagon shaped at the bridge end containing the pickup, and then a long slender square cornered neck out to the patent heads.

"Before he actually made this solid body guitar, he electrified every instrument he could get his hands on: zithers and pianos and Spanish guitars. He would break up two guitars just to get the necks and fretboards and glue them onto a flat top guitar, having three necks with three different tunings. He made a solid body (black walnut) guitar with FIVE sets of strings, five tunings. The guitar was about 24 inches wide and the neck about 20 inches wide. I can remember his demonstrating his "out of this world" guitar at the local Sears-Roebuck store in South Seattle.

"He saw the possibilities of manufacturing these guitars for sale, so he sent in to the U.S. Patent office for information regarding any type of electric stringed instruments. A complete search was made which I recall cost him $300. There were NO types, whatsoever, presented to the U.S. Patent Office, so my dad knew he was the FIRST. However, the chances of patenting an electric pickup would be nil, as Bell & Company had long since covered that.

"**Audiovox Manufacturing Co.** After building a few guitars out of solid black walnut, dad decided he would do all the assembly work and electrical manufacturing, and he contracted Emerald Baunsgard to do the woodworking. Then he started the Audiovox Manufacturing Company. Emerald was a master at inlay work so the black walnut guitars all had inlaid frets, inlaid pearl position markings, and beautiful hand-rubbed finishes. The guitars were very quickly accepted on the market. My dad also made solid body Spanish guitars but they were not readily received.

"**Push Button Tuning, and Pedals.** A sales brochure printed in 1935 in Seattle shows Model 336-Duo, 6-string double neck with the caption 'This instrument is especially designed for professionals and artists. The two necks give this guitar many combinations. The DUO is supplied with Paul Tutmarc's latest invention, Automatic tuning. At the press of a button, ANOTHER TUNING!' The button lever was at the patent head area of the guitar. You could pre-set the amount of pressure that would be put on the string and raise the pitch a half step or a full step. Dad very soon after this started making a pedal guitar. I have one of his early pedal steels, made about 1949. He made it just for me with my name on it. It had three pedals.

"**String Bass.** Dad's first string bass was carved out of solid soft white pine, the size and shape of a cello. To this instrument he fastened one of his friction tape pickups and the first electric bass was created. That was in 1933. The Seattle Post-Intelligencer Newspaper published a photograph of him showing it to a girl. My dad had set out to create an instrument which was small and light-weight, yet capable of producing more sound than several upright acoustic basses. He went on to make a 42-inch long solid body bass out of black walnut, like his guitars, and the electric bass was launched. My father advertised his electric guitars, single and double necked steel guitars, AND his new electric bass in a local school's 1937 yearbook. That certainly establishes a definite date. I played the electric bass in John Marshall Junior High School, here in Seattle, in 1937 and 1938.

"**Amplifiers.** Dad's amplifiers were designed by Bob Wisner. Incidentally, this same Bob Wisner later worked on the atom bomb in Wendover, UT and in Almagordo NM, then with the Boeing Company on the Bomarc missile program, and eventually in Cape Kennedy, with the moon rockets. While the first astronauts were on their way to the moon, Bob Wisner passed away. He never knew they made a successful landing.

"During this time, I had become a steel guitarist under my father's instruction. Sol Ho'opi'i, the great Hawaiian steel guitarist, was my father's idol. It was our joy to meet Sol personally in 1942 and we were all very close for the next 11 years until Sol's death here in Seattle in 1953. It was my pleasure to play with Sol on many occasions. His widow, Anna Ho'opi'i, lives here in Seattle.

Sol Ho'opi'i and Bud Tutmarc playing a Hawaiian steel guitar
duet together, backed by the local band., 1952 Bud Tutmarc photo

"**Pickups, Six Inches in Front of the Bridge.** By 1948 I had begun manufacturing instruments too. I was making a guitar for an excellent Hawaiian guitarist, Ray Morales, who wanted one that would give him more depth of sound on the bass strings. I placed a pickup in various places over the strings and found that putting it about six inches IN FRONT of the bridge gave much more depth of sound. Accordingly, I changed all my pickups on my electric basses to that position. This is still prevalent in basses today. Also, I found that slanting the pickup so that the polepiece would be farther from the bridge under the bass strings and closer to the bridge under the treble strings gave much more depth to the bass strings while not hurting the treble sound of the higher strings. I have a picture of Sol Ho'opi'i holding one of my slanted pick-up guitars in 1952. With Sol passing away in 1953, I certainly have proof of being the first to slant the guitar pickup. You will note that almost every guitar now has a slanted pickup, near the bridge.

"Well, that's about all I can tell you about the first electric guitar, and the FIRST electric bass. My father, Paul H. Tutmarc, was THE MAN!"

Paul H. Tutmarc, Sr. shows his double neck steel guitar to Dick McIntire, 1940
Bud Tutmarc photo

Sol Ho'opi'i, 1952, proudly displays a 6-string steel guitar with slanted pick-up built by Bud Tutmarc. Bud Tutmarc photo

Dickerson - Magnatone

These guitars, small in stature, had a magnificent tone. Their originator, Delbert J. Dickerson, began manufacturing guitars in the 1930's, supplying teachers and schools. The structure of the guitar was simple - a volume control, six strings, with the pickup and magnets built right into the pine or spruce body, covered with a pearlite finish. Identification could be made by the diamond-shaped decal at the tail end. They were small compared to other electric steel guitars: 28 1/4 inches long, 7 1/2 inches wide with a 22 1/2 inch scale length. At the height of their manufacturing career they turned out 200 guitars per week under 10 different brands as ordered by music schools or music outlets. The company sold out in 1944 to Gaston Fator and he later sold it to Magna Electronics who turned out the guitars under the name Magnatone.

Popular steel guitarist Margie Mays plays an ancient 6-string Magnatone Multi-Matic with 8 little buttons. By just pushing one button (at an HSGA convention in Joliet, IL) she had an instant change of tuning, so for the fun of it she demonstrated by changing to several different tunings as she played a song. It seemed like the answer to the pedal steel guitarist's prayers, it was so small and neat and the tuning change was so fast and correct. Only a few were built because of the whirring sound made by the solenoids, unacceptable in a recording studio.

Magnatone 6-string built in the 1940's.
Jyunichi Yoshie photo

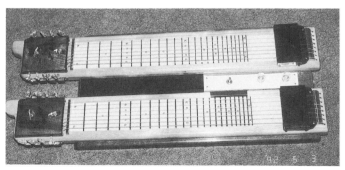

Dick Lloyd's 1949 double 8 Magnatone serial 23129
A. Ruymar photo

128

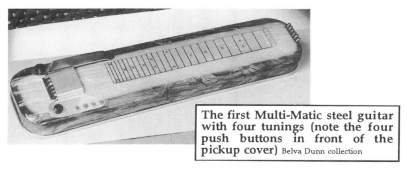

The first Multi-Matic steel guitar with four tunings (note the four push buttons in front of the pickup cover) Belva Dunn collection

6-string Magnatone Multi-matic with eight push-buttons for changing tunings. Played by Margie Mays at HSGA convention in Joliet, 1988 L. Ruymar photo

Dick McIntire (L) and Sol Ho'opi'i (R) discuss the merits of the Dickerson 6-string student model and two Dickerson amplifiers
Belva Dunn photo

A more personal point of view is given in the following, written by the son-in-law of Del Dickerson, Wes Dunn:

"Delbert Dickerson manufactured guitars for the following companies: The Varsity Guitar And Amplifier, The Southern California Music Co., The Oahu Publishing Co., Bronson Publishing Co., and Roland Ball (father of Ernest Ball, the steel guitarist), who now has multiple studios and stores. Each had their own name, not 'Dickerson'.

"Mr. Dickerson made his first steel guitar for his daughter, Belva. It was not long until Sol Ho'opi'i, Belva's instructor, asked Mr. Dickerson to make one for him. Mr. Dickerson applied for a patent and he was ready to go. The Hawaiian boys saw Sol's guitar and amplifier and were impressed so much that Dick McIntire, Sam Koki, Eddie Bush, and many others were soon playing the Dickerson guitar. He would make the guitars in the color of their choice, covered with 'mother of pearl'. Mr. Dickerson specialized in student models, however, as he tried to bring down the cost so that any family could afford one. When he tried to get Belva into the school orchestra, he was refused as they had no sheet music for the steel guitar. This would not stop him! He said, "Give her the first violin part," and with reluctance the director did so. Playing the violin part helped Belva with her fast picking, which amazed even Sol Ho'opi'i, her teacher, from whom she had been taking lessons since the age of seven.

"Years later, when Belva was in high school, Sol decided to leave the 'Memories of Hawai'i' radio broadcast, which was transcribed and sent overseas to our service men. He asked Belva if she would take over for him as steel guitarist, which she did. One evening I thought I would go up to the radio station to see Sol, who was my steel guitar teacher, and for whom I had played standard guitar on various occasions. To my surprise, Sol was not there but I recognized his wife Georgia Stiffler on 'ukulele, brother-in-law Eddie Vance on standard guitar, and two whom I had never met - Belva Dickerson on steel guitar and Elsie Jaggers on vibraphone, who was also starting to take steel guitar lessons from Sol. Eddie told me that he was leaving and wondered if I would take his place on standard guitar, which I did. Belva and I also played for U.S.O. dances and many other occasions. Not too long after, we were engaged and on her 19th birthday, 47 years ago, Belva and I were married.

"When World War II was over Mr. Dickerson decided that he did not want to manufacture guitars any longer, so he sold his patent rights to Gaston Fator, who had several music studios and a store. He manufactured a few and then sold the patent rights to Magnatone.

"One day I asked Mr. Dickerson if he would make Belva a multiple tuning guitar and he said, 'Sure, a push-button guitar, but not pedal.' At this time we had three music studios in Southern California and we were teaching over 600 students per week. Magnatone would have us test out every new guitar and amplifier and so often we would shake our heads and it was 'back to the drawing board'. When they saw Belva's multiple tunings guitar they wanted to start manufacturing them. Mr. Dickerson agreed if they would make only six and let our students buy them and test them. Margie Thompson (now Margie Mays), Belva's favorite student, received the first one and I had Mr. Dickerson OK it for eight push buttons instead of four. Soon our students were playing all six and as usual there were many bugs to be worked out, with Mr. Dickerson the consultant. Magnatone felt it wise, due to technical problems, to discontinue the Multi-Matic guitar.

"Sol Ho'opi'i especially liked the raised hand rest that Mr. Dickerson made on all his guitars. Ernie Tavares, who was working for Fender, stopped by and was fascinated with Belva's push button guitar. He offered Mr. Dickerson a nice sum to build him one, but was refused. The last guitar that Mr. Dickerson made for Belva was an 8-string Console foot pedal guitar that folds and will fit into a compact zippered case, and of course the proud father had to put Belva's name on it!"

The Alkire Eharp

Another ingenious problem solver was Eddie Alkire, a West Virginian, who felt the steel guitar was functionally limited. The story of his publishing and teaching career has been told in an earlier chapter of this book dealing with steel guitar schools. In his search for more harmonic possibilities, in 1939 he developed the 10-string Eharp. Alkire was highly acclaimed as having brought the steel guitar into full status as a musical instrument.

The first three models of the Eharp had ten strings. So successful were they that Alkire continued to improve on them. In 1972 Eddie built a fourth handmade instrument he called the "Superaxe". It had 20 strings and was too heavy. In his fifth instrument called the "Cruiser" he succeeded in reducing the weight by a third. In 1975 he started his sixth instrument made of oak, which he called the "Islander". It was beautiful but still too heavy. If he hoped to carry it to Hawai'i it would have to be lighter than that. So, instrument #7, the "Mini-surfer", a 12-pounder, was born. He premiered this one at the 19th annual convention of the Fretted Instrument Guild of America at Asheville, NC in 1976. He had many more exciting plans for the world of Hawaiian music but was called to meet his maker in 1981. In 1983 he was posthumously inducted into the Steel Guitar Hall of Fame.

10-string
Alkire Eharp
Leo Rajotte collection

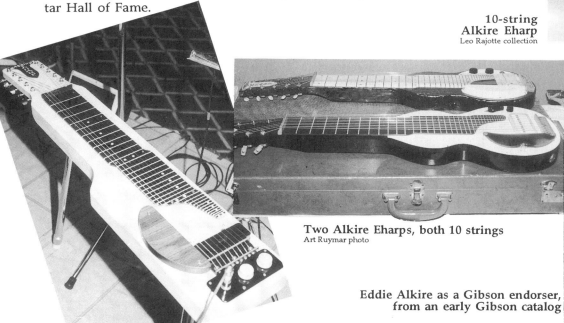

Two Alkire Eharps, both 10 strings
Art Ruymar photo

Eddie Alkire as a Gibson endorser,
from an early Gibson catalog

EDDIE ALKIRE
Easton, Pa.

10-string
Alkire Eharp with hand rest,
on legs Art Ruymar photo

Fender Guitar Co.

From a small garage in Fullerton CA to the giant conglomerate of CBS Columbia which acquired Fender in 1965, the story of Leo Fender is the story of American creativeness and business acumen. The names Stringmaster, Stratocaster and Telecaster are synonymous with the name Fender. A creative genius, Leo Fender began making guitars with pickups as early as 1925, crude as they were (since he was basically a radio repairman). Nothing significant happened until he teamed up with Doc Kaufmann in 1946. The first instrument they built was a steel guitar, brand name "K and F". The K for Kaufman and the F for Fender. In 1946 the partnership broke up and Leo Fender carried on, to become <u>the</u> name in guitars. In later years he produced Musicman electric guitars and amplifiers, also the G.& L. products. They stopped making steel guitars in the 1960's.

The K&F nameplate, mounted on one of the early steels

The Stratocaster design has been credited to the late Freddie Tavares who began employment with Leo Fender in 1953 as a design engineer. Freddie designed the famous body which Rock 'N Roll stars around the world would herald as the ultimate from the fifties until today. A rock guitar designed by a Hawaiian. and they said the twain would never meet!

At the HSGA convention in Joliet IL in 1991, at one time there were 10 Fender necks on stage, so prized are they for their tone. One triple-neck owned by Frank Miller was played by Barney Isaacs of Hawai'i, a second triple Fender was played by Dick Sanft of Florida, and a Fender quad was played by Duke Kaleolani Ching, of California, who actually uses all four necks in any given song. The old style Fender tube amplifier is also highly prized as being the most compatible with Hawaiian steel guitar, giving the richest, most mellow tone.

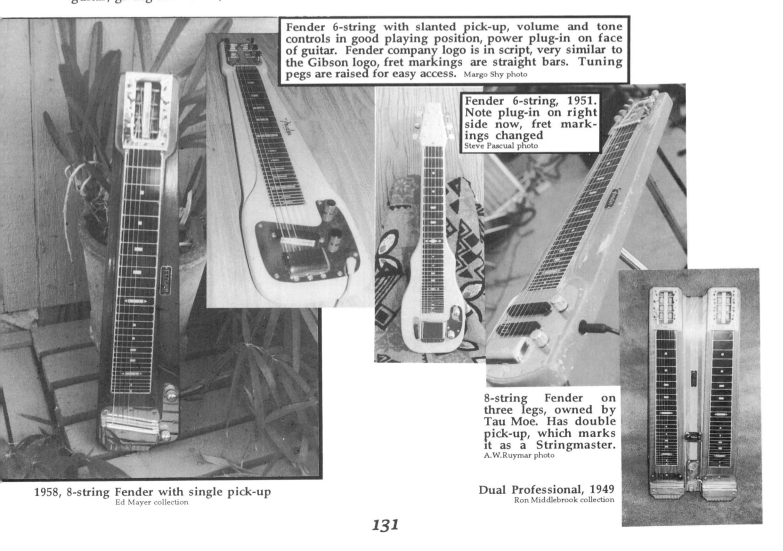

Fender 6-string with slanted pick-up, volume and tone controls in good playing position, power plug-in on face of guitar. Fender company logo is in script, very similar to the Gibson logo, fret markings are straight bars. Tuning pegs are raised for easy access. Margo Shy photo

Fender 6-string, 1951. Note plug-in on right side now, fret markings changed Steve Pascual photo

8-string Fender on three legs, owned by Tau Moe. Has double pick-up, which marks it as a Stringmaster. A.W.Ruymar photo

1958, 8-string Fender with single pick-up
Ed Mayer collection

Dual Professional, 1949
Ron Middlebrook collection

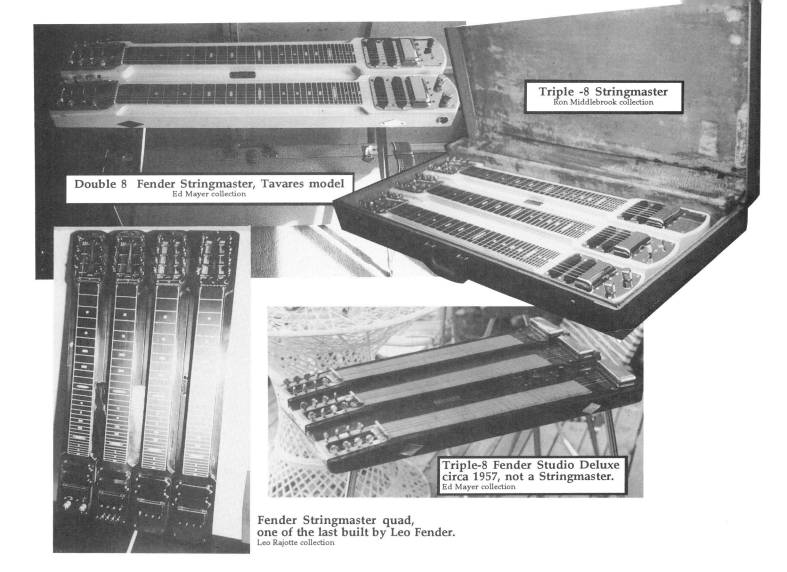

Double 8 Fender Stringmaster, Tavares model
Ed Mayer collection

Triple -8 Stringmaster
Ron Middlebrook collection

Triple-8 Fender Studio Deluxe circa 1957, not a Stringmaster.
Ed Mayer collection

Fender Stringmaster quad, one of the last built by Leo Fender.
Leo Rajotte collection

...And Others

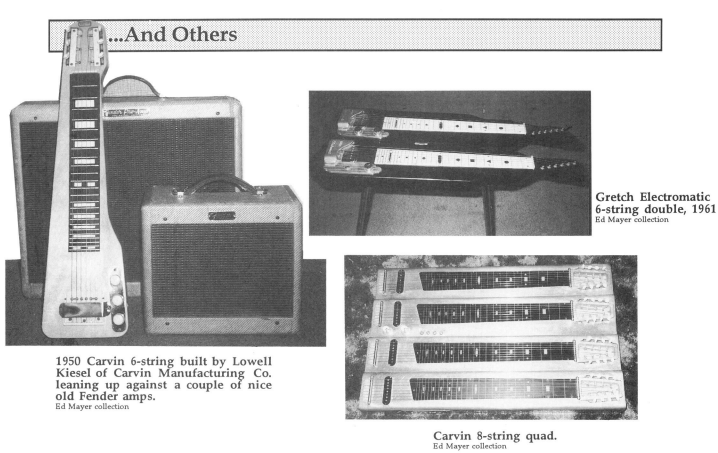

1950 Carvin 6-string built by Lowell Kiesel of Carvin Manufacturing Co. leaning up against a couple of nice old Fender amps.
Ed Mayer collection

Gretch Electromatic 6-string double, 1961
Ed Mayer collection

Carvin 8-string quad.
Ed Mayer collection

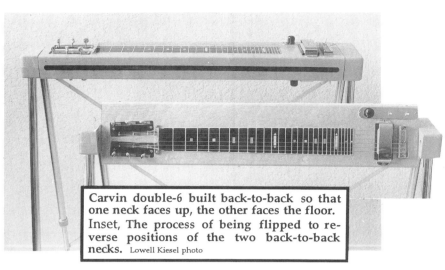

Carvin double-6 built back-to-back so that one neck faces up, the other faces the floor. Inset, The process of being flipped to reverse positions of the two back-to-back necks. Lowell Kiesel photo

Matses "Pro-Steel" 6-string custom built by Matses Steel Guitars, still being produced Chuck Matses photo

Oahu's very first student guitar (acoustic), with adjuster to raise the strings, flat bar, three picks, and 52 lessons Oahu Publications photo

Hollywood lap steel, made in early 1930s. Has small metal plate in sound hole to help amplify the sound. Paper fret board with the frets and all the notes printed on it. Ron Middlebrook collection

Oahu's "Troubador" 6-string electric covered with jewel-like mother-of-pearl material called Lumarith, in a delicate shade of peach. Built by the Dickerson Bros. of Los Angeles, complete with equally beautiful 20-watt amplifier, "El Capitan" Don Wright photo

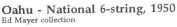

Oahu - National 6-string, 1950
Ed Mayer collection

A set of four Oahu 6-string Leilanis, 1955.
Ed Mayer collection

OAHU
DIANA

Rhapsody in Gold

Must Be Compared To It!

Gold-plated, deluxe style patent heads with patented SafeTiString posts.

Gracefully designed solid wood body—hand rubbed and polished.

Genuine rosewood fingerboard—heavy brass frets.

Full size 25⅛" playing scale.

Fingertip tone and volume controls.

OAHU
DIANA
Rhapsody In Gold

Made So Fine That All Others
Must Be Compared To It!

Gold-plated patented SafTiString posts
Gold-plated tuning keys
Gold-plated patent head covers
Gold "Diana" nameplate
Gold-engraved Clef design
on plastic unit cover

1950's
Kalamazoo
Lap Steel, wood
body finished in
dark burgundy
paint with at-
tached cord,
Steve Evans photo

PRESENTING THE WORLD'S FINEST ELECTRIC HAWAIIAN GUITARS THE "BRONSON BIG THREE"

owned and endorsed by America's foremost Professionals, famous on Radio, Stage and Screen. Truly the "ARTIST GUITARS" of them all. You, too, will agree when you have seen and heard these colorful, beautiful instruments in their superior tone and rich lustrous finish. They do, without the slightest question, pass in beauty, tone, and performance anything we have heretofore presented.

THERE ARE THREE DISTINCTIVE MODELS:

The No. GA-120 BRONSON SUPER ZEPHYR : Guitar is finished in Silver Grey with inlaid tinsel keyboard and trim. The amplifier has six metal tubes, giving an overall gain of 128 D.B. with an undistorted output of 20 watts, using a High Fidelity 12-inch curved speaker cone. It has a frequency response from 40 to 12,000 cycles and accomodations for two instruments and one microphone. Also has a tone control on the amplifier.

PRICE—Guitar and Amplifier.................. $120.00
Strong reinforced case to fit, silk plush lined.... 10.50

The No. GA-100 BRONSON STREAMLINER : Guitar is finished in Maroon-Golden combination. The amplifier has four tubes, so constructed as to give five tube performance. It has a 10-inch High Fidelity speaker, with an undistorted output of 15 watts.

PRICE—Guitar and amplifier $100.00
Strong reinforced case to fit, silk plush lined ... 10.50

The No. GA-495 BRONSON SINGING ELECTRIC : Guitar is finished in Dark Green Marble effect. The amplifier is small and light in weight covered with Rayon Flock in a color to match the Guitar. It is equipped with a High Fidelity 6-inch curved cone speaker. It has three tubes, giving an output of five watts.

PRICE—Guitar and Amplifier........................ $49.50
Special Shaped Keratol Case to fit................. 4.50

Further detailed information and bona fide endorsements will be furnished on request.
If your dealer cannot supply you, write direct to

BRONSON MUSIC CORPORATION
KERR BLDG.,   DETROIT, MICHIGAN
MANUFACTURERS   **DISTRIBUTORS**

c. 1940

Graduate to the Singing Guitar

Electric Hawaiian Guitar Outfit

$37.50 Cash
$4.00 Down

See Inside Back Cover for Sears Easy Terms

Never before has such a high quality outfit been offered at such a low price. Just right for concert or solo playing! Plenty of volume to fill a dance hall. A brand new model designed to save you money. **Guitar:** Latest type magnetic pick-up unit, with separate volume and tone controls on top. Equipped with special electric guitar flat-wound strings. Cable is detachable microphone type. Improved nickel-plated combination bridge and tail piece. Body is selected seasoned hardwood in a 2-tone shaded mahogany finish with brown striping on edge. Rosewood fingerboard, professional type frets. Mother-of-pearl position dots. **Amplifier:** 4 tubes, 2 jacks—one with separate volume control for use with microphone. 8-inch dynamic speaker—6-8 watt output. 110-volt, 60 cycle A.C. only. Oblong hardwood cabinet finished to match guitar. Outfit complete with sturdy brown Keratol covered chipboard Guitar case and illustrated instruction book.

12 F 02302—Complete outfit. Shpg. wt., 26 lbs. .$37.50
▲ 12 F 02307—Guitar and case. Shipping weight, 12 pounds $18.95
▲ 12 F 02308—Amplifier only. Shipping weight, 19 pounds $22.95

Electric Hawaiian Outfit

$55.00 Cash
$5.00 Down

Ⓐ Now you can get the instrument that is a "must" in big name bands. Sells for $85 elsewhere. **Guitar:** Selected seasoned hardwood. Finished in curly grained shaded Mahogany. 23-inch scale, accurately fretted. Improved magnetic style pick-up with string volume balancing device. Separate tone and volume controls. **Amplifier:** Latest type with 3 stages of amplification. 5 tubes. 8-inch dynamic type speaker. 2 input jacks for one instrument and microphone. **Amplifier Cabinet:** Hard wood, covered with brown tweed Keratol. Outfit includes tweed covered Guitar case, rust colored velveteen lined. Instruction book. For 60-cycle, 110-volt A.C.

▲ 12 F 02303—Complete Outfit. Shpg. wt., 28 lbs $55.00
▲ 12 F 02305—Same as above, but Spanish Guitar. Shpg. wt .36 lbs.$59.50
▲ 12 F 02304—Hawaiian guitar only, with case. Shpg. wt., 11 lbs.$24.50
▲ 12 F 02306—Spanish guitar only; with case. Shpg. wt., 16 lbs . $29.50
▲ 12 F 02311—Amplifier only. Shpg. wt., 17 lbs $34.75

Deluxe Electric Guitar

$95.00 Cash
$8.00 Down

Ⓑ *(text partially obscured)* on white celluloid ... 23-in. scale. Separate ... controls. **Amplifier:** ... speaker—bass reflex ... ber—6 tubes. 14 to 16 ... torted output. 4 input ... wood cabinet covered with ... glazed brown tweed material ... volt, 60-cycle A.C. Guitar ... for amplifier.

12F2330F—Complete ... case for guitar. Shpg. wt ... **Spanish Guitar Outfit** ... with fully arched ... size guitar. Maple ba... Spruce top. Celluloid ... With case to match amp... Shipped from factory ... You pay freight from ...
12 F 2332F—Shpg. wt ...
12 F 2331F—Hawaiian ... with case. Shpg. wt., 18...
12 F 2333F—Spanish ... with case. Shpg. wt....
12 F 2334F—Amplifier ... Shipping weight, 40 lb...

Top and Left, Advertisement for "Singing Guitar" in Sears, Roebuck & Co. 1940 Copy says "Put yourself into the spotlight with a singing guitar! A new instrument-fast-growing in popularity- greatly demanded in orchestras, and outstanding for solo playing . . .

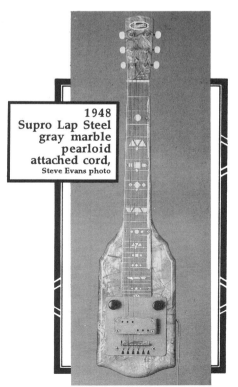

1948 Supro Lap Steel gray marble pearloid attached cord, Steve Evans photo

Hawaiian Electric Mono-Unit

$75.00 Cash
$7.00 Down

Put yourself into the spotlight with a singing guitar! A new instrument—fast-growing in popularity—greatly demanded in orchestras, and outstanding for solo playing. This long-lasting, beautiful-sounding guitar will be an endless source of pleasure as long as you own it. This model is exclusive with Sears! The amplifier is contained in the same cabinet that holds the guitar. **Handy and easy to carry. Hawaiian Style Guitar:** Selected, seasoned maple body, 31½ inches long. Highly polished shaded Mahogany finish with hand inlaid black and white celluloid. Ebonized fingerboard, with mother-of-pearl position dots. 23-inch scale. Latest, improved, built-in super-sensitive pick-up unit. Separate volume and tone controls on top of guitar. Adjustable pole pieces for balancing the tone of each string. **Powerful Amplifier:** 4 stages of amplification with 10 to 12 watts undistorted output. No hum. 6 tubes and large 10-inch high fidelity speaker. Size, 33x9x14 inches. 3 input jacks. Can be used with microphone. Airplane striped Keratol covered wood case with curtain to protect speaker. Complete with illustrated instruction book. **Shipped from factory in Chicago. You pay freight from there. Order from your nearest Mail Order House.**

12 F 2320F—Shipping weight, 35 pounds $75.00

135

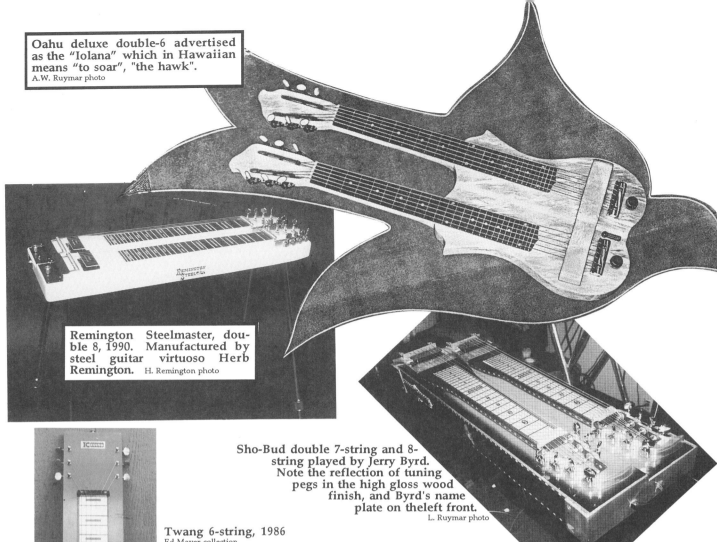

Remington Steelmaster, double 8, 1990. Manufactured by steel guitar virtuoso Herb Remington. H. Remington photo

Sho-Bud double 7-string and 8-string played by Jerry Byrd. Note the reflection of tuning pegs in the high gloss wood finish, and Byrd's name plate on the left front. L. Ruymar photo

Twang 6-string, 1986
Ed Mayer collection

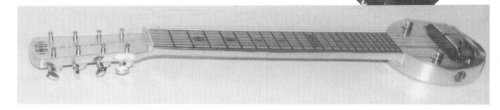

Sho-Bud Jerry Byrd frypan 8-string built in 1980's by Shot Jackson, Nashville. Same design (with horseshoe magnets) as the original Rickenbacker frypan, built in long-scale and short-scale models. Fret markings spell Jerry Byrd's name. A.W. Ruymar photo

Guitars Built In Other Countries

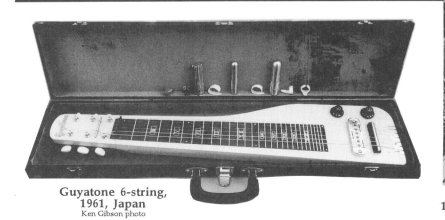

Guyatone 6-string, 1961, Japan
Ken Gibson photo

Höfner, 6-string, 1950, Germany, Celluloid.
Ed Mayer collection

Vox Humana 6-string from the Netherlands, 1952. Ed Mayer photo

Framus 6-string built in Germany George Rout photo

Teisco T.W., double-8 made by Nippon Onpa Kobyo Co. Ltd., Japan, bought in Kuala Lumpur, in 1955. Shown here with its owner Bertie Samuel. B. Samuel photo

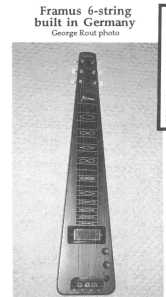

Guyatone 6-string, 1978, built to resemble Tavares' Fender Stringmaster Ed Mayer collection

Teisco, 6-string made in Japan. Very light weight. Owned by Merle Kekuku L. Ruymar photo

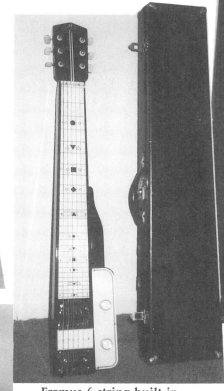

Guyatone 6-string deluxe, 1957. Built in Japan Ed Mayer collection

Framus 6-string built in Germany, 1947 Ed Mayer collection

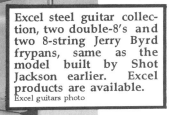

Excel steel guitar collection, two double-8's and two 8-string Jerry Byrd frypans, same as the model built by Shot Jackson earlier. Excel products are available. Excel guitars photo

Excel, Jerry Byrd model, 10-strings, 5 lock levers, made by Japanese steel guitar maker, "Fuzzy" Mitsuo Fujii in 1965 Kiyoshi Kobayashi photo

Hand-Made Originals

Ed Mayer. 6-string "Headless".
Copyrighted, pat. pending.
Ed Mayer collection

Norm English. 25" scale, pearl finish, three screw-in legs. Stringtone lever tuning changer. Three tunings, A, E, C#m   Ken Autenrieth photo

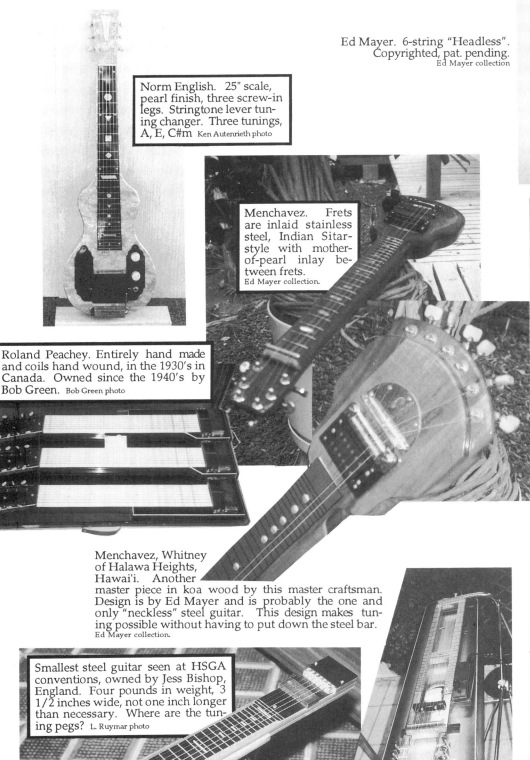

Menchavez. Frets are inlaid stainless steel, Indian Sitar-style with mother-of-pearl inlay between frets.
Ed Mayer collection.

Roland Peachey. Entirely hand made and coils hand wound, in the 1930's in Canada. Owned since the 1940's by Bob Green.   Bob Green photo

Menchavez, Whitney of Halawa Heights, Hawai'i. Another master piece in koa wood by this master craftsman. Design is by Ed Mayer and is probably the one and only "neckless" steel guitar. This design makes tuning possible without having to put down the steel bar.
Ed Mayer collection.

Jimmy Hawton. 8-string quad., 1954-55.. The frets are illuminated by lights inside the guitar, through translucent fretboards, for playing in the dark. May be the only quad built in the 1950's except for Fender's.   L. Ruymar photo

Smallest steel guitar seen at HSGA conventions, owned by Jess Bishop, England. Four pounds in weight, 3 1/2 inches wide, not one inch longer than necessary. Where are the tuning pegs?   L. Ruymar photo

Dr. Pentti Airenne of Finland. This 8-string guitar is acoustic as well as electric. Note the split fretboard with the sound hole evident between the two fretboard parts. Very heavy.   A.W. Ruymar photo

10-string Alkire Eharp with fretboard replaced by a painted woodrose vine, played by Myldred Cooper. Instrument on left is hand-made 10-string Eharp also with woodrose vine instead of fret markings.   M. Cooper photo

138

The Gibson Guitar Co.
Acoustic To Electric

Further to the Lloyd Loar story earlier in this chapter, we received a letter from the Gibson Company. They stated that there were many who claimed to be the first to build the electric guitar, but "Though Gibson later claimed the electric guitar among its many firsts, there were no electric models in the line until four or five years after Dobro and Rickenbacker had introduced electrics on a commercial scale. Lloyd Loar had invented an upright electric bass way back in the 1920's, so Gibson engineers were certainly aware of electric instruments and there were some very early prototypes, but the catalogues through 1935 made no mention of commercial electric models."

In the early days, Gibson did not make any style concessions for Hawaiian acoustic guitars. In about 1918 they began informing customers that, with the purchase of a Spanish guitar, they could also receive "complete Hawaiian steel guitar equipment" free of charge. What they supplied was a steel "nut" to raise the strings, but no picks or steel bar. In 1927 they designated their models L-0, L-1, L-2, and the Nick Lucas Special as being the best for conversion to Hawaiian style. By 1934 a pair of Roy Smeck acoustic Hawaiian guitars plus the Nick Lucas line were designated and equipped especially in the Hawaiian style.

In 1936 they announced their first electric Hawaiian guitar, the EH-150. It had a 6-string maple body with 29 fret markers, one cobalt-magnet straight bar pickup, tone and volume knobs (one on either side of the pickup), a sunburst finish, maple neck, and a bound rosewood fingerboard. The matching EH-150 four-stage six-tube amp was a boxy 15-watt unit with bump protectors on its corners. It had a 10-inch high fidelity ultrasonic reproducer, also known as a speaker. The rear panel was fastened with luggage clasps. Total cost of guitar and amp was $150.00, or $5.00 extra if you wanted a 7-string guitar. The last EH (Electric Hawaiian) models listed were in the 1942 catalogue, EH-185, EH-150, and EH-125 along with their respective amplifiers.

1952 Gibson Custom Deluxe 6-string, differs from the Skylark only in fret markings
Ed Mayer collection

6-string Roy Smeck (Gibson) electric
Kalaya Nilsen photo

Roy Smeck as a Gibson endorser playing an acoustic Gibson guitar

6-string Gibson
Leo Rajotte collection

1951 set of three model BR-9 Gibson student models. Hardwood body finished in ivory with cremona brown trim. Plastic hand rest. Individual pole pieces for balanced tone. Volume and tone controls on far side for fingertip action. Note the numerical fret markings   Ed Mayer collection

1939 6-string Gibson Royaltone with magnesium frame, slanted pick-up. Very similar to EH-185. The only difference is that the EH-185 has tuning pegs turned upward and a coverplate over the bridge.   Ed Mayer collection

6-string Gibson BR6 with authentic position markers, script logo   Kazunori Funao collection

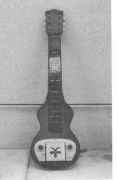

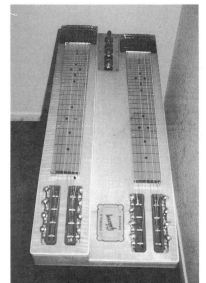

1945 6-string Gibson EH-125. Note the different fret markings on all these models   Ed Mayer collection

Gibson double-8 Console Grande   Ed Mayer collection

1950 Gibson double eight on legs
Ed Mayer collection

Gibson EH150 with slanted pickup, was built as 6, 7, or 8 string models   A. Ruymar photo

Gibson double-8 Console Grande, also available as triple-8. Curly maple body with golden sunburst shading, ivoroid bound edges and silver plastic fingerboards with colored position markers. Body tapers off at tuning end. Catalog does not show what appears to be a pedal device attached to this model.   George Rout photo

140

Epiphone "Varichord"

Another pitch changing steel guitar put on the market (1946) was Epiphone's 7-string "Varichord". Its problem was that the string pulls were manipulated by the player's right hand, which interfered with smooth playing. The instrument could be played on the lap or on a portable stand, but the concept of foot pedals wasn't used by the co-inventors Don Maffei, a Radio City Music Hall guitarist, and Clyde Doerr.

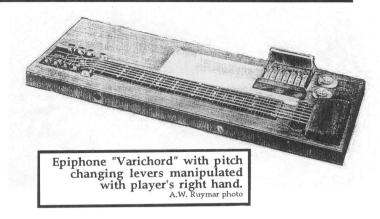

Epiphone "Varichord" with pitch changing levers manipulated with player's right hand.
A.W. Ruymar photo

Epiphone Electar 8-string.
Fret markings differ from 6-string model
Leo Rajotte collection

Epiphone 6-string, 1948
Ed Mayer collection

Pedal Steel Guitars

Gibson's First Pedal Steels

In 1940, the EH-125 Hawaiian steel with mahogany top was introduced, along with the 6-pedal Electraharp, the first successful pedal steel guitar, the design of which is credited to John Moore. Its cabinet was of maple and walnut, mounted on wheels. It was patented in 1939 and eacph pedal could raise or lower any or all of the eight strings in any combination. It was tuned E7th (E.B.G#.E.D.B.G#.E) with pedals for A9, A, C#9, E6, Em7 and E13th. Regardless of pedal changes, it stayed in tune. Pedals had been developed for harps in the early 1700's and perfected by the 1810's so it was a natural outcome to apply them to a steel guitar, considering the limitations posed by the steel bar. Serial E4141-8 was one of the first three built. It was traced to Ed Moldthan of Fort Wayne Indiana, the second was bought by band leader Alvino Rey, and the whereabouts of the third is not known. The price listed in the 1941 catalog was $477. There were no playing instructions issued with the guitars. Perhaps 20 of these guitars were sold when the Pearl Harbor attack caused Gibson to put guitar production "on hold" in order to join the war effort. After the war, in 1949, the Electraharp put on the market by Gibson was inferior in every way, termed by musicians "a piece of junk". Why would Gibson knowingly produce an inferior product? The story goes that they had been threatened with a copyright lawsuit by Harlin Brothers of Indianapolis who had developed the Multi-Kord as early as 1933.

Gibson Electraharp, one of the 20 pre-war models, built with decorated wood cabinet
Hudson Hawk photo

Pedal models built after the war included a 6-string 4-pedal student model Electraharp EH-610, the 8-string 4-pedal Electraharp, the 8-string 6-pedal Electraharp EH-620, the triple 8 Multiharp with 6 pedals, and the double-8 with eight pedals. These later models came without the cumbersome but beautiful maple and walnut cabinet.

Hudson Hawk, the owner of the guitar pictured here, had this to say: "I had gone to the music store to buy a double eight, a Gibson Console Grande. The salesman showed me the Electraharp for $395.00 and I was hooked, even more so when he told me Alvino Rey was using the instrument. Rey is one of my music heroes, and one of the finest gentlemen in the music business.

"On the bottom side of the chassis, stamped in numbers 3/16 of an inch high, are the somewhat blurred numbers 5091 6, as near as I can make out. When I bought it in 1942, I was told it was the seventh and last to be made due to the war. The number seems to indicate that it was the sixth. (Or could it mean 6 pedals?) My Electraharp has eight strings and six pedals located in the front left corner of the cabinet. About a year ago one showed up on a video by a group called Prairie Oyster. It had been rented especially for the video from Gruhn Guitars in Nashville.

"The Electraharp was made from 1938 to 1942, according to information I got from Norlin, Inc. I have seen several models, including one with folding legs and four pedals, a later one having two necks with pedals only on one, and the model I have. The cabinet is permanent and beautiful, with no break-down capability, which means it is difficult to transport.

"Although credit is given to John Moore and Wilbur Marker as the designers, in an interview on the cover of his Big Band Steel Guitar album, (Steel Guitar Record Club #13), Alvino Rey mentions having collaborated on a pulley system with a friend at Gibson named John.

Gibson Electraharp foot pedals, mounted inside the cabinet. Hudson Hawk photo

"In comparison to today's pedal steel guitar, the Electraharp was a snap to set up, tunings wise. Each string was attached to a linkage system, with two bars per string. Going across these bars were six bars connected to the pedals. In them were threaded holes, placed over the string bars, and those contained

Gibson Electraharp tuning mechanism
Hudson Hawk photo

small screws. When the pedal was depressed, the screws caused the strings to be raised or lowered, depending upon in which hole you placed the screw. Tuning was done by simply turning the screw. Changing tunings was a simple matter - you just relocated the screws according to how you wanted to change it. In fact, the ease of tuning was a real blessing since the guitar did not hold tuning very well. On the plus side, the pitch of every string could be changed with one pedal. The more strings activated the more pressure the pedal required. There were no gauged strings on the market back in the forties, so some guesswork was involved when changing individual strings. If you were really flush, you could buy the whole set of Electraharp strings. As I recall, a set of eight strings cost $1.50!"

Jay Harlin And The Multi-Kord

Jay Harlin built the first pedal steel called the "Kalina Multi-Kord" in the late 1939's. The patent was issued Aug. 21, 1947 by Jay D. Harlin. The Harlin Brothers; Jay, Herb, George, Jimmy and Wynn, had a very successful teaching program in Indianapolis, Indiana. They also made lap steels. Jay at this writing is still living in Indianapolis, his brothers have passed away.

Jay Harlin with his first 8 string, 6 pedal steel guitar
John Quarterman photo

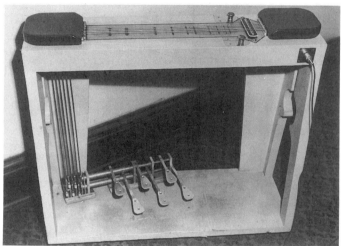

Players view of the first pedal steel, Gibson pickup John Quarterman photo

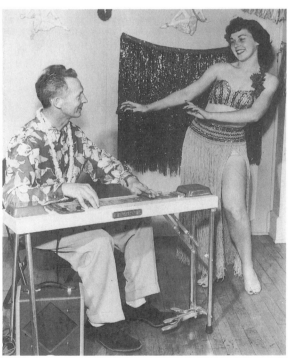

Jay Harlin and Darlene Lamar, Jan. 6, 1952 with Multi-Kord, 4 pedals John Quarterman photo

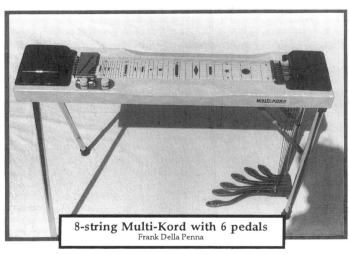

8-string Multi-Kord with 6 pedals
Frank Della Penna

Close-up of 8-string Multi-Kord tuning mechanism
Frank Della Penna

Alvino Rey's Story Of The Invention

In a letter dated February 18, 1993, Alvino Rey recounted his part in the
invention of the pedal steel guitar and the events that led up to it.

"After making a start on 'ukulele at the age of six in San Diego, I began playing the banjo in 1921, finally replacing the great Eddy Peabody, then went to New York in the Big Time. There I studied classic guitar. It wasn't until I heard Andy Sanella, a sax player on staff at NBC, that I heard a very unusual sound - an accoustic steel guitar. He played in E7th. The Gibson Guitar Co. made me a duplicate of his instrument and I went home to San Francisco, on staff with NBC. I was on two very beautiful programs featuring the new steel and pipe organ. "Bridge to Dreamland" and "Blue Moonlight".

"It was in 1931 that I discovered the Rickenbacker electric guitar. I went on stage and played "Song of the Islands" and that started a whole new era for me. Horace Heidt heard me and hired me for five years. It was there that I was featured on every program on the major networks. Heidt promoted the steel guitar in all the arrangements.

"When we arrived in Chicago in 1935, the Gibson company was very much interested in promoting the steel guitar but knew nothing about it so they set up a room in the Lyon and Healy building where I could work. We built many models out of every conceivable material; brass, aluminum, every kind of hard wood. I was not hearing the chords for good music out of six strings so I devised a string changer for the end of the guitar, and then one pedal. Then I went to two necks. I finally made one up on a stand so I could add more pedals.

"It wasn't until 1940 that I met John Moore in Connecticut where he worked at Pratt and Whitney making mock-ups for their airplane motors. I suggested the tunings that I wanted, and he then developed it as

HORACE HEIDT and ALVINO REY
Horace Heidt's Brigadiers

I requested. The guitar was so wonderful that I was convinced it was the answer, a new approach to playing the steel.

"I suggested to John that he go to Gibson with this instrument, which he did and they hired him to develop their many new designs in guitars. As far as I can remember, I received the first guitar and didn't like the looks of the enclosed front so you couldn't see the player's legs work, so I changed everything to fit my needs and I have those other models now and kept most of them.

"I jump now to the Fender Guitar Co. They too wanted to get into the steel market. I spent many months working with Leo along with Freddy Tavares, a wonderful steel player from Hawai'i. Anyway, I worked out several different ways of tuning and utilizing various tuning methods of pulling the strings but we had trouble with the cables. Finally they gave up on the steel when Leo sold the company to CBS. Gene Fields had developed a wonderful steel but they dropped the idea, much against my wishes.

"I never patented any of my ideas, I was just satisfied in getting a better instrument on the market. You might say that I was the first to utilize the foot pedal on the steel guitar. That goes back to the thirties. Everyone calls me the inventor of the pedal steel. I just developed it and introduced it, and hope some day it will be played as a complete musical instrument, not solely as so many think of it as a country instrument and I hope that some day it will not be classed as that."

Alvino Rey with the first Electraharp, about 1941. He lengthened the strings on that model and opened the front so that the foot work could be seen. Alvino Rey photo

144

Frank McPhalen of Vancouver BC ordered one of the earliest Electraharps from the factory. His did not have the wood cabinet and he was told that it was one of three (of that model) built and that the other owners were Alvino Rey and Paul Martin. He was extremely pleased with its performance and played no other steel guitar throughout his professional career.

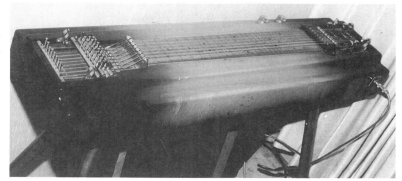

Frank McPhalen's Electraharp model EHP-3 (bought in the early 1940's) has no wooden cabinet, 8 strings and 4 pedals and it stays in tune beautifully. Art Ruymar photo

Pitch changing mechanism on model EHP-3. This section had a plastic cover. Art Ruymar photo

Model EHP-3's tuning keys. This section had a plastic cover. Art Ruymar photo

Frank McPhalen's model EHP-3, with four pedals. Art Ruymar photo

Harmolin Changed Pitch With Hand Levers

Earlier in this chapter you saw National electric guitars with Triplex Chord Changers, but National did not lead the way. Even earlier than the Multi-Kord was the 1932 Harmolin invented by Arthur R. Harmon. It was an acoustic guitar with seven strings, tuned A major low bass except for the fourth string which was a G, making it A7th. There were three levers, the first being mounted to the top of the guitar near the bridge. It controlled the G string, moving it out of the way by dropping it slightly until the player required a 7th chord, when it would push the string up to be level with the other 6 strings. Underneath the neck, lever #2 lowered the second string a half-tone to produce a minor triad on the top three strings, and lever #3 raised the third string a half tone to produce a diminished 7th on the top four strings. The problem was to hold onto the guitar while playing it and pushing the levers, but the Harmolin probably pointed the way to the Fender steels, the Sho-Buds, the Emmons, and so on.

Button-Pushing Devices

Getting away from levers, pedals, and pulls, there were some inventions involving button-pushing. The Hawaiian All-Chord Guitar was advertised by the St. Louis Music Supply Co. in 1935. It was an acoustic 6-string with two buttons placed on the top of the guitar, handy for pushing with the right hand. The instruction was to pull one button to lower the second string for minor chords and to pull the other button for 7th chords. The buttons were placed in easy reach of the picking hand and the player "simply" pushed down a button with his/her palm to disengage it. The buttons were a special attachment that had to be built into the guitar upon request. The guitar came with the built-in attachment, "tone bar", special nut and instruction book, for $25.00.

Earlier in this chapter we discussed Paul Tutmarcs push-button tuner, and last but not least, is the 6-string Magnatone Multi-matic with push-button tuners played by Margie Mays.

Early Pedal Steels, A Final Word

The story of the development of pedal steel guitars will not be dealt with further in this book. It is a large topic and the instrument with its pedals took a different path, into country music. The story is best left to others in that musical genre to tell.

Before we apologize for the inadequacies of the steel guitar, we must note that the Spanish Guitar had its "improvers" as well. In 1903 Edward Stevenson had invented a 9-string harp-guitar-like instrument supported by a stand. It was a standard Spanish guitar (6 strings) with a second neck holding 3 more strings. Four foot pedals controlled the 3-string neck by stopping them at different frets. The player had merely to pluck them to get a variety of additional bass notes. This contraption could have inspired some of the steel guitar inventors referred to earlier in this chapter. There was also a pitch-changing attachment invented by John and Chris Kaufman in 1928. It changed the tuning of a Spanish guitar to a steel guitar tuning by the pulling of a lever which engaged the strings and raised the nut, thereby raising the strings as well.

I would like to share with you a letter received from Walter Carter co-author of "Gruhn's Guide to Vintage Guitars". He says, after discussing the Gibson Electraharp and the Harmolin, "I have seen an acoustic Harlin Brothers guitar with a combination of knee levers and hand levers that pre-dates the Electraharp, I think. In any case, the pedal steel was developed as a result of the need for different tunings. The doubleneck, tripleneck, and even Fender's postwar four-neck models were one avenue that manufacturers took to solve the problem... Aside from the Electraharp and the Harlin Bros. instruments, I know of only one prewar model with pitch-changing capability, and that is the Epiphone Varichord. I have one of these in my personal collection, so they really did exist. It was used by Al Cernet on many albums (according to Al), including some Don Ho records. As I think I mentioned in the Electraharp article, the previous owner of that instrument used the pedals to change tunings but did not change while a note was sounding. That effect would be the death knell for the lap steel, and it occurred on Webb Pierce's recording of 'Slowly' in 1954, with Bud Isaacs playing pedal steel. There were still a few attempts to develop pitch-changing devices on lap steels after that. National's Triplex Chord Changer allowed three different tunings (E7, Cm, and A). I've seen an accessory on a Gretsch lap steel that did the same thing.

"Regarding Lloyd Loar and Vivi-Tone, the earliest evidence I have found of Vivi-Tone electrics is in a January 1933 magazine article - after Rickenbacker's frying pan was introduced."

Picks, Bars, & Accessories

A side from combs, pocket knives, railway bolts and glass tumblers, the very first acoustic guitars were played wih a flat bar, not more than a quarter of an inch wide. Finger picks were metal and the thumb pick of tortoise shell. A metal adapter raised the strings off the fretboard, to convert a Spanish guitar to a Hawaiian guitar.

In the photo at right are the early accessories for Hawaiian steel guitar playing. (A)-Bars have changed radically as you will see. (B)-The metal adapter. (C)-The thumb pick is now made of plastic and most players prefer it to be a bit wider for better grip on the thumb, and prefer the picking tip to protrude further. (D)-Metal finger picks have not changed much, they are usually bent back to shield the tip of the finger. Some players bend them a lot, some players not at all.

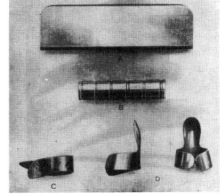

Oahu provided students with this model in three sizes depending on the size of the student's hand

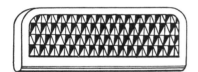

Whaley Royce designed a flat bar with a pattern for better grip.

Whaley Royce flat bar, grooved to fit the thumb on one side and grooved to fit the finger on the other side.

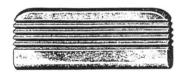

Gibson's answer to providing better grip on the bar was a series of chisled lines on both sides.

Whaley and Royce "Keoki" model provided grip in a different way.

Gibson countered with a similarly shaped bar, still aimed at better grip for the player.

Gibson's "Blue Nose", rounded at both ends, made of polished bronze or of polished steel. This model indicates less attention to grip, more care to produce noiseless movement. Manufacturers experimented with glass, plastic, brass, bronze and other materials in the quest for better tone and sustain.

The "Stevens" bar by Whaley & Royce was made of bronze with heavy nickle plating. It was designed to fit the thumb and two fingers, hoping for a compromise in grip and better movement.

This heavily nickle plated cylindrical bar with sharply cut ends by Whaley and Royce was tricky to hold, easier to slant, but had the nasty habit of catching on the first and second strings when the player pulled it back to the lower strings.

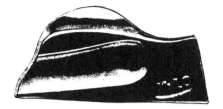

Whaley & Royce's "Kilo" was to be the ultimate in hand and finger fit and there are many who still use this form, or something similar. It was great for grip but the sharp front edge would catch on the strings.

Oahu's "Black Rajah" was very popular and is still treasured by many as their favorite bar. It had a lead core covered by crystallized composition rubber. It was impossible to break, even when dropped on cement.

Gibson's polished chromium cylinder with rounded end for noiseless movement and easier slanting is a current model. Pedal steel guitarists like extra length and more depth to their bars, but most who play eight strings or less prefer the smaller bar with two and seven eighths of an inch length, and five eighths of an inch diameter.

Gibson's "Hawaiian Moon", one piece high test bronze; said to eliminate contact of the fingers with the strings when desired; balanced and shaped to fit the land. Came with a leather case.

Gibson's "Hilo Beach", made of high test bronze. Scooped out on top for ease of comfort. Greatest weight is over the bass strings and the bottom is oval, not round preventing scraping and distortion.

This model, same size as the smaller Gibson referred to above, is great for noiseless movement and easy manipulation. The recessed end provides a place for the thumb to catch in, to push the end forward for a reverse slant. It takes a bit of skill and daring to handle this one.

Unusual bar: This was sent in by Tom Harrington of Tasmania. It was designed for use by a friend who had injured his hand. The loop is large enough for him to slip his index finger through it, and it swivels to permit him to play forward and reverse slants.

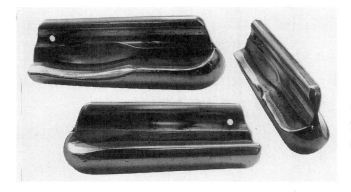

Three views of the bar designed by and used by Rudolf Barten of Cologne, Germany. It is shaped perfectly for his hand.

Sent in by Paul Kerley. "In the 1930's it was thought that the bar should be as heavy as possible to get maximum volume. The bar on the left is 3 & 1/4 inches long, 3/4 inch high, 3/4 inch thick and weighs one pound. Machined cross hatch grooves for good grip. The bar on the right is 3 & 1/4 inches long, 1 & 1/2 inches high, 3/4 inch thick, and weighs 6/10's of a pound. A side view would show that they both are flat bars embedded in cylinders which in their former lives were model "T" Ford Wrist pins. The bar on the left has the cylinder welded to a piece of 3/4 inch bar stock which was then milled. The bar on the right has a piece of 3/4 inch bakelite bolted to the wrist pin. It allowed faster movement and both produced good tone and sustain." The player's sustain is in question.

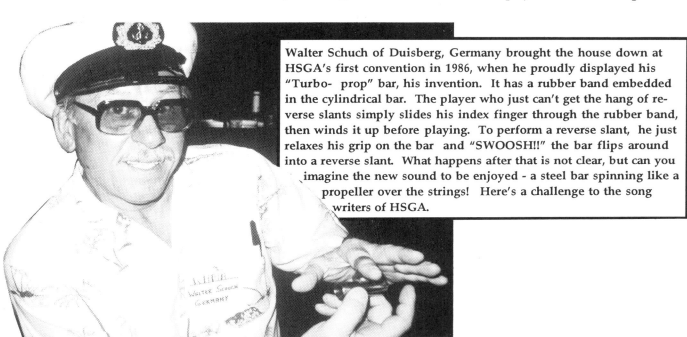

Walter Schuch of Duisberg, Germany brought the house down at HSGA's first convention in 1986, when he proudly displayed his "Turbo- prop" bar, his invention. It has a rubber band embedded in the cylindrical bar. The player who just can't get the hang of reverse slants simply slides his index finger through the rubber band, then winds it up before playing. To perform a reverse slant, he just relaxes his grip on the bar and "SWOOSH!!" the bar flips around into a reverse slant. What happens after that is not clear, but can you imagine the new sound to be enjoyed - a steel bar spinning like a propeller over the strings! Here's a challenge to the song writers of HSGA.

HAWAIIAN STEEL AND PICK KIT

This convenient quality set is furnished in a neat display box. It provides one Professional "Bullet End" NATIONAL Steel, two silver adjustable finger picks, and one silver perforated Thumb pick.

No. 13 Kit
Complete
Each $1.30

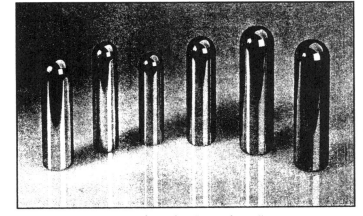

Modern day "Tonebars "
Chromed Steel and Stainless Steel

Chapter 6

Playing Techniques

Publishers Of Music Method Books

by Miro Maximchuk

"Kalani Peterson invented the Peterson Number System in 1916, and published an instruction book. Shortly after, Keoki E. Awai arranged and had published by Sherman-Clay & Co. of San Francisco, two volumes of the 'Superior Collection of Steel Guitar Solos', both in note and Peterson system. Included were nearly thirty selections - all Hawaiian. William J. Smith of the Wm. J. Smith Music Co. published one of the best known Hawaiian guitar methods, 'Kamiki' which is 'Smith' in Hawaiian. Ernest Kaleihōkū Ka'ai, both a composer and arranger, wrote two folios of music 'Songs of Old Hawai'i' (in E7th tuning) and 'Ka'ai's Enchanted Melodies for Hawaiian Guitar' in note and Peterson system.

"In the 1920's, steel guitar instruction courses were offered, consisting of 52 lessons. One was published by the New York Academy of Music and the other by the Hawaiian Conservatory of Music. The New York Academy supplied demonstration records played by Robert Yap, a native Hawaiian of Chinese extraction.

"One of the earliest publishers of sheet music, around 1915, was Roach-Frankland of Cincinnati OH, for whom Ernest Ka'ai arranged many selections. Other publishers were C.S. DeLano in Los Angeles and the Sherman-Clay Company in San Francisco."

These were the first to publish Hawaiian music and steel guitar instruction. Later, hundreds of publishers got into the act, including - believe it or not - the "Sears Home Study Course for Hawaiian Guitar" published exclusively for the Sears, Roebuck and Co. department store, 1938, by M. M. Cole Publishing Co., Chicago. The most prolific of all publishers was the Oahu Publishing Co., discussed in an earlier chapter. Other publishers were; Bob Miller, Inc. New York; Robbins Music Corporation, New York; Calumet Music Co., Chicago; American Hawaiian Teachers, Inglewood, California; Don Santos Publishing, Rochester, New York; Eddie Alkire Publications, Easton, PA.

Considering that the steel guitar has undergone many physical changes during its short life, it is reasonable to assume that parallel changes were made in playing techniques. Many guitarists still enjoy playing in the old style, so the following advice is never out of date. Later in this chapter we will discuss modern methods as they apply to the electric guitar. Although most of us now work with the electric instrument, it is very refreshing and pleasing to the audience if a few numbers are performed on the acoustic guitar. May both styles continue to flourish!

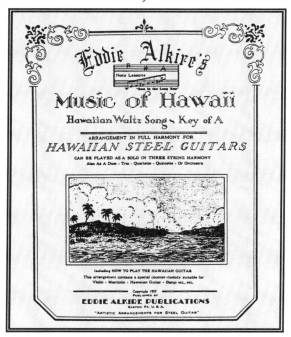

Eddie Alkire Publications, Copyright 1937

Kamiki Hawaiian Guitar Method

This method, printed by Wm. J. Smith & Co., NY in 1916 gave instruction to the steel guitar player based on the use of the flat narrow bar resembling a knife blade, two metal finger picks and a thumb pick, playing an acoustic guitar. The left hand technique was as follows: "Hold the bar loosely between thumb and first finger. All vibration must be stopped by use of the second finger. The third and fourth fingers may be held clear of the strings or may rest firmly upon the strings." The vibrato or tremolo (a very slight oscillation of the steel along the strings back and forth) was to be produced not by arm or wrist movement but by a nervous trembling quiver of the fingers. When playing single string notes on the high, or "E", string, the player was advised to anchor the second and third fingers on the outer edge of the finger board to give steadiness to the vibrating fingers controlling the bar.

The acoustic guitar played in the original way, with flat bar. A.W.Ruymar photo

Thumb picks were not made to fit a woman's thumb so the lady player was advised to cut out the thumb from a pair of gloves, put the glove-thumb on first, then the pick. It would prevent soreness caused by friction. The thumb pick was made of tortoise shell, the finger picks of metal. The two finger picks were referred to as "thimbles". They were to extend only the slightest bit beyond the fingernails, just enough to keep nails from striking strings.

Staccato playing involved the instant stopping of the string after it had been plucked. This was done by raising the bar off the string and blocking the sound by resting the third and fourth fingers of the left hand on the string to stop the vibration. The grace note (plucking the note one fret lower than intended, then sliding it up to the correct bar) was described as "a whiney effect so easy to acquire, but disgusting to musicians and should not be indulged in."

Open string harmonics were to be produced at frets 3, 4, 5, 7, 9, and 12, produced by placing the finger of the left hand at the harmonic point, striking the string and immediately removing the finger from the string.

> Editor's note re: **TREMOLO AND VIBRATO**. The following definitions are taken from the New American Dictionary of Music: " Vibrato: A slight more or less rapid fluctuation of pitch employed by singers and on some instruments to impart warmth and expression. Tremolo: A tremulous effect produced by the rapid repetition of a pitch or chord or the rapid alternation of two pitches of a chord. In reference to the voice, the term sometimes is used as synonymous with vibrato but more often it is restricted to a fluctuation in dynamics, reserving the term 'vibrato' for a fluctuation in pitch." ...My interpretation is that for a steel guitarist vibrato is done with a bar movement and tremolo is done with fingers of the right hand in rapid repeating of a note on one or more strings.

Techniques And Philosophies Of Steel Guitar Playing

by Joe Boudreau, steel guitarist of Lake Elsinore, CA.

"PERFORMANCE POSITION. It is generally agreed that the standing position affords the steel guitarist more flexibility than the sitting position. Even frypan devotees buy portable stands to enjoy freedom of movement. For some, the sitting position fosters the undesirable habit of tapping time with the foot. Rhythm machines and back-up tapes can be the answer for the lonesome foot-tapper.

"Although most players position their instrument about elbow-high, Jerry Byrd plays with his hands well below his elbows. When questioned as to what bearing the standing posture has on the correct use of a foot pedal volume control, Byrd answered, 'I find it easier to take my foot off when desired, which prevents becoming a slave to the volume pedal.'

"FOOT PEDAL VOLUME CONTROL . Music is flat and uninteresting unless there is a change of volume - a crescendo and a decrescendo to accent certain phrases. The best volume control is done by the players' hands, as when playing acoustic guitars. On the first electric instruments the volume control knob was usually in a position where the little finger of the right hand could manipulate it. The player could strike the note with the volume off, then quickly but smoothly turn the volume on. Today foot volume pedals are popular, the better models incorporating a tone control feature as well. Their purpose is to enhance sustain without a noticeable change in volume, and to heighten the expression and feeling of a song.

"Not widely known is the fact that Jerry Byrd uses a customized volume pedal. It operates in reverse of a standard production model by <u>increasing</u> the volume on the up stroke. Conversely, volume is <u>decreased</u> on the down stroke. When questioned about this, Byrd commented, 'You will find it to be smoother when raising your foot than when pushing it down. I use an audio taper control - one that has a <u>smooth, gradual</u> sweep from zero volume to full volume - whereas the linear taper produces a <u>rapid</u> increase of volume in a short space. My control is a 500 meg. audio taper all around, on guitar and pedal.'

"ELECTRONIC TUNERS AND CHANGING TUNINGS. For those of us not gifted with perfect pitch, electronic tuners are easy to use, relatively inexpensive, and reliable for maintaining standard pitch. They are invaluable for pre-tuning silently while waiting backstage, or for visual tuning in noisy settings. By all means, if you must use one, learn to be unobtrusive. It should be stressed however, that electronic tuners must not supplant one's expertise in tuning by ear. Even after tuning each string to the electronic tuner, most players like to do a 'fine tuning' by ear. If a player must change tunings during a performance, it must be done quickly. If you're a novice and cannot do it by ear, leave the electronic tuner connected in the line between the guitar and amplifier, out of sight to the audience. Turn your guitar's volume off and tune visually. Turn the volume back on.

"TUNING THE AMPLIFIER. Good players are meticulous about their amplifier settings. Before a performance they will carefully test their sound, since the size and the acoustic structure of each hall is different. Then, when the hall fills with people the sound seems to be absorbed by their presence and another amplifier adjustment is necessary. This is why we cling jealously to our own familiar equipment.

"STRINGS. Buy strings of the correct gauge number, and keep a supply of spares on hand. Wipe the strings clean after every session to prevent rust caused by residual body acid. Specially treated wiping cloths are available for this purpose. Strings should be replaced at regular intervals. Tired strings will not sing brilliantly and cannot produce clear harmonics. Frequent switching between tunings will greatly shorten string life, especially when stretching a string more than one fret beyond its recommended pitch.

"READING MUSIC WHILE PERFORMING. Many feel that this practice is a major distraction, not only to the player but also to the audience. The performer who does it is locked into the 'student' syndrome. Reading creates the negative impression that the performer is more interested in playing by the book than in giving an individually stylized performance. It might less charitably be seen as a crutch for the unprepared. The entire score, including the harmony chords, must be memorized. Only then can a performer concentrate on playing with feeling, and so imbue the performance with personal style, imagination and confidence.

"As always, there are exceptions. Some professionals are able to read several measures ahead so that reading presents no hindrance to stylistic expression. If a steel guitarist hopes to be hired to play in a top-level professional show he or she must be able to read the score while playing, and have it memorized as well.

"**TABLATURE VS. MUSIC NOTATION.** The advantage of tablature (the number system) is that it is easily read and understood by beginners. However, 'tab' has serious limitations. One cannot learn much about music theory or readily discern the inter-relationship of chords and keys from 'tab'. It is absolutely essential to good musicianship to learn to read standard music notation, but do not let the written music become a crutch or a restraint to your natural musicianship.

"**HARMONY.** Without a working knowledge of harmony, the Hawaiian steel guitarist never will be able to make confident transitions from the melody line to 'runs' and back-up chord progressions. It is a definite advantage to learn to play a rhythm instrument - be it 'ukulele, rhythm guitar, bass, or whatever. While strumming, one is immersed in playing the chord patterns and progressions, and in LISTENING for chord changes. Beginning your career as a steel guitarist by studying the old A major high bass fretboard thoroughly can be a great assist in learning the spellings of chords.

"It is best to learn thoroughly all chord patterns, positions, and progressions, in all the popular keys, in a <u>single basic tuning</u> before attempting to play in other tunings. Assuming that one is motivated, has a good teacher, and understands the need to be focused on a goal while practicing, there remain only the three cardinal rules for becoming proficient on any instrument;

(1) PRACTICE (2) PRACTICE (3) PRACTICE."

The Technique Of Steel Guitar Playing

by Jerry Byrd

"The most indelible impression I want to leave with you is that the Hawaiian steel guitar must be played not only with the head and the hands, but also with the heart. As with any instrument, a musician plays with his head and hands, but an artist plays with head, hands, and heart. That is even more so with the steel guitar, one of the most versatile and expressive instruments in the world.

"**STEEL GUITARS.** In choosing your equipment, my personal preference is a double neck guitar with eight strings on each neck, short scale. That means the distance from the bridge to the nut is 22.5 inches, as opposed to the long scale which is 24.5 inches. I prefer the short scale because it enables the player to make more accurate slants, especially at the lower frets. The most desirable distance between strings is three eighths of an inch.

"**PICKS.** I use two metal finger picks, which can be bought in various gauges. I prefer a Dunlop medium #18. A metal pick can expand and become loose while playing. If the pick is not too hard, you will be able to squeeze it back to its proper shape. I bend the picking section back to fit the roundness of my finger tips. I prefer a plastic wrap-around thumb pick with a rather long picking tip.

"**STEEL BAR.** The steel bar should be two and three - fourths inches long and three quarters of an inch in diameter, rounded at one end and recessed at the other end. The recessed end is for your thumb tip to fit into when controlling the bar in playing slant positions. If your bar is longer, you will have difficulty in slanting correctly.

"**AMPLIFIER.** My personal preference in an amplifier is the older-style tube amp. I use a Fender Twin. I keep the volume set at about 4 on a scale of 1-10, the reverb at 4 as well. I like the treble turned almost off and the bass nearly wide open. The final adjustment in tone is done on the guitar itself, keeping the volume wide open on the guitar.

"**TUNING.** To tune your guitar, it is best to develop your ear rather than to depend on an electronic tuner. A tuner is a valuable tool if you must re-tune while other music is being played, but it's best to develop your musicianship in every possible way. Unless you have the gift of perfect pitch, you must tune your first string to another instrument that you know to be in tune. Tune your second string to your first string by intonation. By that, I mean learn to recognize the interval you desire. If you are tuning to A major, your first string is E, your second string C#. The interval between is a minor third. Pluck the two strings at the same time and keep changing the second string until you hear a minor third. The third string will be an A. Tune it to the second string, C#. The interval separating them is a major third. The sound of the three strings, E.C#.A, is a major triad. Learn to recognize it. Your three bass strings are octaves of the first three strings. Tune each bass string to its octave string. Listen for a "fluttering" sound. When it's gone, your two strings should be in tune, an octave apart.

"**STEEL BAR MANIPULATION.** To hold the bar correctly, turn your left hand palm up. Place the bar on the line between the first two fingers with your thumb on the last half inch of the bar. Turn your hand over and place the bar on the strings. Your thumb stays well back, controlling only the last half inch of the bar. Your first finger should be arched so that the tip of the finger acts as a pivot during slanting and exerts a gentle downward pressure to eliminate string vibration sounds. Your second finger lies on the strings behind the bar, keeping the bar straight. Your hand is anchored to the strings by the last two fingers.

"Your right hand must have the wrist slightly to the left, so that the right edge of your palm is parallel to the frets. (This position helps you to play palm harmonics.) Your thumb and fingers will not be in a straight line, but rather the thumb extends farthest to the left, the first finger a little bit to the right of it, and the second finger farther right again. Your thumb mostly picks forward (away from you) and your two fingers pick backward (toward you, in a hand-closing action). When all three pick at the same time, it's the same action as when closing the lid of a bottle.

"All of your playing style is developed with your hands. When picking a single string passage, use your thumb pick. When double-stopping (picking two strings at a time) use thumb and first finger or thumb and second finger. If the two strings are inside strings (strings lower than the first string) use the thumb and first finger. When triple-stopping, use the thumb and both fingers. Arpeggios or strums are played with the thumb.

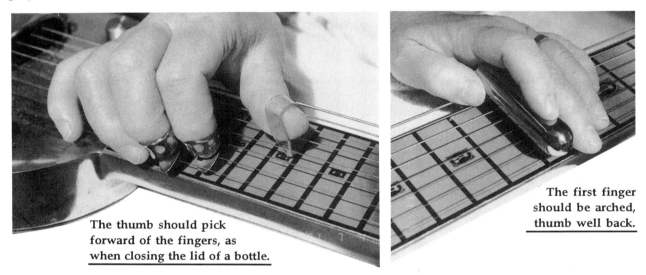

The thumb should pick forward of the fingers, as when closing the lid of a bottle.

The first finger should be arched, thumb well back.

"**MUTING.** Muting is a technique of the palm of your right hand. It is used when the sounding of a certain string is no longer wanted. For example, if the player strikes the first and second string, then wants to move to a position in which the first and third string will be played, the sounding of the second string must be eliminated. It is done by rapidly and imperceptibly damping all strings with the right edge of the right palm just before the second notes (the first and third strings) are plucked. If you are playing a fast passage of single string notes, changing from string to string, you must dampen the sound of each string just as (slightly before) the following note is sounded.

"**DAMPING.** For a novel effect, you can play a series of staccato notes in such a way that the tone is heard but the vibration is immediately cut off to make almost a popping sound. Very lightly lay the edge of the palm of your right hand on the strings as close to the bridge as you can get, and pluck the strings with your thumb. Use normal bar movement.

"**VIBRATO.** The vibrato of your left hand is the greatest single factor that makes your playing unique. Just as we recognize your voice on the telephone, your playing style is recognizable by your vibrato. Be natural, do not make your bar travel too far on either side of the fret. Avoid the 'nanny-goat' sound of vibrating too quickly. The vibrato on the higher frets must be more shallow but the frequency should remain the same. Think of it as using an eraser to rub out a spot. Your wrist doesn't bend, the action is rather with the first two fingers and thumb on the bar, anchored by the last two fingers on the strings.

"**FORWARD SLANT.** Begin by pushing the bar back (to the left) with your thumb so that your thumb is almost at the end of the bar and you can see clearly where the bar contacts the strings, thereby staying on pitch. At the same time, push the bar away from yourself so that your fingers go over the edge of the first string. This movement keeps the rounded end of your bar from dropping between the first two strings. The tip of your first finger (which is arched) keeps the bar positioned correctly on the top string of the slant. To go back to straight-bar position, pull your arm back toward yourself and the bar will naturally straighten.

In a forward slant, push the bar away from you and keep the thumb well back. The first finger acts as a pivot while the other fingers go over the edge. A.W. Ruymar photo

154

To play on the inside (lower) strings, pull the bar down to those strings.
A. W. Ruymar photo

To play a single note passage, tip the bar up so it's not sliding over unused strings.
A. W. Ruymar photo

"REVERSE SLANT. For a reverse slant, the thumb goes to the recessed end of the bar where it has good control, and pushes forward (to the right). The first finger, acting as a pivot, keeps the tip of the bar from losing or gaining pitch. Again, push the tip of the bar outward at the same time so it doesn't slip down between strings.

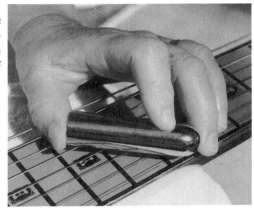

For a reverse slant, the thumb catches in the recessed end of the bar and pushes it forward. The first finger acts as a pivot. A.W. Ruymar photo

"SPLIT STRING SLANT. This is done by permitting the tip of your bar, the rounded nose, to rest <u>between</u> the top two strings, thereby making contact on <u>either side</u> of the bar at any given fret, and placing the bar on a forward slant so that the third or fourth string can be played one fret lower. Example: Top two strings at fret 4, third or fourth string at fret 3. This makes the playing of more chords possible, and of course it can be done not only on the top two strings but on any two adjacent strings, slanted to one fret lower on a selected string below them. This technique was used in tablature arrangements by Alex Hoapili and Andy Iona for the Oahu Publishing Co., 1939.

"HARMONICS. These are musical ornamentation of the most delicate kind. There are many ways to do them, but all harmonics have this in common: the picking of the string and the stopping of the fret (with the finger, palm, or knuckle) must be perfectly synchronized. Just as the pick flies off the string immediately after picking, so must the finger, palm, or knuckle fly off the string immediately after picking in order to produce a harmonic. If it is left on too long, a mutted 'flubbing' sound will be heard. If it is removed too soon, an ordinary note will be heard instead of a harmonic.

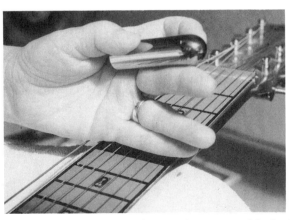

"Finger Harmonics. These have also been called 'natural' and 'open string' harmonics. They are usually played at the 5th, 7th, and 12th frets. They are so-called because the bar is not used at all. Instead, the little finger of the left hand acts as a bar and touches very quickly on the strings at the 5th, 7th, or 12th fret. The right hand plucks the string at the same time. Best results are achieved by moving the right hand as far to the right as possible, allowing for a longer string vibration length. Harmonics on the 12th and 5th frets produce the harmonic notes of the 12th fret, except that those on the 5th fret will be an octave higher. Harmonics on the 7th fret (also 19th fret) will be the harmonic notes of the 7th fret. Those on the 19th fret will be the same as at the 7th fret, not an octave higher as you would expect.

Finger harmonics are done not with the bar but with the finger touching the strings, the finger and side of hand lining up straight with the fret. A. Ruymar photo

<u>"Palm Harmonics.</u> These are a much neglected but very important aspect of steel guitar playing. They provide a change of mood, are very secretive. Don't fight them, don't fear them, just relax and play them easily. Just as we have a nervous tendency to play the next note too soon rather than get the most value from the note we have just played, we're in the habit of tensing up and dreading the palm harmonics. Palm harmonics can be played at any fret, as long as the right edge of your right palm is held parallel to the frets, exactly 12 frets up from the steel bar. The trick is to pluck the string (with

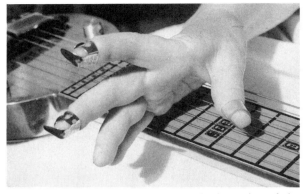

your thumb pick) at exactly the same instant as the palm is placed on the string, and to release the palm quickly enough to allow the harmonic to ring out. If you're quick with the thumb, you can strike several strings at once and produce a harmonic strum. If you're very selective with your right palm, you can pluck two strings with your thumb pick, one of which is a harmonic and the other a natural note. You can also use thumb and finger pick to play strings that are not adjacent, or to play harmonics on a slant. Keep the steel bar right on the fret, do not use vibrato.

Palm harmonics are played with the palm of the right hand exactly twelve frets up from the steel bar. The palm must make a straight line, lined up with the fret. A. Ruymar photo

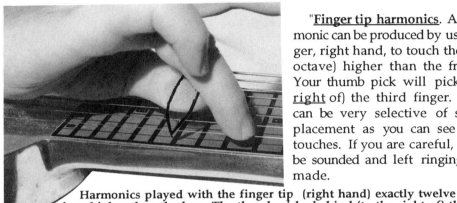

"Finger tip harmonics. A variation of the palm harmonic can be produced by using the tip of the third finger, right hand, to touch the string exactly 12 frets (one octave) higher than the fret where the bar is placed. Your thumb pick will pick the string behind (to the right of) the third finger. With these harmonics you can be very selective of string and precise in finger placement as you can see exactly where the finger touches. If you are careful, a sequence of harmonics can be sounded and left ringing while new ones are being made.

Harmonics played with the finger tip (right hand) exactly twelve frets higher than the bar. The thumb picks behind (to the right of) the finger tip. (These can also be played 7, 5, 4, and 3 frets higher than the bar.) A. Ruymar photo

Knuckle harmonics are done with the knuckle of the right hand little finger twelve frets above the bar (also 7, 5, 4, and 3 frets above the bar). A. Ruymar photo

"Knuckle harmonics. In the same way, you can use the knuckle of your little finger, right hand, to deaden the string and release. With your thumb, you pick the string to the left of the knuckle. These harmonics are the easiest when played with the knuckle 12 frets above the barred fret, but they (and finger tip harmonics) can be used at many other frets to produce higher harmonics, for very special effects. Very few musicians can do this: place your bar at the first fret. Do a harmonic with your finger or your knuckle at the 8th fret, first string. Assuming that the string is tuned to E, the harmonic note you produce will be a high C. Do it at the 6th fret to produce a high F harmonic, at the 5th fret for a high A, and at the 4th fret for a C one octave higher than the C you produced at the 8th fret. With these four notes, you can play 'Taps'. Place your bar at any fret you wish, just remember that these harmonics can be produced by placing the finger or knuckle 7 frets, 5, 4, and 3 frets higher than the bar. That's the secret of the harmonics used in playing 'Whispering Reef'.

"For both palm and knuckle harmonics, some players don't think of placing the hand (palm) 12 frets higher than the bar. Since they can't see exactly where the hand is touching the strings (thumb gets in the way) they prefer to note where their thumb pick was located at the time.

"THE 'P'TAH' SOUND. To keep continuity of sound when changing from one string to another, I like to achieve what I think of as a thread woven in and out of a tapestry, keeping the sound unbroken. I call it the p'tah sound. To move from one string to an adjacent string, let's say for example from the second string on the 5th fret to the first string on the 7th fret, pluck the note at the fifth fret and begin moving your bar up the string toward the seventh fret. Keeping the bar raised so that only the rounded tip is in contact with the strings, about half way along the movement (near the 6th fret), move the bar tip over to the first string. Pluck it, and continue the glide up to the target, the 7th fret. You will have plucked the second note a little early, but your p'tah will sound like an unbroken thread of music. The technique is a bit different, though, when moving between strings that are not adjacent. For example, try moving between the same two frets (the 5th and 7th) but coming from the fourth string to the first string. When the two strings were adjacent you used the tip of the bar. When they are not adjacent you begin by placing the bar flat across the strings. You pluck the first note, on the fourth string, move the bar forward and raise it so that by the time you reach the sixth fret you have only the tip on the first string. Pluck at the sixth fret and continue the glide to the target, the 7th fret.

"For a fluid sound, where possible it's best to keep playing on the same strings by moving the bar up and down the frets, rather than to favor one or two frets and jump from string to string. This is true except where you feel the 'p'tah' effect is desirable.

"**STYLE AND EXPRESSION.** The style you develop comes from what you do between the notes. Do you move directly from one to another? When the same passage is repeated, do you think of a more interesting way to make that same move? How do you handle your vibrato? Changes in volume? Know your tuning very well, know where all the chords are both on the fretboard and in the song. Don't play just what's on the paper, put something of yourself in besides. Even in a fast tempo song, make it sound slow so your listener can relax. Music is an art form. You must communicate with your listener. Most players over-play. They leave their heart at home and throw in every lick, every turn-around, every trick they know into every song they play. Don't do that. Play it simply and from the heart. You want your audience to leave feeling enriched by your music. Listen to yourself when you play. Are you saying something, or just playing notes? Don't compete with other players, be sincere. The Hawaiian steel guitar is the most versatile and expressive instrument I know of. It deserves your best."

Rickenbacker promotional photo of Jerry Byrd

Hawaiian Steel Guitar Tunings

The first known tuning for the Hawaiian steel guitar was the A major low bass tuning in which the player performed both the melody and rhythmic accompaniment much as a zither player does. Soon the solo steel guitarist was replaced by the guitar duo in which one steel guitarist played melody using the A major high bass tuning, and the accompanying guitar was either a steel guitar tuned to A major low bass, or a Spanish guitar. Sol Ho'opi'i was one of the earliest known innovators, having played in A major low bass, A major high bass, and variations of C#m. In "Kealoha's Modern Harmony Method for Hawaiian Steel Guitar" published by Wm. J. Smith Music Co. Inc. (1935) the author, Ylan K. Kealoha, claimed the honor of having invented the A7th tuning. His words intimated that this was the first departure from the A major tuning and that many prominent artists had already adopted it. His tuning differed from A high bass on one string only. The 6th string was tuned to G on the second line of the treble clef, not the low G you would expect on a sixth string. Seven-string guitars were then built, with that same G on the 7th string.

Among the early tunings are E minor and A minor, followed by E7th. Modern day tunings are prolific in their differences. It used to be standard practice to have all 1st strings tuned to "E", but now many people use a lighter gauge 1st string tuned to F#, G, or G#, leaving the "E" to the 2nd string.

For players of the **long scale** guitar (25 1/2" or 26" length of vibrating string), the use of a high A is impossible, as a string built for that pitch would be too thin to tolerate the tension when it's tuned up, to span such a long distance. It would be below the end of the string maker's *table of elongation*. High A on a **short scale** guitar (22 1/2' and 24 1/2") is possible but rarely used.

> A recent survey completed by members of the Hawaiian Steel Guitar Association showed the most popular tuning to be C6 (Am7), followed closely by C6+A7, then E13, C#m in its many variations (C#m9, and C#m7th being the most popular), then A major high bass, C13th, and B11th. Many other tunings were listed but to a lesser degree.

Frank Miller has been able to identify tunings used by early steel guitarists, as follows: (listing the strings from high to low, from 1st to 6th or 8th)

Andy Iona - E major (E.B.G#.B.G#.E), B11, F Major 7th

David Keli'i - first played E7th, then E13th, then C6th with a
Bb on the low strings (which would make it a C13th), and a 6-string B11th.

Danny Stewart - A6th, B11th

Dick McIntire - E7th (E.B.G#.D.B.E) , E Major (E.B.G#.E.B.E), C#m (E.C#.G#.E.B.E).
Later in life he played F#9. (E.C#.G#.E.A#.F#)

Alika Herring - C#m, A major high bass, and others

Sol Ho'opi'i - A major high bass, low bass, and C#m

Tau Moe - C#m, plus many other tunings

Barney Isaacs - C13th (E.C.A.G.E.C.Bb.C), E13th (E.C#.G#.E.D.B.G#.E),
and B11th (E. C#.A. F#. D#. B. F#.B.)

Jules Ah See used mainly the C6 tuning with a Bb (C13th), and many other tunings

Alan Akaka uses C13, B11th (E.C#.A.F#.D#.B.F#.B), plus many other tunings

Jerry Byrd uses his invention, the C6+A7 tuning (E.C.A.G.E.C#.C. low A),
straight C6th, E9th, B11th, and all the others.

Casey Olson uses the C6+A7 or C13th, also B11 with C#on the 6th string.

John Auna plays F#m7th, F#m9th, and C#m+E9th

Merle Kekuku used (1st to 6th) E.C.A.F#.E.C#, which could be called Am6th+F#m7th,
or more simply D9 with added C#. He got an amazing amount of music out of his 6-string Teisco using that tuning, which is strong on minor, 9th, and diminished chords.

Bill Leavitt, in 1986, is credited with inventing the C9+C# tuning (D.C.Bb.G.E.C#.),
especially adapted for Jazz tunes.

Who Was First To Play The C6(Am7) Tuning?

It is difficult to say exactly who did what, as Hawaiian steel guitarists guarded their tunings as professional secrets. Many were known to deliberately put their guitar out of tune when taking a break, so that no one could strum across the strings and guess the secret. Some fathers didn't share even with their sons. We'll make an attempt here, perhaps only to set up a yardstick against which others can measure their information.

The Oahu Publishing Company will serve as a guideline. The one who wrote music arrangements and managed the publishing department, Betty Glynn, reported as follows:

"In the late 1920's, Harry Stanley founded the Honolulu Conservatory of Music in Flint, Michigan and printed a short course of 12 lessons in tablature using the A major low bass tuning. The first two songs were ' Aloha Oe' and 'Nearer My God To Thee'.

"In 1930 the A major low bass course was expanded to 52 lessons. In 1934, I joined the teaching staff in Cleveland and from 1939 to 1985 I was the Oahu music arranger.

"Around the middle 1930's the A major high bass tuning was added for students who were starting to form their own groups accompanied by guitar, 'ukulele, and string bass.

"In the late 1930's and 1940's native Hawaiian groups playing the early electric steel guitars were using the new E7th and C# minor tunings, so these were added to Oahu publications immediately.

"In the 1940's professional steel guitarists invented many new and unusual tunings. Of these C6 (or Am7) was selected to be added to Oahu publications.

"In 1950 the accordion became an instant hit due to Myron Floren and the Lawrence Welk shows. We added accordion lessons and popular sheet music to our extensive catalog."

Margo Shy has the complete set of Oahu publications. The first arrangements in C6 (Am7) shown on her list are: Steel Guitar Rag published in A Major and E Major in 1941, then in C6 (Am7) in 1944. Beyond The Reef was published in C6 (Am7) in 1949. Harbor Lights was written in 1937, first published by Oahu in C#m, E Major, and A Major low bass, then C6 (Am7) in 1950.

Merle Kekuku told us that Tommy Castro was a great innovator, and steel guitarist Joe Custino was ever vigilant to guess Tommy's latest moves. Tommy was the first they knew of to use the straight A minor tuning, E.C.A.E.C.A. Then when he played with the Ray Kinney orchestra on the mainland, Tommy developed a new sound which Joe Custino first identified when he heard Tommy use it on 'Makalapua'. It was E.C.A.G.E.A.E., named Am7 or C6. Up to that time E7th and variations of C#m were in popular use. The 'ukulele tuning most popular in Hawai'i is A.E.C.G. (1st to 4th string), which is also Am7 or C6. Coincidence? The year of this event is not certain.

David Keli'i, playing with Al Kealoha Perry's "Singing Surfriders", recorded Under a Spreading Coconut Tree and Twilight in Hawai'i on Decca record #3484. Some say they detect the C6th (Am7) tuning being used. The problem now is to find out in what year that recording was made. David's very first recordings with the Surfriders were the two albums done on Decca in New York which did NOT contain Under a Spreading Coconut Tree. Eddie Bush is credited with making his first recording in C6 in 1944, but the song is unknown. Alvino Rey's steel guitar method book "Modern Guitar Hawaiian Style" published by Robbins Music Corp, New York in 1937 uses the A7 tuning and "the new E7th tuning". C6 (Am7) was not included.

Some say the first person to publish an arrangement in the C6th (Am7) tuning was Bernie Ka'ai Lewis in his "Golden Gate Folio of Hawaiian Songs". One of the songs, "Manu E" was arranged in C6th - E.C.A.G.E.C., which he called the Am7th tuning. It was published in 1945 Ray Meany's Golden Gate Publications. That may or may not pre-date the Oahu publications. We have a copy of that arrangement. The title is printed as "Manue (The Lure Of The Tropics)" and the other tunings used in the publication are A major low bass, A major high bass, E7th in four variations, A7th, E, Am, Em, C, and C7.

While we were in Hawai'i in 1992, Jerry Byrd showed us a home made recording made by Ron Dearth dated February 1939. The recording is of Jerry Byrd playing Lovely Hula Hands in C6th (Am7). He told us that musicians in those days were using E, E7th, and C#m variations and he came upon the C6th tuning not by hearing someone else use it, but by his own experimentation. He began working on the new tuning early in 1938, and recorded it for the first time on the 1939 recording of Lovely Hula Hands, which was far ahead of anything the Oahu Publishing Co. was offering. He soon added C# to the sixth string, to form his own C6+A7 tuning, E.C.A.G.E.C#.C.A.

Elmer Ridenhour has given us this statement dated July 6, 1992, "I first met Jerry Byrd in 1939 or 1940 at The American Guild of Music convention at Cincinnati Ohio. Jerry and I were back stage and I asked him what tuning he was using to get that beautiful sound. He said he had experimented with and developed his own tuning, a C6th using C.E.G.A. notes.

"At that time all the steel players I knew were using C#m variations or an E7th tuning along with the traditional A tunings. I do know this! The open and closed harmonies, inverted chords and the pure melodic and harmonic progressions as presented by Jerry Byrd were the greatest factor in the development of steel guitar playing today.

"I feel sure there were many experimenting with various combinations of tones for tunings at the same time Jerry was, and events happened to make Jerry's recordings of his music in C6th quickly popular all over the world with everyone wanting to find out where he got that heavenly sound."

Ridenhour's credentials are as follows, "My formal music education began with courses at the University of Virginia and U. of Chicago. I was certified a teacher by the Music Teachers' National Association, helped organize the Virginia Music Teachers' Association, and was president of the Roanoke Music Teachers' Association."

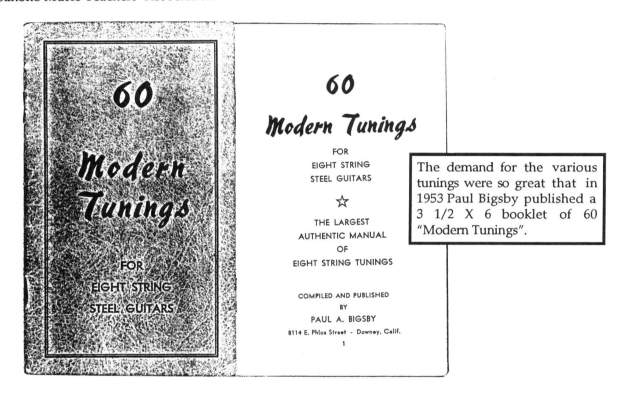

The demand for the various tunings were so great that in 1953 Paul Bigsby published a 3 1/2 X 6 booklet of 60 "Modern Tunings".

Why Do Steel Guitarists Change Tunings?

Why are they constantly in search of the perfect tuning? Human nature - the desire to explore, to experience a new sound, to improve performance, to add a new dimension to the next bragging session with other steel guitarists?? All of those and more. The A major tunings were limited in minor and 7th chords, with only fragments of diminished and augmented chords possible. Some tunings - B11th for example - are great for 9th chords. Some tunings can be "strummed", the low strings can be swept across with the thumb pick to produce great arpeggios of major and 7th chords. These are great in playing waltzes. E13th and A7th are great strum tunings. C6th is considered a good all-round tuning with most chord combinations easily available, but just change the lower strings to what we call the C6+A7 tuning and the 7th chords and diminished chords are more available.

Besides all the practical reasons for selecting a certain tuning, there's the unexplainable charm or the feeling of "rightness" that some tunings have for certain songs. For example: Sand and How D'Ya Do are almost always played in B11th. Maui Chimes and the Hilo March sound best in A major. Very few players will perform Paradise Isle in anything but C#minor. That explains why professional players like to have at least two sets of strings (a double-neck guitar) to play, and still change those two tunings to third and fourth tunings during a performance. However, it is best for the beginner to leave the multiple tuning showmanship to the professionals, to learn two tunings until they are an inseparable part of you.

There are as many possible tunings for the steel guitar as is mathematically possible by multiplying the number of strings by every arrangement of notes in the 12-degree chromatic scale. The number is estimated at 990 on a 6-string guitar. To list them all would be ridiculous. We will list only those which are known to be in use to a large enough extent to be recognized. All tunings listed below will be shown in the high string to low string order: 1st string to 6th or 8th string. Tunings with only 6 strings are the earlier tunings because that's the way the early guitars were built. All 7-string tunings will be shown here extended to 8 strings. All tuning names imply a major chord. If they are not major, such as C#m (C sharp minor) the "minor" is indicated.

How Tunings Are Built.

Let's start with the two original steel guitar tunings:
A low bass - E.C#A.E.A.E
A high bass - E.C#.A.E.C#.A
Both of these tunings contain simply the three notes of the A major triad (A.C#.E.).

A7

To form an A7th tuning, the 7th degree of the A scale, flattened, must be added to the A major tuning. The 7th degree, flattened, is "G". The A7th tuning would therefore be E.C#.A.G.E.A.or E.C#.A.E.C#.G.

Am and Am7

To form an A minor tuning: Lowering the "C#" of any of the above tunings to a "C" would make that tuning A minor . The two possible Am7th tunings (containing the A minor triad plus the flattened 7th) would be: E.C.A.G.E.A or E.C.A.E.C.G. To play any of the above 6 string tunings on an 8-string guitar, the two extra strings added must contain octave duplications of any of the original 6 strings. Example: the two A7th tunings could become E.C#.A.E.C#.A.E.G or E.C#.A.E.C#.A.G.E. You might not like to have your 7th interval, G, on the lowest strings, in which case you might make your 4th string a G, and move the other notes down one string.

A9

To form a "9th" tuning, you must have the 9th degree (which is the same as the 2nd degree) of the A scale, which is a "B", in addition to the minor 7th (or flattened 7th) degree of the scale, which is "G". The A9th tuning would be - E.C#.A.E.C#.A.G.B, or if you like to bring the 9th sound into the middle-range of your music, you could slip the "B" in between the "C#" and the "A" so it would be on the 5th string, or maybe you'd prefer it between the higher C# and A, on the 3rd string. It's a personal choice.

A13

To produce a "13th" tuning. You must add the 13th tone (or degree) of the A scale (which is F#) to an existing A7th tuning or to an A9th tuning.

A11

Let's explore the A11th tuning. To form an 11th chord, the following degrees of the scale are used: 1st (tonic), 3rd, 5th, 7th flattened, 9th, and 11th. Based on the A major scale, the necessary notes to form an 11th chord would be A.C#.E.G.B.D. We're in the habit of tuning the 1st string to E in most tunings. The G and D would appear only once, and A, C#, and E would be repeated in octaves.

When I say that the strings are arranged to the player's liking, the decision is not as simple as it may appear. Beyond making sure that all the required degrees of the scale are represented, the player looks for three adjacent strings to form a minor chord or a 7th chord, or for easy access to diminished and augmented chords. For example, in the B11th tuning (E.C#.A.F#.D#.C#.B.A) the player finds easy access to major chords, 7th chords, and 9th chords on the lower strings, plus a major chord on the top three strings, a minor chord on the 2nd, 3rd, and 4th strings, and a diminished chord on the 3rd, 4th, and 5th strings. That makes B11th a very versatile tuning.

Another consideration when choosing a tuning is the tone quality or the mood that one hears in a tuning, and this quality is not the same to all listeners. Some have said that E9th has a country music sound, but that seems to be true only if the player leans in that direction. Hawaiian minded players can produce the most beautifully Hawaiian sounds on it. For example, listen to Jerry Byrd playing Mama E, Kamalani O Keaukaha, or Kawohikukapulani in E9th. It will definitely not bring the cows home! There are musicians with keen ears who can hear a steel guitar being played and tell you what tuning is being used, and to what note each string is tuned!

Do you see why steel guitar strings are no longer sold in sets, as they were in the early days and as Spanish guitar, mandolin, violin, and many other instrument strings still are? It seems that only steel guitarists cannot decide on a universal tuning (with the exception of Dobro players who stay for the most part with 6 strings tuned D.B.G.D.B.G). Pedal steel guitars have up to 14 strings in all varieties of tunings, so retailers stock strings by gauge numbers, which we will discuss later. The following list represents the most commonly used string arrangements.

Tunings are named 1st to 6th or 8th string order

A Tunings

A high bass. - E.C#.A.E.C#.A
A low bass. - E.C#.A.E.A.E
A7th. - E.C#.A.G.E.A
A7th. - E.C#.A.E.C#.G
A7th. - E.C#.A.E.A.G.E.C#
A7th. - E.C#.A.E.C#.A.G.E
A7th. - A.E.C#.A.E.C#.G.E
Am. - E.C.A.E.A.E
Am. - E.C.A.E.C.A
Am7th. - E.C.A.G.E.A.E
Am7th. - E.C.A.E.C.A.G
A6th. - E.C#.A.F#.E.C#.A.E
A6th. - E.C#.A.F#.E.C#.A.F#
A9th. - E.C#.A.E.C#.A.G.B
A13th. - E.C#.A.E.C#.G.F#.E

B Tunings

B11th. - E.C#.A.F#.D#.C#.B.A
B11th. - E.C#.A.F#.D#.B.F#.B
(related to the A Major and A6th tunings)

C Tunings

C. - E.C.G.E.C.G
C6th. - E.C.A.G.E.C
C6th. - E.C.A.G.E.C.G.E
C7th. - E.C.G.E.C.Bb
C7th. - E.C.G.E.C.Bb.G.E
C9th+C#. - D.C.Bb.G.E,C#
C13th. - E.C.A.G.E.C.Bb.C
C6th+A7. - E.C.A.G.E.C#.C. low A
C#m. - E.C#.G#.E.C#.E
C#m7th. - E.C#.G#.E.B.E
C#m7th.- E.C#.G#.E.C#.B.G#.E
C#m7th+E7th. - E.C#.G#.E.D.C#.B.G#
C#m7th+E9th. - E.C#.G#.F#.E.D.B.G#

D Tunings

D9th. - E.C.A.F#.D.A
D9th. - E.C.A.F#.E.C.A.F#
D9th. - E.C.A.F#.E.C#.A.F#
could also be named D9th+A6th (or D9+F#m7)
D11th. - E.C.A.F#.E.C#.A.G
could also be named D9+A7
These are related to the C6th series.

E Tunings

E high bass. - E.B.G#.E.B.G#
E high inversion. - G#.E.B.G#.E.B
E low bass. - E.B.G#.E.B.E
Em. - E.B.G.E.B.E
E7th. - E.B.G#.D.B.E
E7th.- E.B.G#.E.D.E
E7th. - E.B.G#.E.D.B.G#.E.
E9th. - E.B.G#.F#.E.D.B.G#
E13th. - E.C#.B.G#.E.D.B.G#
E13th. - E.C#.G#.F#.D.B.G#.E

F Tunings

F#9th. - E.C#.G#.E.A#.F#.C#.G#
(related to the C#m tunings)
FM7th+G13th - E.C.A.F.D.B.G.E
(FM7 is translated as an F major chord
with a Major 7th interval, E, as opposed
to the customary flattened or minor 7th, Eb)

G Tunings

G. - D.B.G.D.B.G (Dobro tuning)
G13th. - E.B.G.F.E.D.B.G
G13th - D.B.G.F.E.D.B.G

Scale Tuning

E.C.B.A.G.F.E.

Only the bravest attempt the scale tuning. Jerry Byrd had his double neck ShoBud built especially to accommodate this tuning, with seven strings on the far neck for the scale tuning, and eight strings on the near neck. It is one of Bobby Black's favorite tunings, and Isao Wada San of Japan used it at a Steel Guitar Ho'olaule'a in Hawai'i to make his steel guitar sound exactly like the Japanese koto in his performance of the all-time favorite "Sakura".

Strings By Gauge Number

String gauge charts should be available where strings are sold, but don't expect your dealer to have every string that's listed here. You may have to compromise.

G# .010 or .011
G   .012
F   .013
E   .014 or .015
D   .016
C# .017
C   .017 or .018
B   .019 or .20
A   .022
G# .022 or .023
G   .023 or .024
F# .024
F   .026

below this gauge number, for the best tone all strings should be wound

E   .029 or .030
D# .030
D   .032
C# .034
C   .036
B   .038 or .039
Bb .040
A   .042 or .044
G# .045
G   .048
C (an octave lower) .060
A (an octave lower) .068

The last two should be flat wound, for less scraping sound.

From a 1936 Gibson Catalog

When ordering strings, consider whether you will be changing tunings. If you are in the habit of changing from E9th to E13th, (E9th E.B.G#.F#.E.D.B.G#, E13th E.C#.B.G#.E.D.B.G#) your 2nd string will be changed from B to C#. It would be best to buy a string that is correct for half way between which would be C, gauge .018. Your 3rd string will change from G#.023 to B .019. The median between .019 and .023 would be .021, so that gauge number will perform better tuned to either G# or B, will not sound too thin or be too loose. A wound string is more flexible in that it can be tuned 1 1/2 tones (three frets) higher than the note for which it was made without threatening to break, or lowered one tone (two frets) from its standard pitch without losing tone quality. A plain (unwound) string should be raised or lowered one tone (two frets) only.

Chapter 7

The Hawaiian Steel Guitar Today

Up to this point, we've talked about the Hawaiian steel guitar of the past. Now we'll try to answer the question, "Will it survive another hundred years?" The same question could be asked of the accordion, the zither, the dulcimer, the mandolin, and all the beautiful instruments used in playing folk music of other cultures, except for one difference. In their case, even though rock and country and other musical fads have taken over in their homeland, there is a sizeable nation of people who remember, who still sing the old songs and dance the traditional dances. In Hawai'i, the very existence of the race and its culture hangs by a delicate thread. I believe that we who love the Hawaiian guitar also love the music and the culture that nurtured it. We of the Hawaiian Steel Guitar Association want to be part of its preservation, and we must learn how to do it respectfully, thoughtfully, and let's add "effectively".

In the following articles, we want to show what is being done now to help preserve this beautiful art form. Here's what happened in Sweden in 1991. The steel guitarist in one of the most popular "South Seas" shows ever staged in Sweden has written an account of the event for us.

Paul Abraham And "The Flower Of Hawai'i"

by Thomas Malm, Sweden

"On the 24th of July 1931, a light opera called "Die Blume von Hawai'i", or "The Flower of Hawai'i", was performed in public for the first time. The place was Leipzig, Germany and it became such an immediate success that it was given on sixteen different stages in one year! Paul Abraham, the composer, was a disciple of his compatriot Franz Lehár, in those days the greatest name in the field of light opera. It is quite obvious that Abraham was influenced by his master, but it is also a matter of fact that Lehár used some of Abraham's ideas in his own light operas.

"It was around this time that sound began to be used in movies and Abraham became one of the composers to supply the music, as well as conduct the theater orchestra. 'The Flower of Hawai'i' is his only light opera set in Hawai'i. The story is about how the Hawaiians tried to bring a princess to the throne to be their queen so they could once again have an independent island nation. The princess lived in Paris, where she had a double who was a famous comedienne. So a comedian, Jimmy Boy, brought the princess back to Hawai'i, telling everyone that she was actually his show partner from Paris. During the trip by boat, she fell in love with a captain in the navy. This made it all very complicated, because he had been told to arrest the princess if he could find her, and she was to be married to a Hawaiian prince. All of this, of course, is pure fiction.

"The music consists of typical waltzes, marches, and show tunes of the 1920's and early 1930's, some of them with a Hawaiian theme in the lyrics. Over the years these songs have been recorded many times and Tau Moe, among others, has played Hawaiian steel guitar in this light opera. Some of the LP records where you can find these songs with Hawaiian steel guitar in the orchestra are:

"Goldene Operette: Die Blume von Hawai'i - Victoria und ihr Husar",
Telefunken NTA 516 (all the songs in German).
"Blume von Hawai'i - Maske in Blau", Karussell 635 175 (all the songs in German).
"Blomman från Hawai'i", Lani LALP 543, Yngve Stoor & His Hawaiian Orchestra

" 'The Flower of Hawai'i' is still being shown in Europe, mainly in Germany, but also in Sweden. In 1982 and 1991, I played the Hawaiian steel guitar and 'ukulele in almost 160 performances which were in an open air theatre in Fredriksdal, Helsingborg, here in Sweden. This theatre is in true baroque style and is considered to be the most beautiful in the country. At least 40,000 tickets had been sold before we even began to rehearse in May 1991. The stage was very romantic with a waterfall, three grass shacks without walls (one for the orchestra), and a silhouette model of the Royal Hawaiian Hotel plus a lot of living and plastic flowers and palm trees. The dancers were dressed "Hawaiian style" and their dancing was very beautiful, even if it was not really authentic. Even though the weather was sometimes against us we had to cancel only four performances in 1982 and three and a half in 1991. In the audience we have had many prominent guests. One that I remember especially is Olof Palme, our prime minister who was assassinated in 1986."

It has been said that perhaps our instrument must be more versatile to survive. Does it need more recognition by classical musicians? If so, it must have a music literature to draw from, a demanding course of studies on which to base degree courses, and institutions of higher learning that will include it in their curriculum. (At this date, the only university known to this writer to offer a study of steel guitar is the U. of Maryland, the course under the direction of Dr. Mantle Hood.) Here's the story of one American musician who has taken the steel guitar to the guardians of classical music, the symphony orchestra.

The Polynesian Suite

by Joseph M. Boudreau

"Without a doubt, the 'Polynesian Suite' album represents the ultimate peak ever achieved on the Hawaiian steel guitar. This was the most ambitious recording project ever undertaken to showcase the instrument. Produced in August of 1968, six recording sessions were necessary, three in Mexico City, and three in Nashville. Production costs ran over $25,000.

"Nevertheless, the 'P.S.' is the least known of Jerry Byrd's albums. Even among lovers of the steel guitar, this historical milestone achievement remains largely unknown. Simply too far ahead of its time, it was destined to become Jerry's 'albatross'. It was the brainchild of Boudleaux Bryant and Fred Foster of Monument Records (recently purchased by C.B.S.).

"The 'Polynesian Suite' is a paradox, wrapped in strange circumstances and events, as is attested to by the following pertinent items:

1. Although this entrancing musical quilt is a true symphonic suite consisting of 12 individual segments including an opening and a finalé done in the finest tradition of the Broadway musical stage, its author Boudleaux Bryant was perhaps best known for his work in the field of country music.

2. An accomplished musician, Boudleaux Bryant was, at one time, a violinist with the Atlanta Symphony Orchestra.

3. Bryant conceived and wrote this work especially and specifically for his good friend, Jerry Byrd.

4. Bill Justus, the arranger, was then best known as a writer of rock songs.

5. This album marks the only time known to the writer that a 58-piece symphony orchestra was used to back up a virtuoso soloist on the Hawaiian steel guitar!

6. Jerry Byrd went to the RCA recording studios in Mexico City to oversee the performance of this work by a full symphony orchestra. Understandably, Jerry remembers being in awe at the magnitude of this project and at having to work with so many musicians.

7. During this time, Mexico City underwent a devastating earthquake in which the hotel where Jerry was staying suffered major damage. In fact Jerry, Bryant and his wife Felice, Fred Foster, and Bill Justus all were at great personal peril. According to Jerry, it was a frightening experience.

8. After completing the symphonic track in Mexico City, they returned to Nashville, TN where Jerry completed the steel guitar track at Monument Recording Studios.

9. In the sixth segment of the suite, 'Malay Girl', we have a fine example of Jerry's boundless creativity on the steel guitar. It was thought desirable to produce the sound of the Indian sitar. Jerry was able to simulate this 'feeling' by playing the passage on a Danelectro electric guitar and making the strings contact the frets!!!. I tell you, this guy just won't quit!

For those of you who have never heard the 'Polynesian Suite', I offer my own description of this collectors' album in which the various ethnic races in Hawai'i are saluted musically:

a. 'Invitation To a Luau' Opening. Full symphony with Polynesian drum rhythm. A very interesting movement that sets the tone for all that is to follow.

b. 'Sweet And Sour' Hula tempo with country-western flavor. Polynesian drums in the farmyard! Already we are convinced of Jerry's easy mastery of this medium. Very impressive number.

c. **'Mamola By Moonlight'** Hauntingly beautiful. Reminiscent of 'Moon Of Manakoora' and 'Adventures In Paradise' but has its own distinctive flavor.

d. **'Sake Punch'** Has the quality of 'Sweet And Sour' but on a grander scale. Projects the feel of Broadway's 'South Pacific' and 'Bali Hai'.

e. **'Sand Waltz'** Very beautiful number with full symphony. Easy listening. Infectious Polynesian drum rhythm. As usual, Jerry's performance sparkles!

f. **'Malay Girl'** Malaysian and Indian influences seem equally prominent. Very different. A cameo of Jerry's creativity. Least "Hawaiian" number in feeling.

g. **'Kahala Hula'** Typical popular haole-Hawaiian flavor. Very catchy and bouncy. One is overwhelmed by the total effect of Hawaiian music being performed by a full symphony orchestra with steel guitar. The blend is perfect.

h. **'Pearl Harbor March'** Imagine a full symphony orchestra, complete with steel guitar, as a Polynesian marching band! A very pleasing change of pace - even if one is not overly fond of marches. Adds variety and balance to this colorful musical tapestry.

i. **'Surfside Up'** Does not seem to be aptly named. Opens with a strong modern blues connotation reminiscent of Gershwin's 'An American In Paris', but with Polynesian flavor. Mysterious tinkling Oriental bamboo curtains. Highlights the versatility of the steel guitar.

j. **'Teriyaki'** Strong Oriental flavor with more tinkling bamboo curtains. Conjures up visions of furtive assignations. The feel is a blend of Japanese, Chinese, Korean, and Indian cultures. Polynesian style dim-sum! Yummy!

k **'Diamond Head Hula'** A happy upbeat haole hula. Great Hawaiian feeling. One of my favorites. Easily could stand on its own, as could most of the numbers in this suite. Jerry continues to make all steel guitar players eat their hearts out! What else is new? A scintillating number.

l **'Grande Finalé'** All the previous numbers revisited in grand style. A fitting conclusion to a truly memorable sensory feast.

"The grand feeling of a Broadway South Seas musical runs through the entire suite. All the numbers that comprise the 'Polynesian Suite' present our senses with a continuing tug-of-war in three directions: 1. the beauty of the arrangements, 2. the incredible performance by the entire symphony orchestra, and 3. Jerry Byrd's free-flowing, absolutely spell-binding performance on the steel guitar through the entire suite.

"Unfortunately, only a few of these albums were produced. Today, the 'Polynesian Suite' has become a valued collectors' treasure. If I were to put my own assessment of this album in a nutshell, it would be - - After the 'Polynesian Suite', everything else is down-hill!!"

Steel Guitar Education In Hawai'i Today

HALAU MELE

The following was reported by Dr. G. Kanahele in 'Hawaiian Music and Musicians', 1979.

"In 1975 the Hawaiian Music Foundation made a valiant effort at establishing a school for instruction in Hawaiian music. It was a joint venture with St. Louis High School (a private Catholic-sponsored institution). The school provided the facilities while HMF financed and managed the *halau mele*. It was an eight-week course, two nights weekly. Three courses were offered: slack key guitar, steel guitar, and the making and playing of ancient Hawaiian instruments. The first instructors were William Panui, Jerry Byrd, and Elaine Mullaney. A total of 60 students were enrolled. To ensure that all students had instruments, HMF provided guitars and steel guitars at a nominal fee.

"Following the first course, a second and third were conducted during 1975 with an increase in the number of students, classes, and instructors. Intermediate levels were added to slack key and steel guitar classes, along with new instructors - Clarence Williams and Alan Akaka for steel guitar and George McGuire, Lance Koyama and Danny Akaka for slack key guitar. Efforts were also begun to develop lesson materials and a syllabus.

"Because of the favorable reaction by students, teachers, and officials of St. Louis as well as HMF, at the end of the first year it was agreed to continue the *halau* on a long-term basis. Thus the *halau* began its second year in March 1976.

"A major problem has been the lack of experienced teachers and teaching material. Hence teacher and text development are important aims of the *halau*. Although facilities at St.Louis are adequate for the present, HMF is seeking a permanent site for a Hawaiian Music Academy."

The school lasted a few years, then closed for lack of funding, and shortage of teachers and teaching materials. This was a noble effort and it proved that students would elect to play the steel guitar if the opportunity were given them. It is our hope that another school of the same kind will be established soon, with better funding. In order to keep alive the tradition of Hawai'i's pre-1970's music, we believe that instruction should be given not only on steel guitar but on slack key guitar (kī hō 'alu), 'ukulele, acoustic bass, rhythm back-up on Spanish guitar, and Hawaiian vocals.

As of 1992 steel guitarist Alan Akaka has taken a position as band director at Kamehameha Schools. Perhaps he will be able to stimulate interest among the students. As for post-secondary courses offered on steel guitar in Hawai'i, one might ask, "Why is it that a Hawaiian can study the bagpipes at a university in Scotland but a Scotsman cannot study the Hawaiian steel guitar at a university in Hawai'i?" Both instruments are the "Signature Sound" of their "Homeland", except that the pipes were not born in Scotland, but the steel guitar WAS born in Hawai'i. It's a good question.

Public Instruction

Steel guitar courses are offered on the curriculum at Kamehameha Schools today, but very few students sign up for them. In the Kamehameha Schools continuing education program for adults, listed under "Hawaiian Studies", among other things are listed four hula classes, two levels of slack key guitar (kī hō'alu) guitar, two levels of 'ukulele, and - course #1251 "Guitar Hawaiian Style". It is interesting to note that "Guitar Hawaiian Style" does not mean "steel guitar" in this case. Further on down the list is: "STEEL GUITAR. Introduction to steel guitar. Historical development, tuning, playing techniques. Repertoire to include selections from Hawaiian and American music." The instructor is Grifford Kamaka Tom. This is a new addition to the 1993 curriculum.

Private Lessons

A more continuing and productive effort has been made by Jerry Byrd since he moved from Nashville to the Hawaiian Islands in 1972. Hawaiian music had always been his first choice, which can be seen by the inclusion of at least one Hawaiian song on most of his recordings. He was struck by the very evident lack of steel guitar in public performance in Hawai'i. Steel guitar was at its lowest ebb and he wanted to do something about it. After teaching at St. Louis High School (in Honolulu), he began giving private instruction in a small studio at Harry's Music Store, Wai'alae Ave., Honolulu. He accepts about ten students at any one time and there is much pressure on him to accept more.

Jerry Byrd and his first student,
Alan Akaka work together on many ventures
to bring about the steel guitar's revival.
A. Ruymar photo

His very first student was Alan Akaka. Alan has become one of Hawai'i's foremost steel guitarists along with another of Jerry's students, young Casey Olsen who took Jerry's spot at the Halekulani Hotel's House Without A Key when Jerry decided to retire. Casey plays in his dad's group, the Hiram Olsen Trio with Kalani Fernandes. Casey is the grandson of the late steel guitar virtuoso, Billy Hew Len. The following students of Jerry's are now active on the Hawaiian scene and are the steel guitarists of the future: Greg Sardinha, Eric Kinilau, Denny Hemingson, Isaac Akuna, Paul Kim, Owana Salazar, Anela Kahiamoe, Vinton Castro, Jacqueline Ululani Visser, Pat Carvalho, Nephi Brown, and many more.

To educate steel guitarists outside of Hawai'i as well, Jerry Byrd has written the most comprehensive steel guitar instruction book including rhythm back-up tape recordings. It was printed in both English and Japanese. In 1987 he gave a two-hour seminar at HSGA's first convention in Hawai'i. It was tape recorded and offered for sale to club members the world over, proceeds of the sales going to a scholarship fund, which will be discussed later in this chapter. In 1990 HSGA produced the first and only instruction video for Hawaiian style steel guitar. The instructor was none other than Jerry Byrd. The videos were an instant sell-out and it is the desire of HSGA to put one into the music library of every high school in Hawai'i.

Funding By The Hawai'i State Foundation On Culture And The Arts

Annually, awards are announced to fund the giving of instruction by a Master craftsman to an Apprentice in some aspect of Hawaiian arts and crafts. Under this program, Barney Isaacs has been able to pass on some knowledge of his musical skills, and as a result one of his graduate students, Edward Punua, is an accomplished steel guitarist as well as an all-round musician. Another of Barney's students, Scott Furushima, is well on the way to steel guitar fame. In the 1993 awards, Barney has been given the opportunity to instruct a new student, Lawrence B. Reis, and Henry Kaleialoha Allen of Maui will instruct Kevin Kulakamaka Brown . Clearly, if steel guitar is to make a come-back to popular use in Hawai'i, instruction must be made more readily available to Hawaiian students and we acknowledge with our grateful "Mahalo" the assistance being given by the State Foundation on Culture and the Arts.

Artists In The Schools Program

Steel guitarist Henry Allen in Maui has started a scholarship program, and takes his guitar into school classrooms to demonstrate, instruct, entertain, and inspire the youngsters. On O'ahu, the same classroom work is done by Solomon Kam. On the big island of Hawai'i, John Auna takes his steel guitar charisma to the children. That is possibly the most important single thing that can be done to re-establish the steel guitar as a prominent instrument in Hawai'i.

Before electronic tuners, a musician had to rely on tuning forks and pitch pipes to tune to standard pitch. This unique pitchpipe is "M. Hohner's No. P8 Hawaiian Guitar 'Trutone' pitch pipe. The world's best. Made in Germany." It is designed for the A major low bass tuning.

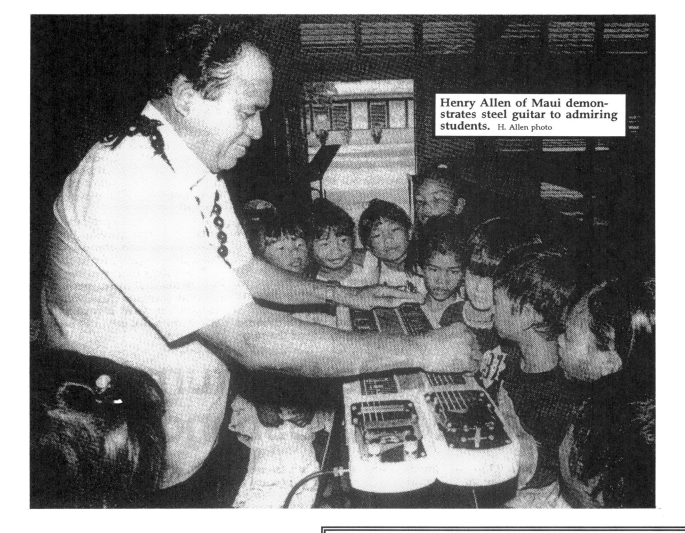

Henry Allen of Maui demonstrates steel guitar to admiring students. H. Allen photo

Steel Guitar Ho'olaule'as

Aside from his one-man battle to provide steel guitar instruction for all and sundry, Jerry Byrd has taken on another important role in Hawai'i. He instigated and produced the Jerry Byrd Steel Guitar Ho'olaule'a. It was an annual event held at the Ala Moana Americana Hotel, a gala concert featuring the best steel guitarists of Hawai'i with an exciting guest or two from overseas. His first Ho'olaule'a was in 1982 and his final was during the year of the steel guitar's centennial, 1989. On that occasion, Hawai'i took the opportunity to say "mahalo" to Manu. Dr. Michael Chun, president of Kamehameha Schools, represented Congressman D. Akaka in presenting the written record of a one-minute address given on the floor of the House of Congress in Washington DC by Mr. Akaka.

Congressional Record

United States of America

PROCEEDINGS AND DEBATES OF THE 101st CONGRESS, FIRST SESSION

Vol. 135   WASHINGTON, WEDNESDAY, APRIL 12, 1989   No. 43

PRAISING JERRY "MANU" BYRD

(Mr. AKAKA asked and was given permission to address the House for 1 minute and to revise and extend his remarks.)

Mr. AKAKA. Mr. Speaker, it is my distinct pleasure to honor a dear friend of mine Jerry "Manu" Byrd during the centennial of the Hawaiian steel guitar. Jerry Byrd is a steel guitarist in the sense that Rembrandt was a painter.

In Hawaiian steel guitar circles, Jerry is known simply as The Great One. Thousands throughout the world have enjoyed his singular musical skill, which brings forth the fantasies and realities of our island paradise: perfumes of tropical flowers, swaying palms, pounding surf, colorful rainbows, surfers, and hula maidens. More importantly, Jerry's steel strings evoke our Hawaiian spirit of aloha.

I feel privileged to join Jerry's many friends and his family in saluting him for his contribution to Hawaii. Jerry has shared his talent so unselfishly, not only with the listening public but with the many students he has taken under his tutelage.

I want to extend a big mahalo to Jerry "Manu" Byrd for all he has done for music and Hawaii.

169

Alan Akaka Carries On

In 1991, Alan Akaka began a new series of steel guitar ho'olaule'as, under the sponsorship of his company, A.I.S. Entertainment. The first two annual concerts were held at the Ala Wai Golf Course Club House during the first week of May, and the third in 1993 was held in the Princess Ke'elikolani Auditorium of Kamehameha Schools. This was his way of bringing steel guitar back to its birth place, to heighten students' awareness of the instrument in the year its inventor was to be honored in the Steel Guitar Hall of Fame, St. Louis MO. If the first concert is an indicator, they will attract an international crowd with enthusiastic support from the kama'ainas for many years to come. Alan Akaka has become the new leader in promoting the Hawaiian steel guitar.

Henry Allen Takes It To Maui

Under the sponsorship of the Maui Intercontinental Resort Hotel in Lahaina, an annual steel guitar ho'olaule'a has become a new tradition. Steel guitarists are invited from other islands, plus a few international guests, to revive and perpetuate the Hawaiian musical tradition on Maui.

John Auna On The Big Island Of Hawai'i

Since the centennial of the steel guitar was celebrated in 1989, steel guitarist John Auna has begun promoting annual steel guitar ho'olaule'as on the Big Island: in the Kona area, in Hilo, and at Honoka'a. This activity provides stimulation for the local steel guitarists who take part, and Auna usually includes a few big name artists from Honolulu.

Spectrum Hawai'i

The people of Hawai'i have begun to recognize the steel guitar again as an integral part of their musical heritage. Recently "Spectrum Hawai'i", a live concert held in the NBC Concert Hall, was filmed. In the show, several famous musical families of the Islands were featured. Included was the music of the late Alvin Isaacs (father of Barney Isaacs), steel guitarist and composer of over 300 songs. The musicans were Barney Isaacs on steel guitar, Benny Kalama on 'ukulele, Aaron Mahi on bass, and Scott Furushima on guitar. Another recent film special, "Hawaiian Rainbows", sponsored by the Music Department, University of Hawai'i, featured Billy Hew Len's steel guitar.

Association For Hawaiian Music

This association was established in 1971 by Dr. George S. Kanahele and friends for the purpose of safeguarding the Hawaiian musical culture. The association began publishing an excellent monthly newsletter, Ha'ilono Mele (News of Hawaiian Music), beginning January 1975. The first editor was Dr Mantle Hood, ethnomusicologist, followed by Jerry Hopkins. It ran for five or six years. AHM promoted special concerts for slack key guitar and for steel guitar, also song writing contests to stimulate public interest.

The club's officers now are: President R. Alex Anderson, Vice President I.B. "Buddy" Peterson, Treasurer Harry S. Dods, and Executive Director Charles Bud Dant. In their 1991 New Year's newsletter they wrote, "... and how do we achieve our goals of preserving the music and culture of Hawai'i and encourage its resurgence throughout the world?? Simple: with the Hawaiian steel guitar! Beginning in early 1991, Hawai'i Public TV, KHET, produced and broadcast two 'Spectrum Hawai'i' programs: one with our President, R. Alex Anderson, his music and his 'ukulele, accompanied by Jerry Byrd on steel guitar and Benny Kalama on guitar and bass. The second 'Spectrum Hawai'i' was an all steel guitar TV show featuring Jerry, Barney 'The Chief' Isaacs, Alan Akaka, and Merle Kekuku along with more wonderful players. Jerry, Barney, Merle and Alan gave some fine narration about instruments, tuning, and styles. We understand that both programs will be broadcast from time to time throughout this year."

The officers of AHM and the board members are a very prestigious group in Hawaiian music circles. With people of their calibre working to preserve and restore the Hawaiian musical culture, the steel guitar's prospects look good.

Hawai'i Calls Again

In March, 1992 an announcement was made in the Honolulu Star Bulletin to the effect that serious discussion had begun to put this world-famous radio show back on the air. Honolulu advertising man Bill Bigelow was reported to have bought the rights to the show from Don McDiarmid. Some of the stars of the show when it closed in 1975 were slated to shine again in the new show. One of those, soprano Nina Keali'iwahamana, was selected as the show's program director. Other vocalists named were Iwalani Kahalewai, sister-in-law of Haunani Iwalani Kahalewai who sang in the original show, and Leilani Kahau. Baritone Gary Aiko (whose mother, Genoa Keawe, sang in the original show) was named as vocalist and bass player, along with Harold Haku'ole on rhythm guitar and George Kuo on slack key guitar. Barney Isaacs, who was there to close the original show in 1975, was mentioned as the steel guitarist.

On July 29th, 1992 the new "Hawai'i Calls" went on a 10-concert tour in and around Tokyo, Osaka, Nagoya, and Kyoto, Japan as a pre-opening goodwill tour. Due to illness, Barney Isaacs was unable to do the tour and steel guitarist Henry Allen of Maui took his place.

On Saturday, October 3rd, 1992 the new Hawai'i Calls show went on the air for the first time since it closed in 1975. Originating from the Tropics Surf Club at the Hilton Hawaiian Village, it was identified as show #2088. The show was hosted by Bill Bigelow in true Webley Edwards style, with vocalist Joe Recca introducing the songs. Important dignitaries made welcoming speeches, and the guest entertainer was Danny Kaleikini.

The show features contemporary Hawaiian music as well as traditional, with different guest artists each week. The last show of each month is broadcast from a different Hawaiian island. Radio stations in many lands are negotiating to carry once again this show that won the hearts of so many millions of people from 1935 to 1975. Once again the steel guitar, known to all the world as the signature sound of Hawai'i, calls "come home, come home to Hawai'i".

In January 1994 the show's name was changed to "The Hawai'i Show" due to problems arising from the use of the original name, and in February 1994 it was changed again to "The Sounds of Aloha". Steel guitarist Casey Olsen and rhythm guitarist Hiram "Jiggs" Olsen came on staff as orchestra leader and his son Casey Olsen replaced Barney Isaacs who retired, due to ill health. Kuhio Yim took the place of George Kuo.

Hawai'i Calls.
(L-R) Bill Bigelow, George Kuo, Harold Haku'ole,
Gary Aiko, Barney Isaacs, Joe Recca,
Nina Keali'iwahamana, Iwalani Kahalewai,
and Leilani Kahau.
Bill Bigelow photo

Steel Guitar Clubs

After reading about the huge steel guitar schools on mainland U.S., their festivals and competitions, the reader will understand that lifetime friendships were formed and steel guitar became a way of life for many people. After the schools folded and the students went about the business of life, there was a feeling of wanting to make it all happen again and to keep in touch with each other.

All over the world there were Hawaiian clubs of all sorts. Some were steel guitar schools, some were for social get-togethers through newsletters and/or organized conventions, many were night clubs. For example: in Holland the Hawai'i Calls Fan Club published a newsletter in English, German, and Dutch for several years beginning in 1959, in England Banjo Mandolin and Guitar magazine was published through the 1930's and 1940's. It served social as well as informative needs and when the magazine ceased to exist its readers carried on as the BMG Tape Club, exchanging tape recorded music and personal greetings on a set routine, still in operation. The Glasgow Hawaiian Club and the London Hawaiian Club were in existence in the 1940's. As early as the 1930's we know of several Australian clubs, the Queensland Hawaiian Club and in Melbourne, the Hawthorn Banjo and Guitar Club. Meanwhile, for social and instructive clubs, for get-togethers and conventions held, the Japanese have been far more dedicated to Hawaiian music and the steel guitar from the 1920's to this day.

Aloha International Steel Guitar Club Magazine

The first of the steel guitar social clubs of Hawaiian interest that we know of in the U.S.A. was started by Rex Mortimer of Altus OK. From January 1966 to February 1968 he published a very professional, very informative quarterly newsletter, the International Steel Guitar Club Magazine. There were no conventions or meetings that we know of. When he died a new club filled the gap.

International Hawaiian Steel Guitar Club

Norman "Red" Moser of South Gate MI was there at the start. It began with a discussion in Red's "Hula Hut", where Dwight Harris, Agnes Nance, and Red met frequently to practice. Red did so much corresponding with steel guitarists across the country exchanging tape recordings and gossiping, the idea came to him that these people should be brought together to meet each other. The club's president and editor Charles E. Moore of Winchester IN had just begun publishing a quarterly newsletter. He agreed to hold the first convention July 12 and 13th in 1975 in the back yard of his home. The convention was so successful a larger place had to be found, so the second year they met in the 4-H Club barn in Winchester, the third year at a roller skating rink, and from then on very successful conventions were held at the Willard Elementary School, Winchester IN. In 1978 Jerry Byrd became their first big name guest artist and the convention exploded in size as a result. That was the year Charlie Hynd and his wife came all the way from Scotland, and Arthur Jones from Wales in the U.K. When Moore retired as editor and president of IHSGC in 1987, he retired the name as well.

Aloha International Steel Guitar Club

A new club was formed immediately, under the presidency of Dirk Vogel who continues to publish a quarterly newsletter under a new name, the Aloha International Steel Guitar Club, holding annual conventions at the same Willard Elementary School in Winchester IN. AISGC carried on inviting steel guitarists from Hawai'i as guests to their annual festivals. Barney Isaacs, Sol Bright, Alan Akaka, and Casey Olsen along with the Hiram Olsen Trio have been their guests.

The Hawaiian Steel Guitar Association

In the meantime, a need was seen for an association which would have a mission to do something positive to restore the popularity of the Hawaiian steel guitar. The HSGA was formed in October of 1985, holding its annual conventions at the Holiday Inn, Joliet IL and an additional convention every second year at the Queen Kapi'olani Hotel in Honolulu, moving to another island during the second week. The club's first president was Joe Boudreau of Lake Elsinore CA who retired from the position in 1986. Steel guitarist Lorene Ruymar of Vancouver BC Canada, who was the vice president at the time, became the new president. Art Ruymar became the new vice president and treasurer. The quarterly newsletter was published during the club's first two years beginning with the January 1986 edition, by Fred Gagner, author of several Spanish guitar method books, living in Scottsdale, AZ. When he retired, Lorene Ruymar assumed editorial duties, beginning with the January 1988 edition, closing with the April 1993 edition.

HSGA had become so large it was no longer possible to run it as a hobby on a volunteered work basis. Therefore in 1993 it was moved to Honolulu under the new presidency of steel guitar virtuoso Alan Akaka, with vice president Jerry Byrd, and newsletter editor Marjorie Scott. Since 1988, HSGA had become a very active promoter of the Hawaiian steel guitar in Hawai'i and around the world. A few of its accomplishments are as follows:

Scholarship Fund. HSGA's first project was to establish a scholarship fund to assist deserving students in Hawai'i to take lessons from Jerry Byrd. Funds are raised by proceeds of sales and by direct donation from members. Through this fund, many young steel guitarists have been helped along their way to success. After moving to Hawai'i, we expect HSGA will become very active in the music education of young Hawaiians. Alan Akaka is a highly skilled music educator, presently employed as bandmaster at Kamehameha Schools. He is bringing music educators onto the HSGA Board of Directors with that goal in mind.

Publicity Campaign. Through tireless letter writing Ruymar has been able to talk to people in the media, in education, in Mayor F. Fasi's office (Honolulu), in Governor John Waihe'e's office (State of Hawai'i), at the Bishop Museum and Hawai'i's two universities, Hawai'i Visitors Bureau, the State Foundation on Culture and the Arts, and so on. All of this campaigning brought about more television and news magazine interviews, live shows, and the inclusion of steel guitar in prestigious activities where it might not have appeared otherwise.

Letter writing campaigns. One example is the Hawaiian cultural exchange with Russia. In 1989 a group of Russian musicians visited Hawai'i, in return for which a large group of Hawaiian entertainers was formed to carry their musical culture to Moscow. Advance news reports did not include a steel guitarist in the group. After firing off some persuasive letters, HSGA was proud to note that steel guitarist Iaukea Bright was included in the show. The second example was when a large party of musicians and entertainers from Hawai'i were to be guests at the Festival of American Folklife at the Smithsonian Institute in Washington D.C., in June of 1989. Again, advance newspaper reports gave detailed lists of who was included and again the steel guitar was not mentioned. HSGA letters were sent immediately to the State Foundation on Culture and the Arts and it wasn't long before both Alan Akaka and Barney Isaacs were approached with an offer. Barney made the trip with the group. Did HSGA play a part in those decisions? We'll never know.

Publishing the information in the HSGA newsletter has resulted in several club members being chosen for the Artists in the Schools program. Henry Allen of Maui, for one, now takes his steel guitar into classrooms and tells the children about the instrument. Barney Isaacs and Edward Punua were successful in receiving a "Master Teacher and Apprentice" grant to enable Edward to take steel guitar lessons from Barney. After graduating Edward, Barney has begun instructing Scott Furushima. Under the same program, John Auna teaches Al Greene Jr.

Concerts in the Park. During the first HSGA convention in Hawai'i in 1987 a special show - free to the public - was sponsored by HSGA at the Bandstand, Kapi'olani Park. Its purpose was to showcase the steel guitarists of the islands. It was a thrilling event, as a large number of top Hawaiian steel guitarists turned out to donate their talent to the cause. It was decided this show must be presented every year to keep up the momentum.

Lei Day Concerts. On May 1st, 1990 the Island steel guitarists of HSGA kept the sweet sounds flowing at the Lei Day celebrations. A bandstand was set up along the parade route where the royal procession would pass, on their way to inspect the leis. The performance was so well received, we have decided to make it an annual event.

Concerts in Shopping Malls HSGA expanded its promotional work of steel guitar to the Ala Moana Shopping Centre's big Centerstage in May of 1993. The large crowds that forgot their shopping to stay and enjoy the whole show gave us the message that this must be done again, with the Royal Hawaiian Shopping Center outdoor stage being our next target. Here is where our young up-coming steel guitarists of Hawai'i must sharpen their skills and become known.

Tourist Demand. When visiting Hawai'i, HSGA members make a point of showing their appreciation to the management when they attend a show that includes steel guitar. If the show does not include steel guitar, they make their feelings known as well. One cannot blame Food and Beverage Managers for not hiring Hawaiian style entertainment complete with steel guitar if they feel there is no tourist demand. We make sure they understand THERE IS a tourist demand. We call it our "Compliment and Complain" campaign. We also write letters to advertising agencies who run commercials on TV that are supposed to represent Hawai'i but do not have the traditional instruments playing the music. We write to airlines who make their money bringing tourists to Hawai'i, yet do not have Hawaiian music on their listening stations and play "the wrong kind" of music in the cabin while passengers wait to disembark. Our next aim is to get the airlines to put an attractive information card in the magazine pockets for passengers to read. The card would remind tourists that much of the charm of the South Seas islands served by this airline is in the music of that culture. Caring guests can do much to show their support.

Other Steel Guitar Clubs

Although the Hawaiian steel guitar has a relatively small following, the pedal steel guitar in country music is flourishing. The clubs listed below are mainly country music oriented, but since the older members cut their musical teeth on Hawaiian style steel guitar, a certain amount of Hawaiian content can be found in all of them.

The **Northwest Steel Guitar Society** may have been the first formed to promote the playing of pedal steel guitar and the Hawaiian steel guitar in country music. It was formed in 1971 and members met each month to instruct and perform for each other. Its first officers were Chubby Howard, Larry DeRocher, and Lee Gillespie.

The following are currently in operation:

Steel Guitar Club, Box 669 Streetsville ON, Canada L5M 2C2. Al Brisco, president and editor.

British Steelies Society, 21 Arnolds Close, Barton-On-Sea, Hants, England BH25 7JW.
    Roy Heap, president and editor

Australian Steel Guitar Association, 355 Lakedge Ave, Berkley Vale NSW Australia 2259.
    Principals Ken Kitching and John Dolan Brown

Pedal Steel Guitar Association (formed in 1973), P.O. Box 248, Floral Park NY 11001.
    Bob Maikel, president and editor

Steel Guitar International (formed in 1978), 9535 Midland Blvd., St. Louis MO 63114.
    DeWitt Scott, president and editor, announced in his July 1994 newsletter that the coming
    October edition of his S.G.I. Enquirer would be his final, after sixteen years of publication.

Steel Guitar World, Box 9297, Spokane WA 99209-9297. Russell K. Rask, editor

Hawaiian music clubs:

Aloha International Steel Guitar Club, P.O. Box 24284 Minneapolis MN 55424.
    Dirk Vogel, president and editor.

Hawaiian Steel Guitar Association, Box 1497, Kailua, HI 96734-1497. Alan Akaka, president.
    Lorene Ruymar, president emeritus, 2090 West 44th Ave. Vancouver B.C. Canada V6M 2E9.,
    editor and author of this book.

Jr. Duravant   Cecil Johnson   Dick Woods

Freddie Sturm and His Hawaiian Ensemble

THUMB PICKS

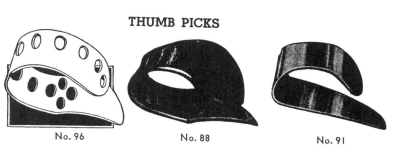

No. 96   No. 88   No. 91

From a 1936 Gibson catalog

Steel Guitar Hall Of Fame

DeWitt Scott, president of Steel Guitar International, is credited with starting the Steel Guitar Hall of Fame in 1978. Plaques and mementos are on display at the Regal Riverfront Hotel, St. Louis. This is the location of Scotty's annual convention which attracts anywhere from 4,000 to 7,000 people. To be worthy of nomination, a steel guitarist must be an outstanding musician and must have contributed to the world of steel guitar, regardless of whether he or she played Hawaiian, country, or another form. Those who have been inducted into the Hall of Fame are as follows:

Jerry Byrd	1978
Leon McAuliffe	1978
Alvino Rey	1978
Herb Remington	1979
Sol Ho'opi'i	1979
Joaquin Murphy	1980
Speedy West	1980
Noel Boggs	1981
Buddy Emmons	1981
Jimmy Day	1982
Dick Ka'aihue McIntire	1982
Eddie Alkire	1983
Ralph Mooney	1983
Don Helms	1984
Bud Isaacs	1984
"Little" Roy Wiggins	1985
Curly Chalker	1985
Harold "Shot" Jackson	1986
Peter Drake	1987
Lloyd Green	1988
Hal Rugg	1989
Billy Bowman	1989
David Keli'i	1990
Bob White	1990
Zane Beck	1991
Tom Brumley	1992
DeWitt Scott	1992
Bob Dunn	1993
Buddy Charleton	1993
Joseph Kekuku	1993
Doug Jernigan	1994
Freddie Tavares	1995

Historic photo of the first three to be inducted into the Steel Guitar Hall of Fame in 1978, *L to R:* Leon McAuliffe, Alvino Rey, Jerry Byrd. In front of them are the bronze plaques which are on display at the Regal Riverfront Hotel, St. Louis MO. Leo Rajotte photo

September 4, 1993 at the Regal Riverfront Hotel in St. Louis MO, Joseph Kekuku is inducted into the Steel Guitar Hall of Fame with full honors as the inventor of the Hawaiian Steel Guitar. Merle and Ronnie Kekuku receive the award from Michael Scott, son of DeWitt Scott, Hall of Fame chairman. Leo Rajotte photo

The exact wording on the Kekuku plaque is:

"STEEL GUITAR HALL OF FAME" (followed by a carved relief of Joseph playing steel guitar, palm trees and grass hut in background) "JOSEPH KEKUKU" (and then in smaller print, with just one spelling error on the great Hawaiian name) "JOSEPH KEKUUPENAKANA-I'AUPUNIOKAMEHAMEHA APUAKEHAU CONSIDERED BY HISTORIANS AS THE INVENTOR OF THE HAWAIIAN STEEL GUITAR. EXPERIMENTED WITH THE DESIGN OF THE COMPONENTS NEEDED TO GIVE BIRTH TO THE "STEEL GUITAR" THAT ARE STILL USED TODAY. BORN 1874 LA'IE, HAWAII, INDUCTED 1993. DIED JAN. 16, 1932. STEEL GUITAR CONVENTION BOARD".

A copy of the plaque was made by H.S.G.A. and presented to Kamehameha Schools in memory of Joseph Kekuku and his nephew Merle Kekuku.

Celebrating The Steel Guitar's Centennial

It was the Hawaiian Steel Guitar Association that observed and publicized the centennial of the invention of the Hawaiian guitar. Although the exact date was difficult to pinpoint since Joseph Kekuku's inventive work took place over a span of years, we chose 1889 as the year to celebrate. That was the year he enrolled at the school and the building of the adaptations took place in the school's workshop. We proposed that date to Elizabeth Tatar, anthropologist at the Bishop Museum who endorsed our decision in a letter of authenticity.

Aside from having a natural desire to celebrate the centennial, we realized that we could do much to attract attention to the guitar through publicity of our activities.

Convention. The main event of the celebration was a convention held at the Queen Kapi'olani Hotel, O'ahu in May of 1989. We truly did attract steel guitarists from many countries around the

B I S H O P   M U S E U M

1525 BERNICE STREET • P.O. BOX 19000-A • HONOLULU, HAWAI'I • 96817-0916 • (808) 847-3511

July 16, 1987

Ms. Lorene Ruymar
President
Hawaiian Steel Guitar Association
2090 West 44th Ave.
Vancouver, B.C.
V6M 2E9

Dear Ms. Ruymar,

Thank you for your letter of July 3 expressing your interest in commemorating the centennial of the invention of the Hawaiian steel guitar. Though it is very difficult in the case of popular musical instruments to place an exact date on their origins, for your purposes I would recommend using 1889, based on D. Mitchell's well-researched contribution in Kanahele (1979), as a workable date.

May I suggest contacting Dr. Ricardo Tremillos, ethnomusicologist at the University of Hawaii-Manoa (Music Department) and Lyn Martin, Folk Arts Coordinator, State Foundation on Culture and the Arts for possible ways to publicize the centennial of the steel guitar.

Sincerely,

Elizabeth Tatar
Associate Anthropologist
Department of Anthropology

cc: Dr. Ricardo Tremillos
    University of Hawaii-Manoa
    Music Department
    Honolulu, Hawai'i 96822
    Ms. Lyn Martin
    Folk Arts Coordinator
    The State Foundation on Culture and the Arts
    335 Merchant St., Rm. 202
    Honolulu, Hawai'i 96813

world and the event was successful and joyful beyond our dreams. The media of Hawai'i gave us all the attention we could hope for and many events were planned by civic groups in Hawai'i as well as in other countries throughout the year, in which the steel guitar was honored.

The Year of Steel Guitar. Mayor Frank Fasi of the City of Honolulu and Governor John Waihe'e of the State of Hawai'i both issued proclamations declaring 1989 to be the Year Of the Steel Guitar.

Postage Stamp. A special request was made of the U.S. Post Office by HSGA and by Honolulu's Mayor Fasi and the State of Hawai'i's Governor Waihe'e to have a special postage stamp issued to commemorate Joseph Kekuku's invention. If accepted, it is expected to appear in 1993 or 1994 when the "Musicians" series goes on sale.

Concerts on the Big Island and in Maui. Steel guitarist John Auna of Kailua, Kona organized a series of concerts and special events in Kona and in Hilo which were well supported by local steel guitarists, guitarists of O'ahu, and by HSGA members. Henry Allen began a series of annual steel guitar ho'olaule'as sponsored by the Maui Intercontinental Resort Hotel, to celebrate the centennial of the steel guitar's invention.

176

OFFICE OF THE MAYOR ✛
CITY AND COUNTY OF HONOLULU ✛

PROCLAMATION

WHEREAS, the Hawaiian Steel Guitar Association is a global communications network comprised of about 300 Hawaiian music enthusiasts; and

WHEREAS, the group was organized to revive the popularity of the musical instrument in much the same way the slack key guitar has enjoyed a resurgence in recent years; and

WHEREAS, toward this end, a scholarship fund has been established to provide formal education for youngsters wishing to pursue musical training; and

WHEREAS, this year marks the centennial anniversary of the invention of the Hawaiian steel guitar with the credit attributed to Joseph Kekuku; and

WHEREAS, although others had made music by sliding combs and glass tumblers up and down the guitar strings, the Kamehameha student is acknowledged as having invented the apparatus in the school's machine shop in 1889; and

WHEREAS, the Hawaiian Steel Guitar Association will hold a convention at the Queen Kapiolani Hotel during May 7-14, 1989,

NOW, THEREFORE, I, FRANK F. FASI, Mayor of the City and County of Honolulu, do hereby proclaim 1989 as

THE YEAR OF THE STEEL GUITAR

in the City and County of Honolulu in special recognition of the 100th anniversary of the authentically Hawaiian musical instrument and urge everyone in our community to support its revival in the islands.

IN WITNESS WHEREOF, I have hereunto set my hand and caused the Seal of the City and County of Honolulu to be affixed.

Done this 8th day of December, 1988, in Honolulu, Hawaii.

FRANK F. FASI, Mayor
City and County of Honolulu

Commemorative Plaque. HSGA designed and produced a special plaque honoring Joseph Kekuku. It was presented to Kamehameha Schools in a ceremony attended by a representative from each country present at the convention. That plaque now hangs in the school's administration offices.

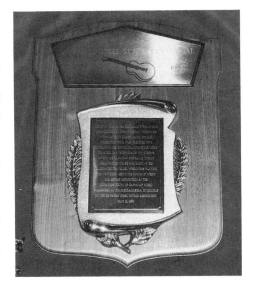

Honorary plaque presented to Kamehameha Schools in honor of their illustrious student.
A.W.Ruymar photo

Proclamation

WHEREAS, 100 years ago Joseph Kekuku enrolled in Kamehameha Schools and through the use of its machine shop developed the first of the genuine steel guitars; and

WHEREAS, he spent his remaining years at Kamehameha perfecting playing techniques and teaching his classmates to play the instrument; and

WHEREAS, Joseph's colleagues spread their skill far and wide, forming schools of their own and teaching the playing of the steel guitar all over the world; and

WHEREAS, the steel guitar is the only uniquely Hawaiian instrument, one which provides the signature sound of the islands; and

WHEREAS, the Hawaiian Steel Guitar Association will hold its worldwide convention May 7 through 14, 1989 at the Queen Kapiolani Hotel in Honolulu; and

WHEREAS, the Association has as its goals the education of Hawaii youth in the playing of the steel guitar and the acquaintance of visitors to the islands with the authentic music of Hawaii;

NOW, THEREFORE I, JOHN WAIHEE, Governor of Hawaii, do hereby proclaim 1989 to be

YEAR OF THE STEEL GUITAR IN HAWAII

and urge all who appreciate authentic Hawaiian music to applaud the steel guitar players and music in our midst.

DONE at the State Capitol, in the Executive Chambers, Honolulu, State of Hawaii, this fifth day of May, 1989.

Other Centennial Projects. Celebration of the centennial gave steel guitarists an opportunity to attract media attention. In Australia, Bill Knox began a video documentary "History of Steel Guitar". In London England, the Institute of Contemporary Arts produced a show "Sliding Around The World" featuring steel guitarists from every continent. Many HSGA members put on their own centennial celebration show in their home town and attracted the attention of local newspapers and TV.

A History of the Steel Guitar to be Written. Best of all, as a centennial project HSGA began collecting data to put this very important book together. It is our hope that music teachers in the Hawaiian school system will refer to it so that future generations will know about the instrument that was invented in Hawai'i and about those great musical ambassadors who went from Hawai'i carrying the spirit of aloha to all parts of the globe. It didn't happen in the same way for other cultures in the South Pacific, but they didn't have the steel guitar.

Proceeds from the sale of this book will be directed to a Trust Fund to assist deserving youngsters in their study of the instruments of traditional (pre-1970's) Hawaiian music. Those instruments are the steel guitar, 'ukulele, kī hō'alu , rhythm back-up guitar, and acoustic bass. Special preference is to be given to steel guitar students, provided they are studying the music of earlier Hawai'i, not following the latest non-Hawaiian music fads. Should there be no Hawaiian music instruction (as described here) established, the fund will be used to give employment and public performance exposure to young Hawaiians who have learned to play the steel guitar but who have not yet begun a professional career in music. This might be done through some form of annual Junior Steel Guitar Ho'olaule'a.

This book is a compilation of many submissions and writings of HSGA club members and others. Those who wrote articles are listed in the index under "Writers". All other sections were written by HSGA's retiring president and editor, Lorene Ruymar who was given the new title "President Emeritus".

Discography Of Steel Guitar

A most comprehensive discography of recorded music featuring steel guitar in all its forms has been written and published by Joe Goldmark, 2259 14th Ave. San Francisco, CA 94116. The 7th edition was completed in 1994, titled "**The International Steel Guitar and Dobro Discography**"

Section 1: lists pop and country steel guitar, songs about the steel guitar, steel instrumentals done by other instruments, and a pop and country steel guitar cross reference. Section 2: Hawaiian steel guitar listings and cross reference. Section 3: Dobro listings and cross reference.

All listings are in alphabetic order by name of steel guitarist or by name of the band, and the recording companies are indicated, with country of origin and serial number. The cross reference section names the band or its leader and lists the names of all steel players who worked with the band at different times. Recordings are listed from Australia, Belgium, Canada, Denmark, England, Fiji, France, Germany, Holland, India, Italy, Japan, Mexico, New Zealand, Norway, South Africa, Sweden, and Switzerland.

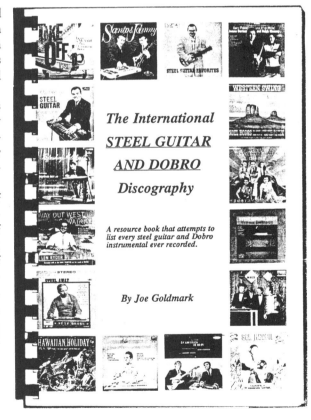

The International
STEEL GUITAR
AND DOBRO
Discography

A resource book that attempts to list every steel guitar and Dobro instrumental ever recorded.

By Joe Goldmark

The Future Of The Hawaiian Steel Guitar

During the 1970's the steel guitar hit its lowest ebb in Hawai'i, to the point that there was only one place where it was played in public on a regular daily basis. That was at the Halekulani Hotel's House Without a Key. Now, due to a new spirit among steel guitarists of the islands, and due also to the work of Jerry Byrd and of the Hawaiian Steel Guitar Association, it appears to be on its way to some degree of revival. The great wave of enthusiasm this instrument caused throughout the world is very evident in Japan. Many of the top artists of Hawai'i make several tours a year to Japan where they are honored and emulated. We hope our North American culture is ready for the pendulum to swing back to sweet music and that the Hawaiians, in their quest to strengthen their cultural roots, will see the steel guitar as being an integral part of their traditional post-European music.

It seems the demand for steel guitarists in the Hawaiian islands is definitely on the increase. Merle Kekuku reported that the Musicians' Union gets requests for steel guitarists every day. There's a better chance the young and untried guitarist will be given a chance. There are now, in 1993, at least seven hotels in the islands where steel guitar is heard on a regular basis. This is a difficult time for all musicians as the karaoke equipment takes over from live performers, but it seems that steel guitar has been out of the public eye for so long, it is now looked on as a refreshing new sound. It appears that the come-back is already well established.

A Bright Future, Through Evolution

by Owana Salazar

"With regard to a genuine concern over the future of the steel guitar in Hawai'i, allow me to share some of my thoughts with you. The steel guitar has much presence in today's performances and recordings. It is especially embraced by contemporary music circles and is utilized with a nouveau performance sound. The mutations in the style of playing contribute to the evolution that is necessary to the future of the Hawaiian Steel Guitar. The evolutionary stylings used in jazz music with the steel are, in essence, the same evolution principle used by contemporary Hawaiian performing artists and musicians.

A large and growing number of mainstream musicians of Hawai'i, in both realms of traditional and contemporary Hawaiian music, include the steel guitar in their recordings and live performances. Artists such as Willie K., Nohelani Cypriano, Tony Conjugacion, Peter Moon, Teresa Bright, Cyril Pahinui, Dennis Pavao, and Diana Aki only name some of the many who incorporate the Hawaiian steel guitar in their music. I believe that one key to the longevity of the Hawaiian Steel Guitar is to embrace this evolution, recognize it and acknowledge its stylized presence as a living link between yesterday and today. Stop worrying and start playing, the Hawaiian Steel Guitar is here to stay!"

Steel guitarist
Owana K. Salazar,
Hawai'i's bright future.
O. Salazar photo

In Conclusion

What would we like to see happening next? We'd like to see Hawaiian youngsters taught more about their excellent musical history, about the great people who played their part in it. We'd like to see instruction on steel guitar offered at institutions of higher learning in Hawai'i. We'd like to see Joseph Kekuku, Sol Ho'opi'i, and other great steel guitarists honored in Hawai'i in the same way that the Olympic swimming champion Duke Kahanamoku is honored. We'd like to see steel guitar recognized once more as an integral part of Hawaiian music. Slack key guitar and 'ukulele enjoy that position, why not the steel guitar? Hawai'i is the birth mother of steel guitar, we in other lands are only adoptive parents. We say, "Don't you see, Hawai'i, how beautiful your child is? Can't you love it again?"

To close, I want to leave you with the words of Tony Todaro in his book 'The Golden Years of Hawaiian Entertainment'. He said, "Kekuku's contribution made Hawaiian music acceptable and every Hawaiian musical group should salute Joseph Kekuku by building their group around the steel - and in the case of a large orchestra, a steel has been used in the past and should still be a must instrument, no matter how small the part.

"Listen closely next time you hear a steel guitar solo - listen and you can hear its haunting strains whispering softly but clearly, 'I am the soul of Hawaiian music. I can be sad - I can be glad; I can be haunting - I can be taunting - but I cannot be neglected and lonely. Play with me, caress me, keep me in tune and I'll give you forever the stars and the moon.' "

Joseph Kekuku'upenakana'iaupuniokamehameha
Apuakehau, inventor of the
Hawaiian steel guitar.
Sam K. Na'inoa photo, courtesy of R. Maximchuk

Courtesy The Experience Music Project, Seattle, Washington

Bibliography
and Suggested Readings

Books:

Bishop Museum "Annotated Catalog of Books & Series in Print".
   Honolulu, Bishop Museum Press, 1988
Blackburn, Bill. "Old Guitar Mania". Anaheim Hills CA. Centerstream Publishing
Brennan, Joseph, "The Parker Ranch of Hawai'i" New York. 1979
Brozman, Bob "The Art and History of National Resonator Instruments".
   Anaheim Hills CA. Centerstream Publishing,
Byrd, Jerry "The Jerry Byrd Instruction Course for Steel Guitar" - A Complete Study
   for the Serious Student. Isao Wada, Oudensha Company Ltd., Kawasaki Japan, 1983.
Carter, Walter. "Gruhn's Guide to Vintage Guitars". Cupertino CA.   Miller Freeman, 1991
Daws, Gavan. "Shoal of Time, A History Of The Hawaiian Islands".
   Honolulu HI. University of Hawai'i Press , 1974.
Evans, Tom and Mary. "Guitars". New York. Paddington Press Ltd., 1977
Fullerton, George. "Guitar Legends". Anaheim Hills CA. Centerstream Publishing.
Goldmark, Joe. "The International Steel Guitar And Dobro Discography".
   San Francisco, CA. Self published, 1994
Hartman, Robert Carl. "The Larsons' Creations, Guitars and Mandolins".
   Anaheim Hills CA. Centerstream Publishing,
Iwanade, Yasuhiko. "The Fender Strat History" Anaheim Hills CA. Centerstream Publishing.
Kanahele, George S. "Hawaiian Music and Musicians, An Illustrated History".
   Honolulu HI. The University Press of Hawaii, 1979
Kanahele, George S. "Pauahi, The Kamehameha Legacy",
   Honolulu HI. Kamehameha Schools Press, 1986
Kasher, Kamohalu and Burlingame, Burl. "Da Kine Sound. Conversations With the People
   Who Create Hawaiian Music". Kailua HI. Press Pacifica, 1978
LaRue, Piercy W. "Hawai'i Island Leaders. Brief Tales of Remarkable Historic Characters".
   Honolulu HI. P.W. LaRue
Ling, Jan "Svensk Folkmusik", 4th edition. Stockholm, Sweden. Bokförlaget Prisma, 1974
Longworth, Mike. "C.F.Martin & Co. Est. 1833. A History".
   Minisink Hills PA. 4 Maples Press Inc., 1987
Middleton, Richard and Horn, David editors. "Popular Music 1: Folk or Popular? Distinctions,
   Influences Continuities".   Cambridge. Cambridge University Press, 1981
Mitchell, Donald D. "Kikā Kila, The Story of the Steel Guitar". Honolulu HI.
   The Hawaiian Music Foundation, 1973
Moseley, Willie G. "Classic Guitars, U.S.A. - A Primer for the Vintage Guitar Collector" .
   Anaheim Hills CA. Centerstream Publishing Co., 1991
"Musical Instruments of the World, An Illustrated Encyclopedia". United Kingdom and U.S.A.
   The Diagram Group, Paddington Press, 1976
Nielsen, Hakon Grüner. "Folkelig vals" . Copenhagen Schønberg. Danmarks Folkeminder No. 22, 1920
Noble, Gurre Ploner "Hula Blues" Honolulu HI. Tongg Publishing Co. Ltd., 1948
Noble, Johnny. "Paradise Of The Pacific", Navy Day Edition. "Origin Of The Steel Guitar" .
   Honolulu HI, E.A.Langton-Boyce, 1943. pp 34-35
Owens, Harry. "Sweet Leilani, The Story Behind the Song".
   Pacific Palisades, CA. Hula House, 1970
Panum, Hortense "The Stringed Instruments of the Middle Ages, Their Evolution and Development". London, England.
   William Reeves, English editiion, 1971
Phillips, Stacy. "The Art of Hawaiian Steel Guitar". Pacific, MO.
   Mel Bay Publications, Inc, 1991
Piercy, LaRue W. "Hawai'i Island Leaders. Brief Tales of Remarkable Historic Characters".
   Kailua Kona HI. Published by the author
Quarterman, John "The History of Dobro Guitars" co-author Tom Gray,
   Anaheim Hills CA. Centerstream Publishing
Roberts, Helen H. "Hawaiian Music" , Hawaiian Annual.   Yale University, 1926 pp 69-80
Roberts, Helen H. "Ancient Hawaiian Music" Honolulu HI. 1926, reissued 1967 with new title
   included "How the Hawaiian Instrument, the 'Ukulele, Received its Name".
   Polynesian Society Journal #11 1931.
Sadie, Stanley. "The New Grove Dictionary Of Music and Musicians." Vol. 8. Washington D.C.
   Grove's Dictionaries of Music Inc. London, New York. Macmillan Press Ltd. 1985
Sadie, Stanley. "The New Grove Dictionary of Musical Instruments" (3 vol.). London,
   New York. Grove's Dictionaries of Music Inc., Macmillan Press Ltd., 1984.
Schmitt, Robert C. "Hawai'i In The Movies 1898 - 1959"
   Honolulu HI. Hawaiian Historical Society, 1988.
Scott, Jay. "Gretsch - The Guitars of the Fred Gretsch Co."
   Anaheim Hills CA. Centerstream Publishing.
Sharpe, A.P. "Spotlight On Hawaii" London, N.I. Maxlove Publishing Co.Ltd., 1944
Smith, Richard R. "The History of Rickenbacker Guitars".
   Anaheim Hills CA. Centerstream Publishing, 1987

Smith, Wm. J. "Kamiki Hawaiian Guitar Method". Wm. J. Smith & Co. New York, 1916
Tatar, Elizabeth. "Strains of Change, The Impact of Tourism on Hawaiian Music."
    Honolulu HI. Bishop Museum Press, 1987
Thrum, Thos G. "The Hawaiian Annual For 1925, Reference Book of Information and Statistics Relating
    To The Territory Of Hawai'i", 51st issue. Honolulu HI. Published by Thos. G Thrum, 1924
Todaro, Tony. "Tony Todaro Presents: The Golden Years of Hawaiian Entertainment.
    1874-1974". Honolulu HI. Tony Todaro Publishing Co., 1974
Toth, Steve. "Dobro Techniques for Bluegrass & Country"
    Anaheim Hills CA. Centerstream Publishing
Toth, Steve. "Dobro Classics Plus"
    Anaheim Hills CA. Centerstream Publishing
Von Tempski, Armine. "Born In Paradise" Woodbridge, CT. Ox Bow Press, 1940
Walin, Stig. "Die Schwedische Hummel: Eine Instrumentenkundliche Untersuchung" .
    Stockholm, Sweden. Nordiska Museet (Nordiska Museets Handlingar: 43), 1952
Westerbeke, Dave. "History of Bigsby Guitars" Anaheim Hills CA. Centerstream Publishing
Westervelt, William D. "Hawaiian Historical Legends". Rutland, Vermont & Tokyo, Japan.
    Charles E. Tuttle Company, 1923
Wheeler, Tom. "American Guitars". Cupertino CA. Miller Freeman Publications
White, Forrest. "Fender, The Inside Story". San Francisco CA. Miller Freeman Publications, 1994
Winters, David. "Artificial and Natural Harmonics for the Guitar" .

Newsletters, Articles, and Periodicals

"About The Steel Guitar" a series by Riley Allen, Page 4 Honolulu Advertiser October 24, 1944.
"Aikanes O Hawai'i, Inc. Monthly Newsletter". Tampa FL. Edited by Cindy Dias
"Aloha International Steel Guitar Club" quarterly newsletters, edited by Dirk Vogel, Minneapolis MN
"Aleki, Sione of Tonga" by Thomas Malm. HSGA newsletter April 1992
"Alkire, Eddy Story". by L. Ruymar, HSGA newsletter October 1988
"Asercion, Carl Kalani " by Beau Sterling. HSGA newsletter October 1990
"Bentley, Alf of Fiji. Autobiography", HSGA newsletter April 1990
"Biographies on Outstanding Guitarists". Sun City AZ. O'ahu Publishing Co. series
"British Steelies Society Newsletter". Barton on Sea, Hants England. Edited by Roy Heap
"Buysman, Bill Biography" by Ray Smith. HSGA newsletter October 1991
"Byrd, Jerry 'Manu'" by Joe Boudreau. HSGA newsletter April 1990
Catalogs of major guitar manufacturers.
"Ching, Duke Kaleolani" by L. Ruymar, HSGA newsletter April 1990
"Elderly Instruments, Acoustic". Lansing MI. Edited by Stan Werbin
"Epiphone Fretted Instruments Catalog" - 1935
"Europe, Steel Guitar in". by Rudolf Barten. HSGA newsletter April 1989, January 1990.
"Fernandes, Kekuka Story" by Murray Storm. HSGA newsletter October 1991
"From The Archives: Hawaiian Records, 75 Years of Change" Ha'ilono Mele November 1978,
    The Hawaiian Music Foundation. Edited by George S. Kanahele
"Gideon, Onni (Tervonen), Steel Guitar in Finland" by Onni Gideon. HSGA newsletter April 1990
"Guitar Player Magazine". Cupertino CA. Miller Freeman Publications, Senior Editor Joe Gore.
"Harmolin" Nov. 1988, "Electraharp" Apr 1989, and "Steel Guitar Technique" July 1989.
    Ha'ilono Mele, Geo Kanahele, Ed. Published by The Hawaiian Music Foundation, Honolulu HI
"Hall of Fame, Steel Guitar." by L. Ruymar, HSGA newsletter April 1990
" Hawai'i Artreach". Honolulu. State Foundation On Culture And The Arts. Edited by Estelle Enoki
"Hawaiian Leader Dies - Lani McIntire". Banjo, Mandolin, Guitar magazine,
    Volume 48 No. 556 August 1951, edited by A.P.Sharpe, London, England
"Hawaiian Steel Guitar Association" quarterly newsletters, edited by Lorene L. Ruymar,
    Vancouver B.C. Canada 1988-1993.
"Hawaiiana Before 1920" - Miro A. Maximchuk, Prince Albert SK.
"He Aha Ka Meahou Ma Kamehameha" Volume 21 No. 3, Winter 1988, published by Kamehameha Schools
"Herring, Alika K. Autobiography". HSGA newsletter, April and October 1991, January 1992
"Hew Len, Billy Story". by Jerry Byrd. HSGA newsletter January and April 1988.
"History of the Steel Guitar According to Charles E. King" Ha'ilono Mele, October 1976
    pages 5, 6.The Hawaiian Music Foundation, edited by Geo. S. Kanahele
"Holck, Jake Story". by L. Ruymar, HSGA newsletter April 1992
"How Steel Guitar Originated" by "Doc" Adams, Honolulu Advertiser January 24, 1932 Page 5.
"Important Announcement" by Sam K. Na'inoa, Los Angeles CA.
    Sam K. Na'inoa's Foundation of Hawaiian Music Studios 78rpm recording
"International Steel Guitar and Dobro Discography, The" by Joe Goldmark,
    San Francisco, CA 94116
"JoaquinMurphy,TheMusician'sMusician"by ErnieBall
"Juju Music" by Mike Perlowin, Steel Guitar World Referral & Exchange, Russell K. Rask editor
"Kaehalio, Mary Agnes Ah See". by L. Ruymar, HSGA newsletter January 1992
"Kaleiali'i, Kale. Autobiography", HSGA newsletter July 1988 and Jan 1989
"Kam, Solomon Story". HSGA newsletter April 1992
"Kapalakiko Productions Calendar of Hawaiian Events". San Francisco CA, Editor Saichi Kawahara
"Ka Wai Ola O Oha" . Office of Hawaiian Affairs, Honolulu HI. World Press Inc.
"Kekuku, Merle". by L. Ruymar, HSGA newsletter July 1989
"Keli'i, David To Steel Guitar Hall of Fame" by Jerry Byrd. HSGA newsletter July and October 1990
"Kolsiana, Ralph. Autobiography", HSGA newsletters Jul 1990, Oct 1990, Jan 1991, Apr 1991, and Jul 1991
"Krontjong Story" by George Wiebenger. HSGA newsletter April 1988
"Learn To Play the Hawaiian Way " by Harry G. Stanley, 1940.
    O'ahu Publishing Co. Cleveland OH

"Life, Kealoha Autobiography". HSGA newsletter July and October 1989
"Lincoln, Bill" by Jerry Byrd. HSGA newsletter January 1990
"Man Who Gave Steel Guitar To Nashville Dies", reprinted from The Detroit News,
    Ha'ilono Mele, November 1979, page 9. Edited by George S. Kanahele
"Masters Of The Steel String Guitar", Spring 1990. John Cephas, Jerry Douglas, Tal Farlow,
    Wayne Henderson, Ledward Ka'apana, and Albert Lee.
    Produced by The National Council For the Traditional Arts
"Mike Keli'iahonui Hanapi" by Emperor Hanapi, Ha'ilono Mele, September 1977, editor George S. Kanahele
"Mitchell, Donald Kilolani" by L. Ruymar, HSGA newsletter April 1990
"Moe, Tau. Autobiography of", HSGA newsletters Jul 1990, Oct 1990, Jan 1991, Apr 1991, and Jul 1991
"Most Controversial Instrument ", by Jerry Byrd, Ha'ilono Mele, October 1980,
    edited by George S. Kanahele, Honolulu
"Mo'okini, Walter. Autobiography of", HSGA newsletter July 1992
"New Zealand Steel Guitar" by Jim Molberg, HSGA newsletter July 1990
"Nicholas, Sonny". by L. Ruymar, HSGA newsletter October 1989
"Old Fisherman Tells How Steel Guitar Originated; Also How 'Ukulele Got Name"
    by "Doc Adams", The Honolulu Advertiser, January 24, 1932
"Origin Of The Steel Guitar" Riley Allen, Honolulu Advertiser, October 17 1944 page 4,
    October 21 1944 page 4, October 23 1944 page 4, and October 24 1944 page 4.
"Pa'alani, Bill" by George Lake, Frank McPhalen. HSGA newsletter January 1990
"Parelius, Art Story". HSGA newsletter January 1992
"Patent Laws" by U.S. Department of Commerce, Section 100 "Definitions of - " U.S.Code Title 35 - Patents
"Pedal Steel Newsletter". Floral Park NY. President Bob Maickel, Editor Doug Mack
"Photography By Billy Howell" Ha'ilono Mele, Volume V Number 1, January 1979, editor George Kanahele, Honolulu
"Polynesian Music & Dance Association". Scarborough ON. Edited by Gladys Warburton
"Pulevai, The Story of the Paradise Islanders". by B. Waters, HSGA newsletter April, July, 1988, January 1989
"Reid, Billy. Salute To The Makuka Kāne". by L. Ruymar, HSGA newsletter January 1991
"Sliding Around The World". by Mike Cooper, Rome Italy. printed in Folk Roots Magazine,
    October 1989 and reprinted in HSGA newsletter January 1990
"Spotlight on Hawai'i" by A. P. Sharpe. Maxlove Publishing Co. Ltd. London, N.I. 1944
"Steel Bar, History of" by Keoki Lake. HSGA newsletter January 1989
"Steel Guitar Australia" edited by Norm A. Bodkin, Tamworth NSW, Australia. May 1987
"Steel Guitar Club of Canada". Streetsville ON. Edited by Al Brisco
"Steel Guitar Development-Part 1, II, III" by Daniel Kahn, Honolulu HI. Ha'ilono Mele,
    The Hawaiian Music Foundation. March 1976, April 1976, May 1976
"Steel Guitar International Enquirer". St. Louis MO. Pulished by DeWitt Scott.
"Steel Guitar Lives On In India" Honolulu HI. Ha'ilono Mele,
    The Hawaiian Music Foundation. February 1981
"Steel Guitar - More Versions" Riley Allen, Honolulu Advertiser, October 1923, 1944
"Steel Guitar World Referral & Exchange" Spokane, WA. Edited by Russell K. Rask
"Sweden, Hawaiian Music in" . by Thomas Malm.
    HSGA newsletter January and April 1989, April 1992
"Tavares, Freddie. A Fond Farewell". by L. Ruymar, HSGA newsletter October 1990
"That Steel Guitar Story" Riley Allen, Honolulu Advertiser, October 21, 1944
"Tremeloa, Hawaiian". by Terry Sullivan, HSGA newsletter April 1989
"Voice of Hawai'i. Hawaiian Newspaper Published Monthly In The State of California". Los Angeles CA.
"Unpublished Notes on the History of Hawaiian Music", Charles E. King.
    Hawaiian Collection, Kamehameha Schools/Bishop Estate, Honolulu, Hawai'i, n.d., pp.375-379, 382.
    Published in Ha'ilono Mele Vol. 2 No. 6, Oct. 1976.

Courtesy The Experience Music Project, Seattle, Washington

Index

H

200

GUITAR INSTRUCTION & TECHNIQUE

GUITAR CHORDS PLUS
by Ron Middlebrook
A comprehensive study of normal and extended chords, tuning, keys, transposing, capo use, and more. Includes over 500 helpful photos and diagrams, a key to guitar symbols, and a glossary of guitar terms.
00000011..$11.95

GUITAR TUNING FOR THE COMPLETE MUSICAL IDIOT (FOR SMART PEOPLE TOO)*
by Ron Middlebrook
A complete book on how to tune up. Contents include: Everything You Need To Know About Tuning; Intonation; Strings; 12-String Tuning; Picks; and much more.
00000002 ....$5.95

INTRODUCTION TO ROOTS GUITAR

by Doug Cox
This book/CD pack by Canada's premier guitar and Dobro* player introduces beginning to intermediate players to many of the basics of folk/roots guitar. Topics covered include: basic theory, tuning, reading tablature, right- and left-hand patterns, blues rhythms, Travis picking, frailing patterns, flatpicking, open tunings, slide and many more. CD includes 40 demonstration tracks.
00000262 Book/CD Pack $17.95
00000265 VHS Video.................................$19.95

KILLER PENTATONICS FOR GUITAR*

by Dave Celentano
Covers innovative and diverse ways of playing pentatonic scales in blues, rock and heavy metal. The licks and ideas in this book will give you a fresh approach to playing the pentatonic scale, hopefully inspiring you to reach for higher levels in your playing. The 37-minute companion CD features recorded examples.
00000285 Book/CD Pack $17.95

LEFT HAND GUITAR CHORD CHART*
by Ron Middlebrook
Printed on durable card stock, this "first-of-a-kind" guitar chord chart displays all forms of major and minor chords in two forms, beginner and advanced.
00000005..$2.95

MELODIC LINES FOR THE INTERMEDIATE GUITARIST
NEW
by Greg Cooper
This book/CD pack is essential for anyone interested in expanding melodic concepts on the guitar. Author Greg Cooper covers: picking exercises; major, minor, dominant and altered lines; blues and jazz turn-arounds; and more.
00000312 Book/CD Pack $19.95

MELODY CHORDS FOR GUITAR*
by Allan Holdsworth
Influential fusion player Allan Holdsworth provides guitarists with a simplified method of learning chords, in diagram form, for playing accompaniments and for playing popular melodies in "chord-solo" style. Covers: major, minor, altered, dominant and diminished scale notes in chord form, with lots of helpful reference tables and diagrams.
00000222..$19.95

MODAL JAMS AND THEORY*

by Dave Celentano
This book shows you how to play the modes, the theory behind mode construction, how to play any mode in any key, how to play the proper mode over a given chord progression, and how to write chord progressions for each of the seven modes. The CD includes two rhythm tracks and a short solo for each mode so guitarists can practice with a "real" band.
00000163 Book/CD Pack $17.95

MONSTER SCALES AND MODES*
by Dave Celentano
This book is a complete compilation of scales, modes, exotic scales, and theory. It covers the most common and exotic scales, theory on how they're constructed, and practical applications. No prior music theory knowledge is necessary, since every section is broken down and explained very clearly.
00000140..$7.95

OPEN GUITAR TUNINGS*
by Ron Middlebrook
This booklet illustrates over 75 different tunings in easy-to-read diagrams. Includes tunings used by artists such as Chet Atkins, Michael Hedges, Jimmy Page, Joe Satriani and more for rock, blues, bluegrass, folk and country styles including open D (for slide guitar), Em, open C, modal tunings and many more.
00000130..$4.95

OPEN TUNINGS FOR GUITAR*

by Dorian Michael
This book provides 14 folk songs in 9 tunings to help guitarists become comfortable with changing tunings. Songs are ordered so that changing from one tuning to another is logical and non-intrusive. Includes: Fisher Blues (DADGBE) • Fine Toast to Hewlett (DGDGBE) • George Barbazan (DGDGBD) • Amelia (DGDGCD) • Will the Circle Be Unbroken (DADF#AD) • more.
00000224 Book/CD Pack $19.95

ARRANGING FOR OPEN GUITAR TUNINGS
NEW
By Dorian Michael
This book/CD pack teaches intermediate-level guitarists how to choose an appropriate tuning for a song, develop an arrangement, and solve any problems that may arise while turning a melody into a guitar piece to play and enjoy.
00000313 Book/CD Pack $19.95

ROCK RHYTHM GUITAR
by Dave Celentano
This helpful book/CD pack cuts out all the confusing technical talk and just gives guitarists the essential tools to get them playing. With Celentano's tips, anyone can build a solid foundation of basic skills to play almost any rhythm guitar style. The exercises and examples are on the CD, in order of difficulty, so players can master new techniques, then move on to more challenging material.
00000274 Book/CD Pack $17.95

SCALES AND MODES IN THE BEGINNING*
by Ron Middlebrook
The most comprehensive and complete scale book written especially for the guitar. Chapers include: Fretboard Visualization • Scale Terminology • Scales and Modes • and a Scale to Chord Guide.
00000010 ....$11.95

SLIDE GUITAR AND OPEN TUNINGS*

by Doug Cox
Explores the basics of open tunings and slide guitar for the intermediate player, including licks, chords, songs and patterns. This is not just a repertoire book, but rather an approach for guitarists to jam with others, invent their own songs, and understand how to find their way around open tunings with and without a slide. The accompanying CD features 37 tracks.
00000243 Book/CD Pack $17.95

SPEED METAL
by Dave Celentano
In an attempt to teach the aspiring rock guitarist how to pick faster and play more melodically, Dave Celentano uses heavy metal neo-classical styles from Paganini and Bach to rock in this great book/CD pack. The book is structured to take the player through the examples in order of difficulty.
00000261 Book/CD Pack $17.95

*Includes tablature

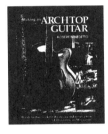